Education and American Culture

ELIZABETH STEINER
ROBERT ARNOVE
B. EDWARD McCLELLAN

Indiana University

Macmillan Publishing Co., Inc.
New York

Collier Macmillan Publishers
London

Copyright © 1980, Macmillan Publishing Co., Inc.

Printed in the United States of America

Macmillan Publishing Co., Inc.
866 Third Avenue, New York, New York 10022

Collier Macmillan Canada, Ltd.

Library of Congress Cataloging in Publication Data
Main entry under title:
Education and American culture.
1. Educational sociology—United States—Addresses,
essays, lectures. 2. Community and school—United
States—Addresses, essays, lectures. 3. Educational
equalization—United States—Addresses, essays,
lectures. 4. Moral education—United States—Addresses,
essays, lectures. 5. Academic freedom—United States—
Addresses, essays, lectures. I. Steiner, Elizabeth.
II. Arnove, Robert F. III. McClellan, Bernard
Edward, (date)
LC191.E4233   370.19′3′0973   79-10755
ISBN 0-02-416770-3

Printing: 1 2 3 4 5 6 7 8   Year: 0 1 2 3 4 5 6

Foreword

George S. Maccia

Professors McClellan, Arnove, and Steiner have undertaken to bring their respective disciplines—history, sociology, and philosophy—to bear on the resolution of educational problems, particularly in reference to schooling in America. The educational problems distinguished are questions as to why educate, whom to educate, what to educate in, and how to educate. Each problem has associated with it a resolutive theme. These themes—education for community, equal educational opportunity, values education, and education through freedom—serve as vehicles for coming to understand and to apply the essential methods and concepts of history, sociology, and philosophy to the resolution of educational problems.

The selection of problems and themes was ingenious, for it enabled responsible and scholarly treatment of educational phenomena. I know of no other collection that brings together without distortion the descriptive and explanatory insights available through history of education and sociology of education and the normative insights available through philosophy of education.

The authors' contributions have provided both methodologically and substantively appropriate content for a course that should provide basic or foundational insights into education. Also they have shown that neither reduction of disciplinary methods or substance nor disparate presentations of disciplines are necessary in a multi-disciplinary approach that is designed to develop understanding of the use of historical, sociological, and philosophical perspectives for education in America. All persons seeking knowledge, as well as those preparing for a professional career in education, will benefit from this volume.

Contents

Problem II: Educate Whom?
Resolutive Theme:
Equal Educational Opportunity

Problem III: Educate in What?
Resolutive Theme:
Values Education

Problem IV: Educate How?
Resolutive Theme:
Education Through Freedom

Perspectives

ON HISTORICAL PERSPECTIVE AND EDUCATIONAL PROBLEMS

B. Edward McClellan

History of education contributes to the understanding and solution of educational problems by extending experience beyond the temporal limits of the immediate present. It not only transfers to children the advantages of old age, as one sage has written, but it conveys to each new generation an organized record of the lives of its predecessors. It allows people to transcend their own time-bound existences, to free themselves from narrow parochialism, and to learn from the triumphs and tragedies of countless men and women who have come before.

By extending experience, history helps people learn to distinguish between the recurrent and the novel, to generalize from the particularities of life, and to find meaning where the uninformed can distinguish no pattern. To the educator, history provides both a fund of knowledge and a way of knowing that can be of enormous value in identifying, understanding, and resolving educational problems.

As a body of knowledge, history is something both more and less than a simple record of the past. It is what people—writing in their own presents—have been able to understand of the past. It is, therefore, a product of an interaction between the present and the past, and, as such, it can be altered either by the discovery of new information or by the refinement of our current understanding.

As a way of knowing, history is a discipline that requires generalization and interpretation as well as the collection and verification of data. Historians do not simply search for information about the past, they attempt to discover connections between events and to make judgments about the meaning of the past events for the present.

In the conduct of their inquiries, historians employ a variety of methodologies, some of them akin to the techniques of humanistic studies, others borrowed from the social sciences. What distinguishes history as a discipline, then, is not its method but its subject and purpose. Historians must always deal with events of the past and must explain them in the specific temporal contexts in which they occur. Unlike scientists who can replicate events in laboratory situations, historians can never manipulate the phenomena they describe. Historians must make sense of events as they happened, and they must do so with documentation that is inevitably partial.

Because history deals with events in their unique contexts, it lacks the power either to prescribe or to predict. If history illuminates the problems of the present, it nevertheless fails to provide adequate grounds for deciding what ought to happen in the future. What is or was, after all, is not necessarily what ought to be. Thus, for example, whether compulsory education ought to be continued is ultimately a question for the philosopher not the historian. Nor does history offer an entirely reliable guide to the probable consequences of particular actions. It may, to be sure, provide some tantalizing clues about the potential effects of policy decisions, but the changing contexts in which even recurrent events take place make the historian at best an imperfect seer. Historians may conclude, for example, that efforts to achieve racial integration in the past have largely failed, but they cannot predict with any certainty that they will fail again in the changed circumstances of the late twentieth century.

Educators will find history of greatest value when they use it cautiously and with a full understanding of its limitations. Wise policymakers will be careful to consider the context in which past events have taken place and will refuse to set limits on the future by treating history as either a prescriptive or predictive discipline. Instead, they will attempt to comprehend the past in all of its complexity, and they will employ their historical understanding to provide a broad perspective in which problems can be more fully understood and justly resolved.

ON SOCIOLOGICAL PERSPECTIVE AND EDUCATIONAL PROBLEMS

Robert Arnove

In two classic statements made over twenty-five years ago, Brookover and Gross described the focus and contribution of sociology to the field of education. According to Brookover, "The sociology of education is the scientific analysis of the social processes and patterns involved in the educational system. This assumes that education is a combination of social acts and that sociology deals with the analysis of human interaction." [1] According to Gross, "What the sociologist has to offer is basically a series of sensitizing and analytic concepts and ideas based on theoretical and empirical analysis that will allow the practitioner to examine in a more realistic and incisive way the multiple forces operating in his [her] social environment." [2]

In this introduction to the sociological study of education as a system of social action and human relations, I shall first discuss what some of these analytic concepts are, what perspectives and paradigms sociologists use, and the nature of sociological imagination.

Analytic Concepts

Concepts can be considered as tools that help us understand phenomena. They are ideas that enable us to focus on selected features of a topic. Sociologists typically use such concepts as culture, socialization, role, status, institution, formal and informal organization, bureaucracy, occupation, and profession to analyze the social interactions that comprise the education system. These concepts illuminate a number of stresses to which educators are subject in formally organized systems of education. For example, there is a clash between schools as agencies of socialization—designed to transmit culture and to bring about developmental changes in individuals so that they may occupy adult roles and perform them competently—and schools as bureaucratic organizations. The conflict resides in the requirements of the

5

learning process for warm, interpersonal relations and attention to the unique learning style of the individual, and the requirements of bureaucracy for impersonal, uniform treatment. Another clash exists between the bureaucratic authority of administrators, based on their position in a hierarchy of offices, and the professional authority of teachers, based on their training in a body of theory related to learning. There are the conflicts teachers experience between administrative requirements to control and regulate students, and the educational mission of fostering freedom and individual development. In the setting of compulsory schooling, which captures students for a prolonged period, demands competitive performances, and systematically evaluates students on not only learning but "social adjustment," students form their own subcultures as means of coping with the pervasive and systematic demands of school authorities. These subcultures—as well as those fostered by school authorities around athletics and other extracurricular activities—may or may not support the learning objectives of an education system. Thus as sociologists have noted, the crises that characterize schooling in American society have little to do with the personal attributes of either teachers, administrators, or students. They arise out of schools as people-processing institutions, which are bureaucratic, and staffed by professionals.[3]

Sociological Perspectives—Imagination

These analytic concepts form part of the perspectives of sociologists who view education at *macro* as well as *micro* levels.[4] Sociologists, as distinguished from other social scientists such as psychologists, study society as a unit of analysis in its own right. Sociologists compare societies over time. They examine the differences and similarities between them—for example, with regard to such processes as stratification, social mobility, and socialization. This macro-level approach is further found in the analyses of the relationships between major social institutions. In the case of the sociological analysis of education, the focus is on how the education system interacts with the family, polity, class structure, and economy. An example of such analysis is the discussion by Durkheim (see Problem I) of the role of schooling in transmitting core values and helping establish a new basis for community in societies undergoing rapid industrialization and urbanization. The role of education—and in particular schooling—in forging a sense of nationhood in newly independent countries is a topic of frequent discussion in the developing areas of Africa, Asia, and Latin America. At the micro-level, sociologists examine schooling and subunits of it, such as the individual classroom, as a self-contained system of values, norms, roles, and statuses (see, for example, the Dreeben article in Problem III). Thus, the previously discussed tensions faced by an educator in a bureaucratic organization, and the student and teacher subcultures that emerge, all constitute part of the micro-analysis of education as a system of social action.

The sociological perspective attempts to generalize about regularity in human affairs by discussing patterns of social behavior as the outcomes of a particular social milieu. While individual motivation and personality attributes are not excluded from such analysis, they are studied in so far as they are affected by extraindividual or contextual phenomena. Characteristics of the individual are conditioned by such social phenomena as expectations as to how someone who occupies a particular position in an institution should act; by collective rates and attributes—such as values held by peers, group morale and cohesiveness; and by the incidence of a phenomenon such as dropout or desertion in a social unit. Durkheim's classic study of suicide, as a case in point, was an attempt to determine how suicide was socially patterned and how it could be explained by such factors as the degree of social cohesiveness of a national society and the institutions in which an individual participated. This analysis of the interrelation between the individual and the collectivity, the part and the whole, is uniquely sociological.

To paraphrase the well-known sociologist C. Wright Mills, when individual troubles are multiplied, they become social ills. Thus, the difficulty encountered by a female or minority college graduate seeking employment may be explained not in relation to imperfections in the individual—i.e., not holding the right certificate, scores on achievement tests, grade point average, personality attributes, and appearance—but in relation to structural characteristics such as the scarcity of employment opportunities, the excessive supply of individuals with college degrees seeking high-status positions, and discrimination in the marketplace.

In *The Sociological Imagination,* Mills noted that few individuals define their troubles in terms of historical change and institutional contradiction: "they cannot cope with their personal troubles in such ways as to control the structural transformations that usually lie behind them."[5] According to Mills the effect of sociological analysis may be both stimulating and liberating:

> By its use men whose mentalities have swept only a series of limited orbits often come to feel as if suddenly awakened in a house with which they had only supposed to be familiar. Correctly or incorrectly, they often come to feel that they can now provide themselves with adequate summations, cohesive assessments, comprehensive orientations. . . . Their capacity for astonishment is made lively again.[6]

Scientific Methods and Paradigms

Within the field of sociology there are competing schools of thought as to the role of sociologists in society, and how the sociologists should go about studying society. Mills, for example, was a foremost representative of a school that advocated that the sociologist be a politically engaged social critic analyzing contemporary social ills. A more orthodox point of view is that sociologists, while not free from value considerations in the selection and analysis of problems, should approximate the role of scientists of society. Whatever their value positions, they should adhere as closely as possible to the canons of the scientific method, to the rigorous and objective study of social phenomena.

For the most part, sociologists agree that if the field is to develop as a science there must be a union of theory with empirical research. But, according to Hurn, "The role of sociologists of education . . . should be broader than the task of weighing evidence against competing theories. They must also examine the intellectual assumptions underlying particular theories that prevail in the field: theories of the determinants of success in school, theories of what schools teach, and theories of the role of schooling in contemporary society." [7]

Recently substantial attention has been given to the analysis of two different approaches or paradigms for studying society and institutions such as education. A paradigm, according to Kuhn in *The Structure of Scientific Revolutions,* is an accepted model or pattern for studying reality. The opposing paradigms have been designated as consensus vs. conflict, and sometimes as functional vs. radical. Briefly, the consensus or functional paradigm, which is traced to Durkheim, examines society as a type of biological organism with its own homeostasis. The emphases in this model of society are on order, stability, and continuity of social arrangements. Social practices and institutions are examined in relation to the contribution they make to the continued survival and well-being of the social system. Presumably most people benefit from the existing social order. By contrast conflict theory examines society as a struggle for power, prestige, and income with only some individuals benefiting from existing social arrangements. At any one time, one group will be dominant and use education and other cultural institutions to maintain its advantage. The paradigm, which derives from the writings of Marx and Weber, emphasizes change and coercion as the salient characteristics of a social system. [8]

In the various sociological sections, we have endeavored to select readings which exemplify one or the other of the two paradigms. The students of this text, then, should be aware of the intellectual assumptions of the different authors, as well as the adequacy of the theory and the empirical findings, in judging the usefulness of the study to an understanding of social forces shaping education.

NOTES

1. Wilbur B. Brookover, "Sociology of Education: A Definition," *American Sociological Review,* **14** (June 1949), 413.

2. Neal Gross, "Some Contributions of Sociology to the Field of Education," *Harvard Educational Review,* **29** (Fall 1959), 286.

3. Sam D. Sieber and David E. Wilder (eds.), *Schools in Society: Studies in the Sociology of Education* (New York: The Free Press, 1973), p. 150; also see Ronald G. Corwin, *Education in Crisis: A Sociological Analysis of Schools and Universities in Transition* (New York: Wiley, 1974), chap. 1.

4. Sieber and Wilder, op. cit., p. 2.

5. C. Wright Mills, *The Sociological Imagination* (New York: Oxford U.P., 1959), p. 4.

6. Ibid., pp. 7–8.

7. Christopher J. Hurn, *The Limits and Possibilities of Schooling: An Introduction to the Sociology of Education* (Boston: Allyn, 1978), p. 25.

8. For further discussion of these paradigms, see ibid., chap. 2; and Ann Parker Parelius and Robert J. Parelius, *The Sociology of Education* (Englewood Cliffs, N.J.: Prentice-Hall, 1978), pp. 4–16.

ON PHILOSOPHICAL PERSPECTIVE AND EDUCATIONAL PROBLEMS

Elizabeth Steiner

When one is uncertain about what to believe, then one is in a problematic state. Unless this doubt is settled, one cannot act. One must pass from doubt to a state of belief. Belief must be fixed. That is to say, problems must be resolved.

As Kant has stated, "the greatest and most difficult problem to which man [the person] can devote himself [herself] is the problem of education."[1] This is patent, because education is a teaching-studenting process and thus one in which the guidance of a person's development is attempted. What a person becomes, therefore, can depend upon education.

The general problem of education is constituted by why-, who-, what-, and how- problems. "Why should a person be educated?" states the problem of the objective of education. Whether education should be for the self or the group is one such problem. "Who should be educated?" states the problem of the student population. An instance would be whether every person should have equal educational opportunity. The problem of the content of education is stated in the question, "What should one be educated in?" The controversy about values education embodies an example of this kind of problem. Finally, "How shall we educate?" raises the problem of method. One such problem is the academic freedom of the student.

A cognitive perspective is a way of conceiving states of affairs and so of coming to belief. A lens to focus observations is necessary, and concepts form such a lens. Percepts without concepts are fuzzy. Without cognitive perspectives, problems cannot be solved.

Since the concepts of philosophy differ in kind from nonphilosophical ones, a philosophical perspective is distinctive. Philosophical concepts are evaluative ones. Evaluative concepts are ideas characterizing states of affairs in regard to their valuableness. But not all evaluative concepts are philosophical; only those that characterize states of affairs in regard to noninstrumental valuableness, i.e., valuableness in terms of intrinsic features. Praxiological concepts are those that characterize states of affairs in regard to instrumental valuableness, i.e., valuableness in terms of extrinsic features. To illustrate, relative to a person's activity, rational would be a philosophical concept and profitable would be a praxiological one. Rational characterizes goodness inherent in human activity, while profitable characterizes goodness effected by human activity—what that activity leads to or is good for. To take good as good for is to commit the pragmatic fallacy: what is effective or what works is necessarily good.

The major philosophical concepts are truth, order, goodness, beauty, and realness. These concepts provide nuclei for the branches of philosophy: truth for epistemology, order for logic, beauty for aesthetics, goodness for ethics and for social or political philosophy, and realness for metaphysics.

Epistemology is that branch of philosophy that characterizes belief states of affairs in terms of truth features. Epistemology enters into a philosophical perspective of education, for one part of a person's development is cognitive and education is a process in which a person's development is guided. Cognitive development is development of beliefs, and pedagogical epistemology provides concepts for evaluating a teaching-studenting process in terms of students coming to true beliefs. These concepts, therefore, relate to the content and method of education. Pedagogical epistemology is one important dimension of a philosophical perspective to resolve educational problems.

Ethics and social or political philosophy are both branches that treat human states of affairs in terms of features of goodness. Ethics, however, focuses on the individual, and social or political philosophy on the relations between individuals. That ethics enters into a philosophical perspective of education is obvious. What is wanted in education is the development of a good person. Ethics of education determines the objective of education. Equally as obvious is social or political philosophy as part of a philosophical perspective of education. Social or political philosophy of education provides concepts for evaluating the goodness of the relation between teacher and student and, where there is more than one student, between students. Moreover, social or political philosophy provides concepts for evaluating education as a right. So these concepts relate both to the method of education and the nature of the student population. Ethics of education and social or political philosophy of education are dimensions also required to resolve educational problems.

Metaphysics is that branch of philosophy that characterizes states of affairs in terms of features of realness. Realness is not to be confused with real in the sense of sensible. An excellent illustration is found in Plato's *Republic* where realness is presented as the ideal person or ideal society both of whom are rational. For Plato the real is the rational not the sensible. This quotation makes this clear:

> "Well," said I, "in heaven, perhaps a pattern of it is indeed laid up, for him that has eyes to see, and seeing to settle himself therein. It matters nothing

whether it exists anywhere or shall exist; for he would practice the principles of this city only, no other." [2]

Science describes real states of affairs in the sense of sensible ones. To take sensible for ideal is to commit the naturalistic fallacy: what has been, is, or will be is necessarily good. Science and philosophy are conflated.

Metaphysics is only indirectly a part of a philosophical perspective of education. Insofar as it is foundational to pedagogical epistemology, logic of education, aesthetics of education, ethics and social or political philosophy of education, it enters into the resolution of educational problems. Plato, to continue the illustration, took the rational to be the real, and thereby made rationality the essential feature of goodness.

Philosophy by providing noninstrumental evaluative concepts gives norms or standards for judging. Hence, philosophy is normative. To again caution about the pragmatic and naturalistic fallacies, these norms are neither norms of effectiveness nor norms that are population tendencies. Norms that are philosophical can result in wisdom, only if used to judge noninstrumental worthwhileness. True beliefs about what is intrinsically valuable in education can be fixed through a philosophical perspective of education, and so the solution of educational problems can be furthered.

NOTES

1. Immanuel Kant, *Education,* trans. Annette Churton (Ann Arbor: University of Michigan Press, 1960), p. 11.

2. W. H. Rouse did the translation and these words of Plato are found in Book 9, 592.

PROBLEM I

Why Educate?

RESOLUTIVE THEME

Education for Community

EDUCATION FOR COMMUNITY: HISTORICAL PERSPECTIVE

B. Edward McClellan

The relationship between education and community poses special problems for the historian, for not only have Americans at various times balanced the needs of the individual and the community in different ways, but they have frequently redefined community itself. Early Puritans, for example, associated the good community with religious conformity and directed their educational efforts toward the conversion of nonbelievers and the suppression of internal dissent. By the end of the eighteenth century, on the other hand, Americans were more tolerant and placed their hopes for a just and harmonious community less on a precise doctrinal purity than on the creation of a broad moral and political consensus.

Subsequent generations of Americans have continued this process of redefinition. Especially at times of profound social change, they have revised in fundamental ways their assumptions about the nature of the good community and the role of education in creating and preserving it. The readings that follow focus on these changing conceptions of education and community, particularly as they have unfolded in the last century and a half.

A broad, interpretive framework for understanding the topic is provided by Robert Wiebe's "The Social Functions of Public Education." Wiebe surveys the multitude of tasks performed by the public school since the early nineteenth century and thereby contributes significantly to an understanding not only of how Americans have redefined community but also how they have attempted at various times to integrate or balance public and private needs and how they have apportioned their loyalty among the various communities to which they have belonged.

Of the changes Wiebe describes, the most traumatic may have been the decline of the small community as the primary locus of collective identity and common endeavor. For generations, Americans had acquired their deepest sense of community from the close personal relationships of everyday life in the town, the county, and the neighborhood. By the end of the nineteenth century, however, industrialization and bureaucratization had largely destroyed this web of personal ties and deprived the small locality of its capacity to elicit public commitment or command the primary loyalty of its citizens. In the absence of these traditional sources of common action, early twentieth-century Americans raised urgent new questions about the possibility of community. Could community exist in the impersonal environment of modern society? Could social cohesion be maintained through democratic and voluntary processes or did industrial society require coercion and authoritarian rule? What new spirit would lead people to respond to collective needs and act in the public interest?

The efforts of modern American educators to deal with these questions is one subject of an important study by Charles Burgess and Merle Borrowman entitled *What Doctrines to Embrace*. This work surveys the thought of a variety of American educators including Thomas Jefferson, William Maclure, William T. Harris, and G. Stanley Hall. In the excerpt printed here, the authors focus on the efforts of the educational philosopher John Dewey to fashion a conception of community appropriate to the conditions of modern industrial society. As historians, Burgess and Borrowman are primarily interested in using Dewey's ideas to illuminate the broad intellectual concerns of a particular time. For a fuller and more exact understanding of Dewey's conception of education and community, the reader should turn to the philosopher's own work. An important excerpt from that work and a brief explication of it from a philosophical perspective appear later in the readings on the problem of community.

The article by Wiebe and the excerpt from Burgess and Borrowman's work complement each other in a way that is important to an understanding of education and community, especially in the twentieth century. Wiebe focuses on educational practice and deals with notions of community only indirectly. Burgess and Borrowman, on the other hand, deal with one influential conception of community without showing in any detail how that conception was embodied in educational practice. Readers will find it necessary to draw connections between the two selections. They may want to ask, for example, how and to what degree the educational practices described by Wiebe reflect the conception of community articulated by Dewey. This question may in turn lead to a more general consideration of the various notions of community embodied by a whole range of educational practices in both the past and the present.

THE SOCIAL FUNCTIONS OF PUBLIC EDUCATION

Robert H. Wiebe

Year by year interest has been growing in a kind of historical inquiry that as yet has no name. It is concerned with the manner in which people have functioned through institutional means, and it takes as its point of departure the values people bring to their actions. Men's behavior—the policies they advocate, the rules they establish, the laws they support—acquires meaning from the beliefs men carry to it. These inquiries have also paid particularly close attention to the place of an institution in a social structure, because they assume that the role of an institution depends upon its fit—the nature of its interaction—within a larger social organization.[1] This essay explores the possible value of such an analysis in the field of public education since the 1830s.[2]

In the spirit of the 19th century evangel, the reformers crusading for common schools in the 1830s and 1840s preached a ritualistic sermon of sin, promise and salvation. The American experiment—perhaps all humanity—had entered a critical phase, they began, with dangers threatening on every side. The truths and traditions that only a generation ago had cemented society were disintegrating before the rush of the masses. "Look at our communities," cried Horace Mann,

> divided into so many parties and factions, and these again subdivided, on all questions of social, national, and international, duty. . . . We want godlike men who can tame the madness of the times, and, speaking divine words in a divine spirit, can say to the raging of human passions, 'Peace, be still;' and usher in the calm of enlightened reason and conscience.

"Grace," "redemption" and "testament," he told an audience of Massachusetts villagers, once the essence of Christian piety, now honored the

Reprinted by permission of the author and *American Quarterly* from pp. 147–164, Vol. XXI, Summer, 1969. Copyright 1969, Trustees of the University of Pennsylvania.

gods of money and credit—debts, mortgages, inheritances. Particularly in the Northeast, the reformers warned of a new industrial feudalism supplanting the old order. "It is a matter of vital importance to manufacturing villages," Henry Barnard reported to the Rhode Island legislature, "to close the deep gulf with precipitous sides, which too often separates one set of men from their fellows, to soften and round the distinctions of society which are nowhere else so sharply defined." Men everywhere echoed the fears of Michael Frank, Wisconsin's leader in educational reform, for "the security of life, the safety of property, and preservation of our liberties and our republican institutions."[3]

Yet, the sermon continued, this was a time of extraordinary promise. "The idea and feeling that the world was made, and life given, for the happiness of all," Mann announced,

> and not for the ambition, or pride, or luxury, of one, or of a few, are pouring in, like a resistless tide, upon the minds of men, and are effecting a universal revolution in human affairs. Governments, laws, social usages, are rapidly dissolving, and recombining in new forms. . . . A new phrase,—the people,—is becoming incorporated into all languages and laws; and the correlative idea of human rights is evolving, and casting off old institutions and customs, as the expanding body bursts and casts away the narrow and worn-out garments of childhood.

The climax—the solution—lay of course in the common school, serving all citizens, stamping them American and unifying the nation. Harness the energy of the masses, show them the truth, and, as Mann grandly predicted, "all the resistless forces of Nature become our auxiliaries and cheer us on to certain prosperity and triumph."[4]

Despite the considerable anxiety it expressed, despite its clamor to control the lower classes by imposing values from above, this was an optimistic message. Both speaker and listener knew they could walk the edge of damnation in the early part of the ritual with assurance that ultimately the path would lead them on to safety. "The eyes of man look forward," Mann declared, "that they may see where they are to go; because Progress is the law of the universe."[5] The very passion for social control was simultaneously a passion for release. The instruments of control were themselves the means of improvement, and reformers predicated the rise of America and of each citizen upon an emancipating discipline of spiritual and physical truths.

They found a ready audience. Even before Thomas Jefferson commentators had associated education with a republican government. By the early 19th century a significant number of Americans already viewed the schools, whether pauper or truly common, as assimilating, stabilizing mechanisms. A waning denominationalism allowed many Americans to think for the first time in terms of general public education, while a reviving religious concern encouraged citizens to propagate basic Protestant morality through some neutral means. By the 1830s, as Wilson Smith, Neil Harris and Fred Somkin have demonstrated, an impressive variety of leaders were urgently seeking a new national cohesion, a source of uniquely American wholeness. They turned naturally to such an agency—more accurately such an idea—as the common school, then imputed to it mystically unifying powers.

But what meaning could that dream of cohesion have in a sprawling, expanding country of autonomous communities? It was one thing for reformers to devise a moral regimen for the schools clustered about Boston, quite another to extend their sway over thousands of communities scattered westward, each with its own norms and its own techniques of discipline. Worries about a rampant decentralization, after all, lay close to the heart of their concern over America's future. In one sense, the answer to this question constitutes the rationale of 19th century public education. First, the reformers believed that they spoke for the nation rather than to it. They assumed that community leaders everywhere shared the same ethical system, the same dedication to public service and the same aspirations to unity. Their task was not to convince people but simply to rouse them, and like-minded legions across the land, community by community, would translate their dream into practice.

Second, their understanding of what would later be called child psychology specified the years under ten—generally from about four to eight—as the critically formative ones. In the fundamental sense of character, success or failure would be determined here. Child psychology was quite literally the inherent logic of the psyche, a linear, step-by-step process so often expressed by the metaphor of a maturing plant. " 'First the blade, then the ear, afterwards the full corn in the ear,' " Mann reminded his listeners. "And in the mind, as in the grain, the blade may be treated so that the full corn will never appear." "[Children] must be taken at the earliest opportunity, if the seeds of good are to be planted before the seeds of evil begin to germinate . . . ," warned Barnard. "Here by kindness, patience, order . . . groups may enjoy the sunshine of a happy childhood at school, and be bound to respectability and virtue, by ties which they will not willingly break." If one could just inculcate the proper habits—those almost infallible signs of an inner morality—when the faculties were tender, the mold of the good man would be set.[6]

By any modern standards, therefore, education within this scheme was strictly elementary. It promised the young child instruction in the three Rs, embellished with what lessons from the Bible, history and geography the community might support, for these basics fulfilled the charge of 19th century popular education. Such a curriculum supplied those essentials assumed to qualify a man as an American citizen and to guarantee a healthy, cohesive republican society.[7] Any extension was predefined a luxury. It was that curriculum—with that justification—which horrified so many white Southerners when the Freedmen's Bureau and private missionaries used it to legitimize the black as a citizen.

Within this framework, the role of the educator was to construct a model environment around the child. The unfolding flower should be touched only by a perfect climate, by exactly the right aphorisms, stories, pictures and songs. Children must "actually [see] the eternal laws of justice, as plainly as we can see the sun in the heavens," said Mann—"as distinctly as if they were geometrical solids," according to Barnard.[8] The famous readers and spellers of the 19th century endured decade after decade precisely because their simple moral lessons were presumed to impress just such images, and their competitors imitated as best they could the same unalloyed didacticism.[9] Educators added minute descriptions of the correct lighting and ventilation, chair arrangement and door location, landscaping and play space, not as ventures in public health or scientific management but as portions of an ideal whole enveloping the impressionable child.[10]

The teacher was another part of that model. Can you picture an individual, Mann asked,

> whose language is well selected, whose pronunciation and tones of voice are correct and attractive, whose manners are gentle and refined, all whose topics of conversation are elevating and instructive, whose benignity of heart is constantly manifested in acts of civility, courtesy, and kindness, and who spreads a nameless charm over whatever circle may be entered? Such a person should the teacher of every Common School be.[11]

Out of school as well as in, the teacher would exemplify, and for this purpose the first normal schools became in their own way schools for models. Educators usually preferred the mothering female for those early, basic years and males only at a later, less plastic stage of the child's development.

The state administrator was the keeper of the model. In a decentralized nation of occasional communication, he articulated the norms of common-school education against which isolated communities could gauge their accomplishments. Americans of the 19th century relied heavily upon inspirational oratory and exhortative literature to provide them not only with the standards they could receive almost no other way but also with the emotional charge to achieve long after the immediate stimulus had gone; and Mann's peerless reputation among the administrators rested upon his unique mastery of these talents. Shrewd men like Barnard knew that whatever the wording of the law they had not an iota of power to coerce the communities.[12] They were to perfect the model and tirelessly, patiently publicize it.

The hodgepodge of schools that emerged was unified only in the loosest sense by this common rationale. It was in countless separate communities rather than in the lecture halls or the legislatures that public education took root, and it was always there that the schools acquired their peculiar form. The leading families of the community in collaboration with the dominant church or churches gave what life they chose to the school delegating subsidiary tasks to it much as they might have to a domestic servant. Where a foreign language predominated, it was spoken in the classroom. Where denominational doctrines mattered, they suffused the instruction. Where indifference prevailed, the schools languished; and where interest rose, the town paid more, cared more for the physical plant and even extended the curriculum. In practical terms the function of the school originated within the community and stopped at its boundaries.

Organization by classes or by types of schools had little relevance in this scheme. Although ambitious educators as part of their model sketched elaborate plans with several stages of schooling, the usual practice was to add and divide classes as it suited local convenience. Even when graded schools became common later in the century, the terms did not carry a fixed meaning from place to place. The Wisconsin high school of the Gilded Age, for example, "was simply the highest department of a graded school," recalled one educator early in the 20th century, "whether that school consisted of three or three times three departments or grades."[13] Schools had delimited, local tasks to accomplish. What use other than convenience could grading serve?

The reformers, in all a tough-minded lot, understood these matters so well they scarcely felt impelled to discuss them. Their vision of national unity required neither a precise uniformity nor a tight administrative surveillance. Only men with an abiding faith in the Aristotelian distinction between accident and essence could dream of cohesion in mid-19th century America. What they could not tolerate were gross violations of the model. In the actual scheme of education, for example, teachers clearly played a subordinate role. It required slight skill to master the rudimentary curriculum, and with the proper texts it seemed not to matter that much if the teacher smiled as his pupils learned of honesty and perseverance from Parson Weems' *Washington*. He could keep order while the discipline of the task and the message of the reader worked their magic. It was rational, in other words, to allocate only a pittance for the teacher, whose low estate and large mixed classes reflected the little anyone other than a few educators expected of him. Reformers fretted endlessly and labored futilely to elevate his standing and improve his quality. Otherwise, they went about their tasks of clarifying, publicizing and encouraging fortified by the belief that truth once abroad contained within itself the irresistible force of its own ultimate triumph.

The heroes of the 1830s and 1840s remained the great names in public education throughout the century because they and the scheme with which they were identified remained relevant. Roughly the same pattern of local control and roughly the same faith in an elementary instruction prevailed in the 1890s. Educational procedure, with poorly paid teachers policing the traditional recitations from the familiar texts, had changed only in degree, not in kind. When William T. Harris, the grand vizier of late-19th century public education, wrote of a curriculum organized "to afford the best exercise of the faculties of the mind, and to secure the unfolding of those faculties in their natural order," he even employed the customary metaphor in stating a hoary truth. The idealist's vision of an education that would place Moral Truth and Reason at its core, habituate the child to goodness at a malleable age, transmit "the inheritance of the race" as a divine obligation, and "lift [the child] into the greater civilization that is around him," all placed Harris and his age beneath the aegis of Horace Mann.[14]

Changes of course had occurred. Even as the reformers of the 1830s had argued the case of a singular American republicanism, others were moving away from the conception of a unique liberty the system of society provided toward a conception of freedom as something the individual found. The educational model that was once to *give* each pupil America's special truths altered subtly to *prepare* the individual so that he could achieve them. During the second half of the century an equally gradual process muted certain ethical overtones peculiar to reform in the 1830s and 1840s and replaced them with the metallic notes of cash value. Once public education had kept company with abolition, temperance and humane treatment for the insane; by the 1880s its more usual companions were industrial productivity and tax policy. Where Horace Mann had assured his audiences that prosperity would naturally follow education's uplifting effect, some of his successors a generation later had shifted the argument so that prosperity now measured education's worth, a worth calculable from tax inputs and student outputs. Education was presumed to be no less moral within its new setting. Morality had simply become more of a commodity, more a quantifiable asset of the marketplace. While public education retained its specifically American, unifying purpose, its points of reference were changing.

The rapid, persistent growth of cities encouraged other, more concrete modifications. Until whites came to determine public education for the freed black, the industrial sections of the city had represented the sole exception to the community-controlled common schools. As Barnard told the Rhode Island legislature in 1845, civilized men had to decide for the urban poor how best to raise them from barbarism.[15] Those decisions from above increased in importance and variety as the slums multiplied. The work ethic, which had long played an especially prominent role in slum education, now more often took the form of so-called practical training in factory skills, and spokesmen for the dispossessed fought these experiments in caste schooling just as the workingmen's groups of the 1830s had. Nevertheless, it was difficult for established Americans to sustain an expensive enthusiasm for lower-class education. Slum dwellers by and large received an indifferent version of the standard fare. Meanwhile, as long as the cities remained a collection of semi-autonomous subdivisions, substantial citizens moved to those areas where they could usually control their own schools as they chose. The patchwork of urban education reflected the general disruptions around it.

Changes in administration developed in conjunction with urban growth. Operating from the twin assumptions that only rigid controls could manage the seething city masses and that only specific, immutable programs of instruction, uniformly applied to every child in every classroom, could produce specific, immutable social results, urban administrators late in the 19th century articulated their model environment in such detail and with such obvious intentions of freezing a fluid society that at times they were able to create the horrors of lock-step routine Dr. Joseph M. Rice discovered in his tour of city schools early in the 1890s. The pre-eminence of William T. Harris, who worshiped a stable society almost as fervently as he did an immortal god, symbolized both the administrator's growing importance as director of the model and his increasing reliance upon form as a barrier rather than a channel to change. Yet the administrator's actual power always remained tenuous in the chaotic cities of the Gilded Age. His primary legacy to the 20th century was not his authority but his very presence. The national recognition accorded popular education and the local pressures to regulate city life had given the administrator a secure, almost honored, position in an era when so few public administrative systems even existed. When dramatic changes in education did arrive, he would be there to consolidate the gains.

A "deluge of discussion" swept education in the years around 1900, announcing in countless ways a revolution within the schools. A series of widely publicized committees evaluated the state of the schools and issued comprehensive recommendations on policy. Following Dr. Rice's hostile appraisal of the traditional common school in 1892 and 1893,[16] public education became a generally accepted subject for the major magazines. A proliferation of citizens' groups, which ranged from a national congress of parents in the 1890s to Chicago's Public Education Association supporting the professional rights of teachers a decade later to the many business associations sponsoring Americanization classes around the First World War, reflected the new, intense concern for education that particularly affected an ambitious, rising urban middle class. Early in the 20th century John Dewey found an alert national audience already eager to read his discussions of a flexible, democratic education, and an innovative administrator such as William Wirt gained almost instantaneous national fame for his experiments in rational schooling in Gary, Indiana. State laws governing local standards were not only strengthened but to an increasing degree applied.

During the 19th century the school had largely arranged its schedule to suit the habits of the community. Now more and more families were expected to bend their habits to a fixed school year, and a multiplying array of social workers, counselors and truant officers stood ready to assist in that hard transition. As attendance mounted, especially in the high school whose enrollment increased fifteen-fold between 1890 and the mid-1920s, it seemed that overnight much of the nation had gone to school and the rest was talking about it.[17]

The standard preface in book after book about the new education was an analysis of what used to be. That had not always been necessary. As late as 1898, George H. Martin in *The Evolution of the Massachusetts Public School System* could merge the decades since Horace Mann into a single modern era. He and his contemporaries had scarcely felt the need to think historically, for the last half-century constituted, in Carl Becker's phrase, their "specious present."[18] Only after a self-conscious break did the past require separate, curious scrutiny.

Almost every explanation the new publicists offered of that break was misleading, a demonstration in itself of their distance from the recent past. Many boasted of a new practicality emanating from their concern for social adjustment. Yet socialization had been the essence of the earlier scheme, and within its own framework of values, it had been as practical as any later one. They talked in addition of the new "stress on developing and perpetuating attitudes, interests, appreciations, and habits" rather than upon "acquiring knowledge as such."[19] Actually, learning for the inherent value of the information was more alien to the old common school, where all lessons carried an ulterior meaning, than the new, where the rising technical requirements of an urban-industrial society demanded considerably higher levels of achievement in the basic subjects. A general conditioning of habits and attitudes was equally central in both. A few publicists, on the contrary, emphasized a fresh sensitivity to the individual. Yet he was an individual located, like his 19th century counterpart, in a smoothly operating total society. The 19th century educator would not have argued with the authoritative statement in *Cardinal Principles of Secondary Education* that the schools should enable "each member [to] develop his personality primarily through the activities designed for the well-being of his fellow members and of society as a whole."[20]

The heart of the change around 1900 was the breakdown of 19th century society. Originating in the major urban centers and spreading to the smaller cities, towns and villages, the capacity—even in many instances the desire—to live apart in a self-contained community collapsed rather suddenly toward the end of the century. In its wake emerged a new order that relied upon increasingly impersonal direction, one attuned to a perpetually shifting interaction of people who would never see each other. Although this fundamental change came over many years, its general drift was clear before the First World War, and its prophets were already calling upon America to re-equip itself for the modern age.

Within this society, the school assumed a radically different role. Rather than an appendage to the visible powers of an inbred community, it became in many instances the only familiar local agency the families in an area could find, the one public institution that might personally connect them with a wider world. Rather than a mirror of values everyone knew, it became the source of those indispensable norms and life styles that were no longer atmospherically available. In the 19th century when the publicist attributed mystical powers to education, many citizens must have responded with a matter-of-fact disbelief, for the common school fulfilled a readily comprehensible function. In the 20th century when the publicist described the new school in matter-of-fact language, citizens increasingly attributed mystical powers to it, for education alone seemed to have that knowledge prerequisite to entering the broader society. Administrators, teachers and their spokesmen transmuted this sense of mystery into the foundations of a new educational profession. These professionals, in turn, won impressive appropriations in a tax-conscious age by means of that same general faith in wizardry.

Along with interpreter and guide—the most important of the new roles—went additional mediating functions as well. In the absence of a viable community, the schools served as a center for such occasions as picnics, group singing and athletic contests that had once been integral to a town's life. They assumed in addition certain secondary tasks of training—in particular those involving such domestic and manual skills as cooking and sewing, woodworking and automobile driving—that were customarily identified with the family, not because the local families had necessarily grown weak but because the functions of the 20th century family had also changed. These many activities, by imitating deep local traditions, gave to some rootless folk the comfortable illusion of an operating community, a myth the neighborly, informal rhetoric of school publicity helped to perpetuate. Privately the administrators knew better. In a manner inconceivable to the 19th century principal, they counseled each other on the techniques of "drawing in" a preoccupied public or of "explaining the school" to a constituency glad to let the experts do the job.[21]

Appropriate to the modern culture they were expected to translate, the schools were systematized and, in a sense, nationalized. As Lawrence Cremin has noted, many Americans early in the century now construed education as a task specifically of the schools rather than of a general society, a reflection of both the school's presumed expertise and a modern society's rational differentiation of functions.[22] For the first time Americans assumed a continuous system of education, running from kindergarten through twelve graded years, and questions of its proper organization became national issues, as the interminable debates over the place of the new junior high school illustrated. Central agencies of education, professionalization and publicity—the major teachers colleges and accrediting agencies, a revitalized National Education Association and a lengthening list of professional journals—set the agenda for discussion and the boundaries of debate throughout the land.

The high school was the core of the new system. Rather than the confusing mixture of college preparatory schools, any grades above the last common-school grade, and a few ventures in industrial apprenticing that had dotted late-19th century America, the new high school was in general outline the same across the nation and always integral to a whole system of education. Conceptually the determinate, dominant high school was an invention of the modern era.

The elementary years, once the sole justification of public education, now served as an appendage that prepared pupils and then fed them into the high schools. In the lower grades, where classes were increasingly organized as simulated little societies—another instance of the schools as surrogate communities—children learned not only the skills to manage advanced subject-matter but, much more important, the undergirding habits of modern society: the omnipresence of impersonal rules, the importance of self-regulated achievement toward a superior's goals, a sophisticated discipline of the clock, the ways to compete while seeming to cooperate, and the like.[23] Morality was no longer a list of maxims; it had become an intricate network of social responses, ones that required years of apprenticeship.

After the conditioning of the elementary grades, pupils on the verge of adulthood were ready to culminate the process in high school. Here they refined their talents as citizens-in-training, especially by applying the general principles of elementary school in a variety of particular situations. In such subjects as a mathematics of the marketplace, a mental hygiene stressing adaptability, and a civics emphasizing their responsibilities and the government's powers, and extracurricularly in such activities as student government and team sports, they were coached in the roles of the modern citizen. The high school, one expert astutely commented, would prepare the adolescent

> as an efficient *user* of products . . . [rather than] as a *producer*. . . . Thus, for example, few individuals in the high school ever hope to become, or could possibly become, journalists, poets, novelists, historians, or essayists. What most of them may become is thoughtful, appreciative readers of journals, poetry, novels, history, or essays. . . . Similarly, in respect to a course in mechanics, or cabinet making, or chemistry . . . few individuals who are in the school will ever have any need for the knowledge of skill which would enable them to build or produce, let us say, an automobile, a living-room chair, or a culture of bacteria. What each one, however, does need to know is how to operate an automobile, once it is built, how to judge of the workmanship,

beauty, and serviceability of a chair once it is manufactured, how to lessen the ever-present menace of harmful bacteria in foods and drinks. . . .[24]

In contrast to the grand planners of the 19th century, those who designed a curriculum of this sort presumed that it would be modified as current needs and tastes changed.

Vocational guidance, the object of extensive discussion and extravagant praise, embodied the second major objective of the high school. Essentially a product of the 20th century, vocational guidance expressed in concrete form a great deal of education's new function as the young citizen's medium into an impersonal society. Its aim before the Second World War was no more than approximate, as those familiar with the Kuder Preference Record and Minnesota Multiphasic Personality Inventory will recognize. But in an age of relatively specialized job categories requiring largely general skills, that kind of broad guidance represented a logical fulfillment of the expert's role.[25]

The psychological theory underpinning this system also reflected the new era. The critical departure from 19th century assumptions came in the 1890s with G. Stanley Hall's celebrated studies of adolescence. From these developed a general view encompassing a whole series of qualitative changes from childhood to maturity. Instead of tending the flower as it unfolded, education found a new idiom for a new orientation. The schools would adapt classroom procedure, ease transitions and note maturation rates in response to a complicated, fluid process of growth. In addition, a modern faith in the unique psychological values of group instruction meant that interaction itself became central in the child's socialization. Theoretically, the 19th century school prepared pupils one by one for life; its successor prepared them in groups.

The modern system, despite the democratic claims of its defenders, more obviously served one class of citizens than had its predecessor. The continual upper-class domination of school boards by itself was just a 20th century adaptation of a 19th century phenomenon. Leading citizens had always controlled public education. The differences lay inside the two schemes. Where the old school had directed its energies, however patronizingly, to all young children in common, the new system was designed to benefit high-school graduates, that minority completing a process whose effects presupposed completion. The parents the new schools cultivated were those of at least a comfortable middle class, hopefully mobile, who sought professional assistance in pushing their children up the ladder. Not only did the life style exemplified in the school fit this level, but as the educational profession rose in stature the instinctive sympathies of teachers and administrators also lay there.[26] The "mechanics and others wanting present employment" who had once patrolled the one-room schools were largely gone.[27]

Radical changes in the 20th century transformed teachers from the town's domestics into experts in the mysteries of guidance, from the subordinate part of a model to the central part of a process. Though administrators sometimes dissented and salaries did not appear to sustain the claim, the teacher was the heart of this system, for she—not the textbooks of yesterday or even the modern lesson-plans and classroom aids—managed the intricate, elusive techniques of socialization. Faith in the self-operating influence of a perfect environment had disappeared. Subject matter, while far more important and much better integrated into the teacher's training, was clearly subsidiary to its social effects. Only the human in charge, responding to situations of the moment, could manipulate the endless details of acculturation.

By all odds the administrator held the most complicated, exacting job within the new system. Rather than ruleskeeper and exhorter, he was now director of a complex institution, commanding attention and money as well as respect. He mediated between the school and a variety of publics. He was the primary educational publicist and the primary politician in a system requiring active yet dutiful constituents—the indispensable legions of the PTA. He himself led the lobby for funds. He was expected to master the sharp language of business acumen yet adopt the modest stance of a disinterested servant. Linking a dream of innocent childhood with a reality of striving adults, he embodied contradictions neither he nor the public could resolve.[28]

Schools varied in infinite ways from this urban-bureaucratic standard. Around the time of the First World War, as the new system was taking form, 60 per cent of America's teachers worked in rural schools, and more than half of these taught alone. A widely deplored "rural problem" replaced in popularity the "city problem" of the previous century, with schools scattered about the countryside lagging in every degree behind the latest innovation. Some areas of the South were just entering the era of the common school while modern schools rose in the cities, and even in many northern and western towns adaptations still only partial as late as the 1950s came grudgingly.[29] The height of open resistance occurred during and immediately after the First World War in the form of the Ku Klux Klan's defense of "The Little Red School House," fundamentalist hostility to scientific atheism in education, and efforts to impose a narrow, uncritical patriotism upon the classroom. Once community leaders had known as a matter of course that their values prevailed in the local schools. Now, as William Jennings Bryan complained a "scientific soviet is attempting to dictate what shall be taught in *our* schools." Spokesmen for the new education prescribed an unnatural urban-industrial remedy of modern curriculum, business efficiency and community leadership for the rural school and expected a suspicious countryside to respond with gratitude.[30]

A familiar mixture of somebody else's practicality and a diluted general education continued to characterize the slum schools of the 20th century, only the irrelevance of rural decency had given way to the irrelevance of modern middle-class socialization. Standardized textbooks, and lesson plans now applied the orderly, accommodating values of the suburb to the world of chance and violence around center city. At the other extreme, the systems of a few wealthy communities and certain metropolitan high schools were responding to the needs of a minority who sought specialized pre-professional training. Yet however well a rare experiment in tracking classes or the demanding curriculum at Bronx High School of Science or even individualized achievement in the Winnetka Plan anticipated a later era, each remained no more than an interesting aberration through the 1930s.[31] Like other deviations, these were still measured against a general, socializing education for modern America.

A skills crisis, first widely recognized in the late 1940s, has now elevated those few pre-professional schools into a new national norm, the full implications of which are still far from clear today. Although the changes generating that crisis had been gathering strength in the 1930s and early 1940s, depression and the presumably abnormal needs of wartime temporarily delayed most people's awareness. Then the cumulative pressures from an increasingly sophisticated industrial technology, a rapidly deepening specialization in all manner of professions and a spreading request for college degrees from other status-conscious occupations released a national cry for trained personnel. Where were the engineers to plan and run the machinery, the scientists to win the Cold War, the doctors to treat every malady, the teachers to manage an exploding population? Professionally-minded critics of the social high school stepped from the shadows to help an appreciative middle-class audience redefine the relationship between education and success. A few years before, success seemed to come to the young man with the right style, the knack. His employer would always train him to the particular job. Now success beckoned to the young man with the advanced degree, that guarantee of specialization opening the doors into industry and the professions. "In these days," stated the Supreme Court in *Brown* v. *Board of Education*, "it is doubtful that any child may reasonably be expected to succeed in life if he is denied the opportunity of an education."[32] More and more Americans could understand this in a new, insistent sense. Education, long correlated with success, appeared suddenly and precisely to *cause* success.

In order to meet that changing relationship, public education was relocated as the subsidiary part of a larger scheme. The school system of twelve integrated steps, once conceived as a whole process uniformly equipping its charges for life—whether they went on to industry, homemaking, commerce or college—would serve instead as a preparatory stage. In a manner vaguely reminiscent of the college preparatory schools of the late 19th century, the high school would now act as a conduit into channels of greater and greater specialization.[33] In fact, life adjustment—that most hallowed of all educational functions—had finally been challenged. At least where training in citizenship and character threatened to steal time from mathematics or science, research projects or writing skills, it fell on the defensive. Increasingly, general socialization was a frill, as alternative means of acculturation through mass media, a commercialized teen-age culture and a broader fund of parental knowledge eased an earlier sense of the family's helplessness before an impersonal society. Educators since the days of Horace Mann who might have disagreed on any other subject would have rebelled in unison against this revolution in priorities.

The curriculum, not the teacher, stood at the center of the new process. Beginning with the sciences and expanding to cover every subject related to professionalization, subject matter underwent perpetual evaluations so that pupils might learn as much as possible as early as possible of the skills they must some day master as specialists. The changes, in other words, were "discipline centered rather than child or society centered. That is, the emphasis is on updating and reorganizing those academic disciplines that are considered basic in the pre-collegiate curriculum."[34] The teacher, important primarily as an adjunct to the new curriculum, was once again an agent. At the same time, however, everyone connected with the school system, while demoted after a period of relative exclusiveness, could receive respect—and funds—unprecedented in educational history if the system served sufficiently well. The achievement race, whipping students, teachers and administrators alike at an ever-faster pace, was that essential.

An ongoing revolution, skills education has won ground very unevenly. Its major victory has been the establishment of a new standard, altering the framework of values even where it has not changed content. What substantive changes it has brought have widened the class differential in the public schools. The new scheme selects a minority already motivated and generally well to-do for favored treatment—often in separate classes—and by the very nature of its objectives then helps to extend the distance between those who remain in the race and those who do not. The runners do not simply finish high school; they continue farther and farther into a world of specialists that eventually lies light-years away from the world of manual labor. Moreover, by sharpening the equation between personal achievement and personal worth, skills education accentuates distinctions that a socializing system had sometimes blurred. Substantial citizens have increasingly moved from city to suburb, from suburb to suburb, in pursuit of such benefits and consequently have contributed to the "growing amount of economic segregation in American public schools since 1940." In 1961, Patricia Sexton reported that "of the nation's 26,500 high schools, a mere 5000 produce 82 per cent of all college students."[35]

Questions of equity and balance have traditionally fallen beyond the scope of the schools. Throughout its history public education has deferred to the leading members of a locality to define its role as they understood society's best interests. The indoctrination in the island communities of the 19th century, the socialization of the early 20th century and the devotion to skills in our time have all been functioned precisely in these terms. What leeway the schools have enjoyed since 1900 has covered the manner of achieving goals, not the goals themselves. The legal setting for the schools and the emotional defenses of local autonomy merely underline the historical record. Such matters would scarcely require emphasis if in this century a vague aura of reform had not come to surround public education, an aura reflecting the primary place of the school in American democratic ideology rather than a comprehension of its place in American social structure. A strong rhetorical tradition, originating with the progressives, has continually raised expectations that the schools, more or less as autonomous agents, could promote a basic national reconstruction if only narrow and timid officials would grow wise and courageous. The burden of this essay is that public education has never even approximated the resources for such independent action, that it has always derived its strength and purpose from institutions around it, and that only a revolution in social relationships would enable the school to fulfill the strange role the rhetoric of reform has set for it.

NOTES

1. Among those who in various ways have participated in such a quest are David Brody, Daniel Calhoun, Stanley Elkins, William Freehling, Paul Goodman, Oscar Handlin, Roy Lubove, Eric McKitrick, David Rothman and James Sterling Young.

2. "Public Schools" and "public education" in this essay exclude all special programs for adults and part-time students and all education at the college and university levels.

3. Horace Mann, *Lectures on Education* (Boston, 1848), pp. 52–53, 231; Henry Barnard, *Report on the Condition and Improvement of the Public Schools of Rhode Island* (Providence, 1846), p. 77; Lloyd P. Jorgenson, *The Founding of Public Education in Wisconsin* (Madison, 1956), p. 45. See also Lawrence A. Cremin, *The American Common School: An Historic Conception* (New York, 1954), pp. 104–5.

4. *Horace Mann on the Crisis in Education,* ed. Louis Filler (Yellow Springs, O., 1965), p. 154; Mann, *Lectures,* p. 117. See also Edward A. Mansfield, *American Education, Its Principles and Elements* (New York, 1854), chaps. i–iii, xii.

5. Filler, *Mann,* p. 175.

6. Mann, *Lectures,* p. 38; Barnard, *Report on Rhode Island,* pp. 73–74. See also J. Orville Taylor, *The District School* (New York, 1834), pp. 37, 98.

7. "The Necessity of Education in a Republican Government," in Mann, *Lectures,* pp. 117–62. Taylor, *District School,* pp. 77, 290–336. Carleton H. Mann, *How Schools Use Their Time: Time Allotment Practice in 444 Cities Including a Study of Trends from 1826 to 1926* (New York, 1926), pp. 14–20.

8. Mann, *Lectures,* p. 125; *Henry Barnard on Education,* ed. John S. Brubacher (New York, 1931), p. 131.

9. Ruth M. Elson, *Guardians of Tradition: American Schoolbooks in the Nineteenth Century* (Lincoln, Neb., 1964).

10. Barnard, *Report on Rhode Island*, appendix XII. Brubacher, *Barnard*, pp. 223 ff. Taylor, *District School*, pp. 223–31.

11. (Horace Mann) *The Massachusetts System of Common Schools: Being an Enlarged and Revised Edition of the Tenth Annual Report of the First Secretary of the Massachusetts Board of Education* (Boston, 1849), p. 86. See also Mansfield, *American Education* pp. 85–95, 246–59; David P. Page, *Theory and Practice of Teaching*, ed. E. C. Branson (New York, 1899), esp. chap. iv.

12. See, for example, Brubacher, *Barnard*, pp. 210, 214.

13. Jorgenson, *Education in Wisconsin*, p. 182.

14. *Report of the Committee of Fifteen on Elementary Education* (New York, 1895), p. 41; John S. Roberts, *William T. Harris: A Critical Study of His Education and Related Philosophical Views* (Washington, D.C., 1924), pp. 27, 121. See also Harris, *Psychologic Foundations of Education* (New York, 1898).

15. See in particular Barnard, *Report on Rhode Island*, p. 34. Michael B. Katz, *The Irony of Early School Reform* (Cambridge, 1968), is an outstanding analysis of class tensions in Massachusetts before the Civil War.

16. Joseph M. Rice, *The Public School System of the United States* (New York, 1893). See also Ellwood P. Cubberly, *The Portland Survey* (Yonkers-on-Hudson, N.Y., 1916). David Tyack graciously helped clarify my interpretation of administrative practices late in the 19th century.

17. The best description of these years is Lawrence A. Cremin, *The Transformation of the School: Progressivism in American Education, 1876–1957* (New York, 1961), Pt. I. See also the valuable information in Edward A. Krug, *The Shaping of the American High School* (New York, 1964); Rush Welter, *Popular Education and Democratic Thought in America* (New York, 1962), chaps. xv, xvi; and Solon T. Kimball and James E. McClellan Jr., *Education and the New America* (New York, 1962), pp. 39 ff.

18. See also Richard G. Boone, *Education in the United States* (New York, 1899).

19. Calvin O. Davis, *Our Evolving High School Curriculum* (New York, 1927), p. 229.

20. U.S. Bureau of Education, Bulletin No. 35 (Washington, D.C., 1918), p. 9. John Dewey, *Democracy and Education* (New York, 1916), is the classic statement of social individualism in this sense. There were, of course, private experiments in highly individualized instruction. Despite attempts by the historian to incorporate them into the mainstream of public education, however, these belong among the increasingly defensive and self-conscious efforts in the 20th century to protect the individual from a hostile, homogenizing environment—an environment that includes public education.

21. See, for example, Arthur B. Moehlman, *Public School Relations* (New York, 1927), and M. E. Moore, *Parent, Teacher, and School* (New York, 1923).

22. *The Genius of American Education* (Pittsburgh, Pa., 1965), pp. 6–7.

23. See, for example, Frederick G. Bonser, *Elementary School Curriculum* (New York, 1922); John L. Horn, *The American Elementary School* (New York, 1923), esp. chap. ii; Lois Coffey Mossman, *Principles of Teaching and Learning in the Elementary School* (Boston, 1929), pp. 1–69. John R. Seeley *et al.*, *Crestwood Heights: A Study of the Culture of Suburban Life* (New York, 1956), is a brilliant examination of the relationship between modern values and education.

24. Davis, *Evolving High School*, pp. 127–28.

25. See, for example, Aubrey A. Douglass, *Secondary Education* (Boston, 1927); National Industrial Conference Board, *Public Education as Affecting the Adjustment of Youth to Life* (New York, 1929), pp. 19 ff.

26. August R. Hollingshead, *Elmstown's Youth: The Impact of Social Classes on Adolescents* (New York, 1949), is an illuminating case study. See also W. Lloyd Warner *et al.*, *Who Shall Be Educated?* (New York, 1944).

27. Henry Barnard, *Normal Schools and Other Institutions, Agencies, and Means Designed for the Professional Education of Teachers* (2 vols., Hartford, Conn., 1851), I, 103.

28. Neal Gross, *Who Runs Our Schools?* (New York, 1958), esp. chaps. ii–v, discusses both the complexity and the uncertainty of the administrator's role.

29. See, for example, Arthur J. Vidich and Joseph Bensman, *Small Town in Mass Society* (Princeton, 1958), chap. vii, and Hollingshead, *Elmstown's Youth, passim.* See also James Agee and Walker Evans, *Let Us Now Praise Famous Men* (Boston, 1960 ed.), p. 291, for a comment on a 19th century common school in rural Alabama during the 1930s.

30. Quoted in Lawrence W. Levine, *Defender of the Faith: William Jennings Bryan: The Last Decade, 1915–1925* (New York, 1965), p. 289. (italics added). See also Thomas J. Woofter, *Teaching in Rural Schools* (Boston, 1917), esp. pp. 59–63.

31. Although Carleton Washburne, the genius of the Winnetka Plan, experimented with individualized learning largely in order to free time for social education, his program nonetheless proved peculiarly relevant to a later era that de-emphasized socialization in favor of individual achievement in skills. See Washburne, *Adjusting the School to the Child* (New York, 1932), esp. chap. i, and Washburne and Sidney P. Marland Jr., *Winnetka: The History and Significance of an Educational Experiment* (Englewood Cliffs, N. J., 1963), esp. Pt. II.

32. 347 U.S. 483 (1954).

33. A renewed scholarly appreciation for the college-oriented Committee of Ten, which studied secondary schools for the National Education Association in the early 1890s, seems related to this recent change in the conception of the modern high school. See, for example, Theodore R. Sizer, *Secondary Schools at the Turn of the Century* (New Haven, 1964), and Lawrence Cremin, "The Revolution in American Secondary Education, 1893–1918," *Teachers College Record,* LVI (Mar. 1955), 295–308.

34. John I. Goodlad, *The Changing School Curriculum* (New York, 1966), pp. 9–10 and *passim.* See also *New Curricula,* ed. Robert W. Heath (New York, 1964).

35. Robert J. Havighurst, "Urban Development and the Educational System," in *Education in Depressed Areas,* ed. A. Harry Passow (New York, 1963), pp. 27 ff; Patricia Cayo Sexton, *Education and Income* (New York, 1961), p. 187.

JOHN DEWEY AND THE GREAT COMMUNITY

Charles Burgess
Merle L. Borrowman

With a generation of intellectuals bred in the atmosphere of small towns of nineteenth-century America and forced in their mature years to wrestle with axiological problems in the impersonal and mechanical blindness of mushrooming megalopoli, Dewey developed a lasting respect for the earlier more intimate method of human intercourse peculiar to rural and small-town America. A restoration of the "face-to-face community," but not of small-town society itself, became for him the life-blood of heightened social attainment and individual dignity, of truly "progressive" change, and of the necessary development of the idea of democracy from its beginnings as a political device to a way of living that embraced equalitarian treatment of man and purposive collective action in all human affairs. Whether he spoke of domestic national life or, as in the following statement, of international relations, his point was the same: "The only way to make headway is to start with the nonpolitical aspects of society—conversation, food, technical meetings, congresses and so on—and end up with politics. But certainly don't start with politics!"[1] On the occasion of his ninetieth birthday the same line of thought, now a fixed aim in Dewey's mind, reappeared: "Democracy begins in conversation."[2]

Jefferson, even Maclure, and William James suggested human goals and methods that became more worthy of support for Dewey than did those proposed by Harris or Hall. None of the former exalted the State over the citizen or failed to support the idea that man, whose nature was plastic, could become a reasoning creature. Education was not a "system of police" to use Daniel Webster's phrase; it was a force of liberation for man. Not to be confused with mere "schooling," education was for Dewey a lifelong experience. Ideally it developed habits of suspended belief, inquiry, and the

Reprinted by permission of the author from pp. 100–112 of Charles Burgess and Merle L. Borrowman, *What Doctrines to Embrace* (Glenview, Ill.: Scott, Foresman and Company, 1969).

willingness to change, by reasoned choice, any and all institutionalized forms of life in response to keener insights about the conditions necessary for the continued elevation of the quality of life. Here was the educational desideratum, then: to involve all members of society in processes meliorative for the human spirit.

By the time Dewey established his experimental school at the University of Chicago (1896) he had adopted a view of progress not unlike that earlier espoused by William Maclure. That is to say, he saw the drive for property, knowledge, and social control as fundamental. Changes in technology that he recognized as evidences of the increased scientific attitude on the part of man, had, he believed, outrun changes in other human institutions. Evil was a function of man's failure to use creative intelligence with respect to these other institutions. Cultural lag, the failure to study and adjust all institutions along with the reorganization of technology, was the source of most problems.

Social disorganization was anathema to Dewey as to Harris and Hall; social order and harmony among men was prized by Dewey as by them. But to him neither the evolutionary outworking of the world soul nor the biological evolution of human instincts could be relied upon to provide this order. What was needed was the deliberate use of cooperative human intelligence, fortified by a scientific attitude and focused upon the relations among social institutions. With the political progressives of his day Dewey saw social reform as a matter of human engineering, with efficiency tempered by humaneness the criteria for success. Though he rejected the state as the embodiment of human virtues and aspirations, he came very close to putting the "community" in its place.

Developments in technology, he argued in *School and Society* (1899), had robbed the family and the village shop of their capacity to aid the young in seeing life whole and integrated. Work had lost its significance, which is to say that one no longer saw intimate relationships between his function as a producer and as a member of a group sharing affection, mutual respect, and common purpose. Academic instruction and scientific inquiry were also now cut off from a direct and immediate connection with the problems and aspirations of men. The pedagogical answer was to re-establish in the school a miniature, embryonic community. By engaging the young in cooperative problem solving, oriented initially around relatively primitive processes of production but following the history of these processes to the contemporary complex level, one could hopefully sharpen a sense of the connectedness and interdependence of modern life and thought.

In *The Child and the Curriculum*, a companion volume to *School and Society*, Dewey addressed himself to the Rousseauvian concern with self-realization. Passages abound in which he waxed eloquent about the case for the child: "The case is of the Child. It is his present powers which are to assert themselves; his present capacities which are to be exercised; his present attitudes which are to be realized."[3] But he was far from Rousseauvian in his criteria about the ultimate image in which child growth should be shaped.

According to *The Child and the Curriculum*, the teacher's sense of the most scientific and efficient ways in which the race has so far developed for responding to problems is crucial in providing direction. Where the experience of the race is not controlling, one's contribution to the group endeavor proves critical. What function a particular child has in a group project will reflect his highly personal interests and capacities, but whether or not it is worthwhile is judged by its value to the common enterprise. The sense of community, which Dewey was most concerned to establish, depended on each child accepting the group's aspiration as his own and allocating esteem to himself and to his peers in terms of service to these aspirations. Of course it was fundamental to Dewey's scheme that the group be "democratic," that all participate in determining what projects are undertaken.

This early Dewey saw changes in the processes for producing and distributing goods and services in the forefront of social change generally. At a time when he momentarily toyed with the recapitulation theory as the possible explanation of this economic evolution, he saw the study of these processes as the most promising clue to organizing instruction. Also at this time one can see emerging something of a Marx-Bellamy orientation: and Dewey himself once suggested that Marx's *Das Kapital* and Bellamy's *Looking Backward* were among the books most markedly shaping his convictions. But Dewey was certainly not at this time a radical social reformer. Nothing in these early proposals need have threatened those in power. Dewey hoped such schools as his would evolve active, productive citizens who would be concerned about social situations, but his was no school for rebels. There is in the early Dewey no call for fundamental assaults on private ownership, nor is there any of the Freudian notion that the basic impulses and desires of the individual might directly clash with institutional social interests.

During the 1920's Dewey's public views began to change. Though later disillusioned with the Soviet experiment, Dewey saw in the revolutionary movements of the twenties new possibilities in the fundamental reforms of political and economic institutions. In that decade he traveled widely—to Russia, Turkey, Mexico, and China. Citizens and government leaders alike stirred Dewey with their enthusiastic, even passionate, efforts to build greater communities in their lands. In Russia, for example, he found the identification of formal education with political propagandizing repugnant; but he also found that "The main effort is nobly heroic, evincing a faith in human nature which is democratic beyond the ambitions of the democracies of the past."[4]

Much of what he found in Leninist Russia therefore

came as a shock. In view of the prevailing idea of other countries as to the total lack of freedom and total disregard of democratic methods in Bolshevist Russia, it is disconcerting, to say the least, to find Russian school children much more democratically organized than our own; and to note that they are receiving . . . a training that fits them, much more systematically than is attempted in our professedly democratic country, for later active participation in the self-direction of both local communities and industries.

Indeed Dewey found in the budding school system of Leninist Russia ideas "from which we might, if we would, learn much more than from the system of any other country."[5]

No clearer "illustration of the ideological distance between Dewey and Hall could be found than in their discussions of "democracy" in the United States and in Russia. "Democracy *everywhere* . . . ," Hall insisted, "tends to the dead level of the average man [whose abilities are sorely limited by heredity], and to the dominance of . . . incompetence and inferiority."[6]

And what of Leninist Russia in Hall's estimation? Hall admitted certain virtues of the new regime; but after weighing them against their accompanying fallacies, he concluded that Bolshevism was "democratization gone mad." It had become a wounded Polyphemus, stumbling in blind pursuit of a classless society. There must be classes in any society, Hall argued. Russia's chances for a successful venture therefore depended upon "The ability of the soviet leaders to organize upward till each class has its proper place."[7] Her leaders must therefore open their eyes to another important maxim: "If the wealth of any land were equally divided, everybody would be poor, not rich."[8] Religion too must be cherished as an asset rather than ostracized as a threat to the State. Selfishness, which Hall saw in evidence at the higher echelons of Russian government, must be obliterated and service and brotherhood be instated.[9] Thus, by abstract tinkering—here discarding a cog, there adjusting a bolt and changing the firing order—Hall tuned up the Bolshevik engine. When he had finished, the engine hummed much like his own ideal State.

Dewey, however, set himself against the authoritarian state ideal and against the social ignorance that permitted changes to proceed in unforeseen, uncontrolled directions. Desperately needed, then, was the creation of responsible channels for change. Opposed to the elitism so dear to Hall, Dewey sought a social order committed to an equality of concern for all its members and to faith in human potential.

Clearly not a "belly liberal"—one who fights for material security *per se*—Dewey charged that

To "make others happy" except through liberating their powers and engaging them in activities that enlarge the meaning of life is to harm them and to indulge ourselves under cover of exercising a special virtue. Our moral measure for estimating any existing arrangement or any proposed reform is its effect upon impulse and habits. Does it liberate or suppress, ossify or render flexible, divide or unify interests? Is perception quickened or dulled? . . . Is thought creative or pushed one side into pedantic specialisms? There is a sense in which to set up social welfare *as an end* of action only promotes an offensive condescension, a harsh interference, or an oleaginous display of complacent kindliness. [But to] foster conditions that widen the horizon of others and give them command of their own powers, so that they can find their own happiness in their own fashion, is the way of social action. Otherwise the prayer of a freeman would be to be left alone, and to be delivered, above all, from "reformers" and "kind" people.[10]

Russia seemed to Dewey to have learned "the way of social action." Not democratization gone mad, but democracy of heroic potential proportions greeted Dewey. The schools and communities supported one another in shaping an enriching life of culture and a shared joy of learning and working together.

Perhaps the most significant thing in Russia, after all, is not the effort at economic transformation, but the will to use an economic change as the means of developing a popular cultivation, especially an esthetic one, such as the world has never known. [And again,] . . . the final significance of what is taking place in Russia [in the 1920's] is not to be grasped in political or economic terms, but is found in change, of incalculable importance, in the mental and moral disposition of a people, an educational transformation. This impression, I fear, deviates widely from the belief of both the devotees and the enemies of the Bolshevik régime. But it is stamped in my mind and I must record it for what is it.

Refreshing too, and enlightened, was the freedom from race and color prejudice that seemed to lend reassuring credence to the plan to bring *all* persons into the cultivated life. Nor was Dewey insensitive to the Russian charge that ". . . a nation that strives for a private culture from which many are excluded by economic stress cannot be a cultivated nation. . . ."[11]

Driven with renewed purpose to explore the obstacles standing between divided Americans and an inheritance of generous union and face-to-face community encounter, Dewey thus severed the democratic spirit from any necessary connection with capitalism.[12] Dewey pondered, "I do not see how any honest educational reformer in western countries can deny that the greatest practical obstacle in the way of introducing into schools that connection with social life which he regards as desirable is the great part played by personal competition and desire for private profit in our economic life." Here was Dewey, who for a generation had been identified with the idea of the school as an integral and integrating institution in the community, now leading himself to the logical conclusion that such interrelationships under capitalism sabotaged the higher purposes of educational reform. He accepted the conclusion in its general form; and continued by noting that the socioeconomic fact of American life "almost makes it necessary that *in important respects school activities should be protected from social contacts and connection, instead of being organized to create them.*" If that were not clear enough, Dewey spelled out the meaning of honest educational reform with unmistakeable clarity, at the same time reaffirming his earlier stress on community values: "The Russian educational situation is enough to convert one to the idea that *only in a society based upon the cooperative principle can* the ideals of educational reformers be adequately carried into operation."[13] In the Russia of the 1920's, at least, intellectuals and educational reformers seemed to be building a potentially enviable community ideal with the power thrust of "a unified religious social faith." What, then, was now the role of honest intellectuals in America? In America intellectuals "have a task that is, if they are sincere, chiefly critical. . . ."[14]

In a sober "Critique of American Civilization," prepared at the request of the Chautauqua in 1928, Dewey resisted prophecy in favor of query and criticism.

> Where are we going? Toward what are we moving? . . . If ever there was a house of civilization divided within itself and against itself, it is ours today. If one were to take only some symptoms and ignore others, one might make either a gloomy or a glowing report, and each with equal justice—as far as each went.

The public and official elements of American life, typified by a general "hardness, a tightness, a clamping down of the lid, a regimentation and standardization, a devotion to efficiency and prosperity of a mechanical and quantitative sort," filled Dewey with "discouragement." But in the ferment on the fringe of what has since been labeled the "Establishment" he took heart. To the "outside" and private circles—focussing upon scattered leaders of the intelligentsia—Dewey looked expectantly for men to write a slogan more noble than "Prosperity is our God." Hopefully the potential cultural dynamism of the private sector would organize its aimless patterns of protest (and bohemianism) into a relevant statement of individual potential and worth. "In saying this," Dewey added, "I do not mean what is sometimes called individualism as opposed to association. I mean rather an individuality that operates in and through voluntary associations."[15] Dismayed by the lethal lethargy of the public sector Dewey saw the main hope for reform in a grass roots impulse of unified private groups. Thus his own energies poured as a testimony to his own action-oriented philosophy. He either attended the birth or encouraged the development of several organizations including the National Association for the Advancement of Colored People, the American Association of University Professors, the American Federation of Teachers, and the League for Industrial Democracy.

All this had taken place before the depression of the 1930's. During that decade, with a nation strife-wracked and simmering with social despera- tion, Dewey made his sharpest attacks upon economic competition, *Carpe diem*. Let the ideal of shared human purpose, of universalized culture, of man dignified now guide the national effort to pull free of the muck of widespread misery. Now, he insisted, reverse the traditional relationship between man and economic machinery. Let technology and production no longer dictate human purpose; but let them now be bent to the task of liberating man from the curse of exploitation and economic competition.

> The actual corrosive "materialism" of our times [Dewey insisted in 1935] does not proceed from science. It springs from the notion, sedulously cultivated by the class in power, that the creative capacities of individuals can be evoked and developed only in a struggle for material possession and material gain. We either should surrender our professed belief in the supremacy of ideal and spiritual values and accommodate our beliefs to the predominant material orientation, or we should through organized endeavor institute the socialized economy of material security and plenty that will release human energy for pursuit of higher values. . . . Regimentation of material and mechanical forces is the only way by which the mass of individuals can be released from regimentation and consequent suppression of their cultural possibilities. . . . Earlier liberalism regarded the separate and competing action of individuals as the means to social well-being as the end. We must reverse the perspec- tive and see that socialized economy is the means of free individual develop- ment as the end.[16]

Where in all this macrocosmic planning did the schools of America fit? To the consternation of social reconstructionists of the 1930's, Dewey re- fused to support their desire to make the schools a center for propagandiz- ing the virtues of the anticipated socialized commonwealth. He continued to insist upon the essentially undemocratic nature of indoctrination. It would be enough—even more than too many teachers were capable of—to focus upon intellectual freedom and thorough understanding of the salient facts of historical and contemporary society.

To be free an individual had to be at liberty to choose between alterna- tives fairly presented. The idea of indoctrination, however innocuously pushed by some social reconstructionists, bode fair to threaten the princi- ple of choice. Freedom of inquiry amounted to social inquiry. All studies should be taught according to the principle that the basis of correlation is social life. Thus too, Dewey explicitly charged the schools with a task that consciously refused to build any fixed social ideal for American youths; schools were to vest in youth the freedom and ability to modify their insti- tutions according to their own best sense of community in the coming day of their own maturity. Dewey recognized and heartily endorsed a twen- tieth-century version of Jeffersonian enthusiasm for viewing societies as ex- periments in living.

Many powerful interest groups, however, consciously restrained free-dom of inquiry. They recognized, Dewey maintained, that if teaching "starts with questions and inquiries it is fatal to all social system-making and programs of fixed ends. . . . It is not easy to imagine the difference which would follow from the shift of thought to discrimination and analys-is."[17] A democratic public required clearly more than mere freedom of in-quiry. Free dissemination of the conclusions of inquiry, free debate, full discussion, and intelligent and intellectually honest persuasion were also essential. Too long had men been led to believe that to be free in one's thought was tantamount to fulfilling the meaning of free inquiry. Mind is not severed from action. Such a notion "presents in fact the spectacle of mind deprived of its normal functioning, because it is baffled by . . . ac-tualities . . . and is driven back into secluded and impotent revery."[18]

The school, then, should foster freedom of expression. Without that suc-cessful effort, social inquiry remained an idle fantasy. Freedom to inquire, to express opinions and render reasoned judgments with impugnity, to combat the oligarchical interests that encouraged social inertia, prejudice, and blind emotion in the interests of mass manipulation—these purposes should guide the efforts of schoolmen. Then all knowledge, unified and directed at social purposes, would make intelligence a community prop-erty. "A fact of community life which is not spread abroad so as to be a common possession is a contradiction in terms. . . . Communication of the results of social inquiry is the same thing as the formation of public opin-ion."[19] A perpetrated lie can thus be *public* opinion in name alone.

But this was far from asserting that the child should dictate his own course of study and activity. Dewey attacked the sentimental and the psycho-analytical advocates of child-centeredness as "stupid." Those who with Harris would be content simply to set the child to memorize lessons in "subject-centered" programs also missed the Deweyan pedagogical point. As Arthur Wirth observed in his provocative study of *John Dewey as Educator*, Dewey

> resisted an either/or choice between values that cluster about "individuality" and those that center about "community." . . . The uniqueness of the *indi-vidual* accounts for values like creativity, challenge, and innovation. Yet the individual is not truly human without the nourishment of community. Un-checked, his freedom can degenerate into self-indulgence, exhibitionism, or anarchistic iconoclasm. *Community* is the source of fellowship, solidarity, hard-won knowledge and supportive traditions. But compulsive concern with these can bring conformity, coercion, and stagnation.[20]

It was Dewey's attempt, one he recognized as "The ultimate problem of all education," to maintain the imperative but fragile balance between "per-missiveness" and "other-directedness."[21]

Ceaseless striving for balance of these interests implied the presence of "democratic methods" in all human relationships. For wherever democracy had failed it had been conceived as

> too exclusively political in nature. It had not become part of the bone and blood of the people in daily conduct. . . . Democratic forms were limited to Parliament, elections and combats between parties. What is happening [in the 1930's] proves conclusively, I think, that unless democratic habits of thought and action are part of the fiber of a people, political democracy is insecure.[22]

But schools failed abysmally wherever their interests in democratic processes found primary expression in student government, bland meandering classroom discussions calculated merely to let each child "have his say," and didactic exercises in social courtesy. Respect for purpose, intelligence, and habits of inquiry had to be sedulously cultivated. How, for example, could schools claim to be preparing youth "for any kind of democratic self-government," Dewey pondered, when schoolmen lacked the courage or knowledge to teach the realities of modern governmental operations? Knowledge of government, as taught when Dewey wrote this critique in 1937, was not

> much connected with how government is actually run, with how parties are formed and managed, what machines are, what gives machines and political bosses their power. In fact, it might be dangerous in some cities if pupils in the schools were given not merely a formal and anatomical knowledge about the structure of the government but also acquired an understanding of how the government of their own community is run through giving special favors and through dealings with industrial powers.[23]

With this example of Dewey's concern for relating an ideal to the actual, one might suspect that he would also require the teacher to align himself with social reconstruction in the interests of widening the democratic tradition. Unwilling to be misunderstood on this crucial point, Dewey spoke of the teacher's position as similar to Hamlet's. The teacher who knew that

> the times are out of joint [could not escape] some responsibility for a share in putting them right. . . . Drifting is merely a cowardly mode of choice. I am not trying here to tell teachers with which of the antagonistic tendencies of our own time they should align themselves—although I have my own conviction on that subject. I am trying only to point out that the conflict is here, and that as a matter of fact [teachers] . . . are strengthening one set of forces or the other. *The question is whether they are doing so blindly, evasively, or intelligently and courageously.* If a teacher is conservative and wishes to throw in his lot with forces that seem to me reactionary and that will in the end, from my point of view, increase present chaos, *at all events let him do it*

intelligently, after a study of the situation and a conscious choice made on the
basis of intelligent study. The same thing holds for the liberal and radical.[24]

But how many teachers understood their own society? How many were
not "unfortunately somewhat given to wanting to be told what to do
. . . ?" Far too many were poorly prepared; they bristled with methodological acumen but lacked clear sense of the purposes of method. "What will
it profit a man to do this, that, and the other specific thing, if he has no
clear idea of why he is doing them, no clear idea of the way they bear upon
actual conditions and of the end to be reached?" Teachers must be intellectually competent; they must understand the process of education. They
must also have the scholarly tenacity to study their society, its antagonistic
forces, its potential future courses. In short, the good teacher is one who in
his desire to become enlightened has fashioned a social theory "of which
educational theory is a part."[25] If but for one generation, teachers would
learn and teach "not merely how society *is* going, but how it *might* be intelligently directed, then," Dewey wistfully added, "I should have no fear
about the future of democracy."[26] Adequate teaching depended upon
more—and more broadly educated—intelligent teachers who possessed
social vision and not a little courage.

Seldom in history had so much been expected of the school teacher. Seldom, when set against these lofty expectations, had teachers looked so
inept. In effect, Dewey's preachments amounted to indictments of teacher
education in particular and the destructiveness of all academic dualisms, as
between the "liberal" and "technical," that flourished in academe.

We have largely ignored the details of Dewey's pedagogical views in
favor of this cursory exploration of the Great Community he envisioned.
Necessarily ignored too have been the developments of Progressive Education and Life Adjustment Education with which Dewey's name has become
so popularly linked.[27] For present limited purposes one should note, however, a peculiar irony in the anxious reappraisals of Progressive Education
and Life Adjustment Education since 1957 and Sputnik. Those who persist
in a defense of Deweyan educational ideals have regularly ignored or failed
to make explicit the relationship Dewey insisted upon establishing between
educational and social theories. The strange anomaly of John Dewey in the
mid-twentieth century is that only the reactionaries of the political right
have regularly identified and publicly described the radical inclinations of
Dewey's thought since World War I.[28] In their frenzy, amounting at times
to group paranoia, American rightists have failed momumentally to discriminate between actual educational developments in twentieth-century
America and Dewey's notions of a suitable education. But it is not to the
credit of those who continue to find their own social purposes growing out
of Dewey's to note that rightists have made the more serious attempts
publicly to analyze Dewey's radical educational and cultural purposes.

Where Deweyan ideas still survive in unregenerate Schools of Education, where he has not been supplanted by those who treat educational processes in a vacuum innocent of social purpose, one suspects that his writings have been similarly edited and truncated. Thus Dewey has largely become the soft-hearted benignitarian, the immobilized cultural relativist who preached "learn by doing" and "child-centeredness." Tiresomely erroneous and timidly misleading clichès survive as perhaps the inevitably misleading legacy of one who ceased to be a man and became a symbol in his own lifetime. "And it is difficult now," Columbia University philosopher Charles Frankel mused in 1960, "to remember that John Dewey was a man, not an institution, a philosopher, and not a social movement."[29]

NOTES

1. James T. Farrell et al., Dialogue on John Dewey, Corliss Lamont, ed. (New York: Horizon Press, 1959), p. 90. Quoted by Herbert Schneider.

2. Ibid., p. 88. Quoted by James T. Farrell.

3. Dewey on Education, Martin Dworkin, ed. (New York: Teachers College Press, 1958), p. 111.

4. Dewey, Impressions of Soviet Russia and the Revolutionary World (New York: New Republic, Inc., 1929), p. 32. These impressions appeared originally as articles in the New Republic.

5. Ibid., pp. 40, 105–108.

6. Hall, Life, pp. 439 f. Emphasis added.

7. Hall, Morale, pp. 328, 337.

8. Hall, Life, p. 535.

9. Hall, Morale, pp. 331, 333.

10. Dewey, Human Nature and Conduct (New York: Henry Holt and Co., 1922), pp. 293 f.

11. Dewey, Impressions, pp. 31, 59, 116. These observations are weakened as evidence if one concludes that they are merely unstudied reactions and truly "impressions." On the other hand, one might take special note of these observations precisely because they are unstudied and unguardedly straightforward.

12. Farrell, Dialogue, p. 124, e.g.

13. Dewey, Impressions, p. 86. Emphasis added.

14. Ibid., p. 121.

15. Dewey, "Critique of American Civilization," in Recent Gains in American Civilization, Kirby Page, ed. (Chautauqua: The Chautauqua Press, 1928), pp. 256 f, 274 ff.

16. Dewey, Liberalism and Social Action (New York: Capricorn Books, 1963), pp. 89 f.

17. Dewey, Individualism Old and New (New York: Capricorn Books, 1962), pp. 164 f.

18. Dewey, Public, p. 167.

19. Ibid., p. 177.

20. Arthur G. Wirth, John Dewey as Educator (New York: John Wiley and Sons, 1966), p. 287.

21. Ibid., p. 297.

22. Dewey, Philosophy of Education (New York: Philosophical Library, 1956), p. 66.

23. Ibid., p. 51.

24. Ibid., p. 71. Emphasis added.

25. Ibid., p. 72.

26. *Ibid.,* p. 53.

27. For a trenchant study of Progressivism in American education, see Lawrence A. Cremin, *The Transformation of the School* (New York: A. A. Knopf, 1962); see also Raymond Callahan, *Education and the Cult of Efficiency* (Chicago: University of Chicago Press, 1962).

28. Countless pamphlets, magazines, and books play the same general theme of Dewey and educational conspiracy. See, e.g., John A. Stormer, *None Dare Call It Treason* (Florissant, Mo., Liberty Bell Press, 1964), esp. ch. VI. This volume was widely circulated during the Johnson-Goldwater Presidential campaign in 1964.

29. Charles Frankel, "John Dewey's Legacy," in *American Scholar,* 29 (Summer, 1960):313.

EDUCATION FOR COMMUNITY: SOCIOLOGICAL PERSPECTIVE

Robert Arnove

The social upheavals of the nineteenth century gave rise to the field of sociology and to the theme of community as an object of study. As a consequence of industrialization, urbanization, nation-building, and secularization a new social order was emerging. These forces contributed to the erosion of the former bases of status, association, and belief. The new discipline of sociology arose as a response to the need to comprehend these changes. The themes that occur in the seminal writings in sociology are those that pertain to the relationship between the individual and the collectivity, to community and the loss of community, to alienation, to progress, and to what Nisbet has called the "rust of progress"—the disenchantment and disillusionment that occur under conditions of rapid social change.

According to Nisbet:

> It was the brilliant French sociologist Emile Durkheim who, at the beginning of the present century, called attention to the consequences of moral and economic individualism in modern life. Individualism has resulted in masses of normless, unattached, insecure individuals who lose even the capacity for independent, creative living.[1]

Durkheim's fundamental concern in his writings on education was with the sources of moral integration and consensus in modern society. For Durkheim, social cohesion was extremely difficult to achieve in industrialized, complex societies characterized by specialization of functions and people bound to one another on the basis of self-interested contractual relations.

What agency would ensure that people were inculcated with the precepts to behave toward one another in a moral way and with consideration of the general social well-being? The answer was formal systems of education. Durkheim viewed education as the means by which society perpetuates the essential conditions of its existence:

46

> Society can survive only if there exists among its members a sufficient degree of homogeneity; education perpetuates and reinforces this homogeneity by fixing in the child, from the beginning, the essential similarities that collective life demands.

And for Durkheim, only State systems of public instruction could insure a universal and secular socializing experience, that would help unify modern, complex societies.[2]

It is interesting to note that the concern of Durkheim with state-building in France in the late nineteenth century should be reflected in the current efforts of the Third World countries of Africa, Asia, and Latin America. These countries are presently attempting to use national systems of public instruction to create a citizenry with common core values and shared allegiances. Schooling, then as now, was looked to as a means of overcoming cleavages of competing regional, religious, ethnic, and social class blocs.

In his arguments concerning the role of public education (schooling), Durkheim exemplifies the functionalist or structural-functional paradigm, which was discussed in the essay on the sociological perspective. Education performs the socially necessary function of perpetuating the values of a society and helping achieve integration. Without these functions a society would not survive. To perform these functions, a special structure emerges—State systems of public instruction, with a common curriculum transmitting a homogeneous body of moral precepts. Teachers are to be exemplars and agents of the moral truths of the greater society.

But, these questions arise: What moral truths are to be propagated? Are they self-evident? Is the State neutral and benevolent? Critical analyses of Durkheim's writings on education, and the functionalist perspective, point out that educational policy and content are not the result of divine revelation or State omniscience.[3] According to conflict theorists, groups intervene to shape the structure and content of education to serve their purposes. Schools are likely to be shaped by social groups to the extent that they possess and exercise power in society.[4] The State itself may be viewed as the agency of dominant groups for legitimating and maintaining their prerogatives (see, for example, the Bowles and Gintis reading in Problem III).

In comparing the Durkheim and the Newmann and Oliver articles we find conflicting points of view. Where Durkheim views State systems of public education as essential to the forging of a sense of community and modern society, Newmann and Oliver see them as agencies that destroy a sense of community and estrange students. Where Durkheim sees schools as agents of social cohesion, Newmann and Oliver view them as places where students are alienated from other age groups, from their neighborhoods, and from one another.

At issue are very different ideas of what community is. Durkheim, whose notion of community is akin to that of the French philosopher Rousseau, views the political community of the nation state as the highest expression of humanity. (According to Rousseau, it is only when individuals submit to the General Will that they can achieve self-fulfillment.) But Newmann and Oliver do not understand community and State as being synonymous. They share the point of view of Nisbet that "community is the product of people working together on problems of autonomy and collective fulfillment of internal objectives, and of the experience of living under codes of authority which have been set in large degree by the persons involved."[5] For Newmann and Oliver, public monopolies of education serving State purposes deny the individual a sense of community and self-realization. As manipulative agents of the State, schools serve State rather than individual needs: by training people to fit into predetermined slots required by the economy they serve the manpower needs of society; by preparing loyal citizens, they serve the political needs of society.

Newmann and Oliver believe that the present structure and functioning of schooling reflects what they call the "great society" concept of American civilization. This concept—which is closely related to unbounded enthusiam for Technology, Automation, Economic Progress (authors' emphases), and bureaucratic forms of management—leads to fragmentation, ideological and aesthetic bankruptcy, depersonalization, and powerlessness.

The authors offer an alternative concept of American civilization: the search for "lost community." According to this alternative model, education is no longer coterminous with schooling. Education becomes the responsibility of a variety of community agencies, and teaching would be undertaken by a diverse array of adults and peers—not just State-certified personnel. Educational activities would be designed to occur within the context of the community as well as within the formal setting of schools.

Elements of the model proposed by Newmann and Oliver are found in a number of educational reform movements of the 1960s and 1970s. Concern with the bureaucratic and indoctrinating aspects of schooling—as well as the substantial number of students who failed in public education—led to a variety of proposals for humanistic and open education, and to calls for community control. An expression of these concerns is found in the alternative schools movement of the past ten years.

The nature of school-community interactions has been a continuing topic of sociological study. For example, a number of classic studies have concentrated on the community power structure and how educational policy is determined by community influentials; another body of literature examines the relationship between social status in the community and how school personnel interact with students from different backgrounds.

The theme of community currently has emerged with regard to the issues of equality of educational opportunity, desegregation, and busing. People clash over these issues and the meaning of community. For some, community is defined in the narrow sense of a neighborhood; for others, community refers to a transcendental moral or political community. These issues not only involve sociological study but enter into the normative and ethical domains of philosophy.

NOTES

1. Robert Nisbet, *Community and Power* (New York: Oxford U.P., 1965), p. 14.

2. See Sam D. Sieber and David E. Wilder, *The School in Society: Studies in the Sociology of Education* (New York: The Free Press, 1973), p. 8; and Charles Bidwell, "Sociology of Education," in *Encyclopedia of Educational Research,* 4th ed., ed. by Robert L. Ebel (London: Macmillan & Co., 1969), p. 1242.

3. Sieber and Wilder, op. cit., and Bidwell, op. cit., p. 1234. However, Durkheim's recently translated *The Evolution of Educational Thought: Lectures on the Formation and Development of Secondary Education in France,* trans. Peter Collins (London: Routledge Paul, 1977) does contain elements of the conflict paradigm. According to Mohamed Cherkaoui—"Bernstein and Durkheim: Two Theories of Change in Educational Systems," *Harvard Educational Review,* **47** (November 1977)—"*The Evolution of Educational Thought* reveals that Durkheim viewed the educational system principally as a powerful weapon in the hands of dominant political groups" (p. 556). For further discussion of Durkheim also see the introductory essay by Jerome Karabel and A. H. Halsey, "Educational Research: A Review and an Interpretation," in their edited collection of readings, *Power and Ideology in Education* (New York: Oxford U.P., 1977), pp. 71–74.

4. See, for example, Economic Commission for Latin America, *Education, Human Resources and Development in Latin America* (New York: United Nations/ECLA, 1968), p. 78.

5. Nisbet, op. cit., p. xv.

EDUCATION: ITS NATURE AND ITS
ROLE

Emile Durkheim

2. Definition of Education

. . .

From these facts it follows that each society sets up a certain ideal of man, of
what he should be, as much from the intellectual point of view as the physical and moral; that this ideal is, to a degree, the same for all the citizens;
that beyond a certain point it becomes differentiated according to the particular milieux that every society contains in its structure. It is this ideal, at
the same time one and various, that is the focus of education. Its function,
then, is to arouse in the child: (1) a certain number of physical and mental
states that the society to which he belongs considers should not be lacking
in any of its members; (2) certain physical and mental states that the particular social group (caste, class, family, profession) considers, equally, ought
to be found among all those who make it up. Thus, it is society as a whole
and each particular social milieu that determine the ideal that education re-
alizes. Society can survive only if there exists among its members a sufficient degree of homogeneity; education perpetuates and reinforces this
homogeneity by fixing in the child, from the beginning, the essential similarities that collective life demands. But on the other hand, without a certain diversity all co-operation would be impossible: education assures the
persistence of this necessary diversity by being itself diversified and specialized. If the society has reached a degree of development such that the
old divisions into castes and classes can no longer be maintained, it will
prescribe an education more uniform at its base. If at the same time there
is more division of labor, it will arouse among children, on the underlying
basic set of common ideas and sentiments, a richer diversity of occupational
aptitudes. If it lives in a state of war with the surrounding societies, it tries

to shape people according to a strongly nationalistic model; if international competition takes a more peaceful form, the type that it tries to realize is more general and more humanistic. Education is, then, only the means by which society prepares, within the children, the essential conditions of its very existence. We shall see later how the individual himself has an interest in submitting to these requirements.

We come, then, to the following formula: *Education is the influence exercised by adult generations on those that are not yet ready for social life. Its object is to arouse and to develop in the child a certain number of physical, intellectual and moral states which are demanded of him by both the political society as a whole and the special milieu for which he is specifically destined.*

3. Consequences of the Preceding Definition: The Social Character of Education

It follows from the definition that precedes, that education consists of a methodical socialization of the young generation. In each of us, it may be said, there exist two beings which, while inseparable except by abstraction, remain distinct. One is made up of all the mental states that apply only to ourselves and to the events of our personal lives: this is what might be called the individual being. The other is a system of ideas, sentiments and practices which express in us, not our personality, but the group or different groups of which we are part; these are religious beliefs, moral beliefs and practices, national or professional traditions, collective opinions of every kind. Their totality forms the social being. To constitute this being in each of us is the end of education.

It is here, moreover, that are best shown the importance of its role and the fruitfulness of its influence. Indeed, not only is this social being not given, fully formed, in the primitive constitution of man; but it has not resulted from it through a spontaneous development. Spontaneously, man was not inclined to submit to a political authority, to respect a moral discipline, to dedicate himself, to be self-sacrificing. There was nothing in our congenital nature that predisposed us necessarily to become servants of divinities, symbolic emblems of society, to render them worship, to deprive ourselves in order to do them honor. It is society itself which, to the degree that it is firmly established, has drawn from within itself those great moral forces in the face of which man has felt his inferiority. Now, if one leaves aside the vague and indefinite tendencies which can be attributed to heredity, the child, on entering life, brings to it only his nature as an individual. Society finds itself, with each new generation, faced with a *tabula rasa,* very nearly, on which it must build anew. To the egoistic and asocial being that has just been born it must, as rapidly as possible, add another, capable of leading a moral and social life. Such is the work of education, and you can readily see its great importance. It is not limited to developing the individual organism in the direction indicated by its nature, to elicit the hidden potentialities that need only be manifested. It creates in man a new being.

This creative quality is, moreover, a special prerogative of human education. Anything else is what animals receive, if one can apply this name to the progressive training to which they are subjected by their parents. It can, indeed, foster the development of certain instincts that lie dormant in the animal, but such training does not initiate it into a new life. It facilitates the play of natural functions, but it creates nothing. Taught by its mother, the young animal learns more quickly how to fly or build its nest; but it learns almost nothing that it could not have been able to discover through its own individual experience. This is because animals either do not live under social conditions or form rather simple societies, which function through instinctive mechanisms that each individual carries within himself, fully formed, from birth. Education, then, can add nothing essential to nature, since the latter is adequate for everything, for the life of the group as well as that of the individual. By contrast, among men the aptitudes of every kind that social life presupposes are much too complex to be able to be obtained, somehow, in our tissues, and to take the form of organic predispositions. It follows that they cannot be transmitted from one generation to another by way of heredity. It is through education that the transmission is effected.

However, it will be said, if one can indeed conceive that the distinctively moral qualities, because they impose privations on the individual, because they inhibit his natural impulses, can be developed in us only under an outside influence, are there not others which every man wishes to acquire and seeks spontaneously? Such are the divers qualities of the intelligence which allow him better to adapt his behavior to the nature of things. Such, too, are the physical qualities, and everything that contributes to the vigor and health of the organism. For the former, at least, it seems that education, in developing them, may only assist the development of nature itself, may only lead the individual to a state of relative perfection toward which he tends by himself, although he may be able to achieve it more rapidly thanks to the co-operation of society.

But what demonstrates, despite appearances, that here as elsewhere education answers social necessities above all, is that there are societies in which these qualities have not been cultivated at all, and that in every case they have been understood very differently in different societies. The advantages of a solid intellectual culture have been far from recognized by all peoples. Science and the critical mind, that we rank so high today, were for a long time held in suspicion. Do we not know a great doctrine that proclaims happy the poor in spirit? We must guard against believing that this indifference to knowledge had been artificially imposed on men in violation of their nature. They do not have, by themselves, the instinctive appetite for science that has often and arbitrarily been attributed to them. They desire science only to the extent that experience has taught them that they cannot do without it. Now, in connection with the ordering of their individual lives they had no use for it. As Rousseau has already said, to satisfy the vital necessities, sensation, experience and instinct would suffice as they suffice for the animal. If man had not known other needs than these, very simple ones, which have their roots in his individual constitution, he would not have undertaken the pursuit of science, all the more because it has not been acquired without laborious and painful efforts. He has known the thirst for knowledge only when society has awakened it in him, and society has done this only when it has felt the need of it. This moment came when social life, in all its forms, had become too complex to be able to function otherwise than through the co-operation of reflective thought, that is to say, thought enlightened by science. Then scientific culture became indispensable, and that is why society requires it of its members and imposes it upon them as a duty. But in the beginning, as long as social organization is very simple and undifferentiated, always self-sufficient, blind tradition suffices, as does instinct in the animal. Therefore thought and free inquiry are useless and even dangerous, since they can only threaten tradition. That is why they are proscribed.

It is not otherwise with physical qualities. Where the state of the social milieu inclines public sentiment toward asceticism, physical education will be relegated to a secondary place. Something of this sort took place in the schools of the Middle Ages; and this asceticism was necessary, for the only manner of adapting to the harshness of those difficult times was to like it. Similarly, following the current of opinion, this same education will be understood very differently. In Sparta its object above all was to harden the limbs to fatigue; in Athens, it was a means of making bodies beautiful to the sight; in the time of chivalry it was required to form agile and supple warriors; today it no longer has any but a hygienic end, and is concerned, above all, with limiting the dangerous effects of a too intense intellectual culture. Thus, even the qualities which appear at first glance so spontaneously desirable, the individual seeks only when society invites him to, and he seeks them in the fashion that it prescribes for him.

We are now in a position to answer a question raised by all that precedes. Whereas we showed society fashioning individuals according to its needs, it could seem, from this fact, that the individuals were submitting to an insupportable tyranny. But in reality they are themselves interested in this submission; for the new being that collective influence, through education, thus builds up in each of us, represents what is best in us. Man is man, in fact, only because he lives in society. It is difficult, in the course of an article, to demonstrate rigorously a proposition so general and so important, and one which sums up the works of contemporary sociology. But first, one can say that it is less and less disputed. And more, it is not impossible to call to mind, summarily, the most essential facts that justify it.

First, if there is today an historically established fact, it is that morality stands in close relationship to the nature of societies, since, as we have shown along the way, it changes when societies change. This is because it results from life in common. It is society, indeed, that draws us out of our selves, that obliges us to reckon with other interests than our own, it is society that has taught us to control our passions, our instincts, to prescribe law for them, to restrain ourselves, to deprive ourselves, to sacrifice ourselves, to subordinate our personal ends to higher ends. As for the whole system of representation which maintains in us the idea and the sentiment of rule, of discipline, internal as well as external—it is society that has established it in our consciences. It is thus that we have acquired this power to control ourselves, this control over our inclinations which is one of the distinctive traits of the human being and which is the more developed to the extent that we are more fully human.

We do not owe society less from the intellectual point of view. It is science that elaborates the cardinal notions that govern our thought: notions of cause, of laws, of space, of number, notions of bodies, of life, of conscience, of society, and so on. All these fundamental ideas are perpetually evolving, because they are the recapitulation, the resultant of all scientific work, far from being its point of departure as Pestalozzi believed. We do not conceive of man, nature, cause, even space, as they were conceived in the Middle Ages; this is because our knowledge and our scientific methods are no longer the same. Now, science is a collective work, since it presupposes a vast co-operation of all scientists, not only of the same time, but of all the successive epochs of history. Before the sciences were established, religion filled the same office; for every mythology consists of a conception, already well elaborated, of man and of the universe. Science, moreover, was the heir of religion. Now, a religion is a social institution.

In learning a language, we learn a whole system of ideas, distinguished and classified, and we inherit from all the work from which have come these classifications that sum up centuries of experiences. There is more: without language, we would not have, so to speak, general ideas; for it is the word which, in fixing them, gives to concepts a consistency sufficient for them to be able to be handled conveniently by the mind. It is language, then, that has allowed us to raise ourselves above pure sensation; and it is not necessary to demonstrate that language is, in the first degree, a social thing.

One sees, through these few examples, to what man would be reduced if there were withdrawn from him all that he has derived from society: he would fall to the level of an animal. If he has been able to surpass the stage at which animals have stopped, it is primarily because he is not reduced to the fruit only of his personal efforts, but cooperates regularly with his fellow-creatures; and this makes the activity of each more productive. It is chiefly as a result of this that the products of the work of one generation are not lost for that which follows. Of what an animal has been able to learn in the course of his individual existence, almost nothing can survive him. By contrast, the results of human experience are preserved almost entirely and in detail, thanks to books, sculptures, tools, instruments of every kind that are transmitted from generation to generation, oral tradition, etc. The soil of nature is thus covered with a rich deposit that continues to grow constantly. Instead of dissipating each time that a generation dies out and is replaced by another, human wisdom accumulates without limit, and it is this unlimited accumulation that raises man above the beast and above himself. But, just as in the case of the cooperation which was discussed first, this accumulation is possible only in and through society. For in order that the legacy of each generation may be able to be preserved and added to others, it is necessary that there be a moral personality which lasts beyond the generations that pass, which binds them to one another: it is society. Thus the antagonism that has too often been admitted between society and individual corresponds to nothing in the facts. Indeed, far from these two terms being in opposition and being able to develop only each at the expense of the other, they imply each other. The individual, in willing society, wills himself. The influence that it exerts on him, notably through education, does not at all have as its object and its effect to repress him, to diminish him, to denature him, but, on the contrary, to make him grow and to make of him a truly human being. No doubt, he can grow thus only by making an effort. But this is precisely bcause this power to put forth voluntary effort is one of the most essential characteristics of man.

4. The Role of the State in Education

This definition of education provides for a ready solution of the controversial question of the duties and the rights of the State with respect to education.

The rights of the family are opposed to them. The child, it is said, belongs first to his parents; it is, then, their responsibility to direct, as they understand it, his intellectual and moral development. Education is then conceived as an essentially private and domestic affair. When one takes this point of view, one tends naturally to reduce to a minimum the intervention of the State in the matter. The State should, it is said, be limited to serving as an auxiliary to, and as a substitute for, families. When they are unable to discharge their duties, it is natural that the State should take charge. It is natural, too, that it make their task as easy as possible, by placing at their disposal schools to which they can, if they wish, send their children. But it must be kept strictly within these limits, and forbidden any positive action designed to impress a given orientation on the mind of the youth.

But its role need hardly remain so negative. If, as we have tried to establish, education has a collective function above all, if its object is to adapt the child to the social milieu in which he is destined to live, it is impossible that society should be uninterested in such a procedure. How could society not have a part in it, since it is the reference point by which education must direct its action? It is, then, up to the State to remind the teacher constantly of the ideas, the sentiments that must be impressed upon the child to adjust him to the milieu in which he must live. If it were not always there to guarantee that pedagogical influence be exercised in a social way, the latter would necessarily be put to the service of private beliefs, and the whole nation would be divided and would break down into an incoherent multitude of little fragments in conflict with one another. One could not contradict more completely the fundamental end of all education. Choice is necessary: if one attaches some value to the existence of society—and we have just seen what it means to us—education must assure, among the citizens, a sufficient community of ideas and of sentiments, without which any society is impossible; and in order that it may be able to produce this result, it is also necessary that education not be completely abandoned to the arbitrariness of private individuals.

Since education is an essentially social function, the State cannot be indifferent to it. On the contrary, everything that pertains to education must in some degree be submitted to its influence. This is not to say, therefore, that it must necessarily monopolize instruction. The question is too complex to be able to be treated thus in passing; we shall discuss it later. One can believe that scholastic progress is easier and quicker where a certain margin is left for individual initiative; for the individual makes innovations more readily than the State. But from the fact that the State, in the public interest, must allow other schools to be opened than those for which it has a more direct responsibility, it does not follow that it must remain aloof from what is going on in them. On the contrary, the education given in them must remain under its control. It is not even admissible that the function of the educator can be fulfilled by anyone who does not offer special guarantees of which the State alone can be the judge. No doubt, the limits within which its intervention should be kept may be rather difficult to determine once and for all, but the principle of intervention could not be disputed. There is no school which can claim the right to give, with full freedom, an antisocial education.

It is nevertheless necessary to recognize that the state of division in which we now find ourselves, in our country, makes this duty of the State particularly delicate and at the same time more important. It is not, indeed, up to the State to create this community of ideas and sentiments without which there is no society; it must be established by itself, and the

State can only consecrate it, maintain it, make individuals more aware of it. Now, it is unfortunately indisputable that among us, this moral unity is not at all points what it should be. We are divided by divergent and even sometimes contradictory conceptions. There is in these divergences a fact which it is impossible to deny, and which must be reckoned with. It is not a question of recognizing the right of the majority to impose its ideas on the children of the minority. The school should not be the thing of one party, and the teacher is remiss in his duties when he uses the authority at his disposal to influence his pupils in accordance with his own preconceived opinions, however justified they may appear to him. But in spite of all the differences of opinion, there are at present, at the basis of our civilization, a certain number of principles which, implicitly or explicitly, are common to all, that few indeed, in any case, dare to deny overtly and openly: respect for reason, for science, for ideas and sentiments which are at the base of democratic morality. The role of the State is to outline these essential principles, to have them taught in its schools, to see to it that nowhere are children left ignorant of them, that everywhere they should be spoken of with the respect which is due them. There is in this connection an influence to exert which will perhaps be all the more efficacious when it will be less aggressive and less violent, and will know better how to be contained within wise limits.

5. The Power of Education. The Means of Influence

After having determined the end of education, we must seek to determine how and to what extent it is possible to attain this end, that is to say, how and to what extent education can be efficacious.

This question has always been very controversial. For Fontenelle, "neither does good education make good character, nor does bad education destroy it." By contrast, for Locke, for Helvetius, education is all-powerful. According to the latter, "all men are born equal and with equal aptitudes; education alone makes for differences." The theory of Jacotot resembles the preceding.

The solution that one gives to the problem depends on the idea that one has of the importance and of the nature of the innate predispositions, on the one hand, and, on the other, of the means of influence at the disposal of the educator.

Education does not make a man out of nothing, as Locke and Helvetius believed; it is applied to predispositions that it finds already made. From another point of view, one can concede, in a general way, that these congenital tendencies are very strong, very difficult to destroy or to transform radically; for they depend upon organic conditions on which the educator has little influence. Consequently, to the degree that they have a definite

object, that they incline the mind and the character toward narrowly determined ways of acting and thinking, the whole future of the individual finds
itself fixed in advance, and there does not remain much for education to
do.

But fortunately one of the characteristics of man is that the innate predispositions in him are very general and very vague. Indeed, the type of
predisposition that is fixed, rigid, invariable, which hardly leaves room for
the influence of external causes, is instinct. Now, one can ask if there is a
single instinct, properly speaking, in man. One speaks, sometimes, of the
instinct of preservation; but the word is inappropriate. For an instinct is a
system of given actions, always the same, which, once they are set in motion by sensation, are automatically linked up with one another until they
reach their natural limit, without reflection having to intervene anywhere;
now, the movements that we make when our life is in danger do not at all
have any such fixity or automatic invariability. They change with the situation; we adapt them to circumstances: this is because they do not operate
without a certain conscious choice, however rapid. What is called the instinct of preservation is, after all, only a general impulse to flee death,
without the means by which we seek to avoid it being predetermined once
and for all. One can say as much concerning what is sometimes called, not
less inexactly, the maternal instinct, the paternal instinct, and even the
sexual instinct. These are drives in a given direction; but the means by
which these drives are expressed vary from one individual to another, from
one occasion to another. A large area remains reserved, then, for trial and
error, for personal accommodations, and, consequently, for the effect of
causes which can make their influence felt only after birth. Now, education
is one of these causes.

It has been claimed, to be sure, that the child sometimes inherits a very
strong tendency toward a given act, such as suicide, theft, murder, fraud,
etc. But these assertions are not at all in accord with the facts. Whatever
may have been said about it, one is not born criminal; still less is one destined from birth for this or that type of crime; the paradox of the Italian
criminologists no longer counts many defenders today. What is inherited is
a certain lack of mental equilibrium, which makes the individual refractory
to coherent and disciplined behavior. But such a temperament does not
predestine a man to be a criminal any more than to be an explorer seeking
adventures, a prophet, a political innovator, an inventor, etc. As much can
be said of any occupational aptitudes. As Bain remarked, "the son of a great
philologist does not inherit a single word; the son of a great traveler can, at
school, be surpassed in geography by the son of a miner." What the child
receives from his parents are very general faculties: some force of attention,
a certain amount of perseverance, a sound judgment, imagination, etc. But
each of these faculties can serve all sorts of different ends. A child endowed
with a rather lively imagination will be able, depending on circumstances,

on the influences that will be brought to bear upon him, to become a painter or a poet, or an engineer with an inventive mind, or a daring financier. There is, then, a considerable difference between natural qualities and the special forms that they must take to be utilized in life. This means that the future is not strictly predetermined by our congenital constitution. The reason for this is easy to understand. The only forms of activity that can be transmitted by heredity are those which are always repeated in a sufficiently identical manner to be able to be fixed, in a rigid form, in the tissues of the organism. Now, human life depends on conditions that are manifold, complex, and, consequently, changing; it must itself, then, change and be modified continuously. Thus it is impossible for it to become crystallized in a definite and positive form. But only very general, very vague dispositions, expressing the characteristics common to all individual experiences, can survive and pass from one generation to another.

To say that innate characteristics are for the most part very general, is to say that they are very malleable, very flexible, since they can assume very different forms. Between the vague potentialities which constitute man at the moment of birth and the well-defined character that he must become in order to play a useful role in society, the distance is, then, considerable. It is this distance that education has to make the child travel. One sees that a vast field is open to its influence.

. . .

Duty remains. The sense of duty is, indeed, for the child and even for the adult, the stimulus *par excellence* of effort. Self-respect itself presupposes it. For, to be properly affected by reward and punishment, one must already have a sense of his dignity and, consequently, of his duty. But the child can know his duty only through his teachers or his parents; he can know what it is only through the manner in which they reveal it to him through their language and through their conduct. They must be, then, for him, duty incarnate and personified. Thus moral authority is the dominant quality of the educator. For it is through the authority that is in him that duty is duty. What is his own special quality is the imperative tone with which he addresses consciences, the respect that he inspires in wills and which makes them yield to his judgment. Thus it is indispensable that such an impression emanate from the person of the teacher.

It is not necessary to show that authority, thus understood, is neither violent nor repressive; it consists entirely of a certain moral ascendancy. It presupposes the presence in the teacher of two principal conditions. First, he must have will. For authority implies confidence, and the child cannot have confidence in anyone whom he sees hesitating, shifting, going back on his decisions. But this first condition is not the most essential. What is important above all is that the teacher really feels in himself the authority the feeling for which he is to transmit. It constitutes a force which he can manifest only if he possesses it effectively. Now, where does he get it from?

Would it be from the power which he does have, from his right to reward and punish? But fear of chastisement is quite different from respect for authority. It has moral value only if chastisement is recognized as just even by him who suffers it, which implies that the authority which punishes is already recognized as legitimate. And this is the question. It is not from the outside that the teacher can hold his authority, it is from himself; it can come to him only from an inner faith. He must believe, not in himself, no doubt, not in the superior qualities of his intelligence or of his soul, but in his task and in the importance of his task. What makes for the authority which is so readily attached to the word of the priest, is the high idea that he has of his calling; for he speaks in the name of a god in whom he believes, to whom he feels himself closer than the crowd of the uninitiated. The lay teacher can and should have something of this feeling. He too is the agent of a great moral person who surpasses him: it is society. Just as the priest is the interpreter of his god, the teacher is the interpreter of the great moral ideas of his time and of his country. Let him be attached to these ideas, let him feel all their grandeur, and the authority which is in them, and of which he is aware, cannot fail to be communicated to his person and to everything that emanates from him. Into an authority which flows from such an impersonal source there could enter no pride, no vanity, no pedantry. It is made up entirely of the respect which he has for his functions and, if one may say so, for his office. It is this respect which, through word and gesture, passes from him to the child.

Liberty and authority have sometimes been opposed, as if these two factors of education contradicted and limited each other. But this opposition is factitious. In reality these two terms imply, rather than exclude, each other. Liberty is the daughter of authority properly understood. For to be free is not to do what one pleases; it is to be master of oneself, it is to know how to act with reason and to do one's duty. Now, it is precisely to endow the child with this self-mastery that the authority of the teacher should be employed. The authority of the teacher is only one aspect of the authority of duty and of reason. The child should, then, be trained to recognize it in the speech of the educator and to submit to its ascendancy; it is on this condition that he will know later how to find it again in his own conscience and to defer to it.

EDUCATION AND COMMUNITY

Fred M. Newmann
Donald W. Oliver

We assume that the most fundamental objective of education is the development of individual human dignity, or self-realization within community. The broadly stated objective can be specified in many ways, emphasizing either individualism or social association. However one defines dignity or fulfillment, the nature of the society within which it develops is critical. As Kateb (1965, p. 456) points out:

> First, the relation between social practices and institutions and the self is not simply one of support or encouragement. To put it that way is to imply that there could be selves without society, that society is at most a device for helping the self to do what it could do alone but only very laboriously, and that eventually the self can outgrow society and be realized in splendid isolation. The plain truth is that without a society there are no selves, that, as Aristotle said, the community is prior to the individual, that the selves to be realized are given their essential qualities by their societies, and that the process of self-realization is a process of continuous involvement with society, as society not only shapes but employs everyone's inner riches. The upshot is that thought about possible styles of life or about the nature of man is necessary to give sense to the idea of individuality. Far from being an oppressive encroachment, social theory (utopian or not) is a basic duty.

Kateb's point applied to education means that educational policy should be based on deliberation and inquiry into needs of the individual within community. Every educator faithful to this premise should be able, therefore, to explicate and clarify the particular conception of society or community upon which he justifies educational recommendations.

Reprinted by permission of *Harvard Educational Review* from pp. 61–88, Vol. 37, No. 1, Winter, 1967.

1. Two Interpretations of Modern American Society

Contemporary American civilization can be interpreted with reference to two general concepts: missing community and great society. The former notices effects of industrialization, urbanization, specialization, and technology that tend to destroy man's sense of relatedness, to disintegrate common bonds, to increase apathy, to depersonalize activities, and to reduce identity and meaning in the human career. In contrast, the vision of a great society exudes a sturdy optimism in man's progress, a desire to accelerate urbanization, technology, and economic development, on the assumption that such inevitable historical forces can be harnessed to make man more free and more secure to allow him to be more "human" than ever before. Education for the great society involves raising teacher salaries, building more schools, using computers and audio-visual devices to supply training and meet the manpower needs of the "national interest." Seen from a missing community perspective, however, major objectives of education involve the creation and nourishment of diverse styles of life which allow for significant choice in the reconstruction of community relationships—formal training and "national interest" are of minor significance. Before delving into the two theories, we must examine the concept of community, for its definition lies at the heart of the distinction between these two views of American civilization.

Redefining Community

Nineteenth century sociologists (and earlier thinkers as well) compared human relationships and groups by referring to a general construct bounded at one end by the concept "community" and at the other by "society" (Tönnies, 1963).[1] The former signifies a closely knit, generally self-sufficient, rural group in which the extended family serves not only the function of procreation but also the functions of economic production, education, recreation, religion, care of the sick and aged, safety, and defense. Individuals in such a group know each other well; they share common experiences and traditions; they depend upon each other and assume responsibility for solving group problems. Style of life varies inappreciably from one generation to the next.

A sharp contrast to this type of group is mass society, characterized by large numbers of people within an urban industrial environment, influenced by many institutions each of which performs the separate functions of education, religion, economic production, defense, medicine, recreation, care of the aged, and legal and political control. People shift their places of residence, change their occupations, and follow living styles quite different from those of previous generations. Because of mobility, specialization, and a rapid rate of change, people have less in common with each other and weaker ties to a basic or primary group; their allegiances and loyalties are diffused among many social units instead of focused on one.

Relationships within a community have been described as "organic," and "natural," while societal relationships are seen as "mechanical," and "rational." Community becomes an end in itself, while society is a means toward other separate ends. Thus did Tönnies distinguish between *Gemeinschaft* (community) and *Gesellschaft* (society), the former based on shared intimacy and interdependence—the folkways and mores of primary groups; the latter signifying impersonal, logical, formally contractual relationships inherent in commerce, science, and bureaucracy. Tönnies helps to clarify the distinction by asserting that in a community, human relationships are characterized by acquaintance, sympathy, confidence, and interdependence; whereas in a society, relationships reveal strangeness, antipathy, mistrust, and independence.

Conventional sociological definitions of community emphasize (a) a set of households concentrated within a limited geographical area; (b) substantial social interaction between residents; and (c) a sense of common membership, of belonging together, not based exclusively on kinship ties. The essential criterion seems to be a psychological one—"a sense of common bond," the sharing of an identity, holding things in common esteem (Inkeles, 1964, pp. 68–9). Communities are frequently identified by references to legal political boundaries, ethnic groups, occupational classifications, or simply areas of residence. Standard definitions fail to distinguish among more specific criteria that *lead to* the development of interaction or a sense of belonging; the above criteria, for example, make it difficult to distinguish between a group and a community. We should like to offer a more differentiated set of criteria, each of which is viewed as a continuum. It is thus possible to have greater and lesser degrees of community depending upon the extent to which each of the criteria described below is fulfilled. These criterial include attributes valued by the authors and encompass characteristics beyond those needed for a minimally adequate definition. For instance, tightly knit groups or communities do not necessarily allow competing factions (attribute 3, below); the Puritans in Massachusetts Bay and the Amish in Pennsylvania are examples. By our definition, such groups constitute less of a community than groups which tolerate more diverse conceptions of "the good life." A community is a group

(1) in which membership is valued as an end in itself, not merely as a means to other ends;

(2) that concerns itself with many and significant aspects of the lives of members;

(3) that allows competing factions;

(4) whose members share commitment to common purpose and to procedures for handling conflict within the group;

(5) whose members share responsibility for the actions of the group;

(6) whose members have enduring and extensive personal contact with each other.

This working definition omits residence, political units, occupations, etc. as necessarily valid boundaries by which to distinguish one community from another.

As we speak of "missing community," we are constantly reminded of the foolishness of wishing for the establishment in the modern world of communities similar to the traditional rural model. We are told either (a) that such communities never did exist; or (b) they may have existed, but they were certainly not very pleasant—on the contrary, that human life in the by-gone community contained anxieties and problems more tragic than the ones we face today; or (c) they may have existed and been delightful, but inevitable forces have pushed them aside and it is impossible to turn back the clock. But these points are irrelevant. Our definition makes no historical claims, nor does it implore a return to days of old. The only claim is that in the modern world, community (as defined above) is missing.

It is not that the number of associations and human groups has decreased. On the contrary, we find more organizations than ever before: professional associations, credit unions, churches, corporations, labor unions, civil rights groups, clubs, as well as families. Yet few, it any, of such groups fulfill our definition of community, mainly because of the relatively special and narrow functions that each of them serves. The emergence of many institutions, each with specialized functions, has created discontinuities, such as the major one described by Nisbet:

> Our present crisis lies in the fact that whereas the small traditional associations, founded upon kinship, faith, or locality, are still expected to communicate to individuals the principal moral ends and psychological gratifications of society, they have manifestly become detached from positions of functional relevance to the larger economic and political decisions of our society. Family, local community, church, and the whole network of informal interpersonal relationships have ceased to play a determining role in our institutional systems of mutual aid, welfare, education, recreation, and economic production and distribution. Yet despite the loss of these manifest institutional functions, we continue to expect them to perform adequately the implicit psychological or symbolic functions in the life of the individual (Nisbet, 1962, p. 54).

What institutions *do* perform psychological or symbolic functions necessary for viable community? In mass society few can be found, and Nisbet traces historical developments that account for their disappearance. He sees at the root of the problem the growth of a centralized economic and political system which, by concentrating on serving *individual* needs, has neglected and eroded community. Objectives of the "great society" are to provide selected products and services: housing, jobs, food, education, medical aid, transportation, and recreation for individuals; and centralized bureaucracies now meet many of these particular needs. But the process of centralization and specialization has caused the breakdown of communication among differing groups, the rise of transient rather than enduring relationships among people, the disintegration of common bonds and the reluctance to share collective responsibility. Whether it is possible to create new forms of community appropriate for urban and industrial society should be of great concern in planning for education. The extent to which one takes this problem seriously depends largely upon whether he accepts a *missing community* or a *great society* frame of reference. These contrasting ways of construing social issues and educational needs are described below. Our intent here is to describe, rather than to defend or justify either view.

The Missing Community

Modern technological society proceeds at an ever increasing rate toward the breakdown of conditions requisite to human dignity. Neither the contented, other-directed, organization man, nor the American female, nor the alienated youth finds genuine integrity or a sense of relatedness to the human community. Experience becomes fragmented, and humans become encapsulated, as occupational specialization and social isolation make it difficult for diverse groups to communicate effectively with each other. Human relationships take on mechanistic qualities and become determined, not by tradition, human feeling, or spontaneous desires, but by impersonal machines or bureacratic flow charts. Career patterns, social roles, and environments change rapidly, producing conflicting demands on the individual, and threatening the establishment of identity. The size, complexity, and interdependence of political and economic institutions dwarf his significance. The destiny of the community appears to be guided either by elite, inaccessible power blocs or by impersonal forces, insensitive to individual protest or opinion. People lack direction and commitment; they betray either lethargic denial of basic problems, ambiguity and conflict regarding value choices, or outright repudiation of a concern for significant choices.[2]

The first theme prominent in the missing community view is *fragmentation* of life. Modern society, it is argued, accelerates a process of specialization, division of labor, and personal isolation, making it difficult for the individual to relate to other human beings outside of a narrow social class or vocational group. The inability to associate or communicate beyond the limits of one's special "place" is destructive to a sense of identity within community, because community demands the ability to perceive (or at least unconsciously assume) relatedness among a variety of people, institutions, events, and stages of life.

Second, and related to fragmentation, is the theme of *change*. In a way, the essence of American character is zeal for change; yet the exponential rate of social change in modern society tends to destroy the essential stability required to establish a sense of relatedness among people. Social change aggravates the difficulties of one generation's relating to the next; it thwarts the opportunity to observe or sense continuity within the human career; and it places considerable strains on the human personality by valuing primarily adjustment and flexibility.

Third, critics decry our present state of *ideological and aesthetic bankruptcy*. It is argued that modern society, through a reverence for technology, cultivates excessive stress on the fulfillment of instrumental values, and pays scant attention to ends or ideals. Mass culture discourages utopian thought; it has slight regard for ideals of beauty and contemplation because it directs its major energy toward producing more products with less effort. This quantitative rather than qualitative emphasis is most evident in the cult of the consumer. Commitment to conspicuous consumption and means of social mobility seem to outweigh commitment to what may be considered more vague or visionary ends such as social justice, personal salvation, or the attainment of inner virtue. Total emphasis on the instrumental and the material (it is argued) is harmful because commitment to more intangible ideals is a prime requisite for building a sense of individual worth.

Fourth, and centrally related to all of these themes, is the trend toward *depersonalization* of experience, typically noted in humanist attacks upon the influence of automation and cybernetics. Delegating to machines a vast number of activities formerly performed by humans may well erode our ability to discriminate the more subtle, less easily communicated differences among human beings—the differences that make each person unique. Not only automation, but a variety of conditions of modern and suburban living (specialization, extreme mobility, geographic isolation of production and consumption) tend to inhibit the development of meaningful interpersonal experience. Outcries against depersonalization—the prospect of man being governed totally by computer-based, predictable decisions—reveal widespread concern over this problem.

Finally, the missing community is characterized by a feeling of *powerlessness*—the sense that no individual has significant control over his own destiny. Powerlessness becomes a central issue in American culture because of its contradiction to premises of liberal political thought; namely that the destiny of the community is determined by the wishes of individuals, by the consent of the governed, rather than by unresponsive elites, aloof bureaucracies, or impersonal forces. But in the face of such conditions as impersonal bureaucracies, the growing influence of corporate structures, and extreme social mobility and change, it is difficult for the individual to see how he affects the determination of social policy or the making of decisions that have profound effects on his life.

Consequences of the above themes can be viewed from a psychological standpoint, leading to internal states of feeling and thought characteristically labeled anomie, alienation, disaffection, identity diffusion, and estrangement of man from himself and community. But a psychological interpretation of these phenomena is difficult to establish for two reasons: first, because of problems in accurately assessing inner psychic conditions, and second, because of the possibility that people may believe themselves to be contented, when in fact they may be unconsciously disillusioned and their community proceeding to a condition of irretrievable disaster. For these reasons, it is particularly important to examine the various themes not only from the standpoint of reports of "how people feel" but also from more analytic examination of the roles and functions of family, religion, occupation; the procedures for attaining justice in metropolitan and bureaucratic environments; and the legal-political arrangements for resolving various kinds of human conflict. In other words, one might see community "missing" in two senses: in terms of individuals' feelings about it, or in terms of a developing institutional framework inimical to the pursuit of human dignity.

The Great Society

Opposed to the missing community interpretation is the more optimistic view that conditions and trends in modern America will lead not to the demise of but to more hopeful forms of self realization. Our economic, political, and social institutions offer virtually unlimited promise for the meeting of material needs, the establishment of justice, and the cultivation of creativity and other elements associated with conceptions of the good life. Having reached a level of high mass consumption, our system may now proceed to stress the development of advanced forms of human service—education, medical care, recreation, psychological counseling, and community planning (Fuchs, 1966). The accelerated growth of technology offers unprecedented opportunity for solving persistent human problems, whether in making work meaningful, extending the life-span, beautifying the countryside, or increasing the motivation of children to learn (National Commission on Technology, Automation, and Economic Progress, 1966). The political system, having zealously guarded basic rights and freedoms, continues on a solid basis of consensus, while still encouraging dissent and experimentation with new approaches to public issues (Schattschneider, 1960; Key, 1966).

The great society interpretation has answers to points raised in the missing community view. We notice a tendency to deny claims made in the latter. For example, evidence is gathered to show that most people work in small firms, rather than large bureaucracies, performing personal human services, rather than manufacturing goods on impersonal assembly lines (Fuchs, 1966). Advances in communications and transportation, far from creating divisive fragmentation, have produced unforeseen possibilities for people of widely differing backgrounds to share common experience. Automation has not produced impersonal, mechanistic individuals, but has freed individuals to be more genuinely human than ever before (Weiner, 1954). People do in fact have power to determine the destiny of the community through their participation in groups designed specifically for the pursuit of given interests. (Bell, 1962, mentions some of the thousands of groups which Americans join—evidence both that man is not alone and that his groups give him power to protect his basic interests.) Rather than apologize for a lack of ideological commitment, one might gather evidence of fervent commitment to basic and traditional American values such as equality of opportunity and general welfare. Programs like the Peace Corps, poverty programs, and civil rights advances attest to this. By reference to figures on the publishing industry and on the state of the arts, one might also argue that aesthetic appreciation and activity begin to flourish more than ever.

Although the great society school would accept the existence of many trends mentioned in the missing community view, it would argue that their effects are beneficial rather than harmful. For example, specialization and division of labor are said to provide additional alternatives or areas of choice never before open to the individual. A highly differentiated and specialized society offers greater possibilities for meeting specific interests, idiosyncratic skills, and desires. Though change does proceed rapidly, it has the refreshing effect of ensuring flexibility, a safeguard against stagnation into fixed styles of living and thinking. Automation and technology also have liberating influences, allowing individuals to pursue interpersonal relationships less constrained by the demands of the environment or material needs. While decisions on important matters may be left in the hands of diffuse bureaucracies or distant "experts," these bureaucratic forms and expert fields of knowledge make helpful contributions in the process of decision-making and management of human affairs.

The optimism inherent in the great society view does not dampen its fervor in attacking a number of social problems. The National Commission on Technology and the American Economy refers to several "social costs and dislocations" caused by technological advance: rapid migration of rural workers to the city, decrease in the number of factory production and maintenance jobs, economic distress due to closing of plants, pollution of the water and air, and 35 million people living below the poverty level. Yet the Commission concludes, "Technology has, on balance, surely been a great blessing to mankind—despite the fact that some of the benefits have been offset by costs. There should be no thought of deliberately slowing down the rate of technological advancement. . . ." (National Commission on Technology, Automation, and Economic Progress, 1966, p. xiii). This report and others (e.g. U.S. Department of Labor, 1966) call for bold and inventive new approaches to the solution of serious social problems, but the basic tasks are seen as unfinished business, or clean-up operations, within a general context of unprecedented prosperity and social accomplishment. There is no tendency to debate or question ultimate goals, but only to confront practical problems of putting existing institutions to work, of devising programs to fulfill unquestioned objectives (such as full employment, higher teacher salaries, or stability in the Negro family). The solution of problems as construed in the great society approach does not require changes in the institutional structure of society at large (Rossiter, 1960).

Two major reasons are offered by proponents of the great socity for not questioning current social trends: (a) much of what is objected to (urbanization, automation, specialization, rapid change, etc.) arises as part of an inevitable stream of social development that has inevitable social costs; and (b) challenging the fundamental premises and organization of the society would result in irrevocable rupture, chaos, and destructive revolution, which would shatter the foundations of modern society rather than improve it. This is what Keniston (1965, p. 433 f.) calls the argument of "psycho-social vice."

Finally, the proponents of great society explain away many of the missing community criticisms. They claim that critics who embrace the missing community view cling to an outdated and inappropriate frame of reference, a characteristically Lockean or Jeffersonian view of society—an agrarian community of yeomen, artisans, and gentlemen aristocrats living a relatively stable existence, close to nature, with deep-rooted personal relationships and a simple social organization whereby individuals exercise power in a way that in fact determines their own destiny. Great society enthusiasts reject the missing community view by pointing out that the concepts of individuality and community take on entirely new meaning in modern society. For example, consent of the governed should not be grounded in the simple-minded notion that each individual can influence decision-makers in government; realistically, influence must be pursued by joining large pressure groups. Or, meaningful work should no longer be judged in terms of obsolete notions of craftsmanship, or pursuing a task from origin to completion; rather, that white collar administrative work within a bureaucracy has important meaning but in a different sense. Modern society cannot be realistically judged through the lenses of what Keniston calls "romantic regression."

Choosing Between Interpretations

An adequate evaluation of the merits of each interpretation requires extended investigation, and this paper is only the beginning of our efforts to
move the inquiry along. The outlined interpretations presented above are
not intended as comprehensive social theories, but as two broadly sketched
descriptive statements which contain, on the one hand, clear overtones of
protest against current social development, and on the other, a self-assured
optimism with the political, economic, and technological character of the
"great society." For the moment, we are more persuaded by the missing
community view. We believe that, in general, the great society orientation
is more sensitive to superficial symptoms than to fundamental problems,
while that of the missing community attacks major issues directly.

By way of example, consider contrasting approaches to the problem of
old age. The great society approach focuses on the attainment of fairly obvious kinds of material needs to reduce direct burdens that the aged can impose on the young: guaranteed medical treatment, guaranteed income,
physical environments suited to the physical capabilities of the aged (fewer
stairs to climb, convenient transportation, moderate climate, etc.). The
missing community approach, however, points up the far-reaching impact
of programs aimed only at such specific needs. In catering to the specific
needs of the aged, we have created entire communities of "senior citizens,"
segregated and literally fenced off from the rest of society. Their physical
isolation helps to reinforce a self-fulfilling mystique about old age which
Rosenfelt (1965, pp. 39–40) describes:

> Health and vigor, it is assumed, are gone forever. The senses have lost their
> acuity. The memory is kaput. Education and new learning are out of the
> question, as one expects to lose his mental faculties with age. Adventure and
> creativity are for the young and courageous. They are ruled out for the old,
> who are, *ipso facto*, timid and lacking in moral stamina. . . .
> While the old person is taking stock of himself, he might as well become
> resigned to being "behind the times," for it is inconceivable he should have
> kept abreast of them. As a worker, he has become a liability. His rigidity, his
> out-of-date training, his proneness to disabling illness, not to mention his irri-
> tability, lowered efficiency and arrogant manner, all militate against the like-
> lihood of his being hired or promoted. . . .
> Nothing is to be expected from the children. They have their own lives to
> lead. Furthermore, they are leading them, like as not, in distant locations,
> bridged only by the three-minute phone call on alternate Sundays, if contact
> is maintained at all. . . . Grandparents make people more nervous than it's
> worth—easier to get a babysitter, and the youngsters like it better that way.

The aged are not only isolated, but clearly discriminated against when it
comes to basic decisions in medical services: the life of a young person is

generally more highly valued (Kalish, 1965). A missing community concern with old age focuses on general questions such as the relationship between the quality of aged life and the nature of community, the meaning of retirement in an age of constantly changing careers and universal leisure, the challenge of creating integral relationships among generations.

As another illustration, consider two ways of construing the problem of the automobile in America. As Detroit increases its auto production, the great society proposes solutions to relatively specific problems: build more highways, clear the polluted air with special devices, and require more effective safety standards. Those viewing the auto from a missing community framework would focus on such issues as (a) the changes in styles of life caused by the auto (e.g. the fact that we may live, work, spend weekends in separate geographic areas) and their implications for "community," (b) the possibility that the auto serves the function of psychological protest against modern society by providing one of the few opportunities for man to enjoy power and freedom and (for young people) privacy, and (c) changes in our sensitivity to the physical environment (the building of highways, gaudy signs, junkyards, parking lots) that affect aesthetic experience and the conservation of natural resources.

The great society neglects basic issues of community by focusing instead on relatively immediate individual needs, and creating *national* organizations to meet them. The President says, "Our goal is not just a job for every worker. Our goal is to place every worker in a job where he utilizes his full productive potential for his own and for society's benefit" (U.S. Department of Labor, 1966, p. xii). The target is the individual worker, the bureaucracy is the Department of Labor, and, of course, we have an eminent national commission on technology and economy which, in a farsighted manner, proclaims that the conditions of work must be humanized, and we must allow for a flexible lifespan of work. Expansive programs are justified and evaluated by reference to the national interest or to "society's benefits."[3] There is, in great society thinking, a huge gap between the concepts of national interest and the dignity of the individual. That gap is the symptom of missing community. The major issues lie *between* obvious economic needs of individuals and the national interest: the problem of creating complex relationships where humans share common bonds which are strengthened not by consensus but by conflict and diversity, relationships in which they associate for enduring and important purposes and in which national interest is only *one* of many competing ways to justify policy. Whereas the missing community view gives these issues highest priority, the great society approach virtually ignores them.

The great society, in its attention to immediate and specific needs, tends to neglect and stifle consideration of basic, long range issues. The missing community view, on the other hand, attunes itself to forces and trends that suggest ominous consequences for the human condition. This, we feel, provides the sort of healthy discontent required to construe and deal with major problems. Our sense of missing community, though clearly influenced by conceptions of former social organization (in this country and other cultures), is *not* based on a nostalgic desire to restore types of communities long obsolete and inappropriate for the modern world. Community is "missing" not in the sense that "old fashioned" ones no longer exist, but in the sense that we have not yet devised conceptions of community that deal with particular challenges of the modern environment. To further explore implications of the missing community view, we shall examine its relevance to trends in American education.

2. A Re-examination of the Premises of Contemporary American Education

The acceptance of existing social trends characteristic of the great society advocate is perhaps one of his more serious limitations. He sees the present as manifesting historically irreversible conceptions of society, e.g., technology, urbanization, or centralization. Desirable outcomes of obvious historical forces are labeled "progress" (e.g. increased leisure), while adverse consequences are called the "price of progress" (e.g. the increasing loss of privacy or the threat of nuclear war). Applied to education, this perspective postulates that we have a type of education, with us here and now, that is obviously consistent with our equalitarian democratic heritage; and although it may have problems, we can build on the foundation that history has provided. But from the missing community point of view, one scrutinizes historical trends as possible *roots* of present problems—roots that may need to be destroyed rather than built upon. The process of evaluating tradition (rather than accepting it as a foundation) allows one to identify a broad range of alternatives and to question the extent to which they may be applicable to present choices. Honest inquiry leads one to ask whether future actions should be built on prior historical choices or whether one might reconsider premises underlying the initial choices themselves.

Because of its apparent inability to re-examine, in either contemporary or historical terms, major premises underlying its approach to education, the great society view manifests a narrow construction of what education is and ought to be. It accepts as given the premises that education is (a) formal schooling, operating as (b) a public monopoly, (c) modeled after the organizational structure and utilitarian values of corporate business. Great society proposals for educational change accept these as traditional, inevitable conditions rather than simply as one peculiar set of options against which a number of alternatives may be continually argued and tested. Below we shall raise questions concerning these premises, questions which suggest that it is time, not simply for "reform," but for a radical re-evaluation of our present conception of education and schooling.

Education as Formal Schooling

To most Americans the term *education* is synonymous with schooling, defined as formal instruction carried on in an institution which has no other purpose. In conventional rhetoric one "gets" an education by going to school. One therefore improves education by improving schools. Whether we read progressive (Dewey, 1900, 1902), traditionalists (Richover, 1960), public educational statesmen (Conant, 1959), prominent professors venturing into curriculum reform (Bruner, 1960), or contemporary analysts of education in America (Kimball & McClellan, 1962; Benson, 1965), we find universal agreement that better education requires better schooling.

Federal and foundation moneys are channeled into hundreds of projects designed to improve instruction in the schools. New approaches to instruction such as team teaching, programmed instruction, the nongraded schools, use of computers, simulation, educational television are all designed as methods for improving schooling. Millions are spent in pre-school training programs to prepare the "disadvantaged" for success in school, to prevent adolescents from dropping out of school, to train teachers to teach in schools. In addition to the traditional elementary-secondary-college sequence of schools, we aim to improve education by creating more schools: summer school, night school, graduate and professional schools.

The proliferation of schools leads one to ponder whether it might be possible to become educated without going through a process of conscious formalized instruction in institutions designed only for that function. Bailyn (1960) notes the emergence of formal schools in the Anglo-American colonies as an historical development responding to radical social changes. He boldly suggests that even before formal schools emerged, people acquired an effective education through less formal processes.

> The forms of education assumed by the first generation of settlers in America were a direct inheritance from the medieval past. Serving the needs of a homogeneous, slowly changing rural society, they were largely instinctive and traditional, little articulated and little formalized. The most important agency in the transfer of culture was not formal institutions of instruction or public instruments of communication, but the family. . . .
> . . . the family's educational role was not restricted to elementary socialization. Within these kinship groupings, skills that provided at least the first step in vocational training were taught and practiced. In a great many cases, as among the agricultural laboring population and small tradesmen who together comprised the overwhelming majority of the population, all the vocational instruction necessary for mature life was provided by the family. . . .

What the family left undone by way of informal education the local community most often completed. It did so in entirely natural ways, for so elaborate
was the architecture of family organization and so deeply founded was it in
the soil of stable, slowly changing village and town communities in which in-
termarriage among the same groups had taken place generation after generation that it was at times difficult for the child to know where the family left off
and the greater society began. . . .
More explicit in its educational function than either family or community was
the church. . . . It furthered the introduction of the child to society by instructing him in the system of thought and imagery which underlay the culture's values and aims. . . .
Family, community, and church together accounted for the greater part of
the mechanism by which English culture transferred itself across the generations. The instruments of deliberate pedagogy, of explicit, literate education,
accounted for a smaller, though indispensable, portion of the process. . . .
The cultural burdens it bore were relatively slight . . . (Bailyn, 1960, pp.
15–19).

The modern American, however, no longer construes family, church, or
other community agencies as vital educational institutions. He is in fact still
in the process of distilling from other institutions their normal educative
functions and transferring them to the school; e.g., vocational training, auto
safety and driver training, rehabilitation of the disadvantaged, early childhood training, homemaking. The consequences of assuming that education
necessarily takes place in school, or *should* take place in school, have been
profound and far reaching, and require serious re-examination.

The allocation of the educational functions of society to a single separate
institution—the school—suggests that such an institution must have a
unique responsibility and that the separation must somehow be intrinsically related to this responsibility. This assumption becomes highly suspect, however, when we look at three important aspects of the separation:
(a) we conceive of education as necessarily "preparation," and we carefully
separate "learning" from "acting," "doing," or productive work; (b) we separate the school environment from the "noninstructional" life of the community at large; and (c) we construe teaching as a specialized occupation,
isolated from the world of action and decision-making—a world that is considered to have no pedagogical function.

Education as Preparation.   The establishment of formal schooling is commonly justified on the ground that we need a specialized institution to
prepare children and youth for life as productive adults. The value of education is seen as instrumental, leading to ends extrinsic from the processes
of formal instruction itself. We get an education *now* so that at some *later*
time we can earn money, vote intelligently, raise children, serve our country, and the like. The preparatory emphasis implies closure—education is
begun and finished. Graduation or commencement signifies the termina-

tion of learning and the beginning of real life. Education in America most often consists of formal training through discrete courses and programs. How many institutions have we designed to foster education, not as preparatory activity but as a legitimate end in itself, insinuated as a continuing integral element throughout one's career?

Preparatory aims of formal schooling are often embedded in a concept of growth. As Bruner remarks, "Instruction is, after all, an effort to assist or to shape growth" (Bruner, 1966, p. 1). To implement such a mandate, schools have isolated children and adolescents from adults and have focused most of the formal training on young people. This, however, betrays a confusion between biological and mental development. Let us assume that the schools should be primarily concerned with mental-emotional development (they can have relatively minor affects on biological growth). First, we wonder whether it is possible to make a useful distinction between people who are "growing" versus those who have "matured" with regard to mental-emotional development. One could argue that adulthood, far from being a period of stable maturity, is no more than a continuing process of mental-emotional growth (and biological change) presenting conflicts and problems of adjustment as "stormy" and challenging as growth during childhood and adolescence. Marriage, child-rearing, occupational decision, pursuit of leisure, adaptation to geographic and occupational change, and adjustment to retirement and death continually demand growth by adults. With the entirety of a human life cycle before us, we would ask, when is mental-emotional maturity reached? If growth, change, and decay continue until death, then why confine education to the early years of biological development?

Second, by assuming young people to be dynamic and growing and adults to be static and ripe, one is led to postulate that adults have needs essentially different from the needs of young people—that conflicts and differences *between* generations are greater than conflicts and differences within a given generation. We would suggest, however, that members of differing generations do have common problems and educational needs, and the needs of members of the same generation may be radically diverse. Compare for example, an unemployed man of 40 with an unemployed teenage dropout, both of whom lack literacy and vocational skills. Could they not share with benefit a common educational experience? Or suppose an oppressed ethnic group is attempting to combat discrimination. Members of that group from all generations face a common problem. Conversely, groups *within* a generation may have quite different educational needs: a 30-year-old mother on public assistance versus a 30-year-old attorney attempting to establish a law practice; or a teenage girl from a broken lower-class home versus a teenage boy from a stable upper-class family.

Our exclusive emphasis on preparation raises another basic question: Is it possible that, in spite of certain commonalities across generations, childhood and adolescence constitute in themselves integral parts of the human career, with certain roles, needs, and behavior that may be quite unrelated to the demands of a future adulthood? Schools are designed mainly to implant in students knowledge, attitudes, and skills revered by adult scholars and educators, yet we can legitimately question why it is necessary to stress almost exclusively adult values before children and youth have attained that biological and social status.

We also note a certain pragmatic folly in education as preparation for future adulthood in the modern world. A leading educational innovator remarks on "the colossal problem of educating youngsters for jobs which do not exist and for professions which cannot be described" (Brown, 1963, p. 14). Is it even possible to prepare children to behave fruitfully in a future world, the dimensions and complexities of which educated adults are presently unable to grasp?

The tendency of formal schooling to isolate children during a period of "preparation" for adulthood has produced a rigid system of age-grading which has as one effect a fractionation of human career. This tends to hinder the development of meaningful relationships among generations and cultivates a fragmented, rather than continuous concept of self. The prevailing conception that children can learn only *from*, rather than with, adults and the forced submission of youth to the rule of adults amplifies the conflict between generations and encourages a posture of dependency, a sense of powerlessness that may carry over from youth to adulthood.

School and the Community at Large. A large portion of school training is separated from, and has no significant effect on students' behavior outside of school mainly because of the isolation of the school establishment from problems, dilemmas, choices, and phenomena encountered beyond school walls. Teachers readily attest to students' capacity to "tune-out" or memorize but not apply lessons taught in school. There is a sense of unreality inherent in living in two discontinuous worlds, if one is to take both seriously.

The progressives tried to handle this separation by bringing more "real life" activities into the school. They tried to match work in school with work in real life, introducing various manual skills and decision-making activities similar to those occurring outside of school. Modern efforts in curriculum reform have pursued the same idea through the development of simulation activities—attempts to make school relevant to more instructional life. But simulation still occurs within *instructional* contexts and is, therefore, detached from actual and significant concerns. It may cultivate an attitude that learning or life or both are synonymous with playing games. The attempt to make school "fun" by exploiting the motivational power of competition or curiosity in children simply avoids the challenge of applying learning to life outside the school. In spite of progressive efforts in the direction of antiformalism (for example, allowing students more individual freedom, emphasizing play and a variety of arts and crafts), they did much to solidify a conception of education as equivalent to formal schooling. In fact, the most dramatic way for the progressive to demonstrate his ideas was to found a new *school*, which soon became isolated from genuine conflicts and decisions of students' lives beyond school walls.

Teaching as a Specialized Occupation. Formal schooling provided the basis for a new specialized "profession of education." As Cremin (1964) points out, the profession was quick to isolate itself from other professions and fields of knowledge. It also built an education establishment dedicated to the study, servicing, and expansion of formal schooling as a separate and discrete institution, often accumulating powerful vested interests irrelevant to the real improvement of education (Conant, 1963, 1964). As an alternative to the unquestioned policy of requiring professionally trained teachers in schools, one might argue that in fact students could gain valuable education from each other and from a variety of "untrained," though interesting individuals, be they blue-collar laborers, politicians, bureaucrats, criminals, priests, atheletes, artists, or whatever. To the extent that schools are staffed by professional educators, learning tends to become isolated from the significant concerns of the community, and the narrower functions and tasks of the *school* come to dominate the broader purposes of education.

Education as Public Monopoly

That schooling was eventually expanded as a stable and universal service through governmental compulsion rather than private voluntary associations, raises questions regarding the political philosophy that underlies such a system. American political thought has traditionally distinguished between society (a collection of various private groupings) and government (the combination of political and legal organs that make up the state). As Tom Paine described the distinction,

> Society is produced by our wants and government by our wickedness: the former promotes our happiness positively; the latter negatively, by restraining vices (quoted in Lindsay, 1943, p. 124).

Lindsay's comments on the distinction illustrate the special value that Americans placed on voluntary associations:

> The English or the American democrat takes it for granted that there should be in society voluntary associations of all kinds, religious, philanthropic, commercial: that these should be independent of the state at least in the sense that the state does not create them. The state may have to control and regu-

late them. Questions concerning their relations with the state are indeed continually turning up, but it is always taken for granted that men form these societies and associations for their own purposes; that their loyalty to such associations is direct; that it therefore does not follow that the state will prevail in any conflict between such associations and the state (Lindsay, 1943, p. 120).

The spirit of this laissez-faire philosophy implies that the state exists to facilitate a plurality of diverse interests inherent in men's *voluntary* associations and enterprises. The commitment of a community representing such a plurality of interests was applied to many domains of experience: to religion where sectarianism flourished; to economic affairs through the development of overlapping and competing business enterprises. Traditional notions of ordered artisan industries controlled by disciplined guilds, agriculture controlled by the feudal lords, mercantile trading policies encouraged and regulated by a central government, monopolistic industry sanctioned by restrictive state charters, all of these institutions fell before the laissez-faire economics practiced in America. It was assumed that the life of the community at large would be infused by the vigor and drive of private enterprise and association, that natural laws of competition and cooperation would prevent any serious conflict between private interests and the public good.

As was not the case in religious institutions and business enterprise, pluralism in the schools was short-lived. The concept of the common school took firm roots in Massachusetts early in the nineteenth century and spread to the other states. The common school was apparently conceived as a deliberate instrument to reduce cultural and religious differences. "The children of all nationalities, religions, creeds, and economic levels would then have an opportunity to mix together in the common schoolroom" (Butts & Cremin, 1953, p. 194). Once the common school was firmly established, pressure grew to establish secondary schools and to open the private academies to all. The schools faced a critical choice: once the common-school concept was accepted, how would the traditional commitment to pluralism be worked out? When children from diverse economic, ethnic, religious, and political backgrounds came together, how would the differences be recognized and handled?

Rapidly increasing, immigration from Europe in the latter half of the nineteenth century and the first decade of the twentieth century created in the common school a major test for the pluralistic philosophy. Some Americans viewed the floodtide of newcomers as an opportunity to renew and invigorate the national and ethnic dimension of American pluralism. In 1915 Horace Kallen sentimentally envisioned

. . . a democracy of nationalities, cooperating voluntarily and autonomously through common institutions in the enterprise of self-realization through the

perfection of men according to their kind. The common language of the commonwealth . . . would be English, but each nationality would have for its
own emotional and involuntary life its own peculiar dialect or speech, its own
individual and inevitable esthetic and intellectual forms. The political and
economic life of the commonwealth is a single unit and serves as the foundation and background for the realization of the distinctive individuality of each
nation that composes it and of the pooling of these in harmony above them
all (Kallen, 1953, pp. 29–30).

But not all Americans had faith in the "distinctive individuality" of national
groups. Fearing that continued cultivation of national differences would be
disruptive to society, the common schools apparently stressed the need for
pooling or assimilating immigrants into a common melting pot.

In addition to tension created by religious sectarianism, free enterprise,
and ethnic diversity, the nineteenth century labored under severe strains
created by the process of rapid industrialization. Evidently the public
school responded to these strains by stressing the common values of routine monotonous work, progress, and the Horatio Alger hope of social mobility.

In the end, public schools attained a virtual monopoly on the life of
youth between ages six and sixteen. This development represents a clear
shift in political philosophy. It signifies a blurring, if not total rejection, of
the distinction between society and government, formerly so crucial to the
American democrat; that is, it indicates a loss of faith in the ability of a
pluralistic system of private associations to provide an education that would
benefit both the individual and his nation.

Perhaps at this point in history it was necessary and useful for the common school to serve a cohesive and integrating function by emphasizing a
common heritage, common aspirations, common learnings, common dress,
and a common routine within the school. One could suggest, in fact, that
the school simply reflected the needs and requirements of the society by
stressing *integrating* elements in the society, rather than the diversity, so
blatant and obvious. Granted that the society might have been on the brink
of disintegration and in need of cohesive institutions at that time, uniformity and confirmity have been continuously characteristic of public education ever since the development of common and secondary schools. One
might argue theoretically that even though education is public and compulsory, it can conceivably encourage and reinforce cultural diversity by providing a wide range of alternative types of education. This, however, has
not been true of public education in America. On the contrary, the schools
have attempted to file down or erase distinctive cultural traits, denying that
important cultural diversity ever existed; the instruction and procedures of
the school reflect a mandate to persuade youth that all groups share a common language, common political and economic institutions, and common
standards of right and wrong behavior. And although it is somewhat more

stylish to recognize the importance of "individual differences," these are construed in psychological rather than cultural terms. In so far as the recent effort to educate slum children has forced us to recognize cultural differences, these are still construed largely as cultural deficiencies.

We are concerned with two general effects of the decision to make education an exclusive, compulsory, public function.[4] The first relates to the way in which the public monopoly has fundamentally altered the nature of childhood and adolescence in America. Young people spend more than half of their working hours from age six to their early twenties trying to meet demands of formal schooling. This has destroyed to a large extent opportunities for random, exploratory work and play outside of a formal educational setting. One could argue that, psychologically, it is most important for youth (and for that matter all humans) to spend a significant portion of their life in spontaneous, voluntary kinds of activity, as in Erickson's (1962) suggestion of a psycho-social moratorium, rather than in regimented, required, planned learning tasks. By denying to students basic responsibility and freedom, public schooling prevents development of a sense of competency in making personal decisions. Though schooling requires large quantities of work ("industry"), its evaluation system generally assumes the work of youth to be inferior to work of adults (teachers). The public institutional milieu of the school discourages the development of intimacy among students, or between students and teachers. Schooling prevents exploratory, experimental activity, it prohibits total involvement in any single interest, it refuses to delegate to students responsibility for seeking their own "education." If public schooling were only one among many major areas of experience for young people, these would be less important criticisms. What makes the criticisms most significant is the fact that schooling has a virtual monopoly on youth's time and energy, possessing the power to suppress the quest for individuation through extra-school activity.

In addition to psychological dangers, the monopoly carries as a second major threat its potential for creating cultural uniformity, destroying diversity in points of view, in styles of life, in standards of taste, and in underlying value commitments. The standard rebuttal for this criticism is to point out that although we do have required public education, it is controlled by local communities, it is not a national system. One can, therefore, have radically diverse types of education, depending upon the unique needs of each community. In theory this answer seems persuasive, but in fact there are a number of forces at work in modern America—mass media, the publishing industry, national curriculum development programs, and professional educators—which combine (however unintentionally) to produce overall institutional similarity. If one examines programs in schools throughout the country, one finds an incredible similarity among curricula of different communities. (The apparent differences between schooling in slums and suburbs cannot be accounted for by assuming that slum dwellers have chosen to have one type of education, suburbanites another.) Although public schooling should not bear all of the responsibility for this cultural uniformity, the fact that it has captive control of youth allows it to accelerate the process of cultural standardization. Our objection to such a trend is based on the assumption that the essence of freedom lies in the opportunity for significant choice, and that choice becomes increasingly limited as individual and cultural differences are blurred or erased.

Given the failure of the school to support a vital pluralistic tradition, one might ask why must education be carried on as a publicly controlled compulsory activity? Law and medicine, certainly as vital as education for society, have remained largely under the control of the private sector. Communication and transmission of knowledge to the community at large, equally important, is accomplished by powerful, but essentially private media industries (books, newspapers, cinema, television). To meet basic subsistence needs, we use a system of production and distribution run mainly by private enterprise. Spiritual-religious activities are exclusively reserved for private associations. Curiously, public schools are required to provide ideological indoctrination (the American Creed) of an order comparable to religious institutions, yet we have refused public support for "religious" education. In the field of citizenship education, the public schools provide instruction for citizen participation in political process, but in fact that instruction is obstructed by myths and misinformation; the most effective training for political life occurs within various private interest groups, or parties.

Education Modeled After Corporate Bureaucracy

Education, having developed into a concept of formal compulsory instruction publicly sponsored, could conceivably have taken many forms. Public schools might have become coordinating agencies which channeled the students into a variety of educational experiences provided by existing political, economic, cultural, and religious institutions. Schools might have become supplementary agencies, like libraries, appended to small neighborhood communities. In the long run, however, education adopted the prevailing institutional structure in the society at large: the factory served by an industrial development laboratory and managed according to production-line and bureaucratic principles. Architecturally, the schools came to resemble factories (instruction carried on first in rooms but more recently in large loft-like spaces, with different spaces reserved for different types of instruction) and office buildings (with corridors designed to handle traffic between compartments of uniform size). Conceivably, schools could have been built like private homes, cathedrals, artists' studios, or country villas.

The schools came to be administered like smooth-running production lines. Clear hierarchies of authority were established: student, parent, teacher, principal, superintendent, and school committeeman, each of whom was presumed to know his function and the limits of his authority. Consistent with the principle of the division of labor, activities were organized into special departments: teaching (with its many sub-divisions), administration, guidance, custodial services, etc. The process of instruction was seen by the administrator as a method of assembling and coordinating standardized units of production: classes of equal size, instructional periods of equal length; uniform "adopted" books and materials that all students would absorb; standard lessons provided by teachers with standardized training. Departures or interruptions in the routine were (and still are) discouraged for their potentially disruptive effect on the overall process (e.g., taking a field trip, or showing a film that requires two periods' worth of time, or making special arrangements to meet with students individually). Conceivably, the schools could have been organized on a much less regimented basis, allowing a good deal of exploratory, random, unscheduled sort of activity. However, as Callahan (1962) persuasively argues, the corporate bureaucratic model, guided by the cult of efficiency, exerted a major influence on the organization and program of public education.

In our view the effects of corporate organization in education lead to three major developments all of which have important contemporary implications: (a) the research and development mentality which limits its attention to finding or building technology and instrumentation to achieve given specifiable goals, rather than questioning or formulating the goals themselves; (b) the increasingly fragmented school environment, which is sliced according to administrative and subject matter categories prescribed by educational specialists rather than according to salient concerns of children, youth, or the larger community; and (c) the trend toward centralized, coordinated decision-making for schools by a combination of agencies in government, business, universities, foundations, and "non-profit" research and development institutes.

The Research and Development Mentality. The great society seeks to build a highly educated final product (a graduate) at the lowest possible cost per unit. Armed with such a mandate, policy makers and educators scurry to devise and implement techniques that will achieve visible "payoffs" in the "terminal behavior" of students. A host of new devices and programs emerge: nongraded schools, advanced placement courses, independent study, programmed instruction, self-administered TV and cinema, computer-based instruction. They are lauded and increasingly in demand for their apparent effectiveness in speeding up the educational process by "individualizing" instruction for students. The Federal government invests millions of dollars through universities, research and development centers, and private industry to produce more efficient methods. Administrators use the techniques both as yardsticks by which to evaluate and as symbols by which to advertise their schools and build their personal reputation. Policy makers and curriculum advisers beg for definite answers concerning which methods are best. But who seeks reasons for the emphasis on acceleration and efficiency? Why read at age three? Why learn quadratic equations at age ten? Why study American history a year or two earlier? Why try to think like an MIT physicist or an anthropologist at all? The research and development mentality thrives on gadgets, engineering metaphors, and the fever of efficiency, but rarely questions the purposes to which its technology is applied.

A new and fashionable manifestation of this general mentality is the current emphasis on systems. The aim of this approach is to describe in schematic (and often mathematical) detail relationships among all components in a system (i.e., a curriculum, classroom, school, or school district) and to evaluate the extent to which given objectives are being achieved by specific components or the system as a whole at certain points of time. Using diagnostic information provided by intensive testing, the job is to build a related set of components and experiences that will lead to specifiable terminal behavior. The general purpose is to *clarify* and *increase* the *effectiveness* of the entire process through which a given input is changed into an output that meets given criteria or standards of performance. The responsibility of systems development is limited to devising techniques for attaining objectives previously fed into the system; the formulation of ultimate aims is delegated to external sources. (The systems engineer boldly proclaims, "You tell us what you want, and we'll program it.") Though one could build a system that would allow for flexibility and even respond to changing objectives, we believe that in essence the systems approach avoids rather than recognizes or deals with the most important problems of education, namely objectives and substance. The excessive concern with technique, rather than a searching examination of ends, results in a tendency to accept as legitimate those objectives that can be translated into operations and those products which can be schematically and quantitatively measured.

Despite its "practical" outlook, the R & D mentality constantly runs up against the "relevancy problem": the fact that children and youth do, in fact, see the content of school as bookish and artificial, unrelated to the decisions and actions that lead to important consequences either in school or in the outside world. Both students and teachers attempt to right the disproportionate emphasis on abstract words and thought by stressing instead concrete procedures that provide a context of action and decision— prompt attendance, assignments completed, tests taken—and success. The progressive approach to the relevancy problem was to abandon rigid work and grade standards without recognizing that these constraints served the fundamental function of providing structure, definition of task, and conse-

quences of decisions that are palpable and immediate. The new R & D pro-
ponent is somewhat more sophisticated: instead of stressing the concrete
procedures associated with abstract verbal tasks, he seeks to simulate the
real tasks of the outside world. Students play war, peace-making, monopoly, empire building, showing all the involvement of adult poker and bingo
players. Although the R & D specialist sees the conceptual relationship between elements of the simulated activity or game and real life decisions,
does the student? Perhaps the student simply learns that adults get their
intellectual kicks out of playing games, rather than dealing with real problems in the noninstructional world. At any rate there is some evidence that
what students learn from playing games is how to play games, not how to
construe either academic or worldly problems more effectively.[5]

Unfortunately, the underlying difficulty cannot be corrected by R & D
specialists. It is a result of the fact that we have chosen to divorce schooling
from problems and choices that have genuine significance for youth and
community. Since the kind of learning we prescribe is not intrinsically important to students, we invent trivial tasks and procedures to capture their
attention, and we contract with engineers and R & D centers to do this as
efficiently as possible. Significant problems and decisions emanate not from
R & D laboratories (questions of basic objectives are beyond their concern),
but from strains and dilemmas in the world beyond school walls. In short,
educational reform must be construed in more fundamental terms than
what is implied in transferring the students attention from nature study to
meal worms.

The Fragmented School Environment. In the spirit of Durkheim's analysis of the effects of division of labor, Thelen comments that one of man's
most important inventions was the development of concepts about how to
organize human activity. But organization requires division and fragmentation which can, at times, have undesirable results:

> We have made hard and fast divisions between thinking and doing, creating
> and applying, planning and acting, preparing and fulfilling. The age of rea-
> son, the development of science, the domination of organization, and the
> simple increase in density of human population have interacted among each
> other to create these divisions. But these divisions have made modern life
> purposeless. For as long as we maintain the division we shall never have to
> find an organizing principle to integrate the parts. The organizing principle
> we have thus succeeded in avoiding is *purpose* (Thelen, 1960, p. 215).

The school, faithful to principles of bureaucratic organization and division of labor, has fostered the development of a number of specialized compartments many of which have no apparent relationship to, or communication with, each other: English, social studies, science, math,
physical education, home economics, industrial arts, guidance. Boundaries

between the departments often arise from legitimate distinctions among subject matter or fields of knowledge, but lack of communication among fields can be attributed to the parochial interests of human beings who place the highest priority on their own area.

Fragmentation may also be seen as arising from underlying disagreements over the fundamental purposes of education. In broad terms we might classify differing objectives as: work skills (competencies required for successful careers and bread-winning), socialization (values and skills necessary to perform in the role of citizenship), psychological guidance (development of mental health), intellectual excellence (acquisition of knowledge and cultivation of various mental abilities). These categories are by no means mutually exclusive, but suggestive of distinguishable factors or values used to support various educational prescriptions. To this list we would add a less commonly stated objective: social reconstruction, that is, the effort to justify schooling as a vehicle for the establishment of a particular social order. Many progressives saw the school as a microcosm of a particular kind of ideal society. Other groups, from Puritans and Amish to Nazis and Communists, have similarly valued schooling as an instrument of social reconstruction.

The corporate educational enterprise tends to minimize conflict among differing objectives and fields of interest; it accommodates a number of philosophies and priorities by establishing isolated compartments, allowing each to pursue its own goals in peaceful co-existence. The "philosophy" of the school is articulated by a simple *listing* of all the differing objectives and course offerings. We have no quarrel with the diversity of objectives and subjects. On the contrary, our commitment to pluralism strongly supports them. We do, however, object to the organizational principle which attempts to minimize conflict by isolating and separating various interests from each other. This attempt has the effect of aggravating fragmentation in community. It discourages tendencies to relate various purposes of man in community within comprehensive social theory; it stifles healthy ferment that might arise from tough public discussion of the merits of different specialties and objectives.

New Corporate Coalitions.   Current efforts to construe education as a system of fully articulated components intended to shape terminal behavior are increasingly evident in mergers among communications, electronics, and publishing industries: Time-Life, Inc. owns television stations, a textbook company, and has recently become associated with General Electric; Xerox owns University Microfilms, Basic Systems, Inc., and American Education Publications; other mergers include RCA with Random House, IBM with Science Research Associates, and Raytheon with D.C. Heath and Company. These companies or their subsidiaries, often with the assistance of university research and development centers, are planning programs, financed by federal funds, to "solve" America's educational problems. Similar coalitions of government, industrial complexes, and universities have long cooperated in the development of America's war hardware and space exploration. The Federal government raises research and development funds, university and industry supply engineering talent and laboratories, and industry manufactures and distributes the final product. A prototype of this pattern applied to education is the urban Job Corps training center, financed by the Federal government which contracted with private corporations to recruit staff, refurbish physical facilities, and manage the centers. Industry then turned to universities to help train personnel, and to advise and evaluate the operation. Presumably this type of coalition could expand its horizons beyond special groups (such as drop-outs, unemployed, pre-school disadvantaged, or Peace Corps and Vista volunteers) and reform all public education in the country at large.

We view with suspicion the emergence of national super-corporations venturing into education production. It signifies most obviously the demise of any hope that education might be rooted in the concerns and pursuits of primary communities. It offers unprecedented possibilities for cultural uniformity, as the large coalitions begin to sketch long-range plans for the production of standardized educational kits or packages to be marketed throughout the nation. The packages will be designed within professionalized and bureaucratized organizations, single-mindedly devoted to educational "projects" as isolated goals. The great society evidently assumes that since the government-industry-university coalition seems to have solved problems of economic affluence and defense, it should therefore be able to solve educational problems.

It should be clear from our basic criticisms that we seriously question this assumption.

. . .

let us summarize the three criticisms we direct at the present education enterprise: (a) it fails to accept as legitimate, or to support, the rich educational potential available in noninstructional contexts—conversely it conceives of education narrowly as mainly formal instruction occurring in schools; (b) by becoming a compulsory public monopoly, it neglects the educational value of diverse public and private associations; (c) it is organized by the model and motivated by the values of corporate industry and bureaucratic civil service.

. . .

NOTES

The authors are indebted to a number of colleagues and students, and to authors listed herein. It is our pleasure to acknowledge the helpful contributions of Robert A. Nisbet, Paul Goodman, Herbert A. Thelen, and Joseph C. Grannis.

1. In the foreword to this edition, P. Sorokin mentions eternal parallels between the work of Tönnies and Confucius, Plato, Aristotle, Cicero, and others. In the introduction, J. C. McKinney and G. P. Loomis discuss analogous concepts in the work of Durkheim, Cooley, Redfield, Becker, Sorokin, Weber, and Parsons.

2. These observations relate to a wide range of phenomena, represented in studies of bureaucracy (Blau, 1956; Whyte, 1956); corporate power (Berle, 1954); political and legal institutions (Mills, 1956; Wheeler, 1965); ideology (Bell, 1962); youth (Friedenberg, 1959, 1963; Goodman, 1956; Keniston, 1965); education (Kimball and McClellan, 1962); work and leisure (Mumford, 1934; Swados, 1957; Veblen, 1957); women (Friedan, 1964); American character (Reisman, 1953; Gorer, 1964); voter behavior (Berelson, Lazarsfeld, & McPhee, 1954); or more generally, the human condition (Arendt, 1958; Royce, 1965). The authors of such studies address themselves to a number of questions, only a few of which are explicitly raised in our characterization of the missing community.

3. See for example, Keppel (1966, Ch. IV), who justifies increased federal spending in education almost entirely on the grounds that it will result in more economic use of human resources; that it is, therefore, in the national interest to make a greater investment in education.

4. The fact that state laws allow youth to fulfill educational obligations by attending private as well as public schools does not diminish the influence of the public monopoly. A relatively small proportion of children do attend private schools (approximately 16 per cent at the elementary level and 11 per cent at the secondary level). Moreover, even private schools must conform to publicly established standards.

5. Unpublished work by Mary Alice White of Teachers College, Columbia University suggests this conclusion.

REFERENCES

In some instances the references below are not to the original editions. Publishers and dates of first publication are within parentheses.

Arendt, Hannah. *The human condition.* New York: Doubleday Anchor, 1958.

Bailyn, B. *Education in the forming of American society: needs and opportunities for study.* New York: Vintage, 1960.

Bell, D. *The end of ideology: on the exhaustion of political ideas in the fifties.* New York: Crowell-Collier, 1962 (Free Press, 1960).

Benson, C. S. *The cheerful prospect: a statement on the future of American education.* Boston: Houghton Mifflin, 1965.

Berelson, B., Lazarsfeld, P. F., & McPhee, W. N. *Voting: a study of opinion formulation in a presidential campaign.* Chicago: University of Chicago Press, 1954.

Berle, A. A. *The twentieth century capitalist revolution.* New York: Harcourt Brace, 1954.

Blau, P. M. *Bureaucracy in modern society.* New York: Random House, 1956.

Brown, B. F. *The nongraded high school.* Englewood Cliffs, N.J.: Prentice-Hall, 1963.

Bruner, J. S. *The process of education.* New York: Vintage, 1960.

Bruner, J. S. *Toward a theory of instruction.* Cambridge, Mass.: Harvard University Press, 1966.

Butts, R. F. & Cremin, L. A. *A history of education in American culture.* New York: Holt, Rinehart and Winston, 1953.

Callahan, R. E. *Education and the cult of efficiency: a study of the social forces that have shaped the administration of the public schools.* Chicago: University of Chicago Press, 1962.

Conant, J. B. *The American high school today.* New York: McGraw-Hill, 1959.

Conant, J. B. *The education of American teachers.* New York: McGraw-Hill, 1963.

Conant, J. B. *Shaping educational policy.* New York: McGraw-Hill, 1964.

Cremin, L. A. *The transformation of the school: progressivism in American education 1876–1957.* New York: Vintage, 1964. (Alfred A. Knopf, 1961)

Dewey, J. *The child and the curriculum* and *The school and society.* Chicago: University of Chicago Press, 1902, 1900.

Erikson, E. H. Youth: fidelity and diversity, *Daedalus,* 1962, Vol. 91 No. 1, 5–27.

Friedan, Betty. *The feminine mystique.* New York: Dell, 1964. (Norton, 1963)

Friedenberg, E. Z. *The vanishing adolescent.* New York: Dell, 1959.

Friedenberg, E. Z. *Coming of age in America: growth and acquiescence.* New York: Random House, 1963.

Fuchs, V. The first service economy. *Public interest,* Winter, 1966, 7–17.

Goodman, Paul. *Growing up absurd.* New York: Vintage, 1956.

Goodman, Paul. *Compulsory mis-education* and *The community of scholars.* New York: Vintage, 1966.

Goodman, Paul & Goodman, Percival. *Communitas: means of livelihood and ways of life.* New York: Random House, 1947.

Gorer, G. *The American people: a study in national character.* New York: Norton, 1964.

Grannis, J. C. Team teaching and the curriculum. In J. T. Shaplin & H. F. Olds, Jr. (Eds.), *Team teaching.* New York: Harper & Row, 1964.

Inkeles, A. *What is sociology: an introduction to the discipline and profession.* Englewood Cliffs, N.J.: Prentice-Hall, 1964.

Jencks, C. Is the public school obsolete? *Public interest,* Winter 1966, 18–27.

Kalish, R. A. The aged and the dying process: the inevitable decisions. *Journal of social issues,* October 1965, *21,* 87–96.

Kallen, H. M. Democracy and the melting pot. In B. M. Ziegler (Ed.), *Immigration: an American dilemma.* Boston: Heath, 1953, 25–34.

Kateb, G. Utopia and the good life. *Daedalus,* Spring, 1965, 454–473.

Keniston, K. *The uncommitted: alienated youth in American society.* New York: Harcourt Brace, 1965.

Keppel, F. *The necessary revolution in American education.* New York: Harper & Row, 1966.

Key, Jr., V. O. *The responsible electorate: rationality in presidential voting, 1936–1960.* Cambridge, Mass.: Harvard University Press, 1966.

Kimball, S. T. & McClellan, J. E. *Education and the new America.* New York: Random House, 1962.

Lindsay, A. D. *The modern democratic state.* London: Oxford University Press, 1943.

Mills, C. W. *The power elite.* New York: Oxford University Press, 1956.

Mumford, D. *Technics and civilization.* New York: Harcourt Brace, 1934.

National Commission on Technology, Automation and Economic Progress, *Technology and the American Economy.* Vol. I. Washington, D.C.: Author, 1966.

Nisbet, R. A. *Community and power.* New York: Oxford University Press, 1962.

Rickover, H. G. *Education and freedom.* New York: Dutton, 1960.

Riesman, D., Glazer, N., & Denny, R. *The lonely crowd: a study in the changing American character.* New York: Doubleday Anchor, 1953. (Yale Univ. Press, 1950)

Rosenfelt, Rosalie H. The elderly mystique. *Journal of social issues,* October 1965, *21,* 37–43.

Rossiter, Clinton. The democratic process. In *Goals for Americans,* the report of the President's commission on national goals and chapters submitted for the consideration of the commission. American Assembly, Columbia University. Prentice-Hall, 1960.

Royce, J. R. *The encapsulated man.* Princeton, N.J.: Van Nostrand, 1965.

Rugg, H. *American life and the school curriculum.* Boston: Ginn, 1936.

Schattschneider, E. E. *The semi-sovereign people: a realist's view of democracy in America.* New York: Holt, Rinehart and Winston, 1960.

Swados, H. *A radical America*. Boston: Little Brown, 1957.

Thelen, H. A. *Education and the human quest*. New York: Harper & Row, 1960.

Tönnies, F. *Community and society*. (Trans. and Ed.) C. P. Loomis, New York: Harper & Row, 1963.

U.S. Department of Labor. *Manpower report of the president and a report on manpower, requirements, resources, utilization, and training*. Washington, D.C.: Author, 1966.

Veblen, T. *The theory of the leisure class*. New York: Mentor, 1957. (The MacMillan Co., 1899)

Webster, H., Freedman, M., & Heist, P. Personality change in college students. In N. Sanford (Ed.), *The American college*. New York: John Wiley, 1962, Chap. 24.

Weiner, N. *The human-use of human beings: cybernetics and society*. Garden City, N.Y.: Doubleday Anchor, 1954.

Wheeler, H. W. *The restoration of politics*. New York: Fund for the Republic, 1965.

Whyte, W. H. *The organization man*. New York: Simon and Shuster, 1956.

EDUCATION FOR COMMUNITY: PHILOSOPHICAL PERSPECTIVE

Elizabeth Steiner

Depending upon whether the sense of community arises from the Latin term *communis* or the medieval Latin term *universitas,* reference is to either fellowship or a body of fellows. In other words, when one thinks of community, one can think of either a quality of living with one another or a grouping of individuals. The latter usually comes to mind when one thinks about community, as in rural community, hometown community, black community, Italian community, Jewish community, Roman Catholic community, mercantile community, scientific community, national community, and international community. Individuals are grouped together because they share certain circumstances: geographic, ethnic, religious, and so on.

Should education be for selves or for groups? Two outstanding philosophers have provided perspectives to help in answering this question.

John Dewey (1859–1952) held that education that was for the self—for self-realization—was for a society that was progressing. To be progressing was to be democratic, and to be democratic was to be rational in the sense of experimental. Education for community, therefore, was education for a grouping of individuals sharing the method of intelligence.

This perspective of Dewey's arose from his ethical, metaphysical, and epistemological views. Dewey's view of the good person was one who is a realizing self. A self is a totality of habits, demands for certain kinds of activities. Selves who are realizing have organized their natural activities (impulses) into demands for true experience. They are using their intelligence as instruments to produce true experience; they are problem-solvers or users of the scientific method; they are experimentalists.

Since Dewey was a pragmatist, reality was taken as experience and truth as progressive experience, experience with a leading quality. Truth then is made, and so emerges. There is no absolute truth, only degrees of truth. Experience was taken as continuous, and hence the experience of one person, past or present, adds to and is part of the total context of experience. The realization of one self depends upon the realization of all other selves. A true total context of experience is progress.

It follows from *education for a democratic community* that the school must be a community that reflects the best aspects of the larger community; otherwise the student will engage in inquiry having no meaning for society. The school must be a democratic community in which the teacher provides opportunities for each student to develop interests in true experiencing, which leads to social progress. Such provision consists of subject matter that leads to information on the context of social life, to discipline that brings intelligence under control for social ends, and to culture that socializes, and consists of motivation that is social in nature (cooperation, reciprocity, and positive personal achievement) and not individualistic in nature (fear, affection, and competition).

Instead of taking community in the sense of a grouping of individuals, Martin Buber (1878–1965) took it in the sense of communion, a quality of living with one another. Education for community, therefore, was education for dialogical relations between persons.

Just as Dewey's perspective arose from his ethical, metaphysical, and epistemological views, so did Buber's arise from his views. There is no ideal according to which each person should pattern one's life, rather each person should make oneself into a genuine character. To make oneself into a genuine character each person must realize in one's whole life with one's whole being the relations possible to one. To do so, a person must become solitary and then overcome solitude through becoming communal.

A person must become solitary, so that one sees oneself as a decision-maker, an originator. But more is required or cosmic and social homelessness results. Individualism understands only a part of a person. In individualism, the person glorifies solitude to save oneself from despair with which one's solitary state threatens one. One plunges into an affirmative reflexion. Origination is not capable of actually conquering the given situation.

A person must become communal without forfeiting questioning power (deciding power) produced by initial solitariness, so that one can realize the relations possible in a given situation. To be communal is not to be collective. In collectivism, a person tries to escape solitude by becoming completely embedded in one of the massive group formations. A person's isolation is not overcome, but one is overpowered and numbed. Collectivism understands a person only as a part. There is no person.

Although Buber was an existentialist, the fundamental fact of existence is neither the individual nor the aggregate. The individual is a fact of existence in so far as he or she steps into an I-Thou relationship. There must be a community. This can only occur, if a person calls upon God to save and perfect God's image in the world. Then the inclusion of a person with a person occurs. A dialogical relation emerges. The elments of a dialogical relation are (1) a relation between two persons, (2) an event experienced by them in common in which at least one actively participates, and (3) no forfeiting of the felt reality of activity while living through the common event from the standpoint of the Other.

It follows from *education for communion* that certain metaphorical conceptions of a student must be rejected. The student must not be conceived as a funnel into which patterns for behaving (being) are poured by a teacher. Even if the teacher is a bearer of assured values (authoritativeness) and not one with a will to power (authoritarianism) nor one with longing (Platonic eroticism), there is still compulsion, which is negative reality. A genuine character does not act from norms or maxims that are transmitted or imposed by will or longing, but is a maker of values, a decision-maker, an originator. Also the student must not be conceived as a pump from which being arises. Freedom is only a starting point. The teacher should select the constructive forces of the world (the world bound up in community; the world turned toward God) and make oneself these. Through education as dialogue, the student becomes related to the effective world that is the teacher.

THE SCHOOL AND SOCIAL PROGRESS

John Dewey

We are apt to look at the school from an individualistic standpoint, as something between teacher and pupil, or between teacher and parent. That which interests us most is naturally the progress made by the individual child of our acquaintance, his normal physical development, his advance in ability to read, write, and figure, his growth in the knowledge of geography and history, improvement in manners, habits of promptness, order, and industry—it is from such standards as these that we judge the work of the school. And rightly so. Yet the range of the outlook needs to be enlarged. What the best and wisest parent wants for his own child, that must the community want for all of its children. Any other ideal for our schools is narrow and unlovely; acted upon, it destroys our democracy. All that society has accomplished for itself is put, through the agency of the school, at the disposal of its future members. All its better thoughts of itself it hopes to realize through the new possibilities thus opened to its future self. Here individualism and socialism are at one. Only by being true to the full growth of all the individuals who make it up, can society by any chance be true to itself. And in the self-direction thus given, nothing counts as much as the school, for, as Horace Mann said, "Where anything is growing, one former is worth a thousand re-formers."

Whenever we have in mind the discussion of a new movement in education, it is especially necessary to take the broader, or social view. Otherwise, changes in the school institution and tradition will be looked at as the arbitrary inventions of particular teachers; at the worst transitory fads, and at the best merely improvements in certain details—and this is the plane upon which it is too customary to consider school changes. It is as rational to conceive of the locomotive or the telegraph as personal devices. The modification going on in the method and curriculum of education is as

This was published originally as a pamphlet by the University of Chicago Press, 1899.

much a product of the changed social situation, and as much an effort to meet the needs of the new society that is forming, as are changes in modes of industry and commerce.

It is to this, then, that I especially ask your attention: the effort to conceive what roughly may be termed the "New Education" in the light of larger changes in society. Can we connect this "New Education" with the general march of events? If we can, it will lose its isolated character, and will cease to be an affair which proceeds only from the over-ingenious minds of pedagogues dealing with particular pupils. It will appear as part and parcel of the whole social evolution, and, in its more general features at least, as inevitable. Let us then ask after the main aspects of the social movement; and afterwards turn to the school to find what witness it gives of effort to put itself in line. And since it is quite impossible to cover the whole ground, I shall for the most part confine myself to one typical thing in the modern school movement—that which passes under the name of manual training, hoping if the relation of that to changed social conditions appears, we shall be ready to concede the point as well regarding other educational innovations.

I make no apology for not dwelling at length upon the social changes in question. Those I shall mention are writ so large that he who runs may read. The change that comes first to mind, the one that overshadows and even controls all others, is the industrial one—the application of science resulting in the great inventions that have utilized the forces of nature on a vast and inexpensive scale: the growth of a world-wide market as the object of production, of vast manufacturing centers to supply this market, of cheap and rapid means of communication and distribution between all its parts. Even as to its feebler beginnings, this change is not much more than a century old; in many of its most important aspects it falls within the short span of those now living. One can hardly believe there has been a revolution in all history so rapid, so extensive, so complete. Through it the face of the earth is making over, even as to its physical forms; political boundaries are wiped out and moved about, as if they were indeed only lines on a paper map; population is hurriedly gathered into cities from the ends of the earth; habits of living are altered with startling abruptness and thoroughness; the search for the truths of nature is infinitely stimulated and facilitated and their application to life made not only practicable, but commercially necessary. Even our moral and religious ideas and interests, the most conservative because the deepest-lying things in our nature, are profoundly affected. That this revolution should not affect education in other than formal and superficial fashion is inconceivable.

Back of the factory system lies the household and neighborhood system. Those of us who are here today need go back only one, two, or at most three generations, to find a time when the household was practically the center in which were carried on, or about which were clustered, all the typical forms of industrial occupation. The clothing worn was for the most part not only made in the house, but the members of the household were usually familiar with the shearing of the sheep, the carding and spinning of the wool, and the plying of the loom. Instead of pressing a button and flooding the house with electric light, the whole process of getting illumination was followed in its toilsome length, from the killing of the animal and the trying of fat, to the making of wicks and dipping of candles. The supply of flour, of lumber, of foods, of building materials, of household furniture, even of metal ware, of nails, hinges, hammers, etc., was in the immediate neighborhood, in shops which were constantly open to inspection and often centers of neighborhood congregation. The entire industrial process stood revealed, from the production on the farm of the raw materials, till the finished article was actually put to use. Not only this, but practically every member of the household had his own share in the work. The children, as they gained in strength and capacity, were gradually initiated into the mysteries of the several processes. It was a matter of immediate and personal concern, even to the point of actual participation.

We cannot overlook the factors of discipline and of character-building involved in this: training in habits of order and of industry, and in the idea of responsibility, of obligation to do something, to produce something, in the world. There was always something which really needed to be done, and a real necessity that each member of the household should do his own part faithfully and in coöperation with others. Personalities which became effective in action were bred and tested in the medium of action. Again, we cannot overlook the importance for educational purposes of the close and intimate acquaintance got with nature at first hand, with real things and materials, with the actual processes of their manipulation, and the knowledge of their social necessities and uses. In all this there was continual training of observation, of ingenuity, constructive imagination, of logical thought, and of the sense of reality acquired through first-hand contact with actualities. The educative forces of the domestic spinning and weaving, of the saw-mill, the grist-mill, the cooper shop, and the blacksmith forge, were continuously operative.

No number of object-lessons, got up as object-lessons for the sake of giving information, can afford even the shadow of a substitute for acquaintance with the plants and animals of the farm and garden, acquired through actual living among them and caring for them. No training of sense-organs in school, introduced for the sake of training, can begin to compete with the alertness and fullness of sense-life that comes through daily intimacy and interest in familiar occupations. Verbal memory can be trained in committing tasks, a certain discipline of the reasoning powers can be acquired through lessons in science and mathematics; but, after all, this is somewhat remote and shadowy compared with the training of attention and of judgment that is acquired in having to do things with a real motive behind and a real outcome ahead. At present, concentration of industry and division of labor have practically eliminated household and neighborhood occupations—at least for educational purposes. But it is useless to bemoan the departure of the good old days of children's modesty, reverence, and implicit obedience, if we expect merely by bemoaning and by exhortation to bring them back. It is radical conditions which have changed, and only an equally radical change in education suffices. We must recognize our compensations—the increase in toleration, in breadth of social judgment, the larger acquaintance with human nature, the sharpened alertness in reading signs of character and interpreting social situations, greater accuracy of adaptation to differing personalities, contact with greater commercial activities. These considerations mean much to the city-bred child of today. Yet there is a real problem: how shall we retain these advantages, and yet introduce into the school something representing the other side of life—occupations which exact personal responsibilities and which train the child with relation to the physical realities of life?

When we turn to the school, we find that one of the most striking tendencies at present is toward the introduction of so-called manual training, shop-work, and the household arts—sewing and cooking.

This has not been done "on purpose," with a full consciousness that the school must now supply that factor of training formerly taken care of in the home, but rather by instinct, by experimenting and finding that such work takes a vital hold of pupils and gives them something which was not to be got in any other way. Consciousness of its real import is still so weak that the work is often done in a half-hearted, confused, and unrelated way. The reasons assigned to justify it are painfully inadequate or sometimes even positively wrong.

If we were to cross-examine even those who are most favorably disposed to the introduction of this work into our school system, we should, I imagine, generally find the main reasons to be that such work engages the full spontaneous interest and attention of the children. It keeps them alert and active, instead of passive and receptive; it makes them more useful, more capable, and hence more inclined to be helpful at home; it prepares them to some extent for the practical duties of later life—the girls to be more efficient house managers, if not actually cooks and sempstresses; the boys (were our educational system only adequately rounded out into trade schools) for their future vocations. I do not underestimate the worth of these reasons. Of those indicated by the changed attitude of the children I shall indeed have something to say in my next talk, when speaking directly of the relationship of the school to the child. But the point of view is, upon the whole, unnecessarily narrow. We must conceive of work in wood and metal, of weaving, sewing, and cooking, as methods of life not as distinct studies.

We must conceive of them in their social significance, as types of the processes by which society keeps itself going, as agencies for bringing home to the child some of the primal necessities of community life, and as ways in which these needs have been met by the growing insight and ingenuity of man; in short, as instrumentalities through which the school itself shall be made a genuine form of active community life, instead of a place set apart in which to learn lessons.

A society is a number of people held together because they are working along common lines, in a common spirit, and with reference to common aims. The common needs and aims demand a growing interchange of thought and growing unity of sympathetic feeling. The radical reason that the present school cannot organize itself as a natural social unit is because just this element of common and productive activity is absent. Upon the playground, in game and sport, social organization takes place spontaneously and inevitably. There is something to do, some activity to be carried on, requiring natural divisions of labor, selection of leaders and followers, mutual coöperation and emulation. In the schoolroom the motive and the cement of social organization are alike wanting. Upon the ethical side, the tragic weakness of the present school is that it endeavors to prepare future members of the social order in a medium in which the conditions of the social spirit are eminently wanting.

The difference that appears when occupations are made the articulating centers of school life is not easy to describe in words; it is a difference in motive, of spirit and atmosphere. As one enters a busy kitchen in which a group of children are actively engaged in the preparation of food, the psychological difference, the change from more or less passive and inert recipiency and restraint to one of buoyant outgoing energy, is so obvious as fairly to strike one in the face. Indeed, to those whose image of the school is rigidly set the change is sure to give a shock. But the change in the social attitude is equally marked. The mere absorption of facts and truths is so exclusively individual an affair that it tends very naturally to pass into selfishness. There is no obvious social motive for the acquirement of mere learning, there is no clear social gain in success thereat. Indeed, almost the only measure for success is a competitive one, in the bad sense of that term—a comparison of results in the recitation or in the examination to see which child has succeeded in getting ahead of others in storing up, in accumulating the maximum of information. So thoroughly is this the prevalent atmosphere that for one child to help another in his task has become a school crime. Where the school work consists in simply learning lessons, mutual assistance, instead of being the most natural form of coöperation and association, becomes a clandestine effort to relieve one's neighbor of his proper duties. Where active work is going on all this is changed. Helping others, instead of being a form of charity which impoverishes the recipient, is simply an aid in setting free the powers and furthering the impulse of the one helped. A spirit of free communication, of interchange of ideas, suggestions, results, both successes and failures of previous experiences, becomes the dominating note of the recitation. So far as emulation enters in, it is in the comparison of individuals, not with regard to the quantity of information personally absorbed, but with reference to the quality of work done—the genuine community standard of value. In an informal but all the more pervasive way, the school life organizes itself on a social basis.

Within this organization is found the principle of school discipline or order. Of course, order is simply a thing which is relative to an end. If you have the end in view of forty or fifty children learning certain set lessons, to be recited to a teacher, your discipline must be devoted to securing that result. But if the end in view is the development of a spirit of social coöperation and community life, discipline must grow out of and be relative to this. There is little order of one sort where things are in process of construction; there is a certain disorder in any busy workshop; there is not silence; persons are not engaged in maintaining certain fixed physical postures; their arms are not folded; they are not holding their books thus and so. They are doing a variety of things, and there is the confusion, the bustle, that results from activity. But out of occupation, out of doing things that are to produce results, and out of doing these in a social and coöperative way, there is born a discipline of its own kind and type. Our whole conception of school discipline changes when we get this point of view. In critical moments we all realize that the only discipline that stands by us, the only training that becomes intuition, is that got through life itself. That we learn from experience, and from books or the sayings of others *only* as they are related to experience, are not mere phrases. But the school has been so set apart, so isolated from the ordinary conditions and motives of life, that the place where children are sent for discipline is the one place in the world where it is most difficult to get experience—the mother of all discipline worth the name. It is only where a narrow and fixed image of traditional school discipline dominates, that one is in any danger of overlooking that deeper and infinitely wider discipline that comes from having a part to do in constructive work, in contributing to a result which, social in spirit, is none the less obvious and tangible in form—and hence in a form with reference to which responsibility may be exacted and accurate judgment passed.

The great thing to keep in mind, then, regarding the introduction into the school of various forms of active occupation, is that through them the entire spirit of the school is renewed. It has a chance to affiliate itself with life, to become the child's habitat, where he learns through directed living; instead of being only a place to learn lessons having an abstract and remote reference to some possible living to be done in the future. It gets a chance to be a miniature community, an embryonic society. This is the fundamental fact, and from this arise continuous and orderly sources of instruction. Under the industrial *régime* described, the child, after all, shared in the work, not for the sake of the sharing, but for the sake of the product. The educational results secured were real, yet incidental and dependent. But in the school the typical occupations followed are freed from all economic stress. The aim is not the economic value of the products, but the development of social power and insight. It is this liberation from narrow utilities, this openness to the possibilities of the human spirit that makes these practical activities in the school allies of art and centers of science and history.

The unity of all the sciences is found in geography. The significance of geography is that it presents the earth as the enduring home of the occupations of man. The world without its relationship to human activity is less than a world. Human industry and achievement, apart from their roots in the earth, are not even a sentiment, hardly a name. The earth is the final source of all man's food. It is his continual shelter and protection, the raw material of all his activities, and the home to whose humanizing and idealizing all his achievement returns. It is the great field, the great mine, the great source of the energies of heat, light, and electricity; the great scene of ocean, stream, mountain, and plain, of which all our agriculture and mining and lumbering, all our manufacturing and distributing agencies, are but the partial elements and factors. It is through occupations determined by this environment that mankind has made its historical and political progress. It is through these occupations that the intellectual and emotional interpretation of nature has been developed. It is through what we do in and with the world that we read its meaning and measure its value.

In educational terms, this means that these occupations in the school shall not be mere practical devices or modes of routine employment, the gaining of better technical skill as cooks, sempstresses, or carpenters, but active centers of scientific insight into natural materials and processes, points of departure whence children shall be led out into a realization of the historic development of man. The actual significance of this can be told better through one illustration taken from actual school work than by general discourse.

There is nothing which strikes more oddly upon the average intelligent visitor than to see boys as well as girls of ten, twelve, and thirteen years of age engaged in sewing and weaving. If we look at this from the standpoint of preparation of the boys for sewing on buttons and making patches, we get a narrow and utilitarian conception—a basis that hardly justifies giving prominence to this sort of work in the school. But if we look at it from another side, we find that this work gives the point of departure from which the child can trace and follow the progress of mankind in history, getting an insight also into the materials used and the mechanical principles involved. In connection with these occupations, the historic development of man is recapitulated. For example, the children are first given the raw material—the flax, the cotton plant, the wool as it comes from the back of the sheep (if we could take them to the place where the sheep are sheared, so much the better). Then a study is made of these materials from the standpoint of their adaptation to the uses to which they may be put. For instance, a comparison of the cotton fiber with wool fiber is made. I did not know until the children told me, that the reason for the late development of the cotton industry as compared with the woolen is, that the cotton fiber is so very difficult to free by hand from the seeds. The children in one group worked thirty minutes freeing cotton fibers from the boll and seeds, and succeeded in getting out less than one ounce. They could easily believe that one person could only gin one pound a day by hand, and could understand why their ancestors wore woolen instead of cotton clothing. Among other things discovered as affecting their relative utilities, was the shortness of the cotton fiber as compared with that of wool, the former being one-tenth of an inch in length, while that of the latter is an inch in length; also that the fibers of cotton are smooth and do not cling together, while the wool has a certain roughness which makes the fibers stick, thus assisting the spinning. The children worked this out for themselves with the actual material, aided by questions and suggestions from the teacher.

They then followed the processes necessary for working the fibers up into cloth. They re-invented the first frame for carding the wool—a couple of boards with sharp pins in them for scratching it out. They re-devised the simplest process for spinning the wool—a pierced stone or some other weight through which the wool is passed, and which as it is twirled draws out the fiber; next the top, which was spun on the floor, while the children kept the wool in their hands until it was gradually drawn out and wound upon it. Then the children are introduced to the invention next in historic order, working it out experimentally, thus seeing its necessity, and tracing its effects, not only upon that particular industry, but upon modes of social life—in this way passing in review the entire process up to the present complete loom, and all that goes with the application of science in the use of our present available powers. I need not speak of the science involved in this—the study of the fibers, of geographical features, the conditions under which raw materials are grown, the great centers of manufacture and distribution, the physics involved in the machinery of production; nor, again, of the historical side—the influence which these inventions have had upon humanity. You can concentrate the history of all mankind into the evolution of the flax, cotton, and wool fibers into clothing. I do not mean that this is the only, or the best, center. But it is true that certain very real and important avenues to the consideration of the history of the race are thus opened—that the mind is introduced to much more fundamental and controlling influences than usually appear in the political and chronological records that pass for history.

Now, what is true of this one instance of fibers used in fabrics (and, of course, I have only spoken of one or two elementary phases of that) is true in its measure of every material used in every occupation, and of the processes employed. The occupation supplies the child with a genuine motive; it gives him experience at first hand; it brings him into contact with realities. It does all this, but in addition it is liberalized throughout by translation into its historic values and scientific equivalencies. With the growth of the child's mind in power and knowledge it ceases to be a pleasant occupation merely, and becomes more and more a medium, an instrument, an organ—and is thereby transformed.

This, in turn, has its bearing upon the teaching of science. Under present conditions, all activity, to be successful, has to be directed somewhere and somehow by the scientific expert—it is a case of applied science. This connection should determine its place in education. It is not only that the occupations, the so-called manual or industrial work in the school, give the opportunity for the introduction of science which illuminates them, which makes them material, freighted with meaning, instead of being mere devices of hand and eye; but that the scientific insight thus gained becomes an indispensable instrument of free and active participation in modern social life. Plato somewhere speaks of the slave as one who in his actions does not express his own ideas, but those of some other man. It is our social problem now, even more urgent than in the time of Plato, that method, purpose, understanding, shall exist in the consciousness of the one who does the work, that his activity shall have meaning to himself.

When occupations in the school are conceived in this broad and generous way, I can only stand lost in wonder at the objections so often heard, that such occupations are out of place in the school because they are materialistic, utilitarian, or even menial in their tendency. It sometimes seems to me that those who make these objections must live in quite another world. The world in which most of us live is a world in which everyone has a calling and occupation, something to do. Some are managers and others are subordinates. But the great thing for one as for the other is that each shall have had the education which enables him to see within his daily work all there is in it of large and human significance. How many of the employed are today mere appendages to the machines which they operate! This may be due in part to the machine itself, or to the *régime* which lays so much stress upon the products of the machine; but it is certainly due in large part to the fact that the worker has had no opportunity to develop his imagination and his sympathetic insight as to the social and scientific values found in his work. At present, the impulses which lie at the basis of the industrial system are either practically neglected or positively distorted during the school period. Until the instincts of construction and production are systematically laid hold of in the years of childhood and youth, until they are trained in social directions, enriched by historical interpretation, controlled and illuminated by scientific methods, we certainly are in no position even to locate the source of our economic evils, much less to deal with them effectively.

If we go back a few centuries, we find a practical monopoly of learning. The term *possession* of learning was, indeed, a happy one. Learning was a class matter. This was a necessary result of social conditions. There were not in existence any means by which the multitude could possibly have access to intellectual resources. These were stored up and hidden away in manuscripts. Of these there were at best only a few, and it required long and toilsome preparation to be able to do anything with them. A high-priesthood of learning, which guarded the treasury of truth and which doled it out to the masses under severe restrictions, was the inevitable
, expression of these conditions. But, as a direct result of the industrial revolution of which we have been speaking, this has been changed. Printing was invented; it was made commercial. Books, magazines, papers were multiplied and cheapened. As a result of the locomotive and telegraph, frequent, rapid, and cheap intercommunication by mails and electricity was called into being. Travel has been rendered easy; freedom of movement, with its accompanying exchange of ideas, indefinitely facilitated. The result has been an intellectual revolution. Learning has been put into circulation. While there still is, and probably always will be, a particular class having the special business of inquiry in hand, a distinctively learned class is henceforth out of the question. It is an anachronism. Knowledge is no longer an immobile solid; it has been liquified. It is actively moving in all the currents of society itself.

It is easy to see that this revolution, as regards the materials of knowledge, carries with it a marked change in the attitude of the individual. Stimuli of an intellectual sort pour in upon us in all kinds of ways. The merely intellectual life, the life of scholarship and of learning, thus gets a very altered value. Academic and scholastic, instead of being titles of honor, are becoming terms of reproach.

But all this means a necessary change in the attitude of the school, one of which we are as yet far from realizing the full force. Our school methods, and to a very considerable extent our curriculum, are inherited from the period when learning and command of certain symbols, affording as they did the only access to learning, were all-important. The ideas of this period are still largely in control, even where the outward methods and studies have been changed. We sometimes hear the introduction of manual training, art and science into the elementary, and even the secondary schools, deprecated on the ground that they tend toward the production of specialists—that they detract from our present scheme of generous, liberal culture. The point of this objection would be ludicrous if it were not often so effective as to make it tragic. It is our present education which is highly specialized, one-sided and narrow. It is an education dominated almost entirely by the mediæval conception of learning. It is something which appeals for the most part simply to the intellectual aspect of our natures, our desire to learn, to accumulate information, and to get control of the sym-

bols of learning; not to our impulses and tendencies to make, to do, to
create, to produce, whether in the form of utility or of art. The very fact
that manual training, art and science are objected to as technical, as tending toward mere specialism, is of itself as good testimony as could be offered to the specialized aim which controls current education. Unless education had been virtually identified with the exclusively intellectual
pursuits, with learning as such, all these materials and methods would be
welcome, would be greeted with the utmost hospitality.

While training for the profession of learning is regarded as the type of
culture, as a liberal education, that of a mechanic, a musician, a lawyer, a
doctor, a farmer, a merchant, or a railroad manager is regarded as purely
technical and professional. The result is that which we see about us everywhere—the division into "cultured" people and "workers," the separation
of theory and practice. Hardly one per cent of the entire school population
ever attains to what we call higher education; only five per cent to the
grade of our high school; while much more than half leave on or before the
completion of the fifth year of the elementary grade. The simple facts of the
case are that in the great majority of human beings the distinctively intellectual interest is not dominant. They have the so-called practical impulse
and disposition. In many of those in whom by nature intellectual interest is
strong, social conditions prevent its adequate realization. Consequently by
far the larger number of pupils leave school as soon as they have acquired
the rudiments of learning, as soon as they have enough of the symbols of
reading, writing, and calculating to be of practical use to them in getting a
living. While our educational leaders are talking of culture, the development of personality, etc., as the end and aim of education, the great majority of those who pass under the tuition of the school regard it only as a narrowly practical tool with which to get bread and butter enough to eke out a
restricted life. If we were to conceive our educational end and aim in a less
exclusive way, if we were to introduce into educational processes the activities which appeal to those whose dominant interest is to do and to make,
we should find the hold of the school upon its members to be more vital,
more prolonged, containing more of culture.

But why should I make this labored presentation? The obvious fact is
that our social life has undergone a thorough and radical change. If our education is to have any meaning for life, it must pass through an equally
complete transformation. This transformation is not something to appear
suddenly, to be executed in a day by conscious purpose. It is already in
progress. Those modifications of our school system which often appear
(even to those most actively concerned with them, to say nothing of their
spectators) to be mere changes of detail, mere improvement within the
school mechanism, are in reality signs and evidences of evolution. The introduction of active occupations, of nature study, of elementary science, of
art, of history; the relegation of the merely symbolic and formal to a secon-

dary position; the change in the moral school atmosphere, in the relation of pupils and teachers—of discipline; the introduction of more active, expressive, and self-directing factors—all these are not mere accidents, they are necessities of the larger social evolution. It remains but to organize all these factors, to appreciate them in their fullness of meaning, and to put the ideas and ideals involved into complete, uncompromising possession of our school system. To do this means to make each one of our schools an embryonic community life, active with types of occupations that reflect the life of the larger society, and permeated throughout with the spirit of art, history, and science. When the school introduces and trains each child of society into membership within such a little community, saturating him with the spirit of service, and providing him with the instruments of effective self-direction, we shall have the deepest and best guarantee of a larger society which is worthy, lovely, and harmonious.

EDUCATION

Martin Buber

"The development of the creative powers in the child" is the subject of this conference. As I come before you to introduce it I must not conceal from you for a single moment the fact that of the nine words in which it is expressed only the last three raise no question for me.

The child, not just the individual child, individual children, but the child, is certainly a reality. That in this hour, while we make a beginning with the "development of creative powers," across the whole extent of this planet new human beings are born who are characterized already and yet have still to be characterized—this is a myriad realities, but also one real-

Reprinted with permission of Macmillan Publishing Co., Inc., from *Between Man and Man* by Martin Buber. Copyright © 1965 by Macmillan Publishing Co., Inc. Also reprinted by permission of Routledge and Kegan Paul Ltd.

ity. In every hour the human race begins. We forget this too easily in face of the massive fact of past life, of so-called world-history, of the fact that each child is born with a given disposition of "world-historical" origin, that is, inherited from the riches of the whole human race, and that he is born into a given situation of "world-historical" origin, that is, produced from the riches of the world's events. This fact must not obscure the other no less important fact that in spite of everything, in this as in every hour, what has not been invades the structure of what is, with ten thousand countenances, of which not one has been seen before, with ten thousand souls still undeveloped but ready to develop—a creative event if ever there was one, newness rising up, primal potential might. This potentiality, streaming unconquered, however much of it is squandered, is the reality *child:* this phenomenon of uniqueness, which is more than just begetting and birth, this grace of beginning again and ever again.

What greater care could we cherish or discuss than that this grace may not henceforth be squandered as before, that the might of newness may be preserved for renewal? Future history is not inscribed already by the pen of a causal law on a roll which merely awaits unrolling; its characters are stamped by the unforeseeable decisions of future generations. The part to be played in this by everyone alive to-day, by every adolescent and child, is immeasurable, and immeasurable is our part if we are educators. The deeds of the generations now approaching can illumine the grey face of the human world or plunge it in darkness. So, then, with education: if it at last rises up and exists indeed, it will be able to strengthen the light-spreading force in the hearts of the doers—how much it can do this cannot be guessed, but only learned in action.

The child is a reality; education must become a reality. But what does the "development of the creative powers" mean? Is *that* the reality of education? Must education become that in order to become a reality? Obviously those who arranged this session and gave it its theme think this is so. They obviously think that education has failed in its task till now because it has aimed at something different from this development of what is in the child, or has considered and promoted other powers in the child than the creative. And probably they are amazed that I question this objective, since I myself talk of the treasure of eternal possibility and of the task of unearthing it. So I must make clear that this treasure cannot be properly designated by the notion of "creative powers," nor its unearthing by the notion of "development."

Creation originally means only the divine summons to the life hidden in non-being. When Johann Georg Hamann and his contemporaries carried over this term metaphorically to the human capacity to give form, they marked a supreme peak of mankind, the genius for forming, as that in which man's imaging of God is authenticated in action. The metaphor has since been broadened; there was a time (not long ago) when "creative" meant almost the same as "of literary ability"; in face of this lowest condition of the word it is a real promotion for it to be understood, as it is here, quite generally as something dwelling to some extent in all men, in all children of men, and needing only the right cultivation. Art is then only the province in which a faculty of production, which is common to all, reaches completion. Everyone is elementally endowed with the basic powers of the arts, with that of drawing, for instance, or of music; these powers have to be developed, and the education of the whole person is to be built up on them as on the natural activity of the self.

We must not miss the importance of the reference which is the starting-point of this conception. It concerns a significant but hitherto not properly heeded phenomenon, which is certainly not given its right name here. I mean the existence of an autonomous instinct, which cannot be derived from others, whose appropriate name seems to me to be the "originator instinct." Man, the child of man, wants to make things. He does not merely find pleasure in seeing a form arise from material that presented itself as formless. What the child desires is its own share in this becoming of things; it wants to be the subject of this event of production. Nor is the instinct I am speaking of to be confused with the so-called instinct to busyness or activity which for that matter does not seem to me to exist at all (the child wants to set up or destroy, handle or hit, and so on, but never "busy himself"). What is important is that by one's own intensively experienced action something arises that was not there before. A good expression of this instinct is the way children of intellectual passion produce speech, in reality not as something they have taken over but with the headlong powers of utter newness; sound after sound tumbles out of them, rushing from the vibrating throat past the trembling lips into the world's air, and the whole of the little vital body vibrates and trembles, too, shaken by a bursting shower of selfhood. Or watch a boy fashioning some crude unrecognizable instrument for himself. Is he not astonished, terrified, at his own movement like the mighty inventors of prehistoric times? But it is also to be observed how even in the child's apparently "blind" lust for destruction his instinct of origination enters in and becomes dominant. Sometimes he begins to tear something up, for example, a sheet of paper, but soon he takes an interest in the form of the pieces, and it is not long before he tries—still by tearing—to produce definite forms.

It is important to recognize that the instinct of origination is autonomous and not derivatory. Modern psychologists are inclined to derive the multiform human soul from a single primal element—the "libido," the "will to power," and the like. But this is really only the generalization of certain degenerate states in which a single instinct not merely dominates but also spreads parasitically through the others. They begin with the cases (in our time of inner loss of community and oppression the innumerable cases) where such a hypertrophy breeds the appearance of exclusiveness, they abstract rules from them, and apply them with the whole theoretical and practical questionableness of such applications. In opposition to these doctrines and methods, which impoverish the soul, we must continually point out that human inwardness is in origin a polyphony in which no voice can be "reduced" to another, and in which the unity cannot be grasped analytically, but only heard in the present harmony. One of the leading voices is the instinct of origination.

This instinct is therefore bound to be significant for the work of education as well. Here is an instinct which, no matter to what power it is raised, never becomes greed, because it is not directed to "having" but only to doing; which alone among the instincts can grow only to passion, not to lust; which alone among the instincts cannot lead its subject away to invade the realm of other lives. Here is pure gesture which does not snatch the world to itself, but exposes itself to the world. Should not the person's growth into form, so often dreamed of and lost, at last succeed from this starting-point? For here this precious quality may be unfolded and worked out unimpeded. Nor does the new experiment lack demonstration. The finest demonstration I know, that I have just got to know, is this Children's Choir led by the marvellous Bakule of Prague, with which our Conference opened. How under his leadership crippled creatures, seemingly condemned to lifelong idleness, have been released to a life of freely moving persons, rejoicing in their achievement, formable and forming, who know how to shape sights and sounds in multiform patterns and also how to sing out their risen souls wildly and gloriously; more, how a community of achievement, proclaimed in glance and response, has been welded together out of dull immured solitary creatures: all this seems to prove irrefutably not merely what fruitfulness but also what power, streaming through the whole constitution of man, the life of origination has.

But this very example, seen more deeply, shows us that the decisive influence is to be ascribed not to the release of an instinct but to the forces which meet the released instinct, namely, the educative forces. It depends on them, on their purity and fervour, their power of love and their discretion, into what connexions the freed element enters and what becomes of it.

There are two forms, indispensable for the building of true human life, to which the originative instinct, left to itself, does not lead and cannot lead: to sharing in an undertaking and to entering into mutuality.

An individual achievement and an undertaking are two very different matters. To make a thing is mortal man's pride; but to be conditioned in a common job, with the unconscious humility of being a part, of participation and partaking, is the true food of earthly immortality. As soon as a man enters effectively into an undertaking, where he discovers and practises a community of work with other men, he ceases to follow the originative instinct alone.

Action leading to an individual achievement is a "one-sided" event.

There is a force within the person, which goes out, impresses itself on the material, and the achievement arises objectively: the movement is over, it has run in one direction from the heart's dream into the world, and its course is finished. No matter how directly, as being approached and claimed, as perceiving and receiving, the artist experiences his dealings with the idea which he faces and which awaits embodiment, so long as he is engaged in his work spirit goes out from him and does not enter him, he replies to the world but he does not meet it any more. Nor can he foster mutuality with his work: even in the legend Pygmalion is an ironical figure.

Yes; as an originator man is solitary. He stands wholly without bonds in the echoing hall of his deeds. Nor can it help him to leave his solitariness that his achievement is received enthusiastically by the many. He does not know if it is accepted, if his sacrifice is accepted by the anonymous receiver. Only if someone grasps his hand not as a "creator" but as a fellow-creature lost in the world, to be his comrade or friend or lover beyond the arts, does he have an awareness and a share of mutuality. An education based only on the training of the instinct of origination would prepare a new human solitariness which would be the most painful of all.

The child, in putting things together, learns much that he can learn in no other way. In making some thing he gets to know its possibility, its origin and structure and connexions, in a way he cannot learn by observation. But there is something else that is not learned in this way, and that is the viaticum of life. The being of the world as an object is learned from within, but not its being as a subject, its saying of I and Thou. What teaches us the saying of Thou is not the originative instinct but the instinct for communion.

This instinct is something greater than the believers in the "libido" realize: it is the longing for the world to become present to us as a person, which goes out to us as we to it, which chooses and recognizes us as we do it, which is confirmed in us as we in it. The child lying with half-closed eyes, waiting with tense soul for its mother to speak to it—the mystery of its will is not directed towards enjoying (or dominating) a person, or towards doing something of its own accord; but towards experiencing communion in face of the lonely night, which spreads beyond the window and threatens to invade.

But the release of powers should not be any more than a *presupposition* of education. In the end it is not the originative instinct alone which is meant by the "creative powers" that are to be "developed." These powers stand for human spontaneity. Real education is made possible—but is it also established?— by the realization that youthful spontaneity must not be suppressed but must be allowed to give what it can.

Let us take an example from the narrower sphere of the originative instinct—from the drawing-class. The teacher of the "compulsory" school of thought began with rules and current patterns. Now you knew what beauty was, and you had to copy it; and it was copied either in apathy or in despair. The teacher of the "free" school places on the table a twig of broom, say, in an earthenware jug, and makes the pupils draw it. Or he places it on the table, tells the pupils to look at it, removes it, and then makes them draw it. If the pupils are quite unsophisticated soon not a single drawing will look like another. Now the delicate, almost imperceptible and yet important influence begins—that of criticism and instruction. The children encounter a scale of values that, however unacademic it may be, is quite constant, a knowledge of good and evil that, however individualistic it may be, is quite unambiguous. The more unacademic this scale of values, and the more individualistic this knowledge, the more deeply do the children experience the encounter. In the former instance the preliminary declaration of what alone was right made for resignation or rebellion; but in the latter, where the pupil gains the realization only after he has ventured far out on the way to his achievement, his heart is drawn to reverence for the form, and educated.

This almost imperceptible, most delicate approach, the raising of a finger, perhaps, or a questioning glance, is the other half of what happens in education.

Modern educational theory, which is characterized by tendencies to freedom, misunderstands the meaning of this other half, just as the old theory, which was characterized by the habit of authority, misunderstood the meaning of the first half. The symbol of the funnel is in course of being exchanged for that of the pump. I am reminded of the two camps in the doctrine of evolution, current in the seventeenth and eighteenth centuries, the animalculists, who believed that the whole germ was present in the spermatozoon, and the ovists who believed it was wholly present in the ovum. The theory of the development of powers in the child recalls, in its most extreme expressions, Swammerdam's "unfolding" of the "performed" organism. But the growth of the spirit is no more an unfolding than that of the body. The dispositions which would be discovered in the soul of a newborn child—if the soul could in fact be analysed—are nothing but capacities to receive and imagine the world. The world engenders the person in the individual. The world, that is the whole environment, nature and society, "educates" the human being: it draws out his powers, and makes him grasp and penetrate its objections. What we term education, conscious and willed, means *a selection by man of the effective world:* it means to give decisive effective power to a selection of the world which is concentrated and manifested in the educator. The relation in education is lifted out of the purposelessly streaming education by all things, and is marked off as purpose. In this way, through the educator, the world for the first time becomes the true subject of its effect.

There was a time, there were times, where there neither was nor needed to be any specific calling of educator or teacher. There was a master, a philosopher or a coppersmith, whose journeymen and apprentices lived with him and learned, by being allowed to share in it, what he had to teach them of his handwork or brainwork. But they also learned, without either their or his being concerned with it, they learned, without noticing that they did, the mystery of personal life: they received the spirit. Such a thing must still happen to some extent, where spirit and person exist, but it is expelled to the sphere of spirituality, of personality, and has become exceptional, it happens only "on the heights." Education as a purpose is bound to be summoned. We can as little return to the state of affairs that existed before there were schools as to that which existed before, say, technical science. But we can and must enter into the completeness of its growth to reality, into the perfect humanization of its reality. Our way is composed of losses that secretly become gains. Education has lost the paradise of pure instinctiveness and now consciously serves at the plough for the bread of life. It has been transformed; only in this transformation has it become visible.

Yet the master remains the model for the teacher. For if the educator of our day has to act consciously he must nevertheless do it "as though he did not." That raising of the finger, that questioning glance, are his genuine doing. Through him the selection of the effective world reaches the pupil. He fails the recipient when he presents this selection to him with a gesture of interference. It must be concentrated in him; and doing out of concentration has the appearance of rest. Interference divides the soul in his care into an obedient part and a rebellious part. But a hidden influence proceeding from his integrity has an integrating force.

The world, I said, has its influence as nature and as society on the child. He is educated by the elements, by air and light and the life of plants and animals, and he is educated by relationships. The true educator represents both; but he must be to the child as one of the elements.

The release of powers can be only a presupposition of education, nothing more. Put more generally, it is the nature of freedom to provide the place, but not the foundation as well, on which true life is raised. That is true both of inner, "moral" freedom and of outer freedom (which consists in not being hindered or limited). As the higher freedom, the soul's freedom of decision, signifies perhaps our highest moments but not a fraction of our substance, so the lower freedom, the freedom of development, signifies our capacity for growth but by no means our growth itself. This latter freedom is charged with importance as the actuality from which the work of education begins, but as its fundamental task it becomes absurd.

There is a tendency to understand this freedom, which may be termed evolutionary freedom, as at the opposite pole from compulsion, from being under a compulsion. But at the opposite pole from compulsion there stands not freedom but communion. Compulsion is a negative reality; communication is the positive reality; freedom is a possibility, possibility regained. At the opposite pole of being compelled by destiny or nature or men there does not stand being free of destiny or nature or men but to commune and to convenant with them. To do this, it is true that one must first have become independent; but this independence is a foot-bridge, not a dwelling-place. Freedom is the vibrating needle, the fruitful zero. Compulsion in education means disunion, it means humiliation and rebelliousness. Communion in education is just communion, it means being opened up and drawn in. Freedom in education is the possibility of communion; it cannot be dispensed with and it cannot be made use of in itself; without it nothing succeeds, but neither does anything succeed by means of it: it is the run before the jump, the tuning of the violin, the confirmation of the primal and mighty potentiality which it cannot even begin to actualize.

Freedom—I love its flashing face: it flashes forth from the darkness and dies away, but it has made the heart invulnerable. I am devoted to it, I am always ready to join in the fight for it, for the appearance of the flash, which lasts no longer than the eye is able to endure it, for the vibrating of the needle that was held down too long and was stiff. I give my left hand to rebel and my right to the heretic: forward! But I do not trust them. They know how to die, but that is not enough. I love freedom, but I do not believe in it. How could one believe in it after looking in its face? It is the flash of a significance comprising all meanings, of a possibility comprising all potentiality. For it we fight, again and again, from of old, victorious and in vain.

It is easy to understand that in a time when the deterioration of all traditional bonds has made their legitimacy questionable, the tendency to freedom is exalted, the springboard is treated as the goal and a functional good as substantial good. Moreover, it is idle sentimentality to lament at great length that freedom is made the subject of experiments. Perhaps it is fitting for this time which has no compass that people should throw out their lives like a plummet to discover our bearings and the course we should set. By truly *their* lives! Such an experiment, when it is carried out, is a neck-breaking venture which cannot be disputed. But when it is talked about and talked around, in intellectual discussions and confessions and in the mutual pros and cons of their life's "problems," it is an abomination of disintegration. Those who stake themselves, as individuals or as a community, may leap and crash out into the swaying void where senses and sense fail, or through it and beyond into some kind of existence. But they must not make freedom into a theorem or a programme. To become free of a bond is destiny; one carries that like a cross, not like a cockade. Let us realize the true meaning of being free of a bond: it means that a quite personal responsibility takes the place of one shared with many generations. Life lived in freedom is personal responsibility or it is a pathetic farce.

I have pointed out the power which alone can give a content to empty freedom and a direction to swaying and spinning freedom. I believe in it, I trust those devoted to it.

This fragile life between birth and death can nevertheless be a fulfilment—if it is a dialogue. In our life and experience we are addressed; by thought and speech and action, by producing and by influencing we are able to answer. For the most part we do not listen to the address, or we break into it with chatter. But if the word comes to us and the answer proceeds from us then human life exists, though brokenly, in the world. The kindling of the response in that "spark" of the soul, the blazing up of the response, which occurs time and again, to the unexpectedly approaching speech, we term responsibility. We practise responsibility for that realm of life allotted and entrusted to us for which we are able to respond, that is, for which we have a relation of deeds which may count—in all our inadequacy—as a proper response. The extent to which a man, in the strength of the reality of the spark, can keep a traditional bond, a law, a direction, is the extent to which he is permitted to lean his responsibility on something (more than this is not vouchsafed to us, responsibility is not taken off our shoulders). As we "become free" this leaning on something is more and more denied to us, and our responsibility must become personal and solitary.

From this point of view education and its transformation in the hour of the crumbling of bonds are to be understood.

It is usual to contrast the principle of the "new" education as "Eros" with that of the "old" education as the "will to power."

In fact the one is as little a principle of education as the other. A principle of education, in a sense still to be clarified, can only be a basic relation which is fulfilled in education. But Eros and the will to power are alike passions of the soul for whose real elaboration a place is prepared elsewhere. Education can supply for them only an incidental realm and moreover one which sets a limit to their elaboration; nor can this limit be infringed without the realm itself being destroyed. The one can as little as the other constitute the educational attitude.

The "old" educator, in so far as he was an educator, was not "the man with a will to power," but he was the bearer of assured values which were strong in tradition. If the educator represents the world to the pupil, the "old" educator represented particularly the historical world, the past. He was the ambassador of history to this intruder, the "child"; he carried to him, as the Pope in the legend did to the prince of the Huns, the magic of the spiritual forces of history; he instilled values into the child or he drew the child into the values. The man who reduces this encounter between the cosmos of history and its eternally new chaos, between Zeus and Dionysos, to the formula of the "antagonism between fathers and sons," has

never beheld it in his spirit. Zeus the Father does not stand for a generation but for a world, for the olympic, the formed world; the world of history
faces a particular generation, which is the world of nature renewed again
and again, always without history.

This situation of the old type of education is, however, easily used, or
misused, by the individual's will to power, for this will is inflated by the authority of history. The will to power becomes convulsive and passes into
fury, when the authority begins to decay, that is, when the magical validity
of tradition disappears. Then the moment comes near when the teacher no
longer faces the pupil as an ambassador but only as an individual, as a static
atom to the whirling atom. Then no matter how much he imagines he is
acting from the fulness of the objective spirit, in the reality of his life he is
thrown back on himself, cast on his own resources, and hence filled with
longing. Eros appears. And Eros finds employment in the new situation of
education as the will to power did in the old situation. But Eros is not a
bearer or the ground or the principle any more than the will to power was.
He only claims to be that, in order not to be recognized as longing, as the
stranger given refuge. And many believe it.

Nietzsche did not succeed in glorifying the will to power as much as
Plato glorified Eros. But in our concern for the creature in this great time
of concern, for both alike we have not to consider the myths of the philosophers but the actuality of present life. In entire opposition to any glorifica-
tion we have to see that Eros—that is, not "love," but Eros the male and
magnificent—whatever else may belong to him, necessarily includes this
one thing, that he desires to enjoy men; and education, the peculiar essence bearing this name which is composed of no others, excludes precisely
this desire. However mightily an educator is possessed and inspired by
Eros, if he obeys him in the course of his educating then he stifles the
growth of his blessings. It must be one or the other: either he takes on
himself the tragedy of the person, and offers an unblemished daily sacrifice, or the fire enters his work and consumes it.

Eros is choice, choice made from an inclination. This is precisely what
education is not. The man who is loving in Eros chooses the beloved, the
modern educator finds his pupil there before him. From this unerotic situation the *greatness* of the modern educator is to be seen—and most clearly
when he is a teacher. He enters the school-room for the first time, he sees
them crouching at the desks, indiscriminately flung together, the mis-
shappen and the well-proportioned, animal faces, empty faces, and noble faces
in indiscriminate confusion, like the presence of the created universe; the
glance of the educator accepts and receives them all. He is assuredly no de-
scendant of the Greek gods, who kidnapped those they loved. But he
seems to me to be a representative of the true God. For if God "forms the
light and creates darkness," man is able to love both—to love light in itself,
and darkness towards the light.

If this educator should ever believe that for the sake of education he has to practise selection and arrangement, then he will be guided by another criterion than that of inclination, however legitimate this may be in its own sphere; he will be guided by the recognition of values which is in his glance as an educator. But even then his selection remains suspended, under constant correction by the special humility of the educator for whom the life and particular being of all his pupils is the decisive factor to which his "hierarchic" recognition is subordinated. For in the manifold variety of the children the variety of creation is placed before him.

In education, then, there is a lofty asceticism: an asceticism which rejoices in the world, for the sake of the responsibility for a realm of life which is entrusted to us for our influence but not our interference—either by the will to power or by Eros. The spirit's service of life can be truly carried out only in the system of a reliable counterpoint—regulated by the laws of the different forms of relation—of giving and withholding onself, intimacy and distance, which of course must not be controlled by reflection but must arise from the living tact of the natural and spiritual man. Every form of relation in which the spirit's service of life is realized has its special objectivity, its structure of proportions and limits which in no way resists the fervour of personal comprehension and penetration, though it does resist any confusion with the person's own spheres. If this structure and its resistance are not respected then a dilettantism will prevail which claims to be aristocratic, though in reality it is unsteady and feverish: to provide it with the most sacred names and attitudes will not help it past its inevitable consequence of disintegration. Consider, for example, the relation of doctor and patient. It is essential that this should be a real human relation experienced with the spirit by the one who is addressed; but as soon as the helper is touched by the desire—in however subtle a form—to dominate or to enjoy his patient, or to treat the latter's wish to be dominated or enjoyed by him other than as a wrong condition needing to be cured, the danger of a falsification arises, beside which all quackery appears peripheral.

The objectively ascetic character of the sphere of education must not, however, be misunderstood as being so separated from the instinct to power and from Eros that no bridge can be flung from them to it. I have already pointed out how very significant Eros can be to the educator without corroding his work. What matters here is the threshold and the transformation which takes place on it. It is not the church alone which has a testing threshold on which a man is transformed or becomes a lie. But in order to be able to carry out this ever renewed transition from sphere to sphere he must have carried it out once in a decisive fashion and taken up in himself the essence of education. How does it happen? There is an elemental experience which shatters at least the assurance of the erotic as well as the cratetic man, but sometimes does more, forcing its way at white-heat into the heart of the instinct and remoulding it. A reversal of the single instinct takes place, which does not eliminate it but reverses its system of direction. Such a reversal can be effected by the elemental experience with which the real process of education begins and on which it is based. I call it experiencing the other side.

A man belabours another, who remains quite still. Then let us assume that the striker suddenly receives in his soul the blow which he strikes: the same blow; that he receives it as the other who remains still. For the space of a moment he experiences the situation from the other side. Reality imposes itself on him. What will he do? Either he will overwhelm the voice of the soul, or his impulse will be reversed.

A man caresses a woman, who lets herself be caressed. Then let us assume that he feels the contact from two sides—with the palm of his hand still, and also with the woman's skin. The twofold nature of the gesture, as one that takes place between two persons, thrills through the depth of enjoyment in his heart and stirs it. If he does not deafen his heart he will have—not to renounce the enjoyment but—to love.

I do not in the least mean that the man who has had such an experience would from then on have this two-sided sensation in every such meeting—that would perhaps destroy his instinct. But the one extreme experience makes the other person present to him for all time. A transfusion has taken place after which a mere elaboration of subjectivity is never again possible or tolerable to him.

Only an inclusive power is able to take the lead; only an inclusive Eros is love. Inclusiveness is the complete realization of the submissive person, the desired person, the "partner," not by the fancy but by the actuality of the being.

It would be wrong to identify what is meant here with the familiar but not very significant term "empathy." Empathy means, if anything, to glide with one's own feeling into the dynamic structure of an object, a pillar or a crystal or the branch of a tree, or even of an animal or a man, and as it were to trace it from within, understanding the formation and motoriality of the object with the perceptions of one's own muscles; it means to "transpose" oneself over there and in there. Thus it means the exclusion of one's own concreteness, the extinguishing of the actual situation of life, the absorption in pure aestheticism of the reality in which one participates. Inclusion is the opposite of this. It is the extension of one's own concreteness, the fulfilment of the actual situation of life, the complete presence of the reality in which one participates. Its elements are, first, a relation, of no matter what kind, between two persons, second, an event experienced by them in common, in which at least one of them actively participates, and, third, the fact that this one person, without forfeiting anything of the felt reality of his activity, at the same time lives through the common event from the standpoint of the other.

A relation between persons that is characterized in more or less degree by the element of inclusion may be termed a dialogical relation.

A dialogical relation will show itself also in genuine conversation, but it is not composed of this. Not only is the shared silence of two such persons a dialogue, but also their dialogical life continues, even when they are separated in space, as the continual potential presence of the one to the other, as an unexpressed intercourse. On the other hand, all conversation derives its genuineness only from the consciousness of the element of inclusion—even if this appears only abstractly as an "acknowledgement" of the actual being of the partner in the conversation; but this acknowledgement can be real and effective only when it springs from an experience of inclusion, of the other side.

The reversal of the will to power and of Eros means that relations characterized by these are made dialogical. For that very reason it means that the instinct enters into communion with the fellow-man and into responsibility for him as an allotted and entrusted realm of life.

The element of inclusion, with whose recognition this clarification begins, is the same as that which constitutes the relation in education.

The relation in education is one of pure dialogue.

I have referred to the child, lying with half-closed eyes waiting for his mother to speak to him. But many children do not need to wait, for they know that they are unceasingly addressed in a dialogue which never breaks off. In face of the lonely night which threatens to invade, they lie preserved and guarded, invulnerable, clad in the silver mail of trust.

Trust, trust in the world, because this human being exists—that is the most inward achievement of the relation in education. Because this human being exists, meaninglessness, however hard pressed you are by it, cannot be the real truth. Because this human being exists, in the darkness the light lies hidden, in fear salvation, and in the callousness of one's fellow-men the great Love.

Because this human being exists: therefore he must really be there, really facing the child, not merely there in spirit. He may not let himself be represented by a phantom: the death of the phantom would be a catastrophe for the child's pristine soul. He need possess none of the perfections which the child may dream he possesses; but he must be really there. In order to be and to remain truly present to the child he must have gathered the child's presence into his own store as one of the bearers of his communion with the world, one of the focuses of his responsibilities for the world. Of course he cannot be continually concerned with the child, either in thought or in deed, nor ought he to be. But if he has really gathered the child into his life then that subterranean dialogic, that steady potential presence of the one to the other is established and endures. Then there is reality *between* them, there is mutuality.

But this mutuality—that is what constitutes the peculiar nature of the relation in education—cannot be one of inclusion, although the true relation of the educator to the pupil is based on inclusion. No other relation draws its inner life like this one from the element of inclusion, but no other is in that regard like this, completely directed to one-sidedness, so that if it loses one-sidedness it loses essence.

We may distinguish three chief forms of the dialogical relation.

The first rests on an abstract but mutual experience of inclusion.

The clearest example of this is a disputation between two men, thoroughly different in nature and outlook and calling, where in an instant—as by the action of a messenger as anonymous as he is invisible—it happens that each is aware of the other's full legitimacy, wearing the insignia of necessity and of meaning. What an illumination! The truth, the strength of conviction, the "standpoint," or rather the circle of movement, of each of them, is in no way reduced by this. There is no "relativizing," but we may say that, in the sign of the limit, the essence of mortal recognition, fraught with primal destiny, is manifested to us. To recognize means for us creatures the fulfilment by each of us, in truth and responsibility, of his own relation to the Present Being, through our receiving all that is manifested of it and incorporating it into our own being, with all our force, faithfully, and open to the world and the spirit. In this way living truth arises and endures. We have become aware that it is with the other as with ourselves, and that what rules over us both is not a truth of recognition but the truth-of-existence and the existence-of-truth of the Present Being. In this way we have become able *to acknowledge*.

I have called this form abstract, not as though its basic experience lacked immediacy, but because it is related to man only as a spiritual person and is bound to leave out the full reality of his being and life. The other forms proceed from the inclusion of this full reality.

Of these the first, the relation of education, is based on a concrete but one-sided experience of inclusion.

If education means to let a selection of the world affect a person through the medium of another person, then the one through whom this takes place, rather, who makes it take place through himself, is caught in a strange paradox. What is otherwise found only as grace, inlaid in the folds of life—the influencing of the lives of others with one's own life—becomes here a function and a law. But since the educator has to such an extent replaced the master, the danger has arisen that the new phenomenon, the will to educate, may degenerate into arbitrariness, and that the educator may carry out his selection and his influence from himself and his idea of the pupil, not from the pupil's own reality. One only needs to read, say, the accounts of Pestalozzi's teaching method to see how easily, even with the noblest teachers, arbitrary self-will is mixed up with will. This is almost always due to an interruption or a temporary flagging of the act of inclusion, which is not merely regulative for the realm of education, as for other realms, but is actually constitutive; so that the realm of education acquires its true and proper force from the constant return of this act and the constantly renewed connexion with it. The man whose calling it is to influence the being of persons that can be determined, must experience this action of his (however much it may have assumed the form of nonaction) ever anew from the other side. Without the action of his spirit being in any way weakened he must at the same time be over there, on the surface of that other spirit which is being acted upon—and not of some conceptual, contrived spirit, but all the time the wholly concrete spirit of this individual and unique being who is living and confronting him, and who stands with him in the common situation of "educating" and "being educated" (which is indeed one situation, only the other is at the other end of it). It is not enough for him to imagine the child's individuality, nor to experience him directly as a spiritual person and then to acknowledge him. Only when he catches himself "from over there," and feels how it affects one, how it affects this other human being, does he recognize the real limit, baptize his self-will in Reality and make it true will, and renew his paradoxical legitimacy. He is of all men the one for whom inclusion may and should change from an alarming and edifying event into an atmosphere.

But however intense the mutuality of giving and taking with which he is bound to his pupil, inclusion cannot be mutual in this case. He experiences the pupil's being educated, but the pupil cannot experience the educating of the educator. The educator stands at both ends of the common situation, the pupil only at one end. In the moment when the pupil is able to throw himself across and experience from over there, the educative relation would be burst asunder, or change into friendship.

We call friendship the third form of the dialogical relation, which is based on a concrete and mutual experience of inclusion. It is the true inclusion of one another by human souls.

The educator who practises the experience of the other side and stands firm in it, experiences two things together, first that he is limited by otherness, and second that he receives grace by being bound to the other. He feels from "over there" the acceptance and the rejection of what is approaching (that is, approaching from himself, the educator)—of course often only in a fugitive mood or an uncertain feeling; but this discloses the real need and absence of need in the soul. In the same way the foods a child likes and dislikes is a fact which does not, indeed, procure for the experienced person but certainly helps him to gain an insight into what substances the child's body needs. In learning from time to time what this human being needs and does not need at the moment, the educator is led to an ever deeper recognition of what the human being needs in order to grow. But he is also led to the recognition of what he, the "educator," is able and what he is unable to give of what is needed—and what he can give now, and what not yet. So the responsibility for this realm of life allotted and entrusted to him, the constant responsibility for this living soul, points him to that which seems impossible and yet is somehow granted to us—to self-education. But self-education, here as everywhere, cannot take place through one's being concerned with oneself but only through one's being concerned, knowing what it means, with the world. The forces of the world which the child needs for the building up of his substance must be chosen by the educator from the world and drawn into himself.

The education of men by men means the selection of the effective world by a person and in him. The educator gathers in the constructive forces of the world. He distinguishes, rejects, and confirms in himself, in his self which is filled with the world. The constructive forces are eternally the same: they are the world bound up in community, turned to God. The educator educates himself to be their vehicle.

Then is this the "principle" of education, its normal and fixed maxim?

No; it is only the *principium* of its reality, the beginning of its reality— wherever it begins.

There is not and never has been a norm and fixed maxim of education. What is called so was always only the norm of a culture, of a society, a church, an epoch, to which education too, like all stirring and action of the spirit, was submissive, and which education translated into its language. In a formed age there is in truth no autonomy of education, but only in an age which is losing form. Only in it, in the disintegration of traditional bonds, in the spinning whirl of freedom, does personal responsibility arise which in the end can no longer lean with its burden of decision on any church or society or culture, but is lonely in face of Present Being.

In an age which is losing form the highly-praised "personalities," who know how to serve its fictitious forms and in their name to dominate the age, count in the truth of what is happening no more than those who lament the genuine forms of the past and are diligent to restore them. The ones who count are those persons who—though they may be of little renown—respond to and are responsible for the continuation of the living spirit, each in the active stillness of his sphere of work.

The question which is always being brought forward—"To where, to what, must we educate?"—misunderstands the situation. Only times which know a figure of a general validity—the Christian, the gentleman, the citizen—know an answer to that question, not necessarily in words, but by pointing with the finger to the figure which rises clear in the air, out-topping all. The forming of this figure in all individuals, out of all materials, is the formation of a "culture." But when all figures are shattered, when no figure is able any more to dominate and shape the present human material, what is there left to form?

Nothing but the image of God.

That is the indefinable, only factual, direction of the responsible modern educator. This cannot be a theoretical answer to the question "To what?," but only, if at all, an answer carried out in deeds; an answer carried out by non-doing.

The educator is set now in the midst of the need which he experiences in inclusion, but only a bit deeper in it. He is set in the midst of the service; only a bit higher up, which he invokes without words; he is set in the *imitatio Dei absconditi sed non ignoti.*

When all "directions" fail there arises in the darkness over the abyss the one true direction of man, towards the creative Spirit, towards the Spirit of God brooding on the face of the waters, towards Him of whom we know not whence He comes and whither He goes.

That is man's true autonomy which no longer betrays, but responds.

Man, the creature, who forms and transforms the creation, cannot create. But he, each man, can expose himself and others to the creative Spirit. And he can call upon the Creator to save and perfect His image.

PROBLEM II
Educate Whom?

RESOLUTIVE THEME
Equal Educational Opportunity

EQUAL EDUCATIONAL OPPORTUNITY: HISTORICAL PERSPECTIVE

B. Edward McClellan

The ideal of equal educational opportunity has occupied a central place in American political rhetoric since the earliest days of the Republic. Americans of the last two centuries have not only declared equality of educational opportunity a worthy end in itself but have proclaimed it an essential condition for the achievement of a stable, cohesive, prosperous, and progressive society.

Equalitarian rhetoric first came to be attached to formal education in the Revolutionary era when Thomas Jefferson, among others, proposed a national system of schooling that would provide scholarships for talented youngsters of modest means who might otherwise have little chance to achieve social prominence. Such a system, thought Jefferson, would bring a measure of equality of opportunity to a society where social station and access to education had so often depended solely on the accidents of birth.

In connecting education with equality, Jefferson and his generation announced a new theme in American thought. During most of the colonial era, Americans had accepted inequality in educational opportunity as a fact of life, a condition as immutable as the inequality of the social structure itself. Few had even imagined that education might be equally accessible to all children or that equal educational opportunity might be the starting point for significant social reform.

Despite the significant break with tradition that it represented, Jefferson's specific proposal was in many ways a relatively modest scheme designed to use rigorous examinations to select a tiny minority of talented youth for leadership positions in a society that remained fundamentally hierarchical. In the middle decades of the nineteenth century, however, Americans turned against rigid hierarchy in the society and began to place less emphasis on the selection of an elite leadership than on the universal and common education of the masses of children. Increasingly, equality in education came to mean not just equal access but equal treatment of all children in a common

123

classroom. In the exuberant rhetoric of this confident democratic age, the school was portrayed as the society's great equalizer, a place where rich and poor studied a common curriculum and achieved an equal start in life.

Equality of treatment remained a powerful ideal throughout the nineteenth century, but, in the early decades of the twentieth, Americans abandoned that commitment and turned to a modern version of the Jeffersonian approach. In a complex industrial society, they reasoned, efficiency required that some children be educated for technical and professional careers, others for lives of less exalted status. Access would still be equal, but treatment would vary according to the abilities and interests of the students involved.

The persistence of the rhetoric of equal educational opportunity in its various forms attests to the preeminent place of the ideal in American popular and political thought. But how influential has this ideal been on educational practice? Has the reality of educational equality approached the promise of the popular rhetoric? The readings that follow suggest that it has not.

In a selection entitled "Unequal Education and the Reproduction of the Social Division of Labor," Samuel Bowles exposes a significant gap between the rhetoric and reality of educational equality. Instead of offering equality of opportunity, Bowles concludes, schooling has served as an elaborate mechanism by which an unequal society has perpetuated itself.

Working from a basically Marxist framework, Bowles focuses primarily on the inequalities arising from social class. But there have been other inequalities in American education as well, as the sad history of racism, ethnocentrism, and sexism attests. Jill K. Conway's "Perspectives on the History of Women's Education in the United States" explores one important area of inequality by examining the discrimination against women in American higher education. Conway's work gives little attention to sex discrimination in public schooling, but the inequalities she finds in higher education have had their clear parallels in the lower grades as well.

As both Bowles and Conway make clear, simple access to educational institutions has never been enough to insure equality of educational opportunity. Readers may wish to explore the various ways in which a relatively accessible educational system has still failed to provide equal opportunity. It may also be useful to ponder the various meanings of equality of educational opportunity and to explore the relationship between equality of educational opportunity and the quest for social and economic justice.

UNEQUAL EDUCATION AND THE REPRODUCTION OF THE SOCIAL DIVISION OF LABOR

Samuel Bowles

The ideological defense of modern capitalist society rests heavily on the assertion that the equalizing effects of education can counter the disequalizing forces inherent in the free-market system. That educational systems in capitalist societies have been highly unequal is generally admitted and widely condemned. Yet educational inequalities are taken as passing phenomena, holdovers from an earlier, less enlightened era, which are rapidly being eliminated.

The record of educational history in the United States, and scrutiny of the present state of our colleges and schools, lend little support to this comforting optimism. Rather, the available data suggest an alternative interpretation. In what follows I argue (1) that schools have evolved in the United States not as part of a pursuit of equality, but rather to meet the needs of capitalist employers for a disciplined and skilled labor force, and to provide a mechanism for social control in the interests of political stability; (2) that as the economic importance of skilled and well-educated labor has grown, inequalities in the school system have become increasingly important in reproducing the class structure from one generation to the next; (3) that the U.S. school system is pervaded by class inequalities, which have shown little sign of diminishing over the last half century; and (4) that the evidently unequal control over school boards and other decision-making bodies in education does not provide a sufficient explanation of the persistence and pervasiveness of inequalities in the school system. Although the unequal distribution of political power serves to maintain inequalities in education, the origins of these inequalities are to be found outside the political sphere, in the class structure itself and in the class subcultures typical of capitalist societies. Thus, unequal education has its roots in the very class structure which it serves to legitimize and reproduce.

Reprinted by permission of the author from pp. 36–64 of *Schooling in a Corporate Society*, edited by Martin Carnoy (New York: David McKay and Co., Inc., 1972).

Inequalities in education are part of the web of capitalist society, and are likely to persist as long as capitalism survives.

The Evolution of Capitalism and the Rise of Mass Education

In colonial America, and in most pre-capitalist societies of the past, the basic productive unit was the family. For the vast majority of male adults, work was self-directed, and was performed without direct supervision. Though constrained by poverty, ill health, the low level of technological development, and occasional interferences by the political authorities, a man had considerable leeway in choosing his working hours, what to produce, and how to produce it. While great inequalities in wealth, political power, and other aspects of status normally existed, differences in the degree of autonomy in work were relatively minor, particularly when compared with what was to come.

Transmitting the necessary productive skills to the children as they grew up proved to be a simple task, not because the work was devoid of skill, but because the quite substantial skills required were virtually unchanging from generation to generation, and because the transition to the world of work did not require that the child adapt to a wholly new set of social relationships. The child learned the concrete skills and adapted to the social relations of production through learning by doing within the family. Preparation for life in the larger community was facilitated by the child's experience with the extended family, which shaded off without distinct boundaries, through uncles and fourth cousins, into the community. Children learned early how to deal with complex relationships among adults other than their parents, and children other than their brothers and sisters.[1]

Children were not required to learn a complex set of political principles or ideologies, as political participation was limited and political authority unchallenged, at least in normal times. The only major socializing institution outside the family was the church, which sought to inculcate the accepted spiritual values and attitudes. In addition, a small number of children learned craft skills outside the family, as apprentices. The role of schools tended to be narrowly vocational, restricted to preparation of children for a career in the church or the still inconsequential state bureaucracy.[2] The curriculum of the few universities reflected the aristocratic penchant for conspicuous intellectual consumption.[3]

The extension of capitalist production, and particularly the factory system, undermined the role of the family as the major unit of both socialization and production. Small peasant farmers were driven off the land or competed out of business. Cottage industry was destroyed. Ownership of the means of production became heavily concentrated in the hands of landlords and capitalists. Workers relinquished control over their labor in return for wages or salaries. Increasingly, production was carried on in large organizations in which a small management group directed the work activities of the entire labor force. The social relations of production—the authority structure, the prescribed types of behavior and response characteristic of the work place—became increasingly distinct from those of the family.

The divorce of the worker from control over production—from control over his own labor—is particularly important in understanding the role of schooling in capitalist societies. The resulting social division of labor— between controllers and controlled—is a crucial aspect of the class structure of capitalist societies, and will be seen to be an important barrier to the achievement of social-class equality in schooling.

Rapid economic change in the capitalist period led to frequent shifts of the occupational distribution of the labor force, and constant changes in the skill requirements for jobs. The productive skills of the father were no longer adequate for the needs of the son during his lifetime. Skill training within the family became increasingly inappropriate.

And the family itself was changing. Increased geographic mobility of labor and the necessity for children to work outside the family spelled the demise of the extended family and greatly weakened even the nuclear family.[4] Meanwhile, the authority of the church was questioned by the spread of secular rationalist thinking and the rise of powerful competing groups.

While undermining the main institutions of socialization, the development of the capitalist system created at the same time an environment—both social and intellectual—which would ultimately challenge the political order. Workers were thrown together in oppressive factories, and the isolation which had helped to maintain quiescence in earlier, widely dispersed peasant populations was broken down.[5] With an increasing number of families uprooted from the land, the workers' search for a living resulted in large-scale labor migrations. Transient, even foreign, elements came to constitute a major segment of the population, and began to pose seemingly insurmountable problems of assimilation, integration, and control.[6] Inequalities of wealth became more apparent, and were less easily justified and less readily accepted. The simple legitimizing ideologies of the earlier period—the divine right of kings and the divine origin of social rank, for example—fell under the capitalist attack on the royalty and the traditional landed interests. The general broadening of the electorate first sought by the capitalist class in the struggle against the entrenched interests of the pre-capitalist period—threatened soon to become an instrument for the growing power of the working class. Having risen to political power, the capitalist class sought a mechanism to ensure social control and political stability.[7]

An institutional crisis was at hand. The outcome, in virtually all capitalist countries, was the rise of mass education. In the United States, the many advantages of schooling as a socialization process were quickly perceived. The early proponents of the rapid expansion of schooling argued that education could perform many of the socialization functions that earlier had been centered in the family and, to a lesser extent, in the church.[8] An ideal preparation for factory work was found in the social relations of the school: specifically, in its emphasis on discipline, punctuality, acceptance of authority outside the family, and individual accountability for one's work.[9] The social relations of the school would replicate the social relations of the work place, and thus help young people adapt to the social division of labor. Schools would further lead people to accept the authority of the state and its agents—the teachers—at a young age, in part by fostering the illusion of the benevolence of the government in its relations with citizens.[10] Moreover, because schooling would ostensibly be open to all, one's position in the social division of labor could be portrayed as the result not of birth, but of one's own efforts and talents.[11] And if the children's everyday experiences with the structure of schooling were insufficient to inculcate the correct views and attitudes, the curriculum itself would be made to embody the bourgeois ideology.[12] Where pre-capitalist social institutions, particularly the church, remained strong or threatened the capitalist hegemony, schools sometimes served as a modernizing counter-institution.[13]

The movement for public elementary and secondary education in the United States originated in the nineteenth century in states dominated by the burgeoning industrial capitalist class, most notably in Massachusetts. It spread rapidly to all parts of the country except the South.[14] In Massachusetts the extension of elementary education was in large measure a response to industrialization, and to the need for social control of the Irish and other non-Yankee workers recruited to work in the mills.[15] The fact that some working people's movements had demanded free instruction should not obscure the basically coercive nature of the extension of schooling. In many parts of the country, schools were literally imposed upon the workers.[16]

The evolution of the economy in the nineteenth century gave rise to new socialization needs and continued to spur the growth of education. Agriculture continued to lose ground to manufacturing; simple manufacturing gave way to production involving complex interrelated processes; an increasing fraction of the labor force was employed in producing services rather than goods. Employers in the most rapidly growing sectors of the economy began to require more than obedience and punctuality in their workers; a change in motivational outlook was required. The new structure of production provided little built-in motivation. There were fewer jobs such as farming and piece-rate work in manufacturing in which material reward was tied directly to effort. As work roles became more complicated and interrelated, the evaluation of the individual worker's performance became increasingly difficult. Employers began to look for workers who had internalized the production-related values of the firm's managers.

The continued expansion of education was pressed by many who saw schooling as a means of producing these new forms of motivation and discipline. Others, frightened by the growing labor militancy after the Civil War, found new urgency in the social-control arguments popular among the proponents of education in the antebellum period.

A system of class stratification developed within this rapidly expanding educational system. Children of the social elite normally attended private schools. Because working-class children tended to leave school early, the class composition of the public high schools was distinctly more elite than the public primary schools.[17] And as a university education ceased to be merely training for teaching or the divinity and became important in gaining access to the pinnacles of the business world, upper-class families used their money and influence to get their children into the best universities, often at the expense of the children of less elite families.

Around the turn of the present century, large numbers of working-class and particularly immigrant children began attending high schools. At the same time, a system of class stratification developed within secondary education.[18] The older democratic ideology of the common school—that the same curriculum should be offered to all children—gave way to the "progressive" insistence that education should be tailored to the "needs of the child." [19] In the interests of providing an education relevant to the later life of the students, vocational schools and tracks were developed for the children of working families. The academic curriculum was preserved for those who would later have the opportunity to make use of book learning, either in college or in white-collar employment. This and other educational reforms of the progressive education movement reflected an implicit assumption of the immutability of the class structure.

The frankness with which students were channeled into curriculum tracks, on the basis of their social-class background, raised serious doubts concerning the "openness" of the social-class structure. The relation between social class and a child's chances of promotion or tracking assignments was disguised—though not mitigated much—by another "progressive" reform: "objective" educational testing. Particularly after World War I, the capitulation of the schools to business values and concepts of efficiency led to the increased use of intelligence and scholastic achievement testing as an ostensibly unbiased means of measuring the product of schooling and classifying students.[20] The complementary growth of the guidance counseling profession allowed much of the channeling to proceed from the students' own well-counseled choices, thus adding an apparent element of voluntarism to the system.

The legacy of the progressive education movement, like the earlier reforms of the mid-nineteenth century, was a strengthened system of class stratification within schooling which continues to play an important role in the reproduction and legitimation of the social division of labor.

The class stratification of education during this period had proceeded hand in hand with the stratification of the labor force. As large bureaucratic corporations and public agencies employed an increasing fraction of all workers, a complicated segmentation of the labor force evolved, reflecting the hierarchical structure of the social relations of production. A large middle group of employees developed, comprising clerical, sales, book-keeping, and low-level supervisory workers.[21] People holding these oc-cupations ordinarily had a modicum of control over their own work; in some cases they directed the work of others, while themselves under the direction of higher management. The social division of labor had become a finely articulated system of work relations dominated at the top by a small group with control over work processes and a high degree of personal au-tonomy in their work activities, and proceeding by finely differentiated stages down the chain of bureaucratic command to workers who labored more as extensions of the machinery than as autonomous human beings.

One's status, income, and personal autonomy came to depend in great measure on one's place in the work hierarchy. And in turn, positions in the social division of labor came to be associated with educational credentials reflecting the number of years of schooling and the quality of education received. The increasing importance of schooling as a mechanism for allo-cating children to positions in the class structure played a major part in legitimizing the structure itself.[22] But at the same time, it undermined the simple processes which in the past had preserved the position and privilege of the upper-class families from generation to generation. In short, it un-dermined the processes serving to reproduce the social division of labor.

In pre-capitalist societies, direct inheritance of occupational position is common. Even in the early capitalist economy, prior to the segmentation of the labor force on the basis of differential skills and education, the class structure was reproduced generation after generation simply through the inheritance of physical capital by the offspring of the capitalist class. Now that the social division of labor is differentiated by types of competence and educational credentials as well as by ownership of capital, the problem of inheritance is not nearly so simple. The crucial complication arises because education and skills are embedded in human beings; unlike physical capi-tal, these assets cannot be passed on to one's children at death. In an ad-vanced capitalist society in which education and skills play an important role in the hierarchy of production, then, the absence of confiscatory inher-itance laws is not enough to reproduce the social division of labor from gen-eration to generation. Skills and educational credentials must somehow be passed on within the family. It is a fundamental theme of this essay that schools play an important part in reproducing and legitimizing this modern form of class structure.

NOTES

Many of the ideas in this essay have been worked out jointly with Herbert Gintis and other members of the Harvard seminar of the Union for Radical Political Economics. I am grateful to them and to Janice Weiss and Christopher Jencks for their help.

1. This account draws upon two important historical studies: P. Aries, *Centuries of Childhood* (New York: Vantage, 1965); and B. Bailyn, *Education in the Forming of American Society* (Chapel Hill: University of North Carolina Press, 1960). Also illuminating are anthropological studies of education in contemporary pre-capitalist societies. See for example, J. Kenyatta, *Facing Mount Kenya* (New York: Vintage Books, 1962), pp. 95–124. See also Edmund S. Morgan, *The Puritan Family: Religion and Domestic Relations in Seventeenth Century New England* (New York: Harper and Row, 1966).

2. Aries, *Centuries of Childhood.* In a number of places, e.g., Scotland and Massachusetts, schools stressed literacy so as to make the Bible more widely accessible. See C. Cipolla, *Literacy and Economic Development* (Baltimore: Penguin Books, 1969); and Morgan, *Puritan Family,* chap. 4. Morgan quotes a Massachusetts law of 1647 which provided for the establishment of reading schools because it was "one chief project of that old deluder, Satan, to keep men from knowledge of the Scriptures."

3. H. F. Kearney, *Scholars and Gentlemen: Universities and Society in Pre-Industrial Britain* (Ithaca, N.Y.: Cornell University Press, 1971).

4. See Bailyn, *Education in the Forming of American Society.* N. Smelser, *Social Change in the Industrial Revolution* (Chicago: University of Chicago Press, 1959).

5. F. Engels and K. Marx, *The Communist Manifesto* (London, England: G. Allen and Unwin, 1951); K. Marx, *The 18th Brumaire of Louis Bonaparte* (New York: International Publishers, 1935).

6. See, for example, S. Thernstrom, *Poverty and Progress: Social Mobility in a 19th Century City* (Cambridge: Harvard University Press, 1964).

7. B. Simon, *Studies in the History of Education, 1780–1870,* vol. I (London, England: Lawrence and Wishant, 1960).

8. Bailyn, *Education in the Forming of American Society.*

9. A manufacturer, writing to the Massachusetts State Board of Education from Lowell in 1841 commented

> I have never considered mere knowledge . . . as the only advantage derived from a good Common School education. . . . (Workers with more education possess) a higher and better state of morals, are more orderly and respectful in their deportment, and more ready to comply with the wholesome and necessary regulations of an establishment. . . . In times of agitation, on account of some change in regulations or wages, I have always looked to the most intelligent, best educated and the most moral for support. The ignorant and uneducated I have generally found the most turbulent and troublesome, acting under the impulse of excited passion and jealousy.

Quoted in Michael B. Katz, *The Irony of Early School Reform* (Cambridge, Mass.: Harvard University Press, 1968), p. 88. See also David Isaac Bruck, "The Schools of Lowell, 1824–1861: A Case Study in the Origins of Modern Public Education in America" (Senior thesis, Harvard College, Department of Social Studies, April 1971).

10. In 1846 the annual report of the Lowell, Mass., School Committee concluded that universal education was "the surest safety against internal commotions" (*1846 School Committee Annual Report,* pp. 17–18). It seems more than coincidental that, in England, public support for elementary education—a concept which had been widely discussed and urged for at least half a century—was legislated almost immediately after the enfranchisement of the working class by the electoral reform of 1867. See Simon, *Studies in the History of Education, 1780–1870.* Mass public education in Rhode Island came quickly on the heels of an armed insurrection and a broadening of the franchise. See F. T. Carlton, *Economic Influences upon Educational Progress in the United States, 1820–1850* (New York: Teachers College Press, 1966).

11. Describing the expansion of education in the nineteenth century, Katz concludes:

> . . . a middle class attempt to secure advantage for their children as technological change heightened the importance of formal education assured the success and acceptance of universal elaborate graded school systems. The same result emerged from the fear of a growing, unschooled proletariat. Education substituted for deference as a source of social cement and social order in a society stratified by class rather than by rank. (M. B. Katz, "From Voluntarism to Bureaucracy in U.S. Education," mimeograph, 1970.)

12. An American economist, writing just prior to the "common school revival," had this to say:

> Education universally extended throughout the community will tend to disabuse the working class of people in respect of a notion that has crept into the minds of our mechanics and is gradually prevailing, that manual labor is at present very inadequately rewarded, owing to combinations of the rich against the poor; that mere mental labor is comparatively worthless; the property or wealth ought not to be accumulated or transmitted; that to take interest on money let or profit on capital employed is unjust. . . . The mistaken and ignorant people who entertain these fallacies as truths will learn, when they have the opportunity of learning, that the institution of political society originated in the protection of property. (Thomas Cooper, *Elements of Political Economy* [1828], quoted in Carlton, *Economic Influences upon Educational Progress in the United States, 1820–1850*, pp. 33–34.)

Political economy was made a required subject in Massachusetts high schools in 1857, along with moral science and civic polity. Cooper's advice was widely but not universally followed elsewhere. Friedrich Engels, commenting on the tardy growth of mass education in early nineteenth-century England, remarked: "So shortsighted, so stupidly narrow-minded is the English bourgeoisie in its egotism, that it does not even take the trouble to impress upon the workers the morality of the day, which the bourgeoisie has patched together in its own interest for its own protection." (Engels, *The Condition of the Working Class in England* [Stanford, Calif.: Stanford University Press, 1968].)

13. See Thernstrom, *Poverty and Progress.* Marx said this about mid-nineteenth-century France:

> The modern and the traditional consciousness of the French peasant contended for mastery . . . in the form of an incessant struggle between the schoolmasters and the priests. (Marx, *The 18th Brumaire of Louis Bonaparte,* p. 125.)

14. Janice Weiss and I are currently studying the rapid expansion of southern elementary and secondary schooling which followed the demise of slavery and the establishment of capitalist economic institutions in the South.

15. Based on the preliminary results of a statistical analysis of education in nineteenth-century Massachusetts being conducted jointly with Alexander Field.

16. Katz, *Irony of Early School Reform* and "From Voluntarism to Bureaucracy in U.S. Education."

17. Katz, *Irony of Early School Reform.*

18. Sol Cohen describes this process in "The Industrial Education Movement, 1906–1917," *American Quarterly,* 20 no. 1 (Spring 1968); 95–110. Typical of the arguments then given for vocational education is the following, by the superintendent of schools in Cleveland:

> It is obvious that the educational needs of children in a district where the streets are well paved and clean, where the homes are spacious and surrounded by lawns and trees, where the language of the child's playfellows is pure, and where life in general is permeated with the spirit and ideals of America, it is obvious that the educational needs of such a child are radically different from those of the child who lives in a foreign and tenement section. (William H. Elson and Frank P. Bachman, "Different Course for Elementary School," *Educational Review* 39 [April 1910]: 361–63.)

See also L. Cremin, *The Transformation of the School: Progressivism in American Education, 1876–1957* (New York: Alfred A. Knopf, 1961), chap. 2, and David Cohen and Marvin Lazerson, "Education and the Industrial Order," mimeograph, 1970.

19. The superintendent of the Boston schools summed up the change in 1908:

> Until very recently (the schools) have offered equal opportunity for all to receive *one kind* of education, but what will make them democratic is to provide opportunity for all to receive such education as will fit them *equally well* for their particular life work. (Boston, *Documents of the School Committee, 1908*, no. 7, p. 53; quoted in Cohen and Lazerson, "Education and the Industrial Order.")

20. R. Callahan, *Education and the Cult of Efficiency* (Chicago: University of Chicago Press, 1962); Cohen and Lazerson, "Education and the Industrial Order"; and Cremin, *Transformation of the School.*

21. See M. Reich, "The Evolution of the U.S. Labor Force," in *The Capitalist System,* ed. R. Edwards, M. Reich, and T. Weisskopf (Englewood Cliffs, N.J.: Prentice-Hall, Inc., 1971).

22. The role of school in legitimizing the class structure is spelled out in S. Bowles, "Contradictions in U.S. Higher Education," mimeograph, 1971.

PERSPECTIVES ON THE HISTORY OF WOMEN'S EDUCATION IN THE UNITED STATES

Jill K. Conway

The lively current debate about developing programs of study which will raise women's consciousness and bring them into American intellectual life on a level of equality with men tends to be ahistorical and to subscribe to many of the unexamined assumptions of American educational history. Among the most revered of these is the interpretation unhesitatingly advanced by historians[1] of education that coeducation automatically was a "liberating experience" for American women and that access to professional education naturally placed women on a level with male professional peers. Advocates of increased participation for women in the creation and trans-

Reprinted by permission of the author and *History of Education Quarterly* from pp. 1–12, Vol. 14, Spring, 1974.

mission of American culture had better examine these assumptions with the skepticism which feminists normally extend to male interpretations of women's experience if they are not to devise a faulty strategy for reform through inability to perceive some of the concealed hazards of the landscape.

Although cultural historians have universally concluded that the development of educational institutions in colonial America and in the young republic of the early national period played a decisive role in the creation of an American democratic culture, little effort has been expended in analysing the impact of these institutions on women's social role or on their consciousness of themselves as independent intellects. To understand the dimensions of this impact we must begin, as in all questions of American cultural history, with the colonial period and the Puritan heritage. Governor Winthrop of Massachusetts Bay gave as succinct an expression of Puritan attitudes to women with aspirations to learning as it would be possible to find in his diary entry after meeting the emotionally disturbed wife of a friend.

> Her husband, being very loving and tender of her was loath to grieve her; but he saw his error, when it was too late. For if she had attended her household affairs, and such things as belong to women, and not gone out of her way and calling to meddle in such things as are proper for men, whose minds are stronger, etc., she had kept her wits, and might have improved them usefully and honorably in the place God had set her.[2]

Although the Puritans placed a high value on literacy for women its purpose was to enable them to study the scriptures under the appropriate male guidance, not to think for themselves as the trial and judgement of Anne Hutchinson vividly illustrates. There was in fact a Puritan prohibition against women publishing books and even so strong-willed a woman as Anne Bradstreet felt called upon to excuse her devotion to writing poetry as an occupation carried out at the expense of sleep after all her household duties and her devotions were finished. Thus the Puritan concern for literacy in women was designed to serve a special purpose, to ensure their salvation, but only in the deviant few did the ability to read encourage an independent and self-directing intellectual life.

The transmission of Enlightenment ideas to the American colonies brought to colonial intellectual life one of the most characteristic debates of Western European thought, designated by the shorthand phrase, the "querrelle des femmes." This was a debate between feminists and antifeminist concerning the extent of women's rationality and the purpose and degree to which the female mind might be educated which had continued from the early Renaissance period through to the Enlightenment. The discussion of this question in 18th century colonial thought was for the most part not original and drew mainly on English and French sources.[3] However, as with so much of his writing, Benjamin Franklin was able to take the European terms of this discussion about female rationality and recast them in uniquely American theories and conclusions. Franklin was willing to abandon the Christian view of the female—as a lesser creation marked by greater impulsiveness and less able to use reason in control of the emotions than men—and to put in its place a view of the female as a rational being engaged in the pursuit of happiness. However the revolutionary potential of such a view was not worked out in his thought because of the biological determinism which was inherent in his view of natural law. Thus it never occurred to Franklin, the archetypal self-made and self-educated man that the freedom to create the self might be extended to women. His *Reflections on Courtship and Marriage* of 1746 instead developed an approach to female education with which Americans were to become familiar.[4] A woman's education, he thought, should develop in her those qualities which would ensure her happiness in marriage since marriage and reproduction were her natural destiny. It was axiomatic for him that women's happiness was to be found in marriage and reason therefore decreed that women should be educated to use their rational powers in the role of wife and mother. In bringing together the consideration of marriage, the pursuit of happiness and the education of women Franklin was squaring up to one of the most troublesome problems which were to perplex the leaders of the revolutionary generation. How could the rational scrutiny of the basis of power and authority in the political realm be undertaken without setting off the kind of radical debate about other patterns of domination and subordination in society which the Revolutionary leaders profoundly wished to leave unquestioned? In particular if the nature of tyranny inherent in monarchical institutions was to be laid bare for all to see how could such matters be duscussed without a consideration of the nature of tyranny within the patriarchal family? If the goal of the individual was to be the pursuit of happiness how could such a pursuit be so defined that women would accept the subordination necessary for harmony in life and order in society? Franklin's answer was to make some concessions toward acceptance of female rationality and to argue for the creation of a system of female education which would make women rationally convinced that their true happiness lay in marriage and would develop in the female mind only those traits and tendencies likely to find satisfaction in domestic life.

Since formal educational institutions for women did not form any part of Franklin's scheme of things the agency by which women were to be educated was to be through their contact during the process of courtship with the more finely disciplined male intellect. Franklin's aspiring suitor came armed with improving books, ready to convey good common sense philosophy, sound moral principles and a grasp of arithmetic. He also came prepared to set limits on the intellectual aspirations of his bride-to-be, to steer her away from the realm of abstract thought because critical intellect would not be conducive to marital happiness, whereas a grasp of accounting would be of practical use in future domestic life.

It only remained for educational theorists to elaborate this view after the Declaration of Independence in accord with the national purpose. The task was ably taken up by Benjamin Rush whose writings on the education appropriate for women in a republic steered clear of the question of female rationality and placed great emphasis on the patriotic duties of republican women.[5] Rush took up another education theme echoes of which were still to be heard in twentieth century discussions of women's education. In a republican society, since all men were equal, there could be no servant class. It followed therefore that women would have to be educated to understand domestic economy because the sound ordering of the household would now become their responsibility. The implicit assignment of women to a service role did not trouble Rush in the slightest since like all his contemporaries he assumed the correctness of the traditional subordination of women, though the upheaval of the Revolution required that this status be squared with republican ideology.

Thus when one looks at the roles taken up by women intellectuals in the early national period, one sees an immediate contrast between the life patterns of women who were to live and work with ideas within the context of American culture and those who took on the role of intellectual in Europe. In Europe the woman intellectual developed her creativity in the hurleyburley of literary life almost to the degree that she was deviant from her society. European women intellectuals were either déclassé (cast out from respectable society, detached from family and family responsibilities, living by their wits as self-supporting individuals) or else they lived a contemplative life in a religious community which was a recognised counter institution for escape from the family.

It was otherwise in the United States in the period from 1790 to 1830 when new roles were emerging for the few women who had somehow acquired education. The early national period was one of intense and anxious questioning about what an appropriate republican culture would be like and about what social forces could be expected to keep republican society stable. The cause for worry and uncertainty about the future came from what was known from classical history of republican societies. Classical parallels suggested that the stability and prosperity of republics rested upon their capacity to maintain virtue and discipline among the citizenry. The United States of the 1790's had no standing army to impart discipline and had recently decided that there should be no national religious establishment which could undertake moral instruction. This meant that the family unit assumed an unprecedented political significance because the family was the only social unit which could be relied on to provide both moral training and discipline for the young of the Republic.

The result of these unique political pressures was the development of a new division of labor between the sexes. Males were thought of as having political and economic responsibilities: they were to be citizens and to provide the economic support for the family. Women had new responsibilities of a very important kind. They were to have the responsibility for the administration of the domestic establishment (something European men and 18th century Americans expected to share with their wives), they were to play the primary role in educating the young, and because of this primary responsibility they were to serve as the moral guardians of the young. This new role for women as guardians of moral standards was unique to American culture. It immediately paved the way for the emergence in the 1830's of the woman teacher who could safely by charged with the education of the young of both sexes.

The first generation of women educators was born in the 1790's when these new cultural forces first began to operate. Their intellectual aspirations thus took them not into deviance but into intense patriotism and affirmation of American values. In explaining their careers they produced the first writing by women on women's education to be published in America. The textbooks, speeches and lectures of Emma Willard and Catharine Beecher[6] were hardly clarion calls to independence for women scholars though both women lived for ideas and supported themselves entirely by their teaching and writing. Both were celebrators of the Republic and of American virtues, both rejoiced in the new calling which republican culture had created for the patriotic woman teacher, and both were impeccably correct in restricting women's teaching role to the moral guidance of the young in insisting that politics, theology and philosophy were the unquestioned concerns of men. This kind of respectability was not unique to women educators. Women moralists and religious writers of the early national period likewise celebrated the family and the moral strength to be derived from maternity though poets like the popular Lydia Sigourney and famous preachers like Mrs. Phoebe Palmer clearly honoured their domestic calling more in prose and sentiment than in hard days in the kitchen or the nursery. Sarah J. Hale, the moralizing editor of *Godey's Lady Book*, likewise earned middle class status though she broke the genteel code about respectable women working because she was such a determined celebrator of the virtues of family life and the responsibilities of women for preserving moral standards.[7] By conforming their concerns as teachers, writers, preachers or publicists to the conventional areas of female expertise and assuming responsibility for the preservation of "respectable" morality, women intellectuals in the early national period took on a role for themselves which was compensatory to that of men's rather than in competition with the work of male scholars, theologians and writers. By doing so they gave actual currency to the theories of writers on women's education like Franklin and Rush and so fostered the belief carried on by their students and readers that women's intellectual life found its purpose in achieving for

American culture some of the tasks which men, because of their economic
and political responsibilities, could not fulfill.

We might expect that this view of the compensatory value of the female
intellect would be modified by the development of coeducational experiments in college education in the 1830's. However, coeducational colleges,
when they came, developed with the same notion of the compensatory role
of the educated woman. Since the early coeducational colleges had as their
goal the training of effective ministers for the West, they aimed to train
women for useful work so that they could function efficiently as the help-
mates of the men who were to evangelise the frontier and keep America
from falling away from Christian culture. The most striking example of an
early coeducational experiment dictated by this practical goal was the
founding of Oberlin College. Oberlin was founded as a manual labour
school which had a farm attached to it where it was expected that men
students could work to produce the crops which were to pay for their education. Shortly after Oberlin was opened, however, it became apparent
that the school would also require a domestic work-force to take care of the
chores of cleaning the residences, producing the means and clearing up afterwards, and laundering and minding the men's clothes. Women students
were thus essential, if real economies were to be achieved in the cost of
providing education. The routine of Oberlin's first women students (so in-
correctly cited as examples of the liberated woman scholar) was as follows.
On Mondays there were no classes held while women students did duty in
the laundry laundering the men's clothes, and carrying out any chores of
mending or repairs that were necessary. No time, however, was set aside
for the laundering and repair of women students' clothes. This was managed in spare time at night after classes. Every day of the week women
students cooked, served meals and waited on tables, thus duplicating in the
college environment the conventional role of the female.

Their presence at Oberlin was compensatory in another important respect. By being there they were thought to contribute to the mental and
emotional balance of the men students, thus ensuring that the male
scholar's time was expended to maximum effect. This is an argument for
coeducation which has a contemporary ring about it as we observe the
adoption of coeducation by the male elite colleges on the ground that the
presence of women (no matter how marginal they may be) is beneficial to
the mental health of men students. Women's presence at Oberlin was justified with disarming frankness for its contribution to the mental health of
the males. After a generation of coeducational experience the essentially
remedial role of the woman student was thus defined. The presence of
women "enkindles emulation; puts each sex upon its best behaviour; almost
entirely expels from the College those mean trickish exploits which so
frequently deprave monastic society, and develops in the College all those
humanizing, elevating influences which God provided for in the well or-

dered association of the sexes together, ..."[8] There was not in the entire discussion of the Oberlin experiment a sustained and serious debate about what coeducation might provide for the training of the female mind, except an adequate preparation for marriage and the capacity to serve as a companion for a frontier minister who might otherwise suffer from cultural deprivation. Women's minds during and after college education were thus considered only from the point of view of the services they might provide for men. We should not therefore be surprised to discover that the coeducational life of Oberlin was not one which encouraged women to think of themselves as the intellectual peers of men. Indeed, those few women's rights advocates who were educated at Oberlin were radicals before they came there and they sustained their interest in feminism in the face of very strong pressures against it during their undergraduate experience. The same conspicuous lack of discussion of the educational purpose of coeducation may be found in the decisions taken during the middle decades of the century to make tax-supported high schools coeducational. The arguments in favour of the movement toward coeducation were strictly economic as were the arguments which finally won admission for women into the midwestern state universities.[9]

We must therefore look elsewhere if we are to locate the causes for the drive towards independent careers for women which was to develop in the post-Civil War period. It was not the product of serious discussion of male and female intellectual equality in coeducational institutions. Instead the experience which proved to be consciousness raising came out of the experience of role conflict which was almost universal for women participants in the anti-slavery movement. Coeducational institutions neatly adapted existing sex roles into their educational goals whereas women activists in the reform movements of the Jacksonian period would not accommodate their moral purpose to the traditionally subordinate position accorded their sex. The women reformers' role conflicts arose from their attempts to act out the now accepted women's role of guardian of society's moral standards through a concern for the situation of slaves rather than through childbearing and teaching. Because of the political implications of the anti-slavery movement they encountered strong opposition as soon as their moral concerns took them beyond the family and the nurturing of the young. Women reformers like the Grimké sisters were forced to recognise that women's supposed moral tasks in society were strictly confined to the domestic sphere and that any effort to confront serious social issues would be constrained by women's subordination in all other areas of intellectual and political life. In attempting to act out women's assigned role of moral guardian within the contentious political sphere of the abolition movement the Grimké's were brought to a radical perception of women's actual subordination with American society and hence toward serious thought about a wide range of feminist issues. This kind of radicalising role conflict for

women reformers was virtually ended with the conclusion of the Civil War
when women's philanthropic concerns were once more directed along
paths of conventional charity. The experience of this early feminist generation however provides us with an insight into the real sources of changing
consciousness for women in the mid-nineteenth century.

In the post-Civil War era the source of important kinds of role conflict
for women came from the establishment of women's colleges on the model
of male elite schools on the East Coast. These women's colleges provided
women with a collective female life and gave them a training for the mind
which was not derivative and did not assume a role for women scholars
compensatory to that of male students. Access to this kind of higher education modelled on the classical and literary curriculum of the male elite
schools produced a batch of women reformers in the 1890's who were different from any preceding generation. They could not accept conventional
marriage because their minds had been trained along lines which required
discipline and independent effort, and they expected to put this training to
a practical use which was not to be found within the narrow confines of
domestic life. Estimates differ about the number who remained single but
approximately sixty to seventy percent of the first generation of graduates
from women's colleges did not marry and many pursued specifically identifiable careers. The search for a career, however, was only briefly and partially radicalizing. Intense conflict was experienced by women of this generation in reaching the decision not to marry and to pursue some
non-domestic career. However, once the decision had been made, the
search for a career did not take women into the life of the déclassé, alienated intellectual because intellectual life was becoming professionalized in
post-Civil War America. Educated women could thus cling to their respectable status and develop new social roles for themselves in founding
the service professions for women. The careers of Jane Addams, Lillian
Wald, and Ida Cannon all illustrate the contribution of the new elite colleges for women to the founding of the service professions. Indeed, of all
the founders of women's professions, only Mary Richmond lacked this kind
of educational background.[10]

Although the founders of the women's professions had developed a
strongly feminist consciousness because of the conflict between the accepted social role for women and the expectations of careers created by
their education, this feminism was not sufficiently radical to produce questioning of the scientific culture of the high Victorian era. In developing service professions for women the pioneering generation continued the acceptance of sex-typed roles for women because evolutionary biology told them
that there was a separate nurturing female temperament which was complementary to that of the male. It is worth remembering that access to
higher education need not liberate the student from the fundamental biases
of Western culture, since women of this generation learned from Darwin

and Spencer that there were biologically determined sexual temperaments, the male being warlike and aggressive and the female being nurturing and passive. The founders of the women's professions built their idea of a proper professional role for women around the systematic development of what they regarded as a biologically determined nurturing female temperament. There was thus no possibility that access to education might liberate them to view themselves as disciplined intellects who could operate without inhibition in traditionally male spheres of competence.

Even when women gained access to scientific and technological education, sex-stereotypes dictated the roles which they defined for the scientifically educated female. The best example of a pioneer woman professional with early access to scientific education may be found in the career of Ellen H. Richards. In 1870 she went to the Massachusetts Institute of Technology as a student of chemistry. Her understanding of her place there is neatly defined in her own words. "Perhaps the fact that I am not a radical or a believer in the all-powerful ballot for women to right all her wrongs and that I do not scorn womanly duties, but claim it as a privilege to clean up and sort and supervise the room and sew things, etc., is winning me stronger allies than anything else."[11] Life in the laboratory did not raise her consciousness. Instead it prompted her to become one of the founders of the home economics movement. In prompting the new field of study for women she claimed that the home was becoming so important a centre of consumption for American society that a housewife with scientific expertise was required to manage it efficiently. Scientific education was thus to be used to bolster and inflate the traditional female domestic role, and in the development of the new field there was no effort to channel women's scientific creativity into more challenging intellectual spheres. Here we see a *reductio ad absurdum* of the unexamined assumption that access to education automatically changes consciousness because contact with scientific education for Ellen Richards merely meant trying to make a profession out of domestic work.

The development of the women's professions should thus be interpreted as a conservative trend by which the potential for change inherent in changed educational experience was still-born and women's intellectual energies were channeled into perpetuating women's service role in society rather than into independent and self-justifying intellectual endeavour. It was also a trend by which the direction and support of most kinds of intellectual enquiry remained unquestionably male-controlled. Thus the development of women's professions has not significantly altered their status in intellectual life nor has it fostered women's intellectual creativity.

It is essential then to grasp that contrary to what educational historians have had to say up to now, it is not access to educational facilities which is the significant variable in tracing the "liberation" of women's minds. What really matters is whether womens' consciousness of themselves as intellects is altered. This did not take place as a result of the development of coeducation in the United States. It did not occur when women entered the service professions. In fact during the great educational changes of the 19th and early 20th century womens' awareness of their own value as intellects was inhibited by their search for a respectable bourgeois professional role. They were ready to expand women's domestic role into some kind of pseudo-scientific profession and willing to see the only legitimate fields for female intellectual effort in extensions of the domestic sphere.

This trend accounts for the relative lack of creativity among the newly educated women professionals so far as thought about women's place in society is concerned. New ideas about women's place in society did not come from the "women's" professions and the research programmes of their professional schools. Instead the revolutionary ideas about women's status came from the developing discipline of anthropology through the endeavours of conventional scholars to develop some general comparative perspective on sexual customs and cultural values. The relative lack of creativity which comes out of women's access to higher education must be stressed because there is a distinct possibility that many of the "women's studies" programmes being developed today will be similarly uncreative. The danger lies in the fact that these programmes will not be productive of change in women's sense of themselves as intellectuals if they assume an inherent female temperament which is intellectually or morally different from that of males. Women's studies programmes will merely produce more sex-typed intellectual activity and no change in women's sense of their involvement in intellectual problems outside a sexually defined sphere of competence. There can be no drive to intellectual power, creativity, and mastery of a discipline while women's intellectual life is still inhibited by the sense that female intellect is in some obscure way complementary to that of men.

In making this point it is necessary to stress that the educational experience of women ought to provide them with some sense of collective life because female sociability is an important precondition for creativity in women's scholarly endeavour just as male sociability has been carefully institutionalised in all communities devoted to higher learning. There can be no question that the development of coeducation in the United States during the mid-nineteenth century deprived women students of the opportunity to experience a self-supporting and self-directing female community, such as existed and continues to exist in the religious and lay schools of many European countries. Experience of a female controlled and directed world is essential, if women are to discover a sense of their own potential for self-directing activity. However, this is an institutional problem having to do with the way in which intellectual activity is organized and pursued. It is not an intellectual problem having to do with different ways of knowing or validating truth.

There is another very practical problem posed by the mushrooming of special women's studies programmes. It is a problem related to the correct strategy to be pursued in encouraging women's intellectual creativity given the manner in which society's resources are channeled toward the support of intellectual life. Should women scholars bore from within established male professions thereby tapping the resources committed to supporting them and attempting to transform the dominant style of intellectual life? Or should they attempt to attract scarce resources to women's programmes which will be staffed by women scholars? Quite apart from the intellectual dangers inherent in such an approach it is tactically weak. Separate and unequal women's programmes will be poorly funded. They are and will continue to be denigrated intellectually and therefore they cannot possibly lead to the establishment of strong female professional identities. They will certainly be among the first expendable academic ventures to be cut when budgets require economies, and their graduates will be the first to be let go when there is any question of professional priorities in the maintenance of established faculties.

This is an unfashionable position to adopt in the current discussion of women's educational needs. However, the history of the women's professions illustrates the dangers inherent in institutionalising certain kinds of feminine intellectual activity within an existing pattern of male controlled professions. The acceptance of any sexual division of labor is bound to channel creativity and to perpetuate existing patterns of socialisation. Only the abandonment of a sexual division of labor in the life of the mind can effectively change women's consciousness of their worth as scholars and creative intellects.

NOTES

1. See for example Thomas Woody, *A History of Women's Education in the United States* (New York, 1929) p. 1, 329 ff. and 11, 224 ff. Woody's interpretation of the impact of higher education on women's status in American society has long remained unchallenged despite the conflict between his general interpretation of the direction of change and the record of individual college histories such as Morris Bishop, *A History of Cornell* (Ithaca, 1962) and Robert S. Fletcher, *A History of Oberlin College from its Foundation Through the Civil War* (Oberlin, 1943), 2 vols.

2. John Winthrop, *The History of New England,* James Savage, ed. (Boston, 1853), p. 2, 216.

3. On the discussion of women's place in the 18th century colonies, see Mary Sumner Benson, *Women in Eighteenth Century America* (Port Washington, 1966).

4. Benjamin Franklin, *Reflections on Courtship and Marriage: In Two Letters to a Friend. Wherein A Practical Plan Is Laid Down For Obtaining And Securing Conjugal Felicity* (Philadelphia, 1746).

5. Benjamin Rush, "Thoughts on Female Education Accommodated to the Present State of Society, Manners and Government in the United States of America," first published in 1787 is most readily available today in Frederick L. Rudolph, ed. *Essays on Education in the Republic* (Cambridge, 1965), pp. 27–40.

6. Emma Hart Willard (1767–1870) founder of Troy Female Seminary and author of many influential school texts on history and geography. See Alma Lutz, *Emma Willard: Daughter of Democracy* (Boston, 1964). Catharine Beecher (1800–1878) founder of Hartford Female Seminary and prolific writer on educational questions. See Mae E. Harveson, *Catharine Esther Beecher, Pioneer Educator* (Philadelphia, 1932).

7. On Lydia Sigourney (1791–1865), see Gordon S. Haight, *Mrs. Sigourney: The Sweet Singer of Hartford* (1930). For the life of Mrs. Phoebe Worrall Palmer (1807–1874) see Richard Wheatley, *The Life and Letters of Mrs. Phoebe Palmer* (1876). The best account of the life of Sarah Josepha Hale, editor of Godey's Lady's Book is Ruth E. Finley, *The Lady of Godey's* (1931).

8. *Oberlin Evangelist,* October 8, 1862. On coeducation at Oberlin, see Fletcher, *A History of Oberlin,* p. 1, 377 ff., and 11, 643 ff.

9. See Woody, *A History of Women's Education,* p. 11, 224 ff. for a discussion of the arguments for and against coeducation.

10. See Jane Addams, *Twenty Years at Hull-House* (New York, 1910), Lillian D. Wald, *The House on Henry Street* (New York, 1915), Ida M. Cannon, *On The Social Frontier of Medicine* (Cambridge, 1952), and Mary Richmond, *The Long View: Papers and Addresses,* sel. and ed. J. C. Colcord and R. Z. S. Mann (New York, 1930).

11. On Ellen H. Richards (1842–1911) see Caroline L. Hunt, *The Life of Ellen H. Richards* (Boston, 1912). For the passage cited, see Hunt, *Life,* 91.

EQUAL EDUCATIONAL OPPORTUNITY: SOCIOLOGICAL PERSPECTIVE

Robert Arnove

The sociological study of equality of educational opportunity (EEO) usually focuses on the relationship between amount and type of schooling and stratification. Stratification refers to the hierarchical ordering of people on such dimensions as wealth, power, and prestige. According to Parelius and Parelius, it is widely assumed that

> "Equality of opportunity" exists when each person, regardless of such ascribed characteristics as family background, religion, ethnicity, race, or gender, has the same chance of acquiring a favorable socioeconomic position.[1]

It should be noted that EEO does not necessarily imply that people will end up equal, but simply that an individual's socioeconomic position will be the result of "a fair and open contest—one in which the winners are those who work hardest and demonstrate the most ability."[2] In this contest, schools play an important role: they test and certify merit, deciding who shall be the winners and losers.

The previous line of reasoning corresponds to the functional or consensus paradigm of society (see p. 8). According to this model, occupations in modern, industrial societies increasingly determine the income, prestige, and power of individuals. What occupations individuals enter, in turn, is primarily determined by the amount and type of schooling they receive. In this view, those who demonstrate great ability in school will be prepared to enter the more lucrative and prestigious professional, managerial, technical, and scientific occupations—whereas those who are less competent will occupy low-level positions in the economy. The higher income that white-collar, professional, and managerial workers earn is justified according to the crucial role that these highly-trained individuals play in modernizing and expanding the economy.[3]

Much of the reform legislation of the 1960s in the United States was based on these notions. According to Mary Jo Bane and Christopher Jencks, reformers assumed that poverty was rooted in differences in cognitive skills of individuals, and that the surest way to improve the life chances of lower class individuals was by raising their academic achievement and level of schooling. To this end, such programs as Head Start, Follow Through, and Upward Bound were established to equip students from so-called disadvantaged backgrounds to compete more effectively with children from mainstream, middle- and upper-income backgrounds. The James S. Coleman study falls within this model: it sets out to study the relationship between quality of schooling and cognitive achievement for different socioeconomic and ethnic groups in American society.

By contrast, adherents of the conflict paradigm point out that inequality has been an integral part of education systems from the very beginnings of publicly funded, compulsory schooling in the United States. While talented *individuals* from working class and minority groups may be able to succeed in school and improve their socioeconomic position, these *groups* as such are denied the opportunities to improve collectively their underclass position vis-à-vis dominant groups. Schools, according to the conflict model, function to perpetuate the existing inequalities in the economy and society. Work in the free enterprise economy is arranged hierarchically: the owners of capital and top management dictate to lower levels of skilled and unskilled workers who have little to do with decisions concerning what is produced, how, and for whom. Schools, in preparing individuals for these different roles, reinforce the existing class structure. Studies and data cited by Bowles and Gintis (see their article in Problem III), indicate that students from different social class backgrounds attend schools where the social relations of learning and the content of instruction vary markedly—the main effect of such differential schooling or socialization is to allocate individuals to futures that are consistent with their social class. According to this point of view, school systems institutionally discriminate against members of underclass groups by neglecting or denigrating their language, values, behaviors, and knowledge. Programs such as Head Start, which attempt to correct for deficiencies in the "cultural background," home life, school-related work habits and skills of working class and minority students, are approaches that simply "blame the victim" for his/her condition in life.[4]

The Bane and Jencks article only partially corresponds to the conflict paradigm. While they criticize the unequal distribution of income in American society, which is rooted in a capitalist economy, Bane and Jencks do not argue the case that schools contribute significantly to inequality across generations (see the Levin critique).

The purpose of describing these paradigms is to provide a framework for viewing and interpreting the readings in this section—the authors' conclusions and the data on which they are based. These paradigms contribute to an understanding of opposing points of view concerning such issues as the inheritance of advantage and equality of access to educational resources.

In the debate over inequality, one critical question concerns the degree to which advantage is passed on from one generation to another. For example, if the social class standing of a family is high in terms of income, occupational status, and educational attainment, will its offspring have greater access to the highest levels of a school system? And what is the effect of family socioeconomic position on the relationship between level of schooling attained and subsequent income and occupational status? While there is some evidence to suggest that schooling in America is becoming increasingly meritocratic—that is, a larger number of academically qualified students from low income backgrounds are able to attend some form of higher education[5]—other researchers point out that these students do not fare as well as those from high income groups.[6] This is the case when students from low income backgrounds have levels of schooling and cognitive achievement equivalent to those from high income backgrounds (see Figure 4, p. 277). By contrast, upper income students, including those who are not academically talented, consistently do better than low income students. They are more likely to attend college and enter the top one fifth of income earners.

Another issue that enters the debate over EEO is whether or not students from different social class and ethnic backgrounds have access to comparable school resources and competent teachers. In this discussion of EEO, the metaphor of a race or contest is frequently used. Are certain students handicapped at the starting line? (The notion of cultural or genetic deficiencies.) Is the race a fair one? Are all the contestants running on the same quality track? (The notion of the quality of schools attended by different economic and ethnic groups.) The Coleman study—which was commissioned by the Office of Education, as mandated by the 1964 Civil Rights Act—set out to examine the conditions of the contest. The study found that, as a general rule, minority students attended schools that were less well endowed and lacking in facilities such as science laboratories that appear to be related to academic achievement. But the most striking, if not startling, conclusion was that the quality of a school has little impact on academic achievement. The social class and racial composition of the student body, family background characteristics, and student attitudes—such as a belief in control over one's destiny—were found to be more substantially associated with academic achievement.

Jencks et al.,[7] using in part data from the Coleman study, similarly conclude that the amount of resources allocated to schooling has little to do with academic achievement. Moreover, Jencks et al. reject the thesis that cognitive achievement and quality of schools attended are major predictors of socioeconomic status.

In *Inequality*, Jencks et al. use the metaphor of a factory in their examination of school effects. The data they marshall indicate that investments in schools cannot be justified in relation to later outcomes such as lifetime earnings. Instead, income is determined by a whole variety of factors—

including luck, personality attributes, social skills, and competencies developed on-the-job. Since the role of schooling in determining economic success is so marginal, they conclude that inequalities in income should be attacked directly through social policies that minimize wage differentials and guarantee an adequate standard of living for all. Schools should not be looked to as agencies for overcoming inequities in the economy.

Social science research characteristically challenges our commonsense interpretations of everyday reality. Certainly the findings of the Coleman and Jencks studies fly in the face of commonly held assumptions concerning the importance of school resources and facilities in determining academic achievement, or the relationship between school success and economic success. Although surprising, the findings nonetheless have been widely discussed, if not accepted, by a substantial number of people—including those who wish to limit financing of public schools or the use of schools as agencies of social reform.

The findings of Coleman and Jencks, however, can be seriously criticized on several grounds. Henry Levin, in his critique of *Inequality* by Jencks et al., has questioned the adequacy of the measurements, the types of variables examined, as well as the assumptions that guided all phases of the research. It is these assumptions that greatly influence the conclusions reached by the researchers. Using a different model of school effects, Hurn notes how the Coleman and Jencks studies can be interpreted differently: "The finding that differences in school quality cannot account for differences in school performance is quite compatible with the argument that virtually all schools reinforce and accentuate already existing inequalities among students."[8]

If this is the case, then, a promising line of inquiry would be to focus on the internal life of schools: on processes such as tracking and counseling; and on the interactions between students and school personnel by which behavior is defined, evaluated, and rewarded. For the most part, Coleman and Jencks follow an input-output or factory model in their research on schools. The researchers measure the effects of inputs (such as family background, intelligence, and student attitudes) on quantifiable concepts (such as academic achievement, years of education attained, and income). In this model, schooling is a black box, about whose inner workings little is known. As Parelius and Parelius note, the research tells us little about the "educational experiences of various groups of children who may, in fact, be attending the same schools and may even be sitting in the same classrooms."[9]

The type of research that sociologists like Hurn advocate would involve an examination of the linkages between what is learned at home and what is taught at school:

   . . . it is clear that an adequate theory linking socialization in the home to success in the student role must specify precisely what qualities are needed for successful performance of that role and, equally importantly, describe the "fit" between socialization and student roles in different kind [sic] of schools.[10]

Such a theory also would comprehend an examination of the relationship between the workings of the larger society and the values and behaviors that are rewarded in school.

In conclusion, the sociological study of EEO involves the analysis of differing interpretations of equality—how they vary over time and social circumstances (the contribution of social history)—and the ways in which social scientists undertake to measure the concept. How equality or inequality is defined and measured is ultimately a matter of ideology and normative judgment. Again, we turn to philosophy for an elucidation of these concerns.

NOTES

1. Ann Parker Parelius and Robert J. Parelius, *The Sociology of Education* (Englewood Cliffs, N.J.: Prentice-Hall, 1978), p. 283.

2. Ibid.

3. For arguments along these lines see Kingsley Davis and Wilbert E. Moore, "Some Principles of Stratification," *American Sociological Review,* **10** (April 1945), 242–249; for a critical interpretation of this point of view see Charles H. Anderson, *Toward a New Sociology: A Critical View* (Homewood, Ill.: Dorsey, 1971), pp. 83–102.

4. William Ryan, *Blaming the Victim* (New York: Vintage Books, 1971).

5. For further discussion, see Christopher J. Hurn, *The Limits and Possibilities of Schooling: An Introduction to the Sociology of Education* (Boston: Allyn, 1978), pp. 96–98.

6. See, for example, William Sewell, "Inequality of Opportunity for Higher Education," *American Sociological Review,* **36** (October 1971), 793–809.

7. The Bane and Jencks article contained in this section is a shortened version of the introduction and conclusions of the book, *Inequality: A Reassessment of the Effect of Family and Schooling in America* (New York: Basic Books, 1972). I, therefore, refer to Jencks et al. in my subsequent discussion of the methodology of the study.

8. Hurn, op. cit., p. 139.

9. Parelius and Parelius, op. cit., p. 315.

10. Hurn, op. cit., p. 169.

EQUALITY OF EDUCATIONAL OPPORTUNITY

James S. Coleman

1.1 Segregation in the Public Schools

The great majority of American children attend schools that are largely segregated—that is, where almost all of their fellow students are of the same racial background as they are. Among minority groups, Negroes are by far the most segregated. Taking all groups, however, white children are most segregated. Almost 80 percent of all white pupils in 1st grade and 12th grade attend schools that are from 90 to 100 percent white. And 97 percent at grade 1, and 99 percent at grade 12, attend schools that are 50 percent or more white.

For Negro pupils, segregation is more nearly complete in the South (as it is for whites also), but it is extensive also in all the other regions where the Negro population is concentrated: the urban North, Midwest, and West.

More than 65 percent of all Negro pupils in the first grade attend schools that are between 90 and 100 percent Negro. And 87 percent at grade 1, and 66 percent at grade 12, attend schools that are 50 percent or more Negro. In the South most students attend schools that are 100 percent white or Negro.

The same pattern of segregation holds, though not quite so strongly, for the teachers of Negro and white students. For the Nation as a whole, the average Negro elementary pupil attends a school in which 65 percent of the teachers are Negro; the average white elementary pupil attends a school in which 97 percent of the teachers are white. White teachers are more predominant at the secondary level, where the corresponding figures are 59 and 97 percent. The racial matching of teachers is most pronounced in the South, where by tradition it has been complete. On a nationwide basis, in

Reprinted from pp. 3, 8–23 of James Coleman et al., *Equality of Educational Opportunity* (Washington: U.S. Office of Education, 1966).

cases where the races of pupils and teachers are not matched, the trend is all in one direction: white teachers teach Negro children but Negro teachers seldom teach white children; just as, in the schools, integration consists primarily of a minority of Negro pupils in predominantly white schools but almost never of a few whites in largely Negro schools.

In its desegregation decision of 1954, the Supreme Court held that separate schools for Negro and white children are inherently unequal. This survey finds that, when measured by that yardstick, American public education remains largely unequal in most regions of the country, including all those where Negroes form any significant proportion of the population. Obviously, however, that is not the only yardstick. The next section of the summary describes other characteristics by means of which equality of educational opportunity may be appraised.

. . .

1.2 The Schools and Their Characteristics

The school environment of a child consists of many elements, ranging from the desk he sits at to the child who sits next to him, and including the teacher who stands at the front of his class. A statistical survey can give only fragmentary evidence of this environment.

Great collections of numbers such as are found in these pages—totals and averages and percentages—blur and obscure rather than sharpen and illuminate the range of variation they represent. If one reads, for example, that the average annual income per person in the State of Maryland is $3,000, there is a tendency to picture an average person living in moderate circumstances in a middle-class neighborhood holding an ordinary job. But that number represents at the upper end millionaires, and at the lower end the unemployed, the pensioners, the charwomen. Thus the $3,000 average income should somehow bring to mind the tycoon and the tramp, the showcase and the shack, as well as the average man in the average house.

So, too, in reading these statistics on education, one must picture the child whose school has every conceivable facility that is believed to enhance the educational process, whose teachers may be particularly gifted and well educated, and whose home and total neighborhood are themselves powerful contributors to his education and growth. And one must picture the child in a dismal tenement area who may come hungry to an ancient, dirty building that is badly ventilated, poorly lighted, overcrowded, understaffed, and without sufficient textbooks.

Statistics, too, must deal with one thing at a time, and cumulative effects tend to be lost in them. Having a teacher without a college degree indicates an element of disadvantage, but in the concrete situation, a child may be taught by a teacher who is not only without a degree but who has grown up and received his schooling in the local community, who has never been out of the State, who has a 10th-grade vocabulary, and who shares the local community's attitudes.

One must also be aware of the relative importance of a certain kind of thing to a certain kind of person. Just as a loaf of bread means more to a starving man than to a sated one, so one very fine textbook or, better, one very able teacher, may mean far more to a deprived child than to one who already has several of both.

Finally, it should be borne in mind that in cases where Negroes in the South receive unequal treatment, the significance in terms of actual numbers of individuals involved is very great, since 54 percent of the Negro population of school-going age, or approximately 3,200,000 children, live in that region.

All of the findings reported in this section of the summary are based on responses to questionnaires filled out by public school teachers, principals, district school superintendents, and pupils. The data were gathered in September and October of 1965 from 4,000 public schools. All teachers, principals, and district superintendents in these schools participated, as did all pupils in the 3d, 6th, 9th, and 12th grades. First-grade pupils in half the schools participated. More than 645,000 pupils in all were involved in the survey. About 30 percent of the schools selected for the survey did not participate; an analysis of the nonparticipating schools indicated that their inclusion would not have significantly altered the results of the survey. The participation rates were: in the metropolitan North and West, 72 percent; metropolitan South and Southwest, 65 percent; nonmetropolitan North and West, 82 percent; nonmetropolitan South and Southwest 61 percent.

All the statistics on the physical facilities of the schools and the academic and extracurricular programs are based on information provided by the teachers and administrators. They also provided information about their own education, experience, and philosophy of education, and described as they see them the socioeconomic characteristics of the neighborhoods served by their schools.

The statistics having to do with the pupils' personal socioeconomic backgrounds, level of education of their parents, and certain items in their homes (such as encyclopedias, daily newspapers, etc.) are based on pupil responses to questionnaires. The pupils also answered questions about their academic aspirations and their attitudes toward staying in school.

All personal and school data were confidential and for statistical purposes only; the questionnaires were collected without the names or other personal identification of the respondents.

Data for Negro and white children are classified by whether the schools are in metropolitan areas or not. The definition of a metropolitan area is the one commonly used by government agencies: a city of over 50,000 inhabitants including its suburbs. All other schools in small cities, towns, or rural areas are referred to as nonmetropolitan schools.

Finally, for most tables, data for Negro and white children are classified by geographical regions. For metropolitan schools there are usually five regions defined as follows:

Northeast—Connecticut, Maine, Massachusetts, New Hampshire, Rhode Island, Vermont, Delaware, Maryland, New Jersey, New York, Pennsylvania, District of Columbia. (Using 1960 census data, this region contains about 16 percent of all Negro children in the Nation and 20 percent of all white children age 5 to 19.)

Midwest—Illinois, Indiana, Michigan, Ohio, Wisconsin, Iowa, Kansas, Minnesota, Missouri, Nebraska, North Dakota, South Dakota (containing 16 percent of Negro and 19 percent of white children age 5 to 19).

South—Alabama, Arkansas, Florida, Georgia, Kentucky, Louisiana, Mississippi, North Carolina, South Carolina, Tennessee, Virginia, West Virginia (containing 27 percent of Negro and 14 percent of white children age 5 to 19).

Southwest—Arizona, New Mexico, Oklahoma, Texas (containing 4 percent of Negro and 3 percent of white children age 5 to 19).

West—Alaska, California, Colorado, Hawaii, Idaho, Montana, Nevada, Oregon, Utah, Washington, Wyoming (containing 4 percent of Negro and 11 percent of white children age 5 to 19).

The nonmetropolitan schools are usually classified into only three regions:

South—As above (containing 27 percent of Negro and 14 percent of white children age 5 to 19).

Southwest—As above (containing 4 percent of Negro and 2 percent of white children age 5 to 19).

North and West—All States not in the South and Southwest (containing 2 percent of Negro and 17 percent of white children age 5 to 19).

Data for minority groups other than Negroes are presented only on a nationwide basis because there were not sufficient cases to warrant a breakdown by regions.

Facilities

The two tables which follow (table 1, for elementary schools, and table 2 for secondary) list certain school characteristics and the percentages of pupils of the various races who are enrolled in schools which have those characteristics. Where specified by "average" the figures represent actual numbers

TABLE 1.
Percent (except where average specified) of Pupils in *Elementary* Schools Having the School Characteristic Named at Left, Fall 1965

Characteristic	Whole Nation						Nonmetropolitan						Metropolitan									
							North and West		South		South-west		North-east		Midwest		South		South-west		West	
	MA	PR	IA	OA	Neg.	Maj.	Neg.	Maj.	Neg.	Maj.	Neg.	Maj.	Neg.	Maj.	Neg.	Maj.	Neg.	Maj.	Neg.	Maj.	Neg.	Maj.
Age of main building:																						
Less than 20 years	59	57	66	61	63	60	48	54	72	34	73	40	31	59	28	63	77	75	52	89	76	80
20 to 40 years	18	18	20	20	17	20	35	13	21	43	17	28	23	23	18	18	11	20	27	10	14	9
At least 40 years	22	24	13	18	18	18	17	32	4	20	9	29	43	18	53	18	12	4	21	1	7	7
Average pupils per room	33	31	30	33	32	29	25	28	34	26	21	31	33	30	34	30	30	31	39	26	37	31
Auditorium	20	31	18	21	27	19	3	5	16	40	14	19	56	40	27	10	20	21	11	1	47	12
Cafeteria	39	43	38	30	38	37	41	33	46	64	47	54	41	45	24	22	34	32	48	38	34	14
Gymnasium	19	27	20	14	15	21	9	8	15	31	15	21	46	49	36	19	6	5	13	17	34	8
Infirmary	59	62	64	77	71	68	52	52	49	44	38	39	74	90	74	79	81	76	59	48	93	96
Full-time librarian	22	31	22	24	30	22	4	13	32	22	5	11	46	43	22	15	38	50	11	12	19	13
Free textbooks	80	82	80	85	84	75	73	56	70	73	99	98	100	98	72	54	84	82	83	65	98	100
School has sufficient number of textbooks	90	87	91	93	84	96	97	99	76	94	97	96	90	97	97	99	74	98	82	84	95	90
Texts under 4 years old	66	68	60	52	67	61	66	51	60	60	47	85	57	56	67	59	71	91	76	53	77	77
Central school library	69	71	72	83	73	72	44	58	74	77	48	75	83	89	57	70	79	69	59	33	81	95
Free lunch program	64	73	66	52	74	59	61	50	87	94	83	70	50	43	42	48	90	85	74	82	65	47

Note: In this Summary section, the group identifications are abbreviated as follows: MA—Mexican American; PR—Puerto Rican; IA—Indian American; OA—Oriental American; Neg.—Negro; and Maj.—majority or white.

TABLE 2.
Percent (except where average specified) of Pupils in Secondary Schools Having the School Characteristic Named at Left, Fall 1965

Characteristic	Whole Nation						Nonmetropolitan										Metropolitan					
							North and West		South		Southwest		Northeast		Midwest		South		Southwest		West	
	MA	PR	IA	OA	Neg.	Maj.	Neg.	Maj.	Neg.	Maj.	Neg.	Mag.	Neg.	Maj.	Neg.	Maj.	Neg.	Maj.	Neg.	Maj.	Neg.	Maj.
Age of main building:																						
Less than 20 years	48	40	49	41	60	53	64	35	79	52	76	44	18	64	33	43	74	84	76	43	53	79
20 to 40 years	40	31	35	32	26	29	15	26	13	33	22	46	41	20	38	37	18	14	16	56	46	19
At least 40 years	11	28	15	26	12	18	21	38	3	15	3	10	40	15	29	20	3	0	6	1	2	3
Average pupils per room	32	33	29	32	34	31	27	30	35	28	22	20	35	28	54	33	30	34	28	42	31	30
Auditorium	57	68	49	66	49	46	32	27	21	36	56	68	77	72	51	44	49	40	67	57	72	45
Cafeteria	72	80	74	81	72	65	55	41	65	78	78	97	88	73	55	54	77	97	75	63	77	79
Gymnasium	78	88	70	83	64	74	51	52	38	63	71	71	90	90	75	76	52	80	70	77	99	95
Shop with power tools	96	88	96	98	89	96	97	96	85	90	88	91	67	97	99	100	89	90	92	97	100	100
Biology laboratory	95	84	96	96	93	94	99	87	85	88	93	96	83	94	100	99	95	100	100	97	100	100
Chemistry Laboratory	96	94	99	99	94	98	98	97	85	91	92	95	99	99	100	100	94	100	96	97	100	100
Physics laboratory	90	83	90	97	80	94	80	90	63	83	74	93	92	99	94	96	83	100	96	97	76	100
Language laboratory	57	45	58	75	49	56	32	24	17	32	38	19	47	79	68	57	48	72	69	97	95	80
Infirmary	65	77	77	69	70	75	47	56	53	45	23	47	96	99	70	83	83	83	74	85	71	87
Full-time librarian	84	93	85	98	87	83	53	58	69	76	67	61	97	99	99	94	96	99	71	63	100	99
Free textbooks	74	79	78	88	70	62	42	53	51	43	94	92	98	91	67	39	58	34	98	97	99	86
Sufficient number of textbooks	92	89	90	96	85	95	99	99	79	91	97	100	94	99	98	100	69	97	94	57	96	96
Texts under 4 years old	58	68	65	55	61	62	77	56	64	54	73	66	55	59	51	67	56	65	99	82	59	67
Average library books per pupil	8.1	6.2	6.4	5.7	4.6	5.8	4.5	6.3	4.0	6.1	8.1	14.8	3.8	5.3	3.5	4.8	4.5	5.7	5.6	3.7	6.5	6.3
Free lunch program	66	80	63	75	74	62	58	54	89	88	61	82	66	52	74	63	79	79	89	52	47	54

rather than percentages. Reading from left to right, percentages or averages are given on a nationwide basis for the six groups; then comparisons between Negro and white access to the various facilities are made on the basis of regional and metropolitan-nonmetropolitan breakdowns.

Thus, in table 1, it will be seen that for the Nation as a whole white children attend elementary schools with a smaller average number of pupils per room (29) than do any of the minorities (which range from 30 to 33). Farther to the right are the regional breakdowns for whites and Negroes, and it can be seen that in some regions the nationwide pattern is reversed: in the nonmetropolitan North and West and Southwest for example, there is a smaller average number of pupils per room for Negroes than for whites.

The same item on table 2 shows that secondary school whites have a smaller average number of pupils per room than minorities, except Indians. Looking at the regional breakdown, however, one finds much more striking differences than the national average would suggest: In the metropolitan Midwest, for example, the average Negro has 54 pupils per room—probably reflecting considerable frequency of double sessions—compared with 33 per room for whites. Nationally, at the high school level the average white has 1 teacher for every 22 students and the average Negro has 1 for every 26 students. (See table 6b.)

It is thus apparent that the tables must be studied carefully, with special attention paid to the regional breakdowns, which often provide more meaningful information than do the nationwide averages. Such careful study will reveal that there is not a wholly consistent pattern—that is, minorities are not at a disadvantage in every item listed, but that there are nevertheless some definite and systematic directions of differences. Nationally, Negro pupils have fewer of some of the facilities that seem most related to academic achievement. They have less access to physics, chemistry, and language laboratories; there are fewer books per pupil in their libraries; their textbooks are less often in sufficient supply. To the extent that physical facilities are important to learning, such items appear to be more relevant than some others, such as cafeterias, in which minority groups are at an advantage.

Usually greater than the majority-minority differences, however, are the regional differences. Table 2, for example, shows that 95 percent of Negro and 80 percent of white high school students in the metropolitan Far West attend schools with language laboratories, compared with 48 and 72 percent, prespectively, in the metropolitan South, in spite of the fact that a higher percentage of Southern schools are less than 20 years old.

Finally, it must always be remembered that these statistics reveal only majority-minority average differences and regional average differences; they do not show the extreme differences that would be found by comparing one school with another.

Programs

Tables 3 and 4 summarize some of the survey findings about the school curriculum, administration, and the extracurricular activities. The tables are organized in the same way as tables 1 and 2 and should be studied in the same way, again with particular attention to regional differences.

The pattern that emerges from study of these tables is similar to that from tables 1 and 2. Just as minority groups tend to have less access to physical facilities that seem to be related to academic achievement, so too they have less access to curricular and extracurricular programs that would seem to have such a relationship.

Secondary school Negro students are less likely to attend schools that are regionally accredited; this is particularly pronounced in the South. Negro and Puerto Rican pupils have less access to college preparatory curriculums and to accelerated curriculums; Puerto Ricans have less access to vocational curriculums as well. Less intelligence testing is done in the schools attended by Negroes and Puerto Ricans. Finally, white students in general have more access to a more fully developed program of extracurricular activities in particular those which might be related to academic matters (debate teams for example, and student newspapers).

Again, regional differences are striking. For example, 100 percent of Negro high school students and 97 percent of whites in the metropolitan Far West attend schools having a remedial reading teacher (this does not mean, of course, that every student uses the services of that teacher, but simply that he has access to them) compared with 46 percent and 65 percent, respectively, in the metropolitan South—and 4 percent and 9 percent in the nonmetropolitan Southwest.

Principals and Teachers

The following tables (5, 6a, and 6b) list some characteristics of principals and teachers. On table 5, figures given for the whole Nation of all minorities, and then by region for Negro and white, refer to the percentages of students who attend schools having principals with the listed characteristics. Thus, line one shows that 1 percent of white elementary pupils attend a school with a Negro principal, and that 56 percent of Negro children attend a school with a Negro principal.

Tables 6a and 6b (referring to teachers' characteristics) must be read differently. The figures refer to the percentage of teachers having a specified characteristic in the schools attended by the "average" pupil of the various groups. Thus, line one on table 6a: the average white student goes to an elementary school where 40 percent of the teachers spent most of their lives in the same city, town, or county; the average Negro pupil goes to a school

TABLE 3.
Percent of Pupils in *Elementary* Schools Having the Characteristic Named at Left, Fall 1965

Characteristic	Whole Nation						Nonmetropolitan						Metropolitan									
							North and West		South		Southwest		Northeast		Midwest		South		Southwest		West	
	MA	PR	IA	OA	Neg.	Maj.	Neg.	Maj.	Neg.	Maj.	Neg.	Maj.	Neg.	Maj.	Neg.	Maj.	Neg.	Maj.	Neg.	Maj.	Neg.	Maj.
Regionally accredited schools	21	27	25	22	27	28	38	29	16	22	59	39	34	24	52	49	21	35	42	23	22	9
Music teacher	31	34	41	33	24	35	22	43	26	17	37	42	34	49	38	32	21	17	23	61	9	13
Remedial reading teacher	41	45	35	41	39	39	37	46	15	11	12	26	73	58	60	17	28	31	18	29	66	70
Accelerated curriculum	34	32	42	37	29	40	47	26	28	24	32	13	34	47	21	28	19	41	34	76	43	73
Low IQ classes	43	44	44	56	54	48	54	48	30	29	47	25	60	51	73	45	48	33	63	66	77	75
Speech impairment classes	41	44	42	58	41	51	34	49	13	11	27	22	59	73	86	67	20	41	34	23	86	82
Use of intelligence test	93	77	90	95	88	95	85	93	80	91	92	90	73	91	97	99	92	100	97	98	98	99
Assignment practice other than area or open	6	11	9	5	12	6	6	1	27	20	26	2	7	4	1	2	12	22	0	0	4	1
Use of tracking	37	47	40	34	44	36	36	28	38	25	38	23	66	50	40	38	45	35	50	48	36	40
Teachers having tenure	68	68	69	79	70	64	70	64	34	49	7	36	100	98	94	76	51	58	64	39	92	90
Principal's salary $9,000 and above	51	52	56	69	51	51	45	34	12	12	22	36	95	86	92	72	30	26	35	14	98	99
School newspaper	23	29	35	37	28	29	39	43	25	26	8	6	28	31	31	24	29	27	22	11	31	31
Boys' interscholastic athletics	55	44	51	47	41	43	71	62	51	51	59	72	22	22	43	46	38	22	43	54	34	22
Girls' interscholastic athletics	35	29	36	32	26	26	37	35	39	38	40	44	19	14	17	17	2	6	29	43	25	18
Band	71	63	64	76	66	72	82	81	39	40	54	76	67	73	77	86	66	85	52	33	95	94
Drama club	26	37	32	33	38	29	43	33	50	31	25	25	34	32	36	29	35	23	33	2	37	36
Debate team	6	4	4	7	5	4	0	3	14	6	10	6	1	3	0	0	3	6	16	8	0	2

TABLE 4.
Percent of Pupils in Secondary Schools Having the Characteristic Named at Left, Fall 1965

Characteristic	Whole Nation MA	PR	IA	OA	Neg.	Maj.	Nonmetropolitan North and West Neg.	Maj.	South Neg.	Maj.	Southwest Neg.	Maj.	Northeast Neg.	Maj.	Midwest Neg.	Maj.	Metropolitan South Neg.	Maj.	Southwest Neg.	Maj.	West Neg.	Maj.
Regionally accredited schools	77	78	71	86	68	76	69	65	40	59	30	62	74	74	75	86	72	81	92	86	100	100
Music teacher, full-time	84	94	88	96	85	88	87	87	65	61	85	77	95	97	96	96	87	100	91	82	99	97
College preparatory curriculum	95	90	96	98	88	96	98	95	74	92	81	83	93	99	99	100	87	100	89	82	100	100
Vocational curriculum	56	50	55	68	56	55	49	64	51	62	52	34	42	35	60	60	58	21	89	80	65	65
Remedial reading teacher	57	76	55	81	53	52	35	32	24	20	4	9	81	66	62	57	46	65	63	62	100	97
Accelerated curriculum	67	60	66	80	61	66	42	46	46	58	25	25	60	82	64	78	72	81	87	55	74	73
Low IQ classes	54	56	50	85	54	49	44	47	23	20	46	12	75	62	86	59	37	34	64	14	98	98
Speech impairment classes	28	58	28	51	21	31	18	33	10	6	1	11	43	44	48	42	0	10	14	3	45	57
Use of intelligence test	91	57	84	86	80	89	87	93	83	90	97	100	59	87	86	86	78	100	94	75	89	92
Assignment practice other than area or open	4	20	9	3	19	4	5	0	32	14	2	0	14	5	0	0	36	9	4	0	0	0
Use of tracking	79	88	79	85	75	74	41	48	55	57	21	24	94	92	74	90	80	80	92	82	99	98
Teachers having tenure	65	86	71	85	61	72	47	73	33	41	2	3	100	98	97	83	50	79	24	15	96	88
Principal's salary $9,000 and above	73	89	73	91	66	72	54	64	31	37	59	63	99	99	76	91	61	46	86	18	100	100
School newspaper	89	95	86	97	80	89	71	72	50	81	67	71	95	93	99	97	87	100	66	94	100	100
Boys' interscholastic athletics	94	90	98	99	95	98	99	99	97	100	96	93	80	95	100	97	93	100	95	100	100	100
Girls' interscholastic athletics	58	33	59	37	57	54	32	32	80	69	89	81	51	60	50	43	45	80	89	97	38	35
Band	92	88	92	98	91	95	90	97	80	76`	84	81	92	97	100	100	93	100	99	100	100	100
Drama club	95	93	89	92	92	93	75	91	87	75	91	88	92	88	93	99	94	94	100	97	100	100
Debate team	51	32	46	50	39	52	43	48	27	36	80	67	27	46	49	69	42	58	68	63	37	48

159

TABLE 5.
Percent of Pupils in Elementary and Secondary Schools Having Principals with Characteristic Named at Left, Fall 1965

Characteristic	Whole Nation MA	PR	IA	OA	Neg.	Maj.	Nonmetro North & West Neg.	Maj.	Nonmetro South Neg.	Maj.	Nonmetro Southwest Neg.	Maj.	Metro Northeast Neg.	Maj.	Metro Midwest Neg.	Maj.	Metro South Neg.	Maj.	Metro Southwest Neg.	Maj.	Metro West Neg.	Maj.
Elementary schools:																						
Negro principal	16	27	11	12	56	1	13	0	86	2	69	1	9	1	28	0	94	2	64	0	3	0
Majority principal	79	71	80	77	39	95	79	90	7	91	24	97	86	97	69	94	1	97	29	100	95	99
Principal with at least M.A.	85	84	77	86	84	80	69	69	65	64	86	91	98	90	98	92	83	74	95	85	96	94
Principal would keep neighborhood school despite racial imbalance	62	52	58	52	45	65	58	67	39	67	58	67	38	53	61	80	48	71	78	67	29	53
Principal approves compensatory education	66	68	61	72	72	59	63	60	61	46	52	58	76	64	82	63	67	46	75	52	92	76
Principal would deliberately mix faculty for:																						
Mostly minority pupils	40	48	38	47	48	43	31	44	41	43	43	35	56	37	51	40	43	44	52	45	61	57
Mixed pupils	34	46	31	42	44	35	46	40	37	35	35	26	50	32	50	34	40	28	46	23	52	42
Almost all majority pupils	17	30	15	25	35	14	19	13	29	3	18	3	48	18	42	15	34	7	33	1	41	37
Secondary schools:																						
Negro principal	9	12	7	3	61	1	8	0	85	0	68	0	22	0	36	4	97	0	82	0	10	0
Majority principal	89	81	91	76	37	95	79	87	10	94	25	98	75	99	64	95	3	100	18	100	90	99
Principal with at least M.A.	91	97	94	94	96	93	89	85	92	90	90	90	97	97	100	100	97	93	94	86	100	100
Principal would keep neighborhood school despite racial imbalance	49	37	50	33	32	56	54	49	41	73	27	52	25	53	48	55	18	91	80	64	14	28
Principal approves compensatory education	80	83	73	94	78	71	73	59	66	55	81	49	75	79	71	79	80	57	100	80	100	100
Principal would deliberately mix faculty for:																						
Mostly minority pupils	56	47	61	70	54	58	50	53	41	49	57	43	41	50	46	71	53	42	85	86	92	65
Mixed pupils	35	41	45	57	37	40	40	39	36	19	37	7	37	37	18	56	57	32	47	46	82	55
Almost all majority pupils	22	32	23	43	39	14	17	9	23	1	32	1	35	20	14	29	48	0	70	1	78	26

TABLE 6A.
Characteristics of Teachers in the *Elementary* Schools Attended by the Average White and Minority Pupil— Percent of Teachers with Characteristic Named at Left, Fall 1965

Characteristic	Whole Nation						Nonmetropolitan						Metropolitan									
							North & West		South		Southwest		Northeast		Midwest		South		Southwest		West	
	MA	PR	IA	OA	Neg.	Maj.	Neg.	Maj.	Neg.	Maj.	Neg.	Maj.	Neg.	Maj.	Neg.	Maj.	Neg.	Maj.	Neg.	Maj.	Neg.	Maj.
Percent teachers who spent most of life in present city, town, or county	37	54	35	39	53	40	34	40	54	55	40	31	64	51	55	39	69	37	35	18	24	24
Average teacher verbal score[1]	22	22	22	23	20	23	23	24	17	22	20	22	22	23	22	23	19	23	21	24	22	24
Percent teachers majored in academic subjects	19	18	17	21	17	16	16	18	12	14	16	22	19	17	17	15	18	16	9	7	23	22
Percent teachers who attended college not offering graduate degrees	39	41	37	32	53	37	48	38	63	47	44	30	45	38	39	40	72	46	44	26	22	21
Percent teachers attended college with predominantly white student enrollment	79	70	85	83	39	97	81	99	9	97	28	93	73	97	75	97	7	95	43	98	82	96
Average educational level of teacher's mother (score)[2]	3.7	3.5	3.7	3.8	3.5	3.7	3.4	3.5	2.9	3.5	3.6	3.7	3.6	3.7	3.7	3.6	3.5	4.2	3.8	3.8	4.1	4.2
Average highest degree earned[3]	3.1	3.1	3.1	3.1	3.2	3.0	2.8	2.8	3.1	3.0	3.4	3.3	3.2	3.1	3.1	3.0	3.2	3.0	3.5	3.2	3.3	3.1
Average teacher-years experience	13	12	12	12	13	12	12	13	14	16	14	13	11	11	11	11	14	10	13	11	11	10
Average teacher salary ($1,000's)	5.9	6.0	6.1	6.6	6.0	6.0	5.8	5.7	4.7	5.0	5.5	5.4	7.2	7.1	7.0	6.5	5.2	5.0	5.9	5.1	7.8	7.3
Average pupils per teacher	30	30	30	28	20	28	26	25	32	27	23	26	27	26	29	28	28	30	30	42	30	31
Percent teachers would not choose to move to another school	58	57	59	59	55	65	56	60	49	73	57	64	53	64	49	63	61	76	63	59	55	66
Percent teachers plan to continue until retirement	44	42	41	39	45	37	42	35	50	51	57	55	31	32	34	31	51	34	48	46	41	34
Percent teachers prefer white pupils	27	21	26	20	7	37	22	32	6	57	10	45	8	18	12	37	1	57	12	48	8	31
Percent teachers approve compensatory education	56	59	56	64	61	56	53	56	55	47	53	44	69	66	65	55	59	49	56	54	73	66
Percent Negro teachers	19	30	14	15	65	2	17	1	90	2	75	1	31	2	40	2	96	4	65	1	22	2
Percent White teachers	78	67	83	79	32	97	99	99	8	96	24	96	67	97	58	98	2	96	32	98	69	95

[1] Score is the average number of correct items on a 30-item verbal facility test. [2] Educational attainment scored from 1–8 (lowest to highest); 4 represents high school graduate. [3] Highest degree earned scored from 1–6 (lowest to highest); 3 represents a Bachelors degree.

TABLE 6B.

Characteristics of Teachers in the Secondary Schools Attended by the Average White and Minority Pupil, Fall 1965

Characteristic	Whole Nation						Nonmetropolitan						Metropolitan										
							North & West		South		Southwest		Northeast		Midwest		South		Southwest		West	
	MA	PR	IA	OA	Neg.	Maj.	Neg.	Maj.	Neg.	Maj.	Neg.	Maj.	Neg.	Maj.	Neg.	Maj.	Neg.	Maj.	Neg.	Maj.	Neg.	Maj.
Percent of teachers who spent most of life in present city, town, or county	31	55	31	36	41	34	20	23	38	48	35	28	62	49	34	31	52	41	37	19	22	25
Average teacher verbal score[1]	23	22	23	23	21	23	23	24	19	23	22	24	22	23	22	23	21	23	21	24	23	24
Percent of teachers majored in academic subjects	37	40	39	40	38	40	39	36	37	35	30	32	40	46	35	41	42	41	25	36	38	41
Percent of teachers who attended colleges not offering graduate degrees	26	27	27	20	44	31	33	31	52	44	32	17	25	29	38	34	64	42	42	22	16	13
Percent of teachers who attended colleges with predominantly white student enrollment	90	86	92	86	44	48	90	99	15	99	31	98	85	98	75	97	8	97	29	99	90	95
Average educational level of teacher's mother (score)[2]	3.8	3.5	3.8	3.7	3.6	3.8	3.6	3.8	3.3	3.8	3.7	3.8	3.5	3.5	3.7	3.8	3.8	4.3	3.4	3.7	4.1	4.0
Average highest degree earned[3]	3.4	3.5	3.4	3.6	3.3	3.4	3.2	3.2	3.2	3.2	3.4	3.4	3.5	3.5	3.4	3.4	3.2	3.3	3.4	3.3	3.6	3.5
Average teacher years experience	11	11	10	11	11	10	9	10	10	12	11	11	12	11	11	10	12	8	11	9	11	11
Average teacher salary ($1,000's)	6.8	7.6	6.8	7.7	6.4	6.6	6.0	6.3	4.9	5.2	5.8	5.6	7.8	7.6	7.2	7.2	5.5	5.4	6.1	5.5	8.8	8.3
Average pupils per teacher	23	22	23	24	26	22	20	20	30	25	21	20	24	20	25	24	26	25	25	26	23	23
Percentage of teachers would not choose to move to another school	49	48	48	48	46	51	39	42	42	59	48	63	51	55	45	49	50	62	55	51	42	47
Percentage of teachers plan to continue until retirement	36	41	34	40	38	33	25	28	35	36	43	43	44	38	37	31	36	23	37	30	44	41
Percentage of teachers prefer white pupils	26	13	24	13	8	32	28	28	8	58	15	48	8	14	11	31	2	52	7	38	10	21
Percentage of teachers approve compensatory education	61	67	60	68	66	60	55	62	60	49	59	50	72	67	67	58	67	54	67	49	72	70
Percent Negro teachers	10	16	8	6	59	2	11	2	85	2	70	1	18	2	35	2	3	1	77	0	14	2
Percent White teachers	87	81	88	76	38	97	88	97	13	98	27	98	79	96	64	97	99	99	20	97	82	94

[1] Score is the average number of correct items on a 30-item verbal facility test. [2] Educational attainment scored from 1–8 (lowest to highest); 4 represents high school graduate. [3] Highest degree earned scored from 1–6 (lowest to highest); 3 represents a Bachelors degree.

where 53 percent of the teachers have lived in the same locality most of their lives.

Both tables list other characteristics which offer rough indications of teacher quality, including the types of colleges attended, years of teaching experience, salary, educational level of mother, and a score on a 30-word vocabulary test. The average Negro pupil attends a school where a greater percentage of the teachers appears to be somewhat less able, as measured by these indicators, than those in the schools attended by the average white student.

Other items on these tables reveal certain teacher attitudes. Thus, the average white pupil attends a school where 51 percent of the white teachers would not choose to move to another school, whereas the average Negro attends a school where 46 percent would not choose to move.

Student Body Characteristics

Tables 7 and 8 present data about certain characteristics of the student bodies attending various schools. These tables must be read the same as those immediately preceding. Looking at the sixth item on table 7, one should read: the average white high school student attends a school in which 82 percent of his classmates report that there are encyclopedias in their homes. This does not mean that 82 percent of all white pupils have encyclopedias at home, although obviously that would be approximately true. In short, these tables attempt to describe the characteristics of the student bodies with which the "average" white or minority student goes to school.

Clear differences are found on these items. The average Negro has fewer classmates whose mothers graduated from high school; his classmates more frequently are members of large rather than small families; they are less often enrolled in a college preparatory curriculum; they have taken a smaller number of courses in English, mathematics, foreign language, and science.

On most items, the other minority groups fall between Negroes and whites, but closer to whites, in the extent to which each characteristic is typical of their classmates.

Again, there are substantial variations in the magnitude of the differences, with the difference usually being greater in the Southern States.

1.3 Achievement in the Public Schools

The schools bear many responsibilities. Among the most important is the teaching of certain intellectual skills such as reading, writing, calculating, and problem solving. One way of assessing the educational opportunity of-

TABLE 7.
For the Average Minority and White Pupil, the Percent of Fellow Pupils with the Specified Characteristics, Fall 1965

Level of School and Pupil Characteristic	Whole Nation						Nonmetropolitan						Metropolitan									
							North and West		South		Southwest		Northeast		Midwest		South		Southwest		West	
	MA	PR	IA	OA	Neg.	Maj.	Neg.	Maj.	Neg.	Maj.	Neg.	Maj.	Neg.	Maj.	Neg.	Maj.	Neg.	Maj.	Neg.	Maj.	Neg.	Maj.
Elementary schools:																						
Mostly white classmates last year	59	52	66	63	19	89	59	91	17	91	19	72	33	87	26	91	7	91	27	91	20	86
All white teachers last year	75	68	77	74	53	88	71	89	53	87	57	84	60	89	52	88	49	89	51	89	52	85
Encyclopedia in home	62	57	64	70	54	75	62	72	36	65	48	64	71	84	60	80	51	80	57	72	64	83
Secondary schools:																						
Mostly white classmates last year	72	56	72	57	10	91	77	96	12	94	23	88	41	90	40	89	4	95	14	96	35	81
All white teachers last year	73	57	75	57	25	89	79	93	11	93	23	90	44	84	45	88	3	92	16	95	46	79
Encyclopedia in home	77	76	75	82	69	82	76	78	52	75	66	75	82	87	80	86	67	88	73	83	78	83
Mother high school graduate or more	49	47	50	53	40	58	51	58	23	45	44	48	51	63	49	63	37	58	41	49	53	65
Taking college preparatory course	36	38	35	41	32	41	29	35	22	33	28	32	39	53	43	46	34	44	29	31	34	46
Taking some vocational course	27	30	28	32	27	23	22	24	23	20	25	20	30	20	28	25	27	16	37	38	35	30
2½ years or more of science	36	38	38	38	39	42	41	41	41	38	47	39	43	55	32	38	43	43	42	31	26	34
1½ years or more of language	37	41	35	43	35	40	29	30	25	26	19	23	49	60	36	44	38	44	34	23	37	50
3½ years or more of English	77	73	80	76	69	83	68	78	66	89	75	84	79	91	73	79	67	89	71	87	62	72
2½ years or more of math	47	45	44	47	44	49	40	39	43	46	50	52	47	63	41	50	46	55	58	45	37	47

TABLE 8.
For the Average Minority and White Pupil, the Percent of Fellow Pupils with the Specified Characteristics, Fall 1965

Secondary School Pupil Characteristic	Whole Nation						Nonmetropolitan										Metropolitan					
							North and West		South		Southwest		Northeast		Midwest		South		Southwest		West	
	MA	PR	IA	OA	Neg.	Maj.	Neg.	Maj.	Neg.	Maj.	Neg.	Maj.	Neg.	Maj.	Neg.	Maj.	Neg.	Maj.	Neg.	Maj.	Neg.	Maj.
Mother not reared in city	45	33	44	33	45	42	58	50	64	65	53	61	25	19	35	32	45	42	48	60	34	33
Real father at home	77	71	75	84	64	83	80	84	65	84	64	85	67	83	70	84	58	84	55	84	62	74
Real mother at home	90	88	90	89	85	92	90	92	82	93	82	94	88	92	90	92	83	92	83	94	86	88
Five or more brothers and sisters	28	27	30	27	44	20	30	24	56	23	54	23	25	15	34	19	48	13	47	17	36	21
Mother expects best in class	48	49	45	42	62	43	47	39	71	55	67	54	50	41	49	38	69	49	71	51	53	41
Parents daily discuss school	47	46	44	42	49	47	44	44	51	51	52	54	50	52	44	45	53	53	51	43	43	44
Father expects at least college graduate	38	34	35	37	38	37	36	32	33	37	39	44	33	39	36	38	39	44	45	45	37	40
Mother expects at least college graduate	41	39	39	41	44	41	41	35	42	40	48	45	38	42	43	41	48	45	52	50	43	44
Parents attend PTA	36	38	34	37	51	37	36	40	59	37	50	34	43	37	45	36	61	44	42	26	36	30
Parents read to child regularly before he started school	25	28	24	24	30	26	26	24	30	25	32	23	32	31	27	27	33	29	31	21	26	27

fered by the schools is to measure how well they perform this task. Standard achievement tests are available to measure these skills, and several such tests were administered in this survey to pupils at grades 1, 3, 6, 9, and 12.

These tests do not measure intelligence, nor attitudes, nor qualities of character. Furthermore, they are not, nor are they intended to be, "culture free." Quite the reverse: they are culture bound. What they measure are the skills which are among the most important in our society for getting a good job and moving up to a better one, and for full participation in an increasingly technical world. Consequently, a pupil's test results at the end of public school provide a good measure of the range of opportunities open to him as he finishes school—a wide range of choice of jobs or colleges if these skills are very high; a very narrow range that includes only the most menial jobs if these skills are very low.

Table 9 gives an overall illustration of the test results for the various groups by tabulating nationwide median scores (the score which divides the group in half) for 1st-grade and 12th-grade pupils on the tests used in those grades. For example, half of the white 12th-grade pupils had scores above 52 on the nonverbal test and half had scores below 52. (Scores on each test at each grade level were standardized so that the average over the national sample equaled 50 and the standard deviation equaled 10. This means that for all pupils in the Nation, about 16 percent would score below 40 and about 16 percent above 60.)

With some exceptions—notably Oriental Americans—the average minority pupil scores distinctly lower on these tests at every level than the average white pupil. The minority pupils' scores are as much as one stan-

TABLE 9.
Nationwide Median Test Scores for 1st- and 12th-grade Pupils, Fall 1965

Test	Puerto Ricans	Indian Americans	Mexican- Americans	Oriental Americans	Negro	Majority
1st grade:						
Nonverbal	45.8	53.0	50.1	56.6	43.4	54.1
Verbal	44.9	47.8	46.5	51.6	45.4	53.2
12th grade:						
Nonverbal	43.3	47.1	45.0	51.6	40.9	52.0
Verbal	43.1	43.7	43.8	49.6	40.9	52.1
Reading	42.6	44.3	44.2	48.8	42.2	51.9
Mathematics	43.7	45.9	45.5	51.3	41.8	51.8
General information	41.7	44.7	43.3	49.0	40.6	52.2
Average of the 5 tests	43.1	45.1	44.4	50.1	41.1	52.0

Racial or Ethnic Group

dard deviation below the majority pupils' scores in the 1st grade. At the 12th grade, results of tests in the same verbal and nonverbal skills show that, in every case, the minority scores are farther below the majority than are the 1st-graders. For some groups, the relative decline is negligible; for others, it is large.

Furthermore, a constant difference in standard deviations over the various grades represents an increasing difference in grade level gap. For example. Negroes in the metropolitan Northeast are about 1.1 standard deviations below whites in the same region at grades 6, 9, and 12. But at grade 6 this represents 1.6 years behind; at grade 9, 2.4 years; and at grade 12, 3.3 years. Thus, by this measure, the deficiency in achievement is progressively greater for the minority pupils at progressively higher grade levels.

For most minority groups, then, and most particularly the Negro, schools provide little opportunity for them to overcome this initial deficiency; in fact they fall farther behind the white majority in the development of several skills which are critical to making a living and participating fully in modern society. Whatever may be the combination of nonschool factors—poverty, community attitudes, low educational level of parents—which put minority children at a disadvantage in verbal and nonverbal skills when they enter the first grade, the fact is the schools have not overcome it.

Some points should be borne in mind in reading the table. First, the differences shown should not obscure the fact that some minority children perform better than many white children. A difference of one standard deviation in median scores means that about 84 percent of the children in the lower group are below the median of the majority students—but 50 percent of the white children are themselves below that median as well.

A second point of qualification concerns regional differences. By grade 12, both white and Negro students in the South score below their counterparts—white and Negro—in the North. In addition, Southern Negroes score farther below Southern whites than Northern Negroes score below Northern whites. The consequences of this pattern can be illustrated by the fact that the 12th-grade Negro in the nonmetropolitan South is 0.8 standard deviation below—or, in terms of years, 1.9 years behind—the Negro in the metropolitan Northeast, though at grade 1 there is no such regional difference.

Finally, the test scores at grade 12 obviously do not take account of those pupils who have left school before reaching the senior year. In the metropolitan North and West, 20 percent of the Negroes of ages 16 and 17 are not enrolled in school—a higher dropout percentage than in either the metropolitan or nonmetropolitan South. If it is the case that some or many of the Northern dropouts performed poorly when they were in school, the Negro achievement in the North may be artificially elevated because some of those who achieved more poorly have left school.

1.4 Relation of Achievement to School Characteristics

If 100 students within a school take a certain test, there is likely to be great variation in their scores. One student may score 97 percent, another 13; several may score 78 percent. This represents variability in achievement within the particular school.

It is possible, however, to compute the average of the scores made by the students within that school and to compare it with the average score, or achievement, of pupils within another school, or many other schools. These comparisons then represent variations between schools.

When one sees that the average score on a verbal achievement test in school X is 55 and in school Y is 72, the natural question to ask is: What accounts for the difference?

There are many factors that may be associated with the difference. This analysis concentrates on one cluster of those factors. It attempts to describe what relationship the school's characteristics themselves (libraries, for example, and teachers and laboratories, and so on) seem to have to the achievement of majority and minority groups (separately for each group on a nationwide basis, and also for Negro and white pupils in the North and South).

The first finding is that the schools are remarkably similar in the way they relate to the achievement of their pupils when the socioeconomic background of the students is taken into account. It is known that socioeconomic factors bear a strong relation to academic achievement. When these factors are statistically controlled, however, it appears that differences between schools account for only a small fraction of differences in pupil achievement.

The schools do differ, however, in their relation to the various racial and ethnic groups. The average white student's achievement seems to be less affected by the strength or weakness of his school's facilities, curriculums, and teachers than is the average minority pupil's. To put it another way, the achievement of minority pupils depends more on the schools they attend than does the achievement of majority pupils. Thus, 20 percent of the achievement of Negroes in the South is associated with the particular schools they go to, whereas only 10 percent of the achievement of whites in the South is. Except for Oriental Americans, this general result is found for all minorities.

The inference might then be made that improving the school of a minority pupil may increase his achievement more than would improving the school of a white child increase his. Similarly, the average minority pupil's achievement may suffer more in a school of low quality than might the average white pupil's. In short, whites, and to a lesser extent Oriental Americans, are less affected one way or the other by the quality of their schools than are minority pupils. This indicates that it is for the most disadvantaged children that improvements in school quality will make the most difference in achievement.

All of these results suggest the next question: What are the school characteristics that are most related to achievement? In other words, what factors in the school seem to be most important in affecting achievement?

It appears that variations in the facilities and curriculums of the schools account for relatively little variation in pupil achievement insofar as this is measured by standard tests. Again, it is for majority whites that the variations make the least difference; for minorities, they make somewhat more difference. Among the facilities that show some relationship to achievement are several for which minority pupils' schools are less well equipped relative to whites. For example, the existence of science laboratories showed a small but consistent relationship to achievement, and table 2 shows that minorities, especially Negroes, are in schools with fewer of these laboratories.

The quality of teachers shows a stronger relationship to pupil achievement. Furthermore, it is progressively greater at higher grades, indicating a cumulative impact of the qualities of teachers in a school on the pupil's achievements. Again, teacher quality seems more important to minority achievement than to that of the majority.

It should be noted that many characteristics of teachers were not measured in this survey; therefore, the results are not at all conclusive regarding the specific characteristics of teachers that are most important. Among those measured in the survey, however, those that bear the highest relationship to pupil achievement are first, the teacher's score on the verbal skills test, and then his educational background—both his own level of education and that of his parents. On both of these measures, the level of teachers of minority students, especially Negroes, is lower.

Finally, it appears that a pupil's achievement is strongly related to the educational backgrounds and aspirations of the other students in the school. Only crude measures of these variables were used (principally the proportion of pupils with encyclopedias in the home and the proportion planning to go to college). Analysis indicates, however, that children from a given family background, when put in schools of different social composition, will achieve at quite different levels. This effect is again less for white pupils than for any minority group other than Orientals. Thus, if a white pupil from a home that is strongly and effectively supportive of education is put in a school where most pupils do not come from such homes, his achievement will be little different than if he were in a school composed of others like himself. But if a minority pupil from a home without much educational strength is put with schoolmates with strong educational backgrounds, his achievement is likely to increase.

This general result, taken together with the earlier examinations of school differences, has important implications for equality of educational opportunity. For the earlier tables show that the principal way in which the school environments of Negroes and whites differ is in the composition of their student bodies, and it turns out that the composition of the student bodies has a strong relationship to the achievement of Negro and other minority pupils.

This analysis has concentrated on the educational opportunities offered by the schools in terms of their student body composition, facilities, curriculums, and teachers. This emphasis, while entirely appropriate as a response to the legislation calling for the survey, nevertheless neglects important factors in the variability between individual pupils within the same school; this variability is roughly four times as large as the variability between schools. For example, a pupil attitude factor, which appears to have a stronger relationship to achievement than do all the "school" factors together, is the extent to which an individual feels that he has some control over his own destiny. Data on items related to this attitude are shown in table 10 along with data on other attitudes and aspirations. The responses of pupils to questions in the survey show that minority pupils, except for Orientals, have far less conviction than whites that they can affect their own environments and futures. When they do, however, their achievement is higher than that of whites who lack that conviction.

Furthermore, while this characteristic shows little relationship to most school factors, it is related, for Negroes, to the proportion of whites in the schools. Those Negroes in schools with a higher proportion of whites have a greater sense of control. This finding suggests that the direction such an attitude takes may be associated with the pupil's school experience as well as his experience in the larger community.

THE SCHOOLS AND EQUAL OPPORTUNITY

Mary Jo Bane
Christopher Jencks

Americans have a recurrent fantasy that schools can solve their problems. Thus it was perhaps inevitable that, after we rediscovered poverty and inequality in the early 1960s, we turned to the schools for solutions. Yet the schools did not provide solutions, the high hopes of the early-and-middle 1960s faded, and the war on poverty ended in ignominious surrender to the *status quo*. In part of course, this was because the war in Southeast Asia turned out to be incompatible with the war on poverty. In part, however, it was because we all had rather muddleheaded ideas about the various causes and cures of poverty and inequality.

Today there are signs that some people are beginning to look for new solutions to these perennial problems. There is a vast amount of sociological and economic data that can, we think, help in this effort, both by explaining the failures of the 1960s and by suggesting more realistic alternatives. For the past four years we have been working with this data. Our research has led us to three general conclusions.

First, poverty is a condition of relative rather than absolute deprivation. People feel poor and are poor if they have a lot less money than their neighbors. This is true regardless of their absolute incomes. It follows that we cannot eliminate poverty unless we prevent people from falling too far below the national average. The problem is economic inequality rather than low incomes.

Second, the reforms of the 1960s were misdirected because they focused only on equalizing opportunity to "succeed" (or "fail") rather than on reducing the economic and social distance between those who succeeded and those who failed. The evidence we have reviewed suggests that equalizing opportunity will not do very much to equalize results, and hence that it will not do much to reduce poverty.

Reprinted by permission of *Saturday Review* from pp. 37–42, Vol. 55, September 16, 1972.

Third, even if we are interested solely in equalizing opportunities for economic success, making schools more equal will not help very much. Differences between schools have very little effect on what happens to students after they graduate.

The main policy implication of these findings is that although school reform is important for improving the lives of children, schools cannot contribute significantly to adult equality. If we want economic equality in our society, we will have to get it by changing our economic institutions, not by changing the schools.

Poverty and Inequality

The rhetoric of the war on poverty described the persistence of poverty in the midst of affluence as a "paradox," largely attributable to "neglect." Official publications all assumed that poverty was an absolute rather than a relative condition. Having assumed this, they all showed progress toward the elimination of poverty, since fewer and fewer people had incomes below the official "poverty line."

Yet, despite all the official announcements of progress, many Americans still seemed poor, by both their own standards and their neighbors'. The reason was that most Americans define poverty in relative rather than absolute terms. Public-opinion surveys show, for example, that when people are asked how much money an American family needs to "get by," they typically name a figure about half what the average American family actually receives. This has been true for the last three decades, despite the fact that real incomes (incomes adjusted for inflation) have doubled in the interval.

During the Depression the average American family was living on about $30 a week. A third of all families were living on less than half this amount, which made it natural for Franklin Roosevelt to speak of "one-third of a nation" as ill-housed, ill-clothed, and ill-fed. By 1964 mean family income was about $160 a week, and the Gallup poll found that the average American thought a family of four needed at least $80 a week to "get by." Even allowing for inflation, this was twice what people had thought necessary during the Depression. Playing it safe, the Johnson administration defined the poverty line at $60 a week for a family of four, but most people felt this was inadequate. By 1970 inflation had raised mean family income to about $200 a week, and the National Welfare Rights Organization was trying to rally liberal support for a guaranteed income of $100 a week.

These changes in the definition of poverty were not just a matter of "rising expectations" or of people's needing to "keep up with the Joneses." The goods and services that made it possible to live on $15 a week during the Depression were no longer available to a family with the same real income ($40 a week) in 1964. Eating habits had changed, and many cheap foods had disappeared from the stores. Housing arrangements had changed, too. During the Depression many people could not afford indoor plumbing and "got by" with a privy. By the 1960s privies were illegal in most places. Those who still could not afford an indoor toilet ended up in buildings that had broken toilets. For these they paid more than their parents had paid for privies.

Examples of this kind suggest that the "cost of living" is not the cost of buying some fixed set of goods and services. It is the cost of participating in a social system. It therefore depends in large part on how much other people habitually spend to participate in the system. Those who fall far below the norm, whatever it may be, are excluded. Accordingly, raising the incomes of the poor will not eliminate poverty if the cost of participating in "mainstream" American life rises even faster. People with incomes less than half the national average will not be able to afford what "everyone" regards as "necessities." The only way to eliminate poverty is, therefore, to make sure everyone has an income at least half the average.

Arguments of this kind suggest not only that it makes more sense to think of "poverty" as a relative rather than an absolute condition but that eliminating poverty, at least as it is usually defined in America, depends on eliminating, or at least greatly reducing, inequality.

Schooling and Opportunity

Almost none of the reform legislation of the 1960s involved direct efforts to equalize adult status, power, or income. Most Americans accepted the idea that these rewards should go to those who were most competent and diligent. Their objection to America's traditional economic system was not that it produced inequality but that the rules determining who succeeded and who failed were often unfair. The reformers wanted to create a world in which success would no longer be associated with skin color, economic background, or other "irrelevant" factors, but only with actual merit. What they wanted, in short, was what they called "equal opportunity."

Their strategy for achieving equal opportunity placed great emphasis on education. Many people imagined that if schools could equalize people's cognitive skills this would equalize their bargaining power as adults. Presumably, if every one had equal bargaining power, few people would end up very poor.

This strategy for reducing poverty rested on a series of assumptions that went roughly as follows:

1. Eliminating poverty is largely a matter of helping children born into poverty to rise out of it. Once families escape from poverty, they do not fall back into it. Middle-class children rarely end up poor.

2. The primary reason poor children cannot escape from poverty is that

they do not acquire basic cognitive skills. They cannot read, write, calculate, or articulate. Lacking these skills, they cannot get or keep a well-paid job.

3. The best mechanism for breaking this "vicious circle" is educational reform. Since children born into poor homes do not acquire the skills they need from their parents, they must be taught these skills in school. This can be done by making sure that they attend the same schools as middle-class children, by giving them extra compensatory programs in school, by giving their parents a voice in running their schools, or by some combination of all three approaches.

Our research over the last four years suggests that each of these assumptions is erroneous:

1. Poverty is not primarily hereditary. While children born into poverty have a higher than average chance of ending up poor, there is still an enormous amount of economic mobility from one generation to the next. A father whose occupational status is high passes on less than half his advantage to his sons, and a father whose status is low passes along less than half his disadvantage. A family whose income is above the norm has an even harder time passing along its privileges; its sons are typically only about a third as advantaged as the parents. Conversely, a family whose income is below average will typically have sons about a third as disadvantaged as the parents. The effects of parents' status on their daughters' economic positions appear to be even weaker. This means that many "advantaged" parents have some "disadvantaged" children and vice versa.

2. The primary reason some people end up richer than others is not that they have more adequate cognitive skills. While children who read well, get the right answers to arithmetic problems, and articulate their thoughts clearly are somewhat more likely than others to get ahead, there are many other equally important factors involved. The effects of I.Q. on economic success are about the same as the effects of family background. This means, for example, that if two men's I.Q. scores differ by 17 points—the typical difference between I.Q. scores of individuals chosen at random—their incomes will typically differ by less than $2,000. That amount is not completely trivial, of course. But the income difference between random individuals is three times as large and the difference between the best-paid fifth and the worst-paid fifth of all male workers averages $14,000. There is almost as much economic inequality among those who score high on standardized tests as in the general population.

3. There is no evidence that school reform can substantially reduce the extent of cognitive inequality, as measured by tests of verbal fluency, reading comprehension, or mathematical skill. Eliminating qualitative differences between elementary schools would reduce the range of scores on

standardized tests in sixth grade by less than 3 per cent. Eliminating qualitative differences between high schools would hardly reduce the range of
twelfth-grade scores at all and would reduce by only 1 per cent the disparities in the amount of education people eventually get.

Our best guess, after reviewing all the evidence we could find, is that
racial desegregation raises black elementary school students' test scores by
a couple of points. But most of the test-score gap between blacks and
whites persists, even when they are in the same schools. So also: Tracking
has very little effect on test scores. And neither the overall level of resources available to a school nor any specific, easily identifiable school policy has a significant effect on students' cognitive skills or educational attainments. Thus, even if we went beyond "equal opportunity" and allocated
resources disproportionately to schools whose students now do worst on
tests and are least likely to acquire credentials, this would not improve
these students' prospects very much.

The evidence does not tell us why school quality has so little effect on
test scores. Three possible explanations come to mind. First, children seem
to be more influenced by what happens at home than by what happens in
school. They may also be more influenced by what happens on the streets
and by what they see on television. Second, administrators have very little
control over those aspects of school life that do affect children. Reallocating
resources, reassigning pupils, and rewriting the curriculum seldom change
the way teachers and students actually treat each other minute by minute.
Third, even when the schools exert an unusual influence on children, the
resulting changes are not likely to persist into adulthood. It takes a huge
change in elementary school test scores, for example, to alter adult income
by a significant amount.

Equal Opportunity and Unequal Results

The evidence we have reviewed, taken all together, suggests that equalizing opportunity cannot take us very far toward eliminating inequality. The
simplest way of demonstrating this is to compare the economic prospects of
brothers raised in the same home. Even the most egalitarian society could
not hope to make opportunities for all children appreciably more equal
than the opportunities now available to brothers from the same family.
Looking at society at large, if we compare random pairs of individuals, the
difference between their occupational statuses averages about 28 points on
the Duncan "status scale" (the scale runs from 0 to 96 points). The difference between brothers' occupational statuses averages fully 23 points on
this same scale. If we compare men's incomes, the difference between random pairs averaged about $6,200 in 1968. The difference between brothers'

incomes, according to our best estimate, probably averaged about $5,700. These estimates mean that people who start off equal end up almost as unequal as everyone else. Inequality is not mostly inherited: It is re-created anew in each generation.

We can take this line of argument a step further by comparing people who not only start off in similar families but who also have the same I.Q. scores and get the same amount of schooling. Such people's occupational statuses differ by an average of 21 points, compared to 28 points for random individuals. If we compare their incomes, making the additional assumption that the men have the same occupational status, we find that they differ by an average of about $5,300, compared to $6,200 for men chosen at random.

These comparisons suggest that adult success must depend on a lot of things besides family background, schooling, and the cognitive skills measured by standardized tests. We have no idea what these factors are. To some extent, no doubt, specialized varieties of competence, such as the ability to hit a ball thrown at high speed or the ability to persuade a customer that he wants a larger car than he thought he wanted, play a major role. Income also depends on luck: the range of jobs available when you are job hunting, the amount of overtime work in your plant, good or bad weather for your strawberry crop, and a hundred other unpredictable accidents.

Equalizing opportunity will not, then, do much to reduce economic inequality in America. If poverty is relative rather than absolute, equalizing opportunity will not do much to reduce poverty, either.

Implications for Educational Policy

These findings imply that school reform is never likely to have any significant effect on the degree of inequality among adults. This suggests that the prevalent "factory" model, in which schools are seen as places that "produce" alumni, probably ought to be abandoned. It is true that schools have "inputs" and "outputs," and that one of their nominal purposes is to take human "raw material" (*i.e.*, children) and convert it into something more "useful" (*i.e.*, employable adults). Our research suggests, however, that the character of a school's output depends largely on a single input, the characteristics of the entering children. Everything else—the school budget, its policies, the characteristics of the teachers—is either secondary or completely irrelevant, at least so long as the range of variation among schools is as narrow as it seems to be in America.

These findings have convinced us that the long-term effects of schooling are relatively uniform. The day-to-day internal life of the schools, in contrast, is highly variable. It follows that *the primary basis for evaluating a*

*school should be whether the students and teachers find it a satisfying place
to be.* This does not mean we think schools should be like mediocre summer camps, in which children are kept out of trouble but not taught anything. We doubt that a school can be enjoyable for either adults or children
unless the children keep learning new things. We value ideas and the life
of the mind, and we think that a school that does not value these things is a
poor place for children. But a school that values ideas because they enrich
the lives of children is quite different from a school that values high reading
scores because reading scores are important for adult success.

Our concern with making schools satisfying places for teachers and children has led us to a concern for diversity and choice. People have widely
different notions of what a "satisfying" place is, and we believe they ought
to be able to put these values into practice. As we have noted, our research
suggests that none of the programs or structural arrangements in common
use today has consistently different long-term effects from any other. Since
the character of a child's schooling has few long-term effects, and since
these effects are quite unpredictable, society has little reason to constrain
the choices available to parents and children. If a "good school" is one the
students and staff find satisfying, no one school will be best for everyone.
Since there is no evidence that professional educators know appreciably
more than parents about what is good for children, it seems reasonable to
let parents decide what kind of education their children should have while
they are young and to let the children decide as they get older.

Short-term considerations also seem decisive in determining whether to
spend more money on schooling or to spend it on busing children to
schools outside their neighborhoods. If extra resources make school life
pleasanter and more interesting, they are worthwhile. But we should not
try to justify school expenditures on the grounds that they boost adult earnings. Likewise, busing ought to be justified in political and moral terms
rather than in terms of presumed long-term effects on the children who are
bused. If we want an integrated society, we ought to have integrated
schools, which make people feel they have a stake in the well-being of
other races. If we want a society in which people are free to segregate
themselves, then we should apply that principle to our schools. There is,
however, no compelling reason to treat schools differently from other social
arrangements, including neighborhoods. Personally, we believe in both
open housing and open schools. If parents or students want to take buses to
schools in other neighborhoods, school boards ought to provide the buses,
expand the relevant schools, and ensure that the students are welcome in
the schools they want to attend. This is the least we can do to offset the effects of residential segregation. But we do not believe that forced busing
can be justified on the grounds of its long-term benefits for students.

This leads to our last conclusion about educational reform. Reformers
are always getting trapped into claiming too much for what they propose.

They may want a particular reform—like open classrooms, or desegregation, or vouchers—because they think these reforms will make schools more satisfying places to work. Yet they feel obliged to claim that these reforms will also reduce the number of nonreaders, increase racial understanding, or strengthen family life. A wise reformer ought to be more modest, claiming only that a particular reform will not harm adult society and that it will make life pleasanter for parents, teachers, and students in the short run.

This plea for modesty in school reform will, we fear, fall on deaf ears. Ivan Illich is right in seeing schools as secular churches, through which we seek to improve not ourselves but our descendants. That this process should be disagreeable seems inevitable; one cannot abolish original sin through self-indulgence. That it should be immodest seems equally inevitable; a religion that promises anything less than salvation wins few converts. In school, as in church, we present the world as we wish it were. We try to inspire children with the ideals we ourselves have failed to live up to. We assume, for example, that we cannot make adults live in desegregated neighborhoods, so we devise schemes for busing children from one neighborhood to another in order to desegregate the schools. We all prefer conducting our moral experiments on other people. Nonetheless, so long as we confine our experiments to children, we will not have much effect on adult life.

Implications for Social Reform

Then how *are* we to affect adult life? Our findings tell us that different kinds of inequality are only loosely related to one another. This can be either encouraging or discouraging, depending on how you look at it. On the discouraging side, it means that eliminating inequality in one area will not eliminate it in other areas. On the encouraging side, it means that inequality in one area does not dictate inequality in other areas.

To begin with, genetic inequality is not a major obstacle to economic equality. It is true, that genetic diversity almost inevitably means considerable variation in people's scores on standardized tests. But this kind of cognitive inequality need not imply anything like the present degree of economic inequality. We estimate, for example, that if the only sources of income inequality in America were differences in people's genes, the top fifth of the population would earn only about 1.4 times as much as the bottom fifth. In actuality, the top fifth earns seven times as much as the bottom fifth.

Second, our findings suggest that psychological and cultural differences between families are not an irrevocable barrier to adult equality. Family background has more influence than genes on an individual's educational attainment, occupational status, and income. Nonetheless, if family background were the only source of economic inequality in America, the top fifth would earn only about twice as much as the bottom fifth.

Our findings show, then, that inequality is not determined at birth. But they also suggest that economic equality cannot be achieved by indirect efforts to manipulate the environments in which people grow up. We have already discussed the minuscule effects of equalizing school quality. Equalizing the amount of schooling people get would not work much better. Income inequality among men with similar amounts of schooling is only 5–10 per cent less than among men in general. The effect is even less if we include women.

If we want to eliminate economic inequality, we must make this an explicit objective of public policy rather than deluding ourselves into thinking that we can do it by giving everyone equal opportunity to succeed or fail. If we want an occupational structure which is less hierarchical and in which the social distance between the top and the bottom is reduced, we will have to make deliberate efforts to reorganize work and redistribute power within organizations. We will probably also have to rotate jobs, so that no individual held power very long.

If we want an income distribution that is more equal, we can constrain employers, either by tax incentives or direct legislation, to reduce wage disparities between their best- and worst-paid workers. We can make taxes more progressive, and we can provide income supplements to those who do not make an adequate living from wages alone. We can also provide free public services for those who cannot afford to buy adequate services in the private sector. Pursued with vigor, such a strategy can make "poverty" (i.e., having a living standard less than half the national average) virtually impossible. Such a strategy would also make economic "success," in the sense of having, say, a living standard more than twice the national average, far less common than it now is. The net effect would be to make those with the most competence and luck subsidize those with the least competence and luck to a far greater extent than they do today. Unless we are prepared to do this, poverty and inequality will remain with us indefinitely.

This strategy was rejected during the 1960s for the simple reason that it commanded relatively little popular support. The required legislation could not have passed Congress, nor could it pass today. That does not mean that it is the wrong strategy. It simply means that, until we change the political and moral premises on which most Americans now operate, poverty and inequality will persist at pretty much their present level. Intervention in market processes, for example, means restricting the "right" of individuals to use their natural advantages for private gain. Economic equality requires social and legal sanctions—analogous to those that now exist against capricious firing of employees—against inequality within work settings. It also requires that wage rates, which Americans have traditionally viewed as a "private" question to be adjudicated by negotiation between (unequal) individuals or groups, must become a "public" question subject to political control and solution.

In America, as elsewhere, the long-term drift over the past 200 years has been toward equality. In America, however, the contribution of public policy to this drift has been slight. As long as egalitarians assume that public policy cannot contribute to equality directly but must proceed by ingenious manipulations of marginal institutions like the schools, this pattern will continue. If we want to move beyond this tradition, we must establish political control over the economic institutions that shape our society. What we will need, in short, is what other countries call socialism. Anything less will end in the same disappointment as the reforms of the 1960s.

THE SOCIAL SCIENCE OBJECTIVITY GAP

Henry Levin

Inequality: A Reassessment of the Effect of Family and Schooling in America by Christopher Jencks and Marshall Smith, Henry Acland, Mary Jo Bane, David Cohen, Herbert Gintis, Barbara Heyns, Stephan Michelson (Basic Books).

About a century ago the books of Horatio Alger, Jr., began to enthrall the nation. Typically they revolved around a fifteen-year-old boy who made his fortune by somehow being in the right place at the right time. When the child of a rich man was drowning, there was one of Alger's boys to save him; when a wealthy man lost his wallet, one of Alger's honest but impoverished heroes would find it. This familiar plot repeated itself in over 120 books that sold some twenty million copies.

Reprinted by permission of *Saturday Review* from pp. 49–51, Vol. 55, November 11, 1972.

Now the Horatio Alger myth has been resurrected, not by a latter-day novelist, but by a group of social scientists at the Harvard University Center for Educational Policy Research. Their conclusion is not rendered in the sentimental and repetitive prose of the Alger parables. Rather it is stated in the precise-sounding terminology of the social sciences. Thus, Christopher Jencks and his colleagues conclude in *Inequality* that computerized analyses employing immense sources of data have shown that "neither family background, cognitive skill, educational attainment, nor occupational status explains much of the variation in men's incomes."

Instead we are told that economic success depends primarily on competencies and chance factors that are almost unrelated to one's class of origin, genes, or schooling. As the authors noted in a recent summary of their work in *SR Education* (October), their results suggest that "school reform is never likely to have any significant effect on the degree of inequality among adults."

Christopher Jencks and his colleagues have published an important book. It is provocative and controversial and addresses a subject of great social significance. *Inequality* is a landmark publication for other reasons. It has been accompanied by a prepublication promotion that is normally reserved only for bestsellers by established novelists. The findings of the book have been widely disseminated, and they are likely to be heavily debated for some time to come. Moreover, the volume is important because Jencks has earned substantial recognition in his own right as an imaginative writer and thinker on important social issues—and because he and his colleagues have direct access to federal policy makers through their numerous federally funded institutes engaged in educational policy studies. The book, therefore, gives the reader insight into some of the premises on which those policies are based.

At the outset Jencks notes two concepts of equality: equality of opportunity and equality of results. He suggests that most people are willing to accept a world with unequal incomes and status if they believe that these differences are based on such merits as ability, training, industriousness, and so on. Most people regard equality of opportunity to compete for life's unequal rewards as a social objective, and schools represent a major instrument to attain that goal. Accordingly, Jencks weighs the relative importance of inequalities in school resources, genetic endowments, and family backgrounds—and, surprisingly, finds that they are not strongly related to economic outcomes. They do not account for a person's income in his adult life.

The authors proceed to draw two major conclusions from their analyses. First, since inequalities in schooling, test scores, and family background do not appear to be strongly related to differences in income, "equality of opportunity" in an economic sense already exists. While we should attempt to make schools more pleasant places for young people, we should not view them as important social instruments for obtaining equality of results. Second, as long as the available economic and occupational roles provided by society are so unequal, large inequalities in economic outcomes will persist. Therefore, Jencks and his colleagues argue that, if we wish to reduce large inequalities in income between rich and poor—the top fifth of the population receives seven times what the bottom fifth receives—we should redistribute income directly by increasing the taxes of the rich and raising the minimum incomes provided for the poor.

The second conclusion seems eminently reasonable from a technical point of view. If we wish to improve the distribution of income, we should adopt policy measures that affect income directly. Yet, if the nature of our society is such that the present, large inequalities in income have existed for almost fifty years, it is difficult to believe that there is a powerful enough political coalition to effect a major redistribution. (Witness the recent decision by Congress to postpone welfare reform for several years.)

We might consider whether the competition for the present unequal rewards is a fair one as Jencks and his coauthors imply. This is the single most crucial finding of the book, since it represents the basis for the authors' derogation of social policies aimed at improving equality of opportunity. Stated explicitly, the lack of relationship between family background, schooling, and test scores with income leads to the conclusion that policies to alter schools and family background will have little impact on eliminating economic inequalities.

Certainly, Jencks's assertion that the advantages with which one starts life have little to do with one's economic success seems to defy empirical verification for both the very poor and the very rich, although it may reflect accurately substantial mobility in the middle class. Surveys of the poverty population suggest that the "permanently poor" (in contrast with the transient poor, such as students, or the elderly who are living on pensions and social security payments) were themselves born into impoverished households and have low educational attainments. The very rich also seem to be able to sustain their position from generation to generation. Only the tumultuous economic upheaval associated with the Great Depression provided any appreciable movement from riches to rags, and only the calamity of World War II seemed to provide any appreciable movement from rags to riches over the last half-century. To assert that the forces of luck and other random factors give the children of the poor about the same chance in life as the children of the rich is in substantial conflict with this evidence.

In addition, many previous studies by economists on the subject have found that both schools and family background appear to have substantial effects on earnings. How is it possible, then, that Jencks's conclusions are in such sharp contrast to those of other researchers? The answer seems to lie in differences in interpretation and in the treatment of the data. For example, some differences that Jencks interprets as small ones would not seem trivial to other observers. Even according to the findings presented in the book, an extra year of elementary or secondary schooling appears to boost future income by about 4 per cent, an extra year of college by about 7 per cent, and a year of graduate school by about 4 per cent. According to these data a comparison of high school graduates and college graduates, who were otherwise identical, would show the college graduates earning about 30 per cent more than their less-educated peers. Jencks apparently believes that such differences are small, but two men separated by such income disparities might not agree. Thus, part of the conflict appears to revolve around the rather subjective issue of what magnitudes are important.

Clearly, the more serious discrepancies between Jencks and other researchers appear to be due to differences in the statistical treatment of data. The book's principal finding on the inefficacy of schools is that test scores, family background, and related factors account for only 12–15 per cent of differences in income. In contrast, other studies have found that from one-third to one-half of the variance in income can by explained by these and similar influences; according to their results, we should seriously consider the policy implications of improving the distribution of schooling.

It is not difficult to find the sources, of the differences between these studies and that of Jencks. In fact, the *Inequality* study omitted data that would have improved considerably the amount of variance in income inequality. The most notable of these omissions include data on age and place of residence.

Ordinarily, when economists attempt to explain the determinants of income or earnings, they are concerned with *real* difference, not just artificial differences that are due to variations in price levels. Much of the differences in income among the various regions of the United States is really attributable to differences in the cost of living. The U.S. Bureau of Labor Statistics found that in 1970 the annual costs of a four-person urban family at an intermediate standard of living varied from about $9,200 in Austin, Texas, to over $12,000 in the New York area and almost $13,000 in Honolulu. There are also large differences within metropolitan areas and regions. Thus, much of what appear to be differences in income among a national population are really due to differences in price levels and do not represent differences in *real* incomes. In order to adjust for these effects, other studies have done their analyses within regions or have adjusted the data for the place of residence. Jencks's failure to do this resulted in a substantial overstatement of the "unexplained" variance in income relative to that of other studies.

A second omission that biases Jencks's results is the failure to include the age of the income recipient. Persons with the same educational and family background show large differences in their income over the life cycle. In the early stages of a career incomes rise briskly as individuals advance through on-the-job training, experience, and occupational upgrading. Peak earnings and advancement are reached at about forty-five to fifty years of age, and at this point many workers and self-employed professionals begin to withdraw from the labor market through early retirement or a reduction of hours worked. Thus, earned incomes decline considerably over the latter segment of the life cycle. Since Jencks's income data are based upon white, nonfarm men, twenty-five to sixty-four years of age, they include large components of income differences that are due to this normal life-cycle phenomenon. His failure to adjust the estimates for the age of the worker will serve to increase the amount of "unexplained" variations in income. Researchers usually treat this adjustment as a matter of standard procedure.

Finally, the fact that Jencks's data include income from property, social security, pensions, and other sources also tends to weaken the relationship between schooling, family background, and income. The statistical treatment in *Inequality* uses virtually the same variables to explain the income of the fully productive worker as it does the one who is retired and receives only a pension or social security payments. It uses the same attributes to explain the 15–20 per cent of income that is derived from nonproperty sources such as rents, dividends, and interest, even though such income is not derived from employment. Thus, the statistical formulation itself does not lend itself to explaining components of income that have little to do with individual labor-market productivity. Jencks does not take these important adjustments into account.

Further, the Jencks approach to explaining differences in income does not take noncognitive personality traits into account—even though recent research has found that schools and family appear to have a greater impact on the development of attitudes and values such as independence and conformity than on test scores. Such attributes appear to play an important role in determining social and economic outcomes. Jencks agrees that noncognitive traits ". . . play a larger role than cognitive skills in determining economic success or failure." Yet he omits such effects because of his stated inability to assess and measure them.

The result of all these omissions is to understate seriously the ways in which incomes vary systematically with differences in schooling and family background. If Jencks had corrected the data for such idiosyncrasies and if he had included data on place of residence, age, and noncognitive attributes, his formulation would probably have explained from three to four times as much of the inequality in income as did the more naïve formulation he actually used.

In a sense this example illustrates the fragility of social-science research in complex areas where theories are mere speculations and the techniques of analysis are subject to wide differences in application, usage, and interpretation. Jencks concluded that, because such a small portion of the variance in income was explained statistically by the family-background, schooling, and test-score variables, differences in income must be due primarily to differences in luck and competences that are not related to an individual's educational and family experiences. Yet the obvious alternative explanation is that the omission of important variables, as well as problems in the quality of the data, were the culprits and that differences in family and schooling do indeed affect economic success of adults.

Though Jencks gives the impression that his results are derived strictly from his statistical model and social-science methodology, in fact, the application of that model and its methodology are based upon numerous judgments and opinions. The omission of important variables because of "ignorance of their effects," the casual ordering of the variables, assumptions of linear relationships and normal distributions, the scavenging and use of data collected for other purposes and the questionable treatment of their measurement errors, as well as the ambiguity of many of the results, means that the actual findings and interpretations are at least as much a product of the value perspectives and opinions of the researcher as they are of this methodology and data. Unfortunately, the values and biases of the researcher are built into his procedures and interpretations at every stage.

Using similar data and techniques of analysis, Jencks's colleagues at Harvard, Herbert Gintis and Samuel Bowles, have found powerful support for the theory that social class and income inequality are indeed transmitted from generation to generation by rather powerful noncognitive effects of both family background and schools. They have constructed their model on the assumption that the vast inequality in society is a reflection of the class structure that corresponds to men's relations to the means of production under a system of monopoly-capitalism. In this Marxian model, schools and other institutions work to reproduce the social division of labor and the class structure. Placed in this context, the data and methods used by Jencks would engender very different interpretations. For example, in the Bowles-Gintis context the fact that society spends about twice as much on the schooling of the rich child as on the poor one hardly seems an innocuous accident.

In contrast, Jencks feigns neutrality in the important value issues of how society functions. Schools, family, and the distribution of income appear to operate in a conceptual vacuum, and Jencks seems to shy away from any socio-political-economic theory that might relate them. This places the reader in a position of having to evaluate conclusions based upon statistical evidence that in turn could be derived and interpreted in many different ways. Unless we know the overall value perspectives of the author, it is very difficult to ascertain why he interpreted the data in the particular way he did in the face of many possible alternative explanations.

Despite the lack of a clear ideological framework, this is an important book. It reminds us that, if we wish to create greater equality of incomes, a direct approach to the redistribution of income is the simplest way to achieve that goal. Moreover, *Inequality* contains some of the most stimulating discussions available on a large number of educational and social issues, and at least this reviewer believes that most of the conclusions relating to the cognitive effects of schools and the nature of IQ are convincing, even though he is not persuaded that family background and schooling are unrelated to economic outcomes.

The book also underlines the need for much more research on the nature, formation, and role of noncognitive traits in determining social and economic outcomes, as well as better overall social theories that would enable us to link the many disparate pieces of statistical evidence. Finally, it is only fair to warn the general reader that, despite the social-science terminology and formidable footnotes and appendices, the interpretations of the data must necessarily follow largely from the perspectives of the author rather than from an objective, computerized analysis. The crude state of the social-science art means that at the present time objectivity is unattainable.

EQUAL EDUCATIONAL OPPORTUNITY: PHILOSOPHICAL PERSPECTIVE

Elizabeth Steiner

Equality, as well as fraternity, is an essential feature of a democratic community. In such a community, not only are individuals associated because they share the method of intelligence, but certain individual rights are honored. Among these rights are the right to be educated. The right to be educated is the right to develop one's intelligence.

The question arises as to the criterion for membership in a democratic community. Should humanness alone suffice or should inherited or acquired characteristics, e.g., property or achievement, be required? W. T. Blackstone, a contemporary philosopher, argues that humanness alone should be the criterion, and hence that education is a human right. Class or merit, therefore, should be irrelevant to the possession of the right to be educated.

Another question is associated with the criterion of humanness. Who is human? To answer this question, the essential features of a human must be set forth. Accidental features must be sorted from essential ones. Plato (427–347 B.C.) in *The Republic* argued that sex was an accidental feature. Differences in physical not intellectual capacity can be attributed to sexual differences. Since intellectual capacity is an essential feature of humanness while physical capacity is not, females as well as males should count as human and be educated.

Given answers to the questions relative to the possession of the right to be educated, other questions arise with respect to how education as a right is to be accorded. What constitutes equality in educational treatment? Are all to be treated the same? If there is to be differential treatment, then what is to be the criterion for such treatment? Blackstone also addresses these questions. Differential treatment, he asserts, should be based upon the intellectual capacity of each individual. As intellectual capacities differ so should treatment.

Answers to the previous philosophical questions about equality of educa-

187

tional opportunity provide the ideal. However, ideals should be actualized. As Blackstone recognizes, actualization depends upon answers to factual and scientific questions. What is the situation with respect to equality of educational opportunity? If the situation is not ideal, what educational and other related conditions, e.g., social and economic, must be instituted to bring about the development of each individual's intellectual capacity? These questions are addressed in the historical and sociological articles in this section.

THE EQUALITY OF WOMEN

Plato

Nevertheless, I continued, we are now within sight of the clearest possible proof of our conclusions, and we ought not to slacken our efforts.

No, anything rather than that.

If you will take your stand with me, then, on this point of vantage to which we have climbed, you shall see all the forms that evil takes, or at least all that it seems worth while to look at.

Lead the way and tell me what you see.

What I see is that, whereas there is only one form of excellence, imperfection exists in innumerable shapes, of which there are four that specially deserve notice.

What do you mean?

It looks as if there were as many types of character as there are distinct varieties of political constitution.

How many?

Five of each.

Will you define them?

Yes, I said. One form of constitution will be the form we have been describing, though it may be called by two names: monarchy, when there is one man who stands out above the rest of the Rulers; aristocracy, when there are more than one.[1]

True.

That, then, I regard as a single form; for, so long as they observe our principles of upbringing and education, whether the Rulers be one or more, they will not subvert the important institutions in our commonwealth.

Naturally not.

Such, then, is the type of state or constitution that I call good and right,

From *The Republic of Plato* translated by F. M. Cornford and published by Oxford University Press (1941). Reprinted by permission of the publisher.

and the corresponding type of man. By this standard, the other forms in which a state or an individual character may be organized are depraved and wrong. There are four of these vicious forms.

What are they?

Here I was going on to describe these forms in the order in which, as I thought, they develop one from another, when Polemarchus, who was sitting a little way from Adeimantus, reached out his hand and took hold of his garment by the shoulder. Leaning forward and drawing Adeimantus towards him, he whispered something in his ear, of which I only caught the words: What shall we do? Shall we leave it alone?

Certainly not, said Adeimantus, raising his voice.

What is this, I asked, that you are not going to leave alone?

You, he replied.

Why, in particular? I inquired.

Because we think you are shirking the discussion of a very important part of the subject and trying to cheat us out of an explanation. Everyone, you said, must of course see that the maxim 'friends have all things in common' applies to women and children. You thought we should pass over such a casual remark!

But wasn't that right, Adeimantus? said I.

Yes, he said, but 'right' in this case, as in others, needs to be defined. There may be many ways of having things in common, and you must tell us which you mean. We have been waiting a long time for you to say something about the conditions in which children are to be born and brought up and your whole plan of having wives and children held in common. This seems to us a matter in which right or wrong management will make all the difference to society; and now, instead of going into it thoroughly, you are passing on to some other form of constitution. So we came to the resolution which you overheard, not to let you off discussing it as fully as all the other institutions.

I will vote for your resolution too, said Glaucon.

In fact, Socrates, Thrasymachus added, you may take it as carried unanimously.

You don't know what you are doing, I said, in holding me up like this. You want to start, all over again, on an enormous subject, just as I was rejoicing at the idea that we had done with this form of constitution. I was only too glad that my casual remark should be allowed to pass. And now, when you demand an explanation, you little know what a swarm of questions you are stirring up. I let it alone, because I foresaw no end of trouble.

Well, said Thrasymachus, what do you think we came here for—to play pitch-and-toss or to listen to a discussion?

A discussion, no doubt, I replied; but within limits.

No man of sense, said Glaucon, would think the whole of life too long to spend on questions of this importance. But never mind about us; don't be faint-hearted yourself. Tell us what you think about this question: how our

Guardians are to have wives and children in common, and how they will bring up the young in the interval between their birth and education, which is thought to be the most difficult time of all. Do try to explain how all this is to be arranged.

I wish it were as easy as you seem to think, I replied. These arrangements are even more open to doubt than any we have so far discussed. It may be questioned whether the plan is feasible, and even if entirely feasible, whether it would be for the best. So I have some hesitation in touching on what may seem to be an idle dream.

You need not hesitate, he replied. This is not an unsympathetic audience; we are neither incredulous nor hostile.

Thank you, I said; I suppose that remark is meant to be encouraging.

Certainly it is.

Well, I said, it has just the opposite effect. You would do well to encourage me, if I had any faith in my own understanding of these matters. If one knows the truth, there is no risk to be feared in speaking about the things one has most at heart among intelligent friends; but if one is still in the position of a doubting inquirer, as I am now, talking becomes a slippery venture. Not that I am afraid of being laughed at—that would be childish—but I am afraid I may miss my footing just where a false step is most to be dreaded and drag my friends down with me in my fall. I devoutly hope, Glaucon, that no nemesis will overtake me for what I am going to say; for I really believe that to kill a man unintentionally is a lighter offence than to mislead him concerning the goodness and justice of social institutions. Better to run that risk among enemies than among friends; so your encouragement is out of place.

Glaucon laughed at this. No, Socrates, he said, if your theory has any untoward effect on us, our blood shall not be on your head; we absolve you of any intention to mislead us. So have no fear.

Well, said I, when a homicide is absolved of all intention, the law holds him clear of guilt; and the same principle may apply to my case.

Yes, so far as that goes, you may speak freely.

We must go back, then, to a subject which ought, perhaps, to have been treated earlier in its proper place; though, after all, it may be suitable that the women should have their turn on the stage when the men have quite finished their performance, especially since you are so insistent. In my judgement, then, the question under what conditions people born and educated as we have described should possess wives and children, and how they should treat them, can be rightly settled only by keeping to the course on which we started them at the outset. We undertook to put these men in the position of watch-dogs guarding a flock. Suppose we follow up the analogy and imagine them bred and reared in the same sort of way. We can then see if that plan will suit our purpose.

How will that be?

In this way. Which do we think right for watch-dogs: should the females guard the flock and hunt with the males and take a share in all they do, or should they be kept within doors as fit for no more than bearing and feeding their puppies, while all the hard work of looking after the flock is left to the males?

They are expected to take their full share, except that we treat them as not quite so strong.

Can you employ any creature for the same work as another, if you do not give them both the same upbringing and education?

No.

Then, if we are to set women to the same tasks as men, we must teach them the same things. They must have the same two branches of training for mind and body and also be taught the art of war, and they must receive the same treatment.

That seems to follow.

Possibly, if these proposals were carried out, they might be ridiculed as involving a good many breaches of custom.

They might indeed.

The most ridiculous—don't you think?—being the notion of women exercising naked along with the men in the wrestling-schools; some of them elderly women too, like the old men who still have a passion for exercise when they are wrinkled and not very agreeable to look at.

Yes, that would be thought laughable, according to our present notions.

Now we have started on this subject, we must not be frightened of the many witticisms that might be aimed at such a revolution, not only in the matter of bodily exercise but in the training of women's minds, and not least when it comes to their bearing arms and riding on horseback. Having begun upon these rules, we must not draw back from the harsher provisions. The wits may be asked to stop being witty and try to be serious; and we may remind them that it is not so long since the Greeks, like most foreign nations of the present day, thought it ridiculous and shameful for men to be seen naked. When gymnastic exercises were first introduced in Crete and later at Sparta, the humorists had their chance to make fun of them; but when experience had shown that nakedness is better uncovered than muffled up, the laughter died down and a practice which the reason approved ceased to look ridiculous to the eye. This shows how idle it is to think anything ludicrous but what is base. One who tries to raise a laugh at any spectacle save that of baseness and folly will also, in his serious moments, set before himself some other standard than goodness of what deserves to be held in honour.

Most assuredly.

The first thing to be settled, then, is whether these proposals are feasible; and it must be open to anyone, whether a humorist or serious-minded, to raise the question whether, in the case of mankind, the feminine nature is capable of taking part with the other sex in all occupations, or in none at all, or in some only; and in particular under which of these heads this business of military service falls. Well begun is half done, and would not this be the best way to begin?

Yes.

Shall we take the other side in this debate and argue against ourselves? We do not want the adversary's position to be taken by storm for lack of defenders.

I have no objection.

Let us state his case for him. 'Socrates and Glaucon,' he will say, 'there is no need for others to dispute your position: you yourselves, at the very outset of founding your commonwealth, agreed that everyone should do the one work for which nature fits him.' Yes, of course; I suppose we did. 'And isn't there a very great difference in nature between man and woman?' Yes, surely. 'Does not that natural difference imply a corresponding difference in the work to be given to each?' Yes. 'But if so, surely you must be mistaken now and contradicting yourselves when you say that men and women, having such widely divergent natures, should do the same things?' What is your answer to that, my ingenious friend?

It is not easy to find one at the moment. I can only appeal to you to state the case on our own side, whatever it may be.

This, Glaucon, is one of many alarming objections which I foresaw some time ago. That is why I shrank from touching upon these laws concerning the possession of wives and the rearing of children.

It looks like anything but an easy problem.

True, I said; but whether a man tumbles into a swimming-pool or into mid-ocean, he has to swim all the same. So must we, and try if we can reach the shore, hoping for some Arion's dolphin or other miraculous deliverance to bring us safe to land.[2]

I suppose so.

Come then, let us see if we can find the way out. We did agree that different natures should have different occupations, and that the natures of man and woman are different; and yet we are now saying that these different natures are to have the same occupations. Is that the charge against us?

Exactly.

It is extraordinary, Glaucon, what an effect the practice of debating has upon people.

Why do you say that?

Because they often seem to fall unconsciously into mere disputes which they mistake for reasonable argument, through being unable to draw the distinctions proper to their subject; and so, instead of a philosophical exchange of ideas, they go off in chase of contradictions which are purely verbal.

I know that happens to many people; but does it apply to us at this moment?

Absolutely. At least I am afraid we are slipping unconsciously into a dispute about words. We have been strenuously insisting on the letter of our principle that different natures should not have the same occupations, as if we were scoring a point in a debate; but we have altogether neglected to consider what sort of sameness or difference we meant and in what respect these natures and occupations were to be defined as different or the same. Consequently, we might very well be asking one another whether there is not an opposition in nature between bald and long-haired men, and, when that was admitted, forbid one set to be shoemakers, if the other were following that trade.

That would be absurd.

Yes, but only because we never meant any and every sort of sameness or difference in nature, but the sort that was relevant to the occupations in question. We meant, for instance, that a man and a woman have the same nature if both have a talent for medicine; wheras two men have different natures if one is a born physician, the other a born carpenter.

Yes, of course.

If, then, we find that either the male sex or the female is specially qualified for any particular form of occupation, then that occupation, we shall say, ought to be assigned to one sex or the other. But if the only difference appears to be that the male begets and the female brings forth, we shall conclude that no difference between man and woman has yet been produced that is relevant to our purpose. We shall continue to think it proper for our Guardians and their wives to share in the same pursuits.

And quite rightly.

The next thing will be to ask our opponent to name any profession or occupation in civic life for the purposes of which woman's nature is different from man's.

That is a fair question.

He might reply, as you did just now, that it is not easy to find a satisfactory answer on the spur of the moment, but that there would be no difficulty after a little reflection.

Perhaps.

Suppose, then, we invite him to follow us and see if we can convince him that there is no occupation concerned with the management of social affairs that is peculiar to women. We will confront him with a question: When you speak of a man having a natural talent for something, do you mean that he finds it easy to learn, and after a little instruction can find out much more for himself; whereas a man who is not so gifted learns with difficulty and no amount of instruction and practice will make him even remember what he has been taught? Is the talented man one whose bodily powers are readily at the service of his mind, instead of being a hindrance?

Are not these the marks by which you distinguish the presence of a natural gift for any pursuit?

Yes, precisely.

Now do you know of any human occupation in which the male sex is not superior to the female in all these respects? Need I waste time over exceptions like weaving and watching over saucepans and batches of cakes, though women are supposed to be good at such things and get laughed at when a man does them better?

It is true, he replied, in almost everything one sex is easily beaten by the other. No doubt many women are better at many things than many men; but taking the sexes as a whole, it is as you say.

To conclude, then, there is no occupation concerned with the management of social affairs which belongs either to woman or to man, as such. Natural gifts are to be found here and there in both creatures alike; and every occupation is open to both, so far as their natures are concerned, though woman is for all purposes the weaker.

Certainly.

Is that a reason for making over all occupations to men only?

Of course not.

No, because one woman may have a natural gift for medicine or for music, another may not.

Surely.

Is it not also true that a woman may, or may not, be warlike or athletic?

I think so.

And again, one may love knowledge, another hate it; one may be high-spirited, another spiritless?

True again.

It follows that one woman will be fitted by nature to be a Guardian, another will not; because these were the qualities for which we selected our men Guardians. So for the purpose of keeping watch over the commonwealth, woman has the same nature as man, save in so far as she is weaker.

So it appears.

It follows that women of this type must be selected to share the life and duties of Guardians with men of the same type, since they are competent and of a like nature, and the same natures must be allowed the same pursuits.

Yes.

We come round, then, to our former position, that there is nothing contrary to nature in giving our Guardians' wives the same training for mind and body. The practice we proposed to establish was not impossible or visionary, since it was in accordance with nature. Rather, the contrary practice which now prevails turns out to be unnatural.

So it appears.

Well, we set out to inquire whether the plan we proposed was feasible and also the best. That it is feasible is now agreed; we must next settle whether it is the best.

Obviously.

Now, for the purpose of producing a woman fit to be a Guardian, we shall not have one education for men and another for women, precisely because the nature to be taken in hand is the same.

True.

What is your opinion on the question of one man being better than another? Do you think there is no such difference?

Certainly I do not.

And in this commonwealth of ours which will prove the better men—the Guardians who have received the education we described, or the shoe-makers who have been trained to make shoes?[3]

It is absurd to ask such a question.

Very well. So these Guardians will be the best of all the citizens?

By far.

And these women the best of all the women?

Yes.

Can anything be better for a commonwealth than to produce in it men and women of the best possible type?

No.

And that result will be brought about by such a system of mental and bodily training as we have described?

Surely.

We may conclude that the institution we proposed was not only prac-ticable, but also the best for the commonwealth.

Yes.

The wives of our Guardians, then, must strip for exercise, since they will be clothed with virtue, and they must take their share in war and in the other social duties of guardianship. They are to have no other occupation; and in these duties the lighter part must fall to the women, because of the weakness of their sex. The man who laughs at naked women, exercising their bodies for the best of reasons, is like one that 'gathers fruit unripe,'[4] for he does not know what it is that he is laughing at or what he is doing. There will never be a finer saying than the one which declares that what-ever does good should be held in honour, and the only shame is in doing harm.

That is perfectly true.

NOTES

1. The question whether wisdom rules in the person of one man or of several is unim-portant. In the sequel the ideal constitution is called kingship or aristocracy (the role of the best) indifferently. Cf. 540 D, p. 262, and 587 D, p. 315 f.

2. The musician Arion, to escape the treachery of Corinthian sailors, leapt into the sea and was carried ashore at Taenarum by a dolphin, Herod, i, 24.

3. The elementary education of Chap. IX will be open to all citizens, but presumably carried further (to the age of 17 or 18, see p. 259) in the case of those who show special promise.

4. An adapted quotation from Pindar (frag. 209, Schr.).

HUMAN RIGHTS, EQUALITY, AND EDUCATION

W. T. Blackstone

In the United States there is very little debate or disagreement over whether the right to an education is a human right or over whether all persons should receive equality of educational opportunity. Education is seen not only as a right but as a necessity made compulsory. True, Senator Goldwater and others remind us that the Constitution of the United States says nothing about education; but as Senator Eugene McCarthy points out, it does say a lot about human dignity, happiness and inalienable rights.[1] Quite plainly the right to an education or equality of educational opportunity has been taken to be entailed by these fundamental principles. However, there has been and continues to be considerable disagreement over what is meant by the human right to an education or equality of educational opportunity, and consequently, over what conditions the fulfillment of which would assure that right or equality.

In this paper I will consider these issues. My procedure will be both analytic or conceptual and normative. First, I will present a brief analysis of the general concepts, "human rights" and "equality of treatment." Then I will extend this analysis more specifically to education as a human right and equal educational opportunity. I will also offer several normative arguments and recommendations, which themselves involve reference to recently documented empirical facts, and conclude by giving a brief summary

Reprinted by permission of the executrix of the estate of the author and *Educational Theory* from pp. 288–296, Vol. 1, No. 3, Summer, 1969.

of what I consider to be the limits of the rational adjudication of moral issues of this type.

The analysis offered, I believe, *is* a morally neutral explication. My normative conclusions, though, are the result of two elements: (1) certain value commitments, which I think are *essential* for anyone who subscribes to the ethic of democracy, but which go in a certain direction *within* that ethic (what I mean by "within" I will make clear as I proceed) and (2) the acceptance of certain empirical states of affairs.

I do not think that the concepts, equality and human rights, are identical, though they do cross at important junctures. Historically, equality has been held to be one of several human rights, as by John Locke. Others have held that equality is the only human right. This seems to be what is held by H. L. A. Hart in his thesis that the equal right to be free is the only natural right.[2] My thesis is that equality is used in several different senses, and *one* of those uses is identical to the notion of a *human* right. This is my reason for treating both of these concepts together in this paper. In effect I want to show that the same sort of problems confront the notion of a "human right" as confront the notion of "equality" (that is, a key use of this concept) and, *mutatis mutandis,* the same problems confront the notion of a "human right to education" as confront the notion of "equality of educational opportunity." I turn first to the concept of human rights.

The Concept of Human Rights

Presumably what differentiates human rights from legal rights is that the latter are the permissions, entitlements, and prohibitions embodied in statute law and which are enforceable by reference to that law, whereas the former may or may not be so embodied or recognized by law and in fact hold independently of laws or social conventions. Human rights are those rights which one possesses simply in virtue of the fact that one is human. They also hold independently of special, acquired characteristics, such as wealth, education, moral character, and so on. No acquired characteristics whatever are relevant and hence, human beings are not gradable in regard to the *possession* of these rights. All that is required is that one be human.

This entails nothing about what constitutes the fulfillment of a given human right for a given person on a given occasion. Human rights theorists have never insisted on identity of treatment as necessary for the fulfillment of a human right. They have insisted in fact that there are multiple grounds which require and justify differential treatment of persons (in fulfilling their human rights), that identical treatment in many cases is improper and unfair, and that consequently careful attention to the circumstances and capacities of persons, and rational *judgment*, is required to properly fulfill a human right. The fact that one is human therefore, and *qua* this fact possesses human rights, entails little about how one should be treated on a given occasion. It seems to me to entail only that one should be treated as any other human being who is similar to oneself in all *relevant* respects. And this is vacuous indeed until criteria of relevance for differential treatment are spelled out.

The problem, then, as I see it, with the concept of human rights is twofold: (1) criteria for being human must be laid down so that we know which beings have human rights (and though this seems a simple problem I will show in a moment with an example that it is not) and (2) criteria of relevance which justify differential treatment in according a person his human right must be specified. These problems are related but let me speak to (1) first.

What are the criteria for being human? Not criteria for being a brilliant, efficient, or productive human but just human? Well, skin pigmentation, the length of nose, and cranium size seem to be accidental features. Are there any essential ones? I am not so sure that human nature has an *essence* which distinguishes it from other animal natures. Perhaps the difference lies in having the capacity or potentiality for a certain range of qualities and activities.[3] Man differs from other animals in that his rational capacities and perceptual apparatus give him this range—the ability to choose, use concepts and reason—which other animals lack. On this analysis the problem of who is human and therefore has human rights boils down to who has these capacities and potentialities.

What about an imbecile or a moron or a madman? Are they human and do they possess human rights? We say that they do—only that they have impaired capacities. However, and this is the point I want to make here, the notion of "human" can be used in a more flagrantly normative way as Friedrich Nietzsche does when he insists that one is *really* human only if one's capacities are at a certain level—the level of the *ubermensch* or superman.[4] The implication of this for the existence and accordance of human rights is tremendous. In Nietzsche's "master-morality" the scope of rights and duties are severely restricted, depending on one's "slave" or "ubermensch" status. Those persons or bodies without "ubermensch" qualities can in fact be used as a scaffolding for the further elevation and use of those with these *really* human qualities. Everything hangs on what is built into the concept "human."

The Nietzschian thesis can perhaps best be formulated as a choice of criteria of relevance for differential treatment in according rights. That is, instead of simply reading certain bodies out of the human race, what is done is the setting of criteria of relevance for differential treatment so that the characteristics of "slaves" and "ubermensch" are constitutive aspects of the criteria. Then the rules justify including or excluding or qualifying the treatment of certain persons.

Most anything *can* be justified. It depends entirely on the criteria chosen. The question is which criteria *ought* to be chosen and used, for the question of what is *relevant* is in large part normative. This is the crucially important problem and I will return to it. But first I want to offer a brief analysis of the concept of equality (as promised) and show that the same problem of justifying criteria of relevance for differential treatment which confronts the notion of human rights also confronts the principle of equality.

Equality of Treatment

I am not here concerned with uses of equality as a descriptive concept but only with prescriptive uses, in particular with the classical principle which has played such a key role in moral and political contexts over the centuries and formulated by Aristotle in these words, "Equals are to be treated equally: unequals unequally,." and by others as "Everyone is to count for one and no more than one" and "all men are equal" (in the sense of being entitled to equal consideration). As with the human rights norm, this principle is vacuous until criteria of relevance for differential treatment are filled in. It prescribes simply that all persons are to be treated alike and that no person is to be given better treatment or special consideration or privilege unless justifying reasons can be given for such differentiation. It precribes that all human beings, no matter what natural or acquired characteristics they possess, no matter how unequal their endowments and conditions, are entitled to the same relative care and consideration. The principle does not prescribe identical treatment of persons—unless those persons and circumstances are similar in all *relevant* respects. The problem, however, is specifying, and *justifying* criteria of relevance for differential treatment. Again, it is plain that everything in the way of the treatment of persons hangs on those criteria. And here is the rub, for these are fundamental differences in the criteria proposed—at least in their order of priority.

Let me spell this out just a little. The claim that certain criteria are relevant involves both descriptive and prescriptive aspects. The descriptive aspect poses no special problem. It amounts roughly to the assertion that certain factors are causally related to given ends, and as such is straightforwardly verifiable. For example, to assert that I.Q. is relevant to educability is to assert such a causal relationship. The prescriptive aspect of judgments of relevance, on the other hand, poses difficult problems. A host of different *general* criteria of relevance has been recommended by Aristotle, Nietzsche, Karl Marx, Franklin Delano Roosevelt, and so on. They include "merit," "need," "worth to society" and so on. Each of these normative criteria can be explicated or unpacked in different ways. Aristotle and Nietzsche do not agree on what constitutes "merit." But let us ignore the ambiguity of these notions for a moment and concentrate simply on the general, contrasting criteria of "merit" and "need." If "merit" is taken as a general and fundamental criterion of relevance for differential treatment, this amounts to the formulation not only of criteria for particular evaluations of how to treat people but also of a general concept of what society should be like. If "need," on the other hand, is given primary emphasis, then we have different guidelines for treating people and for a different concept of a desirable society.

I am *not* arguing here that criteria of merit and criteria of need are mutually exclusive. Obviously they are not and one can accept both—and other criteria. It would be an odd world, indeed, in which merit-criteria did not exist. I am arguing that the *moral priority* or emphasis in one's scale of relevant criteria or reasons for differential treatment entails very important differences in guidelines for treating people—for distributing goods and services—and for one's concept of a desi*rable* society.

Need-Criteria Priority

Now let us ask this question: Can we justify the claim that need-criteria (admittedly the concept of "need" needs analysis but this is not the place to do it) should take moral priority over criteria of merit and other criteria? For the most part we in this country at least subscribe to this moral priority. We say in a host of contexts, involving medical treatment, legal treatment, basic living conditions and so on that all human beings ought to be accorded a certain mode of treatment *qua* the fact of humanness, *qua* the fact of equality in that sense, and that acquired characteristics, inherited circumstances or rank and wealth, and worth to society are irrelevant in according these modes of treatment. In other words we do, at least on a doctrinal level, espouse the moral priority of need-criteria, and a good case can be made that this priority is fundamental to the democratic ethic. But is there an argument which will justify this priority or must it simply be a fundamental postulate?

There is an argument implicit in Plato's *Republic* which I think is forceful. Plato there holds that differential treatment on the basis of merit is inescapable but that fairness requires that, first, all be given the opportunity to develop those meritorious qualities. For Plato this involves the fulfillment of certain basic human needs and educational opportunities. Frankena recently argued the same point, that merit cannot be the most basic criterion for distributive justice because "a recognition of merit as the basis of distribution is justified only if every individual has an equal chance of achieving all the merit he is capable of. . . ."[5] The point is that giving priority to merit-criteria is like pretending that everyone is eligible for the game of goods-distribution, while knowing that many individuals, through no fault of their own, through circumstances and deficiencies over which they have no control, cannot possibly be in the game.

The Human Right to Education

Now assuming that human rights extend to education or that equality extends to educational opportunity, what is entailed by what we have just argued concerning criteria of merit, need, and so on? First, if education is seen as a human right, then all are entitled to it simply *qua* the fact of being human. Criteria of merit, however conceived, such as I. Q. or wealth or social class are irrelevant in regard to the *possession* of this right. Such capacities and conditions are certainly relevant, however, in how education as a right is to be *accorded*. There is no question that these capacities and conditions are causally related to the educability of persons or to the extent to which any given person can be educated. If the above argument on the moral priority of need and capacity-criteria is accepted, then the *ideal* fulfillment of the human right to education entails providing those conditions, social, economic, and educational, which will enable each person to fulfill his capacities. It may be that such ideal fulfillment is impossible in some circumstances—due to extreme scarcity of goods and services. It may be that it is possible but that, for a variety of reasons, available goods and services are not properly distributed. What constitutes proper distribution in any given case is a complex matter of three premises or components: (1) norms or criteria of relevance for differential treatment *and an order of priority* among those criteria, (2) empirical facts which bear on the needs, abilities, and circumstances of the person or persons involved, and (3) knowledge of the goods and services *available* for distribution.

I will not concentrate on knowledge of available goods and services. This is obviously essential for proper judgment about distribution. Since these goods vary greatly from one country to another, this fact alone results in great variability in distribution. It would be unreasonable in practice, for example, to insist on the fulfillment of the right of everyone to a university education in India, whereas it might well be reasonable in the United States. It is conceivable, in fact, that goods of various types be so limited or scarce that the very notion of a right to certain goods or of equality of treatment loses its significance. The same holds for conditions of extreme abundance, for no occasion for pressing a right would ever arise if everyone's needs could be satisfied simply by reaching out or asking. This, I take it, is Hume's point about the conditions which give talk about "justice," and I assume, "rights," its point and significance. Rights talk, then, and claims for equal treatment, presuppose conflicts of interests and a world in which there is neither a complete abundance of need-fulfilling resources nor a complete lack of such resources.

Normative Criteria and Empirical Facts

Concerning (1) norms, I have suggested that *genuine* democrats are committed to need-criteria priority, and I will indicate what seems to me to be entailed by this. I want to indicate these entailments by briefly focusing on (2) certain empirical facts or issues.

There are a host of factual issues which must be resolved by sociological and educational research before we can come up with the needed factual premises which, together with our normative principles or commitments, will yield a conclusion about what ought to be done to properly accord the human right to an education or equality of educational opportunity. These facts will vary greatly from one country, or religion, to another. My focus here will be on some facts in the United States recently dramatized by the Coleman Report, an 800 page document which is the result of the second largest piece of social science research ever conducted.[6]

A serious obstacle to progress is fulfilling the human right to education in America, and elsewhere, is the absence of adequate, tested information on how well our schools are fulfilling the educational needs of our children and where they are failing to do so. I am not a sociologist or an educational researcher so I am not about to presume to tell you what school factors are of central importance in equalizing educational opportunity or fulfilling the human right to education. The variables involved here are exceedingly complex. But the need for reliable information is plain. This is clear from the furor kicked off by the recent Coleman Report on *Equality of Educational Opportunity*. This survey investigated the relationships of pupil achievement with various aspects of pupil background and some forty-five measures that describe the schools attended. This is undoubtedly the most elaborate data collection projected conducted thus far. One of its conclusions, not entirely surprising to me, is that the differential effects of schools on pupil achievement "appear to arise not principally from factors that the school system controls, but from factors outside the school proper."[7] This report has been criticized for its almost exclusive use of verbal ability as a criterion of academic achievement (a criterion known to be far more a product of a child's home rather than his school). Henry Dyer, Director of The Educational Testing Service argues that it pays little attention "to the kinds of achievement on which the schools have traditionally focused," and that other criteria in other studies (he cites that of Shaycroft[8]), related specifically to the subjects studies in school, show that among schools there are substantial differences in effects, even when socio-economic differences are accounted for.[9] Dyer concludes that the results of the Coleman Report "have the unfortunate, though perhaps inadvertent, effect of giving school systems the false impression that there is not much they can do to improve the achievement of their pupils."[10]

Now I am not so sure that the Report gives this impression, but the point I want to stress is that we frequently have fundamental disagreements about what can and what cannot be done by schools to insure equal educational opportunity. Much more research needs to be done to provide this essential factual data about the key causal factors in the home, community, and school related to educability. In some cases it may be difficult, if not impossible, to separate the variables centering around home and community from those of the school, but we must press our demand for knowledge here to the limit. We desperately need a truer assessment of the key factors related to equality of educational opportunity.

We have known for years that there is massive inequality in public school education, which cuts not only along racial lines but also socioeconomic lines. Achievement tests show that minority group students of the lower socio-economic class score significantly lower on a variety of tests than middle-class whites, and that far from providing equal educational opportunity, our schools in many cases are not even equipping students to function well in our society. One significant conclusion of the Coleman Report, as I read it, is that we *cannot expect* the schools alone to provide this opportunity, that although the schools can and do mold and shape a student, the *massive* inequality which confronts us can be overcome only by confronting those variables in the non-school environment. As the report points out, the achievement differences between racial and ethnic groups simply are not lessened with more years of schooling.

Normative Recommendations

The upshot of all this is that we cannot meaningfully confront the problem of educational equality without confronting the problem of social and economic equality. Given a social order in which there are very wide differences in living standards, in which even minimal living conditions are not satisfied for a substantial percentage of the population, and in which the children of low income families must become wage-earners in their early teens, the mere formal access to primary and secondary education will never provide equality of educational opportunity. If, *as we profess,* social class and wealth, not to speak of skin pigmentation, are irrelevant in the distribution of education (irrelevant, *not* in the causal sense, but in the sense that they ought not count as factors in regard to the *possession* of rights), then we must institute the necessary social and economic changes which will ameliorate these conditions inherited by so many of our children. More than compensatory programs of education, decreased student-teacher ratios, better facilities, improved teacher quality, and so on are required. What is also required are certain fundamental social and economic changes in our society, changes which can overcome the impoverishment and socially hostile-to-education conditions of the home and community.

This is a tall order, and it cannot be done overnight. And we should not make the mistake of seeing the inequality problem as essentially a racial one. There are millions of poor whites and some rich Negroes. What is required is not merely an end to racism but an end to the political powerlessness of poor people no matter what their color. This will undoubtedly require fundamental changes in the distribution of political power among social and economic classes.

What is at stake is the promise of democracy. Educated and productive citizens constitute the basis of democratic stability, and our public schools have constituted the principal instrument in making such citizens. But whatever success our public school system has had in the past, it is clearly failing today in many instances, especially in many large city ghettos. There is considerable truth in Kenneth Clark's remark that "American public schools have become significant instruments in the blocking of economic mobility and in the intensification of class distinctions rather than fulfilling their historic function of facilitating such mobility. In effect, the public schools have become captives of a middle class who have failed to use them to aid others to move into the middle class." [11]

The cost of changing this in terms of money will be high but we cannot afford not to do it. It will also involve giving preferential treatment to the poor and the deprived; and though this preferential treatment is justified on relevant grounds (given the ethic of democracy), such a policy will result in conflicts of interest, for it will detract from the interest of other classes. It will increase the competition for good jobs and some who now obtain those jobs almost by default may not like the competition.

It will also cost us in terms of freedom. Any new social or economic strictures decrease the area of free choice for man. The 18th century debate on the conflict of equality and freedom did have a point. But again the cost here is worth the product, and we must be willing to admit that on occasion, many of our most cherished values do conflict, and choice must be made.

How far are we willing to go in order to remove the causes of inequality? How far should we go? Getting rid of these causes will require a fantastic array of social policies, including birth control, pre-school environment control, housing regulations, and perhaps a guaranteed minimum income. Our society is clearly moving in the direction of these policies. How far we *will* go can be only a rough guess. How far we *ought* to go requires a continuous debate within the framework of our ethical and normative commitments, one which recognizes that equality of treatment, though a basic value within the ethic of democracy is not the only such value; that there are other basic values such as individual freedom, which may and do conflict with equalitarian considerations and which necessitate a choice, and a loss, *to some extent*, of one of these values. I do not believe that ethical choice is a one-principle affair, and, in my opinion, efforts to reduce all morally relevant considerations to one principle, such as that of utility, have failed. This fact leaves us with the possibility of fundamental conflicts of value, not only with opponents *outside* of the democratic ethic, such as Nietzsche, but *within* the democratic ethic itself. The conflict "within" involves differences not only in priority (or degrees of priority) among criteria of relevance for the differential treatment of persons but also on priority choice when such values as equality *and* freedom conflict.

NOTES

This paper was read at a Symposium on Education and Ethics at the University of Georgia, May 17–18, 1968.

1. See Eugene McCarthy, "My Hope for the Democrats," *Saturday Review*, November 5, 1966, p. 50.

2. H. L. Hart, "Are There Any Natural Rights?" in *Society, Law and Morality*, ed. Frederick Olafson (Englewood Cliffs, New Jersey, 1961). First published in the *Philosophical Review*, Vol. LXIV (1955).

3. See S. I. Benn and R. S. Peter's discussion of this in *The Principles of Political Thought* (New York, 1964). Originally published in 1959 as *Social Foundations of the Democratic State.*

4. See especially Nietzsche's *The Geneology of Morals* and *Beyond Good and Evil.*

5. William Frankena, "Some Beliefs About Justice" (The Lindley Lecture, University of Kansas, 1966).

6. James S. Coleman, *et al. Equality of Educational Opportunity* (Washington, D.C.: United States Government Printing Office, 1966).

7. *Ibid.,* p. 312.

8. Marion F. Shaycroft, *The High School Years: Growth in Cognitive Skills* (Pittsburgh, Pennsylvania: American Institutes for Research and School of Education, University of Pittsburgh, 1967).

9. Henry Dyer, "School Factors and Equal Educational Opportunity," *Harvard Educational Review,* Vol. 38, 1968, p. 46.

10. *Ibid.*

11. Kenneth B. Clark, "Alternative Public School Systems," *Harvard Educational Review,* Vol. 38, 1968, p. 101.

PROBLEM III
Educate in What?

RESOLUTIVE THEME
Values Education

VALUES EDUCATION: HISTORICAL PERSPECTIVE

B. Edward McClellan

The emergence of a modern, pluralistic, and largely secular society in America has elevated questions about the proper role of moral instruction in the nation's public schools into one of the paramount educational issues of the day. Some theorists argue that the religious, cultural, and ideological diversity of the society makes education in morality a virtually impossible task for the public school. They suggest that schools should emphasize the development of cognitive and social skills and leave responsibility for moral education to such institutions as the family and the church. Others contend that the moral domain is far too important to be ignored in public education. Whatever the problems, they argue, schools must find a way to deal forthrightly with questions of morality and to treat moral concerns as an integral part of a whole educational fabric.

To Americans of an earlier day this debate would have seemed bizarre, for until the end of the nineteenth century most people simply assumed that morality lay at the core of all education. In that fundamentally religious age, both individual salvation and social stability were thought to rest largely on the diffusion of sound moral values, and no institution of education, including the public school, was free of responsibility for moral development.

What controversy existed on the question of moral education in this era focused not on the place of morality in schooling but rather on the manner of teaching it. Here the major dispute arose in the early nineteenth century when the proliferation of Protestant denominations and the rapid growth of the Catholic population created concern about whether the public school should allow moral education to include the teaching of specific religious creeds. Protestants generally favored a public schooling in which moral education would be based on a nondenominational Christianity and reenforced by the daily reading of scriptures. Catholics, on the other hand, were skeptical about the possibility of teaching moral values apart from sectarian doctrines and church traditions. Offended by a public schooling that seemed only to teach an ill-disguised Protestantism, Catholics eventually created a separate, parochial system where they were able to integrate moral and religious education on their own terms.

As traditional Protestants and Catholics debated the merits of their particular schemes in the late nineteenth century, a new approach to moral education emerged to challenge the fundamental assumptions of both groups. Born of a rapidly modernizing society, this approach gained prominence in the early part of the twentieth century. It rejected the notion that morality should be rooted in the fixed doctrines of revealed religion and proposed instead to teach students an ethical sensitivity based on emergent human values.

Articulation of this new approach at once enlarged and reshaped the controversy over moral education. Ironically, as the debate widened to include the conflict between modernists and traditionalists, the actual influence of moral education in the schools steadily declined. Twentieth-century educators, disturbed by the controversial character of moral questions and preoccupied by the vocational and social needs of industrial society, increasingly favored curricula that emphasized cognitive development and the skills of interpersonal relationships. By the middle decades of the century, it sometimes appeared that deliberate efforts to provide moral instruction in the public schools might disappear altogether. Many educators, of course, would have welcomed such a development, but others were determined to restore consideration of moral questions to a place of importance in the school's curriculum. If, by the late 1970s, these educators had still brought about little real reform in educational practice, they had at least succeeded in initiating a thoughtful reexamination of the issues surrounding the place of moral instruction in the public schools.

The readings that follow trace the history of moral education in the schools from the early nineteenth century to the present. My article, "Moral Education and Public Schooling," provides an overview of the changing place and character of moral education in the nation's public elementary and secondary schools. It pays particular attention to the social and cultural contexts in which various approaches to moral education have developed Neil McCluskey's "America and the Catholic School" focuses more narrowly on the debate between Catholics and Protestants and on the emergence and development of the parochial school system.

By focusing on the deliberate and systematic efforts to teach moral values, these readings neglect the subtle, often unconscious moral education that takes place when schools demand certain kinds of behavioral conformity or teach such instrumental values as efficiency or congeniality. Fortunately, the readings on sociology that follow focus precisely on this subtle inculcation of values and thereby provide an indispensable supplement to the selections in history. Readers may find it interesting to try to distinguish between educational practices that openly attempt to deal with moral questions and those that impart values indirectly. This effort should provide a useful perspective from which to consider the philosophical questions about what moral education should be and how it should be provided.

MORAL EDUCATION AND PUBLIC SCHOOLING

B. Edward McClellan

The stable communities of eighteenth-century America educated their young slowly, almost casually. In this world, where children were expected to remain in the towns of their birth and where fathers still held power to affect the wealth and status of sons, no sense of urgency required that moral education be accomplished early or quickly. Nor was there need to apportion precise institutional responsibilities for moral training. Children learned from families, churches, schools, and other agencies in an almost infinite variety of patterns. Sometimes they acquired their values informally—from older brothers and sisters, from neighbors, from the rhythms of community life itself; sometimes, they spent long periods in formal educational settings. But, always, they learned in ways that combined the formal and informal as particular circumstances rather than general principles dictated. In this fluid, flexible system, no one pattern of moral education set a standard by which others could be judged. No scheme of stages measured its progress or directed its pace. No age defined the time in which it had to be accomplished.[1]

It was the disappearance of eighteenth-century stability and the collapse of its methods of moral education that formed the context for the emergence of the public school system in the middle decades of the nineteenth century. The erosion of the old patterns began in the last years of the eighteenth century and the early decades of the nineteenth, when a surge of geographical mobility dramatically transformed the character of American life. Encouraged by an end to restrictions on westward movement, by the growing ease of transportation, and by a blossoming urban prosperity, increasing numbers of Americans abandoned the stability of familiar towns to strike out for new territories. Searching for wealth, freedom from old restrictions, or simply for the thrill of movement itself, they marched in endless streams from east to west, from town to town, from

This paper appeared in a modified form in *Viewpoints*, Vol. 51, No. 6 (November, 1975), pp. 1–15.

village to city. As they moved, they shattered the traditional stability of community life and destroyed the familiar patterns of moral education. In this new, freewheeling society, where children often left their homes at the brink of adulthood, communities lost the capacity to train their young slowly. Now, if values were to be taught and behavior shaped, the task had to be accomplished well before the child could move beyond the protective environment of his home community into a world of strange people, restless activity, and alluring evils.

As Americans began to prepare their sons and daughters for life away from home, moral education acquired a quality of definition it had never had in the eighteenth century. The most obvious dimension of that definition was time. Once a task that extended well into adulthood, perhaps even to the end of life itself, now moral education assumed the temporal limits of childhood. "The germs of morality," wrote Horace Mann, "must be planted in the moral nature of children, at an early period of their life."[2] To fail in those critical years was to miss an opportunity unlikely to be recaptured except in the extraordinary environment of the penitentiary, the reformatory, or the asylum. To succeed, on the other hand, was to prepare the child for a whole lifetime of virtue, to make him like "those oaks" that "preserve their foliage fresh and green, through seasons of fiery drought, when all surrounding vegetation is scorched to a cinder."[3] Combining a faith in the malleability of the child with a pessimism about the reformability of adults, nineteenth-century Americans simply assumed that the alteration of early habits—good or bad—was "as little probable as that 'the Ethiopian should change his skin, or the leopard his spots.' "[4]

By imposing narrow temporal limits on moral education, Americans forced a sharpening of the lines of institutional responsibility as well. No longer could society afford the variegated patterns and informal methods of a more casual era. A process so compressed by time required the intense, specialized efforts of designated agencies. Accordingly, nineteenth-century Americans made moral education the special responsibility of the family and the school, the two institutions most adaptable to the need for offering intensive training to young children. "The most dangerous transition in a youth's life," declared one educator,

> is that which carries him from the authoritative control of the family and the school to the responsibility of untried liberty. The shores of this perilous strait of human life are strewn with wrecked manhood.
>
> The home-life and the school-life of the child should prepare him for this transition to freedom by effective training in self-control and self-guidance, and, to this end, the will must be disciplined by an increasing use of motives that quicken the sense of right and make the conscience regal.[5]

Beyond the efforts of these two agencies, men found few institutional resources to guard against the ever-present temptations of an unstable world.

Consequently, they placed extraordinary demands on both family and school and, in the process, profoundly altered the institutional context of moral education.

By all standards, primary responsibility rested with the family. "Having ordained that man should receive his character from education," proclaimed one parents' guide of the 1830s,

> it was ordained that early instruction should exert a decisive influence on character, and that during this important period of existence, children should be subject to the change of their parents.[6]

Within the family itself, the mother was usually expected to act as the chief agent of moral training.[7] "By the plan of creation and the providence of God," declared Dr. Donald Drake, a Cincinnati physician and popular speaker on domestic education, "it is the peculiar duty of the mother, to watch over her child for many of the first years of its life; and on her more than the father rests the responsibility."[8] In the mother's hands, warned Samuel Goodrich, author of childrens' literature and parents' manuals, lay the greatest power for shaping the character of the child:

> You have a child on your knee. Listen a moment. Do you know what that child is? It is an immortal being; destined to live forever! It is destined to be happy or miserable! And who is to make it happy or miserable? You—the mother! You, who gave it birth, the mother of its body, are also the mother of its soul for good or ill. Its character is yet undecided; its destiny is placed in your hands.[9]

At a time when early moral education seemed to hold the only key to the perpetuation of virtue, no one was more clearly identified with the critical task than the mother.

If the family bore primary responsibility for moral education, however, it shared a significant part of its burden with the school. In fact, the school's role in moral training grew at roughly the same pace as the family's. Once, schooling had played only a marginal part in training the society's young; now, men assigned it vast new duties, gave it the support of public funds, and made it into a significant instrument of moral education. As its responsibilities grew, the school acquired a distinct and important place in an increasingly standardized pattern of childhood education. In the eighteenth century, the school had served a relatively small clientele who often stretched an elementary education over ten to fifteen years; now, it was expected to serve masses of students and provide them with an early, systematic, and intensive training.[10]

As an institution that both supplemented the efforts of the family and served the interests of the state, the public school of the nineteenth century was expected to perform a variety of functions. Because it brought children of all social stations into the same classroom, for example, many men saw it as a powerful democratizing force. Others expected it to erect barriers against social disorder, to promote national cohesion, or to encourage commerce and industry. At the core of all of its tasks, however, lay moral education, for even when men defined the goals of public schooling in political or economic terms, they invariably accepted moral education as the proper means to achieve their ends. In this society so free of traditional institutional restraints, moral training seemed equally important to the creation of the diligent worker, the responsible citizen, and the virtuous man. Thus, conceptions of private morality and good citizenship simply merged in the nineteenth-century mind. "There is the simple but momentous syllogism," declared one educator.

> Free schools are for good citizenship, and good citizenship demands the fullness of manhood. Therefore, to culture youths in the fullness of manhood is the express object of free schools.[11]

Nothing revealed the centrality of moral education to the public school enterprise so clearly as the overwhelming preference for women teachers. Women were the acknowledged experts in moral training in the nineteenth century, and Americans insisted that, when possible, they teach the early grades of public schooling. "A great part already, and it is hoped that a greater part hereafter, of the business of instruction in schools," declared Boston educator George B. Emerson, "must be performed by females. Everything indicates the natural adaptation of the female character to this vocation."[12] What qualified particular women for teaching positions was their character and reputation rather than any special training or even their general level of education. Although school leaders constantly tried to upgrade the pedagogical skills of teachers, even tough-minded reformers were willing to forgive a woman "her ignorance of syntax and low level of scholarship" if she had "common sense and a good heart."[13]

Aside from serving as a proper moral model, the central task of the teacher was to insure good behavior in the classroom and thereby encourage the early development of the habits essential to the virtuous life. "The first requisite of the school is order," declared William T. Harris:

> each pupil must be taught to conform his behavior to the general standard, and repress all that interferes with the function of the school. In the outset, therefore, a whole family of virtues are taught the pupil, and taught them so thoroughly that they become fixed in his character.[14]

Following the rules of faculty psychology and the logic of the Protestant ethic, teachers rewarded regularity, punctuality, self-restraint, industry, and respect for others and punished slovenliness, inattention, and disorderly behavior. Where the right faculties and good habits could be "drawn forth" by kindness and gentle encouragement, educators typically favored such an approach; but where the rod seemed in order they were rarely reluctant to resort to it.[15]

As teachers worked to shape the proper habits, textbooks taught the simple rules of nineteenth-century morality. Early exercises emphasized "carefully chosen maxims and selections" meant to be "committed to memory and deeply engraved by frequent repetition." It was these simple sayings, educators hoped, that would forever form the "points of attachment around which the experiences of life crystallize." Beyond such elementary rules, students learned of the alluring disguises of temptation and the dangers of straying from the path of virtue by reading ever more complicated "stories selected for the lesson they teach and talked over in such a way to develop the moral judgment in applying familiar principles."[16]

The values themselves were a blend of traditional Protestant morality and nineteenth-century conceptions of good citizenship. Textbooks taught "love of country, love of God, duty to parents, the necessity to develop habits of thrift, honesty, and hard work in order to accumulate property, the certainty of progress [and] the perfection of the United States."[17] Famous spellers and readers, like those of Noah Webster and William Holmes McGuffey, warned ominously of the dangers of drunkeness, luxury, self-pride, and deception and promised handsome earthly rewards for courage, honesty, truthfulness, and "cheerful submission to lawful authority."[18] From every facet of their training, children learned that failure followed inevitably from wickedness and that worthwhile achievements came only from "a good conscience, a proper use of opportunities and a firm belief that God will help those who bravely strive to do their duty."[19]

Although most of these values had been familiar to generations of Protestants, nineteenth-century Americans gave their morality a peculiarly rigid quality. Lacking the informal corrective processes of a stable community life, they attempted to implant absolute rules as inflexible guides to behavior. In a world so free of external restraints, they simply assumed that only an internalized set of rules could guarantee individual virtue and social safety. The goal of moral education in this context was

> to build up a partition wall—a barrier—so thick and high, between the principles of right and wrong, in the minds of men, that the future citizens will not overleap or break through it. A truly conscientious man, whatever may be his desire, his temptation, his appetite, the moment he approaches the boundary line which separates right from wrong, beholds an obstruction—a barrier—more impassable than a Chinese wall. He could sooner leap the ocean, than transgress it.[20]

Always afraid that the slightest deviation from the society's norms might lead to a whole pattern of wickedness, nineteenth-century Americans left no grey areas in their moral training, no room for interpretation, no flexibility to apply values as shifting contingencies might dictate. Only absolute rules rigidly adhered to, they believed, could protect against the enormous temptations of the day.

The character of life in nineteenth-century America rarely challenged the reliability of rigid moal rules or the easy equation of virtue with reward. The relative simplicity of social organization allowed men to operate in the various spheres of community life without any significant sense of ethical disjunction; every area of daily endavor—the home, the school, the church, the job—rewarded the familiar virtues in roughly similar proportions. Although a persistent mobility led nineteenth-century Americans to make frequent economic and social adjustments, it seldom required equivalent moral accommodations. As long as men stayed within certain ethnic and religious boundaries, they could move from community to community, even from rural village to urban neighborhood, without ever altering their conceptions of right and wrong. Moreover, since movement often carried men up the social ladder as well as across territory, it was only natural to assume that virtue usually achieved its appropriate material reward.

With the emergence of a complex corporate and bureaucratic society in the first quarter of the twentieth century, however, the simple equations of nineteenth-century morality began to make less and less sense to a growing number of Americans. The first to challenge the relevance of the old values were those who benefited most from the new scheme of things, men whose wealth, influence, prestige, or independence had grown in the greatest proportions. The vast majority of these men stood at the top of the new order, often organized into prestigious and powerful professional groups; among them were doctors, lawyers, college professors, school administrators, labor leaders, business executives, engineers, and the like. In a variety of important ways, these men experienced a world very different from the community life of nineteenth-century America. From their place in the vanguard of change, they dealt with a society in an apparent state of perpetual and fundamental transformation. What they encountered was not simply the ceaseless activity of geographical mobility, but technological and social change of such a magnitude that it seemed to require constant reevaluation of the rules of human conduct.

While this new pattern of change challenged traditional assumptions about the permanence of values, a sharp division of life by function destroyed an older sense of wholeness. Now, as men moved from one sphere of activity to another, they encountered in each place a different set of rules.[21] At work, for example, they expected to interact smoothly, almost mechanically, in a basically impersonal setting. There, they were judged by their efficiency rather than their reputations and rewarded for competence rather than character. At home, on the other hand, close personal relationships and intense emotional involvements required an entirely different set of expectations and rewards.[22] To be a father, a professional, a community leader, and a consumer in this new world meant to act in four different spheres and to perform each function by separate rules.

From the experience of these corporate elites and newly conscious professional groups emerged a new approach to the meaning of virtue and the process of moral education. Among the first to articulate that approach were many of America's most prominent educational leaders, men associated with the best universities, the most influential journals, and the largest teachers' associations. Supported by a powerful constituency of America's new elites, these educators began early in the century to raise serious questions about the form and content of traditional moral training and to translate the new orientation into specific proposals for reform. Although this effort to create a new approach to moral education was only one strand of a much more general reform movement, it was always a central and clearly identifiable theme.

What distressed educational reformers most about nineteenth-century moral training was its rigidity. In a world where social patterns as well as technologies changed so rapidly, they believed, traditional rules could never serve as adequate guides to moral behavior. "Relativity must replace absolutism in the realm of morals as well as in the spheres of physics and biology," declared the *Tenth Yearbook* of the National Education Association's Department of Superintendence.

> This, of course, does not involve the denial of the principles of continuity in human affairs. Nor does it mean that each generation must repudiate the system of values of its predecessor. It does mean, however, that no such system is permanent; that it will have to change and grow in response to experience. The day of authoritarianism, in the historical sense, is past.[23]

Modern man, observed the reformers, needed the capacity to move easily from today's challenge to tomorow's, from one sphere of activity to another, and to observe in each circumstance a different set of rules. No single code of absolutes could possibly equip the child for a life that called for such adaptability. Instead, a world of complexity required a conception of virtue that allowed men to respond flexibly to a variety of enormously different situations. "Character education," declared the *Tenth Yearbook,*

> consists of constructive reactions to life situations without thought on the part of the individual as to whether his reaction in a particular situation is one calculated to bring about his own self-improvement.[24]

If the school were to prepare its students to live ethically in the fractured world of modern America, thought the reformers, it would have to do more than offer a new, updated set of rules; it would have to both teach a method for making moral judgments and cultivate an ethical sense, an "ability to know what is right in any given situation."[25]

A conception of virtue that emphasized flexible response to changing contingencies required a standard by which to judge the moral act, and, in the scheme proposed by twentieth-century reformers, that standard was social consequence. In the nineteenth century, men had measured their actions against rules sanctioned by religion and tradition and firmly implanted in highly developed and rigid superegos. Moreover, nineteenth-century Americans had lived in a world predictable enough to allow them to assume that context rarely altered the consequence of an action. But, in the twentieth century, with its tight spheres of specialized functions, men knew that similar actions often had strikingly different effects. To apply the rules of the corporation to the process of child rearing, for example, was to commit an unpardonable cruelty. In such a world, argued the reformers, the ethical life required the careful exercise of a moral imagination, an "ability to picture vividly the good or evil consequences to self and to others of any type of behavior." [26]

In place of the simple moral arithmetic students had learned in nineteenth-century schools, reformers now proposed to teach an elaborate calculus of social consequence. To accomplish the task, they envisioned an education that stretched beyond the years of early childhood well into late adolescence. Moral judgment, they believed, required a subtle and extended training carefully calibrated to correspond to the slow, natural stages of psychological development. In addition, reformers assumed that the burden of the new moral education would rest primarily with the school. Although parents could still teach the habits and values of family life itself, only the school, they believed, had the resources to prepare children for life beyond the home.

The complex processes of the new moral education required a far more sophisticated method than the drill and repetition of nineteenth-century indoctrination. If the school were to prepare children to respond flexibly and ethically to the contingencies of a fractured and ever-changing world, reformers argued, it would have to guide its students through a variety of intricate problems and social situations designed to present moral dilemmas and evoke ethical responses. The focus for such modern moral training could never be "some traits to be expressed, some rules of conduct, some ideal of truth or beauty." Instead, the

> center of attention is to be the situation. The need for character is all bound up in the event itself. It is tangible and concrete and real. It cannot be escaped or relegated to copy books. Life is one situation after another, and each situation has possibilities of richer and poorer living, of greater or less integration of values. [27]

In the classroom, teachers would have to employ a whole variety of new techniques to develop the capacity for moral judgment. "The cultivation of the child's moral imagination" required

story-telling, socialized discussions, including debates; directed study; drama-
tization; excursions; laboratory and library technics; testing and mastery exercises; the management of routine details; and teaching through projects.[28]

Outside the classroom, schools would have to construct still other arenas
for learning—athletic contests, student governments, social clubs, and the
like. By placing the child in such a variety of social environments, reformers hoped to accomplish a complex moral apprenticing that would
prepare students for the peculiar problems of life in the modern world.

At its highest level of abstraction, the reform conception of moral education appeared to offer only a new, rational technique for making ethical
decisions without reference to a roster of fixed rules or desirable character
traits. In its specific details, however, the new scheme was primarily a program for socializing students in the habits and values of elite life in corporate America. Socialization, to be sure, was a far more subtle process
than indoctrination, but it came no closer to the ideal of moral autonomy,
as some of its proponents claimed. Instead, the new approach simply used
a different method to teach a different, more modern set of values. If it no
longer employed the rigid standards of nineteenth-century morality, it nevertheless had its own list of desirable traits—e.g., efficiency, industry, respect for expertise, adaptability, and cooperativeness—and it emphasized
them with the same consistency that an earlier approach had stressed the
value of sobriety.[29]

Since the new moral education taught precisely the traits that made for
success in elite and professional circles, it quickly gained the support of the
most powerful and influential elements in Americans society. Yet, it won
ground in the schools only gradually and unevenly and never entirely
supplanted the older scheme. To the surprise of many of its strongest proponents, the new approach was met with indifference or hostility by a large
number of Americans, especially those who lived at the margins of the new
corporate system or who operated at its lowest levels. To the factory la-
borer, for example, the old meaning of character and the rigid disciplines of
the nineteenth-century classroom often made more sense than the more
socialized situations designed to prepare for a world of work where men
could expect to make significant choices.[30] To many religious fun-
damentalists, country-dwellers, and others, the new moral education
seemed not only irrelevant but actually threatening, an attempt on the part
of a manipulative elite to substitute scientific-rationalism for religion, to destroy the fundamental values that had given meaning to their lives, or to
deprive them of their only psychic rewards in a world that also denied
them a decent measure of power, status, and independence.

Most supporters of the new approach to moral education dismissed such
resistance to their reform as the lingering effects of ignorance and supersti-
tion. In a variety of minor ways, however, some of them have condoned a

differential moral training that continued to teach traditional values to those outside elite circles. It was not uncommon, for example, for elites to sanction compensatory education programs that used the techniques of radical behaviorism—techniques almost identical to those suggested by faculty psychology—to teach the same rigid habits that nineteenth-century schools had so strongly emphasized. Acting either out of a conviction that the old training made better laborers or on the assumption that some people were simply not equipped for a more advanced morality, these men—perhaps unknowingly—contributed to the failure of their own reform. Yet, despite their complicity, resistance to the new approach was primarily a genuine expression of the disaffected groups themselves. It was these groups that did most to preserve traditional moral education and who most consistently opposed the imposition of the new patterns on their children.

Since the early twentieth century, tension between the reformers and the defenders of tradition has periodically erupted into bitter public controversy. For the most part, the battles have been fought in countless local school districts, with defenders of more traditional training usually resisting the incursion of reformist programs. In Dayton, Tennessee; Kanawha County, West Virginia; and thousands of less celebrated localities, new doctrines, new procedures, and new textbooks have precipitated some of the stormiest confrontations in the history of American local politics. On occasion, the issues have occupied a national stage as well. Court decisions limiting prayer and Bible-reading in the schools, for example, have led to vigorous, though unsuccessful, national movements to amend the Constitution and restore "God-given moral absolutes" to the classroom.[31]

Despite such highly charged encounters, however, Americans have usually been able to contain the conflict by requiring schools to offer something to all sides in the dispute. The organizational patterns of the twentieth-century school, to be sure, have strongly favored the reform approach. Schools have, in fact, employed all manner of new teaching techniques, added extra-curricular activities, confronted students with complexity, and subjected them to the impersonal rules of a bureaucratic institution. Yet, at the same time, most of them have reserved a place in their programs for the old character education, and, in many states, legislation has actually required special courses in morality. In his 1929 survey of New York schools, J. Cayce Morrison found some form of traditional moral education in virtually every classroom.[32] And, despite the best efforts of reformers since that time, subsequent studies throughout the century have confirmed the persistence of the pattern he found.[33]

What has emerged from this history of conflict and accommodation is a public schooling that allows different schemes to exist side-by-side in a patchwork that makes sense only when viewed as the political and social compromise that it is. Ironically, the very tensions that have prevented schools from adopting a single, integrated approach to moral training might have had an enormously liberating impact on public education. Had educators been allowed to take the issues of the conflict itself into the classroom, they might finally have made the public school an arena for the open and critical discussion of moral questions, a necessary if not sufficient condition for a rational moral education. Instead, as opposing camps shouted slogans at each other outside the schools, administrators kept a sterile peace inside, fulfilling their duties to a grateful public by placing the need for social peace above the quest for a moral training that would go beyond both indoctrination and socialization and attempt to educate autonomous and rational moral men.

NOTES

1. An overview of this scope requires a special kind of acknowledgement. My approach to the topic has been heavily influenced by Robert H. Wiebe, "The School as an Agency of Culture," unpublished address to the Midwest History of Education Society, 1971; Robert H. Wiebe, *The Segmented Society* (New York: Oxford U.P., 1975); and Solon T. Kimball and James E. McClellan, Jr., *Education and the New America* (New York: Random, 1962).

2. Horace Mann, untitled editorial remarks, *The Common School Journal,* **1** (November 1838), 14.

3. Ibid.

4. T. J. Biggs, "Lecture on Domestic Education," *Transactions of the Fifth Annual Meeting of the Western Literary Institute and College of Professional Teachers, 1835* (Cincinnati, The Executive Committee, 1836), p. 52.

5. Emerson E. White, "Moral Training in the Public School," *The Journal of Proceedings and Addresses of the National Education Association, 1886* (New York: N.E.A., 1887), p. 131.

6. Samuel G. Goodrich, *Fireside Education* (New York: F. J. Huntington, 1838), p. 72.

7. The significance of the mother's new role was suggested by Wiebe, "The School as an Agency of Culture." See also Stanley K. Schultz, *The Culture Factory: Boston Public Schools, 1789–1896* (New York: Oxford U.P., 1973), pp. 50–52; Anne L. Kuhn, *The Mother's Role in Childhood Education: New England Concepts, 1830–1860* (New Haven: Yale U.P., 1947).

8. Daniel Drake, "Discourse on the Philosophy of Family, School and College Discipline," *Western Literary Institute Transactions, 1834* (Cincinnati: Josiah Drake, 1835), p. 47.

9. Goodrich, op. cit., p. 169.

10. For an excellent account of the old patterns, see Warren Burton, *The District School As It Was, Scenery Showing, and Other Writings* (Boston: T. R. Marvin, 1852), pp. 2–152.

11. Harry F. Harrington, "What Should Be the Leading Object of American Free Schools?" *NEA Proceedings, 1873* (Peoria, Ill.: N.E.A., 1873), p. 222.

12. George B. Emerson, "On the Education of Females," *The Introductory Discourse and the Lectures Delivered Before The American Institute of Instruction, 1831* (Boston: Hilliard, Gray, Little, and Wilkins, 1832), p. 28.

13. Eli Tappan, "Examination of Teachers," *NEA Proceedings, 1883* (Boston: N.E.A., 1884), pp. 7–8.

14. William T. Harris, "Moral Education in the Common Schools," *All Lectures, 1884* (Boston: Willard Small, 1884), pp. 33–34.

15. National Council of Education, "Report of the Committee on Elementary Education," *NEA Proceedings, 1886* (New York: N.E.A., 1887), p. 268.

16. J. W. Stearns, "The Public Schools and Morality," *NEA Proceedings, 1885* (New York: N.E.A., 1886), p. 89.

17. Ruth M. Elson, *Guardians of Tradition: American Schoolbooks of the Nineteenth Century* (Lincoln, Neb.: U. of Neb., 1964), p. 338.

18. Frederick A. Packard, *The Daily Public School in the United States* (Philadelphia: Lippincott, 1866), p. 19, 34. See also Robert H. Wiebe, "The Social Functions of Public Education," *American Quarterly*, **XXI** (Summer 1969), 150; Roscoe L. West, *Elementary Education in New Jersey: A History* (Princeton: Van Nostrand, 1964), p. 72.

19. Samuel W. Burnside, "On the Classification of Schools," *All Lectures, 1833,* (Boston: Carter, Hendee and Co., 1834), p. 74.

20. Mann, untitled editorial remarks, p. 49.

21. For a brilliant treatment of the division of life by function, see Wiebe, *The Segmented Society,* pp. 24 ff.

22. See Kimball and McClellan, op. cit., chap. 2.

23. National Education Association, Department of Superintendence, *Tenth Yearbook: Character Education* (Washington, D.C.: N.E.A., Dept. of Superintendence, 1932), p. 11. This yearbook was the Report of a Commission on Character Education.

24. Ibid.

25. National Education Association, *Report of the Committee on Character Education,* U.S. Bureau of Education, *Bulletin,* No. 7 (Washington, D.C.: G.P.O., 1926), p. 1.

26. Ibid.

27. NEA, *Tenth Yearbook,* p. 57.

28. Ibid., p. 202.

29. See Wiebe, "Social Functions of Public Education," p. 158; John R. Seeley et. al., *Crestwood Heights: A Study of the Culture of Suburban Life* (New York: Basic, 1956).

30. For an excellent treatment of the attitudes of laborers see Samuel Bowles, "Unequal Education and the Reproduction of the Social Division of Labor," in Martin Carnoy (ed.), *Schooling in a Corporate Society: The Political Economy of Education in America* (New York: McKay, 1972), pp. 36–64.

31. The words are those of Alice Moore, a member of the Kanawha Valley School Board and a defender of the old approach to moral education. See *Christian Crusade Weekly*, **XXV** (March 30, 1975), 1, 4.

32. J. Cayce Morrison, *Character Building in New York Public Schools: An Analysis of Practices Reported by Teachers and Supervisory Officers for the School Year, 1928–1929.* (Albany: State U. of N.Y., 1933).

33. See, for example, Henry Lester Smith, *Character Education: A Survey of Practice in the Public Schools of the United States* (Texarkana, Arkansas-Tex.: Palmer Foundation, 1950).

AMERICA AND THE CATHOLIC SCHOOL

Neil G. McCluskey

VI

Catholics in America were caught up in a painful dilemma. They were as eager to send their children to school as their Protestant neighbors, but in good conscience, they could not. Literacy, knowledge, skills—these were the steps to the full sharing of all that was the American dream. But the common schools had not been designed with Roman Catholic children in mind. These schools, for whose support Catholics were taxed, smacked strongly of Protestantism, with their Protestant books, hymns, prayers, and, above all, their Protestant Bible. Catholics sought to alleviate their plight in two ways. They asked that Catholic youngsters be excused from classroom reading of the Protestant Bible and similar devotional practices and that school taxes paid by Catholics be used to educate their children in church schools.

In the matter of Bible reading, Catholics found no legal redress. On the contrary, strong legal support for the religious status quo in the public schools was supplied by an 1854 ruling of the Maine Supreme Court (*Donahue* v. *Richards*), permitting school officials to require the reading of the King James version of the Bible, a precedent which was not successfully challenged until near the close of the century.

The effort by Catholics to obtain a share of the tax money collected for the schools likewise failed. Their brief was set forth with dignity and clarity by the New York Catholics in 1840. Speaking for the entire Catholic community, the spokesmen informed the Board of Aldermen that as Catholics:

> They bear, and are willing to bear, their portion of every common burden;
> and feel themselves entitled to a participation in every common benefit.

Reprinted by the permission of the publisher from pp. 12–25 of "America and the Catholic School" in *Catholic Education in America: A Documentary History* (New York: Teachers College, Columbia University, 1964).

This participation, they regret to say, has been denied them for years back, in reference to Common School Education in the city of New York, except on conditions with which their conscience, and, as they believe their duty to God, did not, and do not leave them at liberty to comply.[1]

One result of this Catholic agitation was that New York City's common schools were shortly taken over by the State from the private group calling itself the Public School Society. Yet this was no solution to the root problem of parental freedom of choice in education. The move was, however, a large step toward the inevitable secularization of the schools. The pattern of no funds for denominationally controlled schools was set—and has endured, with minor exceptions, down to the present day.

The great Protestant majority was easily persuaded that Catholic efforts to eliminate the Protestant Bible from the schools and to get public money for their own schools represented a concerted attack on the foundations of the republic. It was simply taken for granted that the Bible and the flag symbolized America and that an attack on one was an assault on the other. Since nativism looked to Protestant Christianity as the source and guarantee of its moral influence, it was easy enough to turn Catholic efforts for accommodation in the area of education into an occasion for a crusade.[2]

The voices of the moderates from either side who were willing to discuss compromises were quickly drowned out. Bigots and extremists—at times on the Catholic side, too—carried the day. The 1830's saw the burning of the Charleston Convent and Maria Monk's "Awful Disclosures." In the 1850's, there were the Philadelphia riots, the demonstrations during the tour of the pope's representative, Archbishop Bedini, the tarring and feathering of the Jesuit John Bapst, the Massachusetts law for the inspection of the convents of nuns, and the riots and bloodshed of Louisville's "Bloody Monday." The Civil War broke up the politically powerful Know-Nothing movement, but the forces of nativism banded together again in the 1880's to form the American Protective Association.

This is the dark side of the story of the public school movement and reflects little credit on the land of religious liberty.[3] In fairness, however, as Orestes A. Brownson tried to explain to his fellow Catholics, Protestant antipathy toward things Catholic was a complex matter.[4] With the arrival on American shores of hundreds of thousands of Irish and German Catholics, the name "Catholic" began to conjure up much more than simply a religious affiliation. These people were not just Catholics, but foreigners with a different look and a strange accent to them. Their cheap labor flooding the market posed an economic threat. They were people of the ghetto, the slum, and the saloon. When they refused to patronize the common schools and set up separate institutions for their children, sometimes schools where a foreign tongue was the principal language (as in the case of the German schools), perceptive Protestants saw them as a menace to the American way.[5]

VII

But the Protestants of the nation had—and have—their own dilemma to face. In opposing Catholic influence in the public schools, they were forced to stand by and watch helplessly, as all religious influence disappeared and a totally secular philosophy moved in. Traditionally, the American people have come to look upon the schools as the most efficient means of transmitting to children the public philosophy which undergirds our society. They have insisted that the school assume a proper responsibility for developing the child's character or, to phrase it for the modern ear, for inculcating moral and spiritual values. But the history of the public school has made it plain that this mandate, however feasible in the past, is impossible to discharge any longer. The common school is assigned a responsibility for character education, but whatever Christian consensus formerly existed as to the nature of this chore has long since disappeared.

In the 1840's, it was relatively easy: character formation was based upon the morality and inspiration of the Christian Bible. In teaching religion the public school was not to favor any one sect in the community but to inculcate the generally agreed upon moral and religious truths of all Protestants, as given in the Bible. This compromise was originally intended to safeguard the rights of conscience and the constitutional exercise of religious freedom by individuals, as well as to protect the equal position of the Protestant churches and sects in the common schools. There was no question of a philosophy of education hostile to religious teaching as such.

In the mid-nineteenth century, however, important figures in the educational world began to argue with success that by its very nature the school is completely secular and hence incompetent to enter the sphere of religious education. This position was not dictated by hostility toward religion or religious education; it was rather concerned with the most appropriate occasion for efficient instruction in religion and with safeguarding the rights of private conscience. (In effect, this position also provided a logical basis for denying a share of public funds to religious schools.) In method, spirit, and content, it was urged, secular truth is necessarily antagonistic to the acquisition of religious truth, to the extent that the two cannot be taught under the same roof. Moreover, those who argued this position frankly acknowledged the religious fragmentation of society. Thus, Bishop Spalding could say: "I am willing to assume and to accept as a fact that our theological differences make it impossible to introduce the teaching of any religious creed into the public school. I take the system as it is,—that is, as a system of secular education. . . ."[6]

The current understanding of "secular," however, is vastly different from its meaning for the men of Bishop Spalding's day. Until quite recent years, moral and spiritual values were universally assumed to be rooted in some kind of religious value system. Despite sectarian differences, American leadership could count on general acceptance of a theistically based natural law, upon which was reared the unity of what men considered a "Christian" nation. This included belief in the existence of a Creator, who was the source of the justice and the rights defined in the nation's first great political documents.

The naturalist philosophy of scientific humanism propounded in this century by John Dewey and others has had much to do with emptying the concept of "secular" of its theistic-natural law content. Dewey advanced a "scientific" substitute for the traditional concept of religion, which he judged would be more in keeping with the exigencies of modern democratic society. Since his empirical pragmatist philosophy limited reality to the natural order, no place was left for supernatural religion either within or outside the school.

Today, the ethics of total secularism or scientism have largely replaced the moral values of the Judaeo-Christian tradition as the basis for character formation in public education. It has become impossible for the schools in most areas to teach what many parents believe should be taught their children. Parents and church people have yielded step by step to the importuning of minority groups, not simply pushing to remove all religious influence from the schools, but working to erect the kind of legal "wall" between the churches and the state school that would make it impossible for church groups to collaborate in any way with the public schools.

To assert this is not to ignore the central problem, namely, the limitations inherent in the idea of one *common* school serving a religiously pluralistic society. The coexistence within the same society of groups holding fundamentally different views regarding the nature and destiny of man has made for an impasse in the approach to the moral side of education. For in the final analysis, moral and spiritual values are built upon what men hold as ultimate or supreme in life. Obviously, it is only in an ideal society, wherein men agree freely and completely about ultimate values, that a common approach to the moral side of education can be readily found.

For a long period in our history, there was some basis for a general agreement on values and their sanctions. The Old World legacy of Greco-Roman natural law and of the central religious concepts of the Judaeo-Christian tradition was almost universally accepted and was widely operative in American society. There was agreement on what constitutes the basis and general content of a Christian philosophy of character education, despite quarrels over the version of the Bible upon which this should be based. However, the fragmentation of the Protestant churches multiplied differences over dogma both among Protestants themselves and with the Catholics, whose increasing numbers each decade gave them a louder voice. Non-European religious groups established themselves. New groups arose whose ultimates derived from a secular and humanistic rather than a Christian tradition. All these factors entered into the historical process which has resulted in the official secularization of large sectors of American public education.

VIII

The compromise approach of Horace Mann contained the principle of its own dissolution. The precious little common ground that once existed among Unitarians, Methodists, Congregationalists, Catholics, Jews, and deists gradually eroded. The positive doctrinal elements regarding church organization, sacraments, and the mission of Christ had to be strained out of the common-school religion piece by piece to avoid offending dissenters. Such a process of attrition inevitably worked to the advantage of groups holding a minimum of positive doctrine or none at all. A blandly Christian flavor that contented Unitarians could only dismay Congregationalists and Episcopalians. The soup in time got so thin that it pleased no palate. Belief in God, the Golden Rule, and the Bible were all that long survived this process of disintegration.

When the Bible in the classroom became an object of contention between Protestants and Catholics, and later between Christians and non-Christians, the courts banned Bible-reading in eight states. The 1963 ruling of the United States Supreme Court has stopped the practice in thirteen other states, where it was required, and in twenty-five more, where it was permitted. In recent years, public school exercises formally expressing belief in God have also been under steady attack. The *Engel* v. *Vitale* decision of the same tribunal in 1962 ended the optional recitation of a privately composed prayer in New York State. Yet the process of total secularization of the common school has been a consistent one—the working out of an inner logic whose final outcome is not yet in view. In some measure due to Catholic intransigence, the compromise idea that began life so hopefully in the 1840's has become bankrupt. America's public schools are no longer either Protestant or Christian. They are no longer religiously oriented. They are officially secular.

Faced with the ultimate question of whether religion is the starting point and essence of true education, the public school has had to adopt a theoretical neutrality between those who believe in the God of the Western tradition and those who do not. Yet the public school is not really neutral, for it gives an equivalent denial to the question by actually taking another starting point and aiming at another goal. What is worse, the public school, by default, facilitates the entry of a naturalist religion of democracy, or secularist cult of society, into the vacuum, so that only the child from a secularist family can feel perfectly at home in the common public schools. By default, civic or political virtue has become practically the exclusive goal of public school education. In other words, these schools exist primarily to produce good citizens. It can be granted that within a religiously divided society a common school by itself cannot easily achieve a broader goal. The point to be made here, however, is that the philosophy of public school education is being dictated by those forces in society which, wanting no other goal for it, have nearly succeeded in quarantining the public school from the churches and church-related organizations.[7]

In retrospect, it is only fair to point out that secularists are not the only ones responsible for what took place in the public schools. Sectarian bitterness and denominational jealousies greatly neutralized the influence of religion in the schools. The resulting impasse has facilitated the entry into the schools of a philosophy of moral and spiritual values completely divorced from religion, while advocates of a climate favorable to a religiously based moral and spiritual program in the public schools have been able to glorify the ideal of the uncommitted mind and the uncommitted conscience, or that vaguest of all ideas—humanitarianism. As a result, the American public school is now unable or unwilling to take a stand on, or perhaps even to confront, the central questions regarding the meaning of man: his origin, his purpose, his destiny. Even with all the good will in the world, public school teachers are less and less free, not simply to answer, but often even to ask, the great questions about God, conscience, duty, rights, and the future life.

IX

The central problem, we repeat, is the contradiction inherent in the very idea of one common school attempting to serve a religiously pluralistic society. Correlative to this problem has always been the place of the independent, church-related school in the total scheme of things. There are those who resent the growth of the Catholic school and regard it as a threat to the public school. When they oppose any kind of public support for Catholic schools, they have recourse to that argument which calls parochial school education "divisive" or "un-American" or "undemocratic." In reality, the opposition is not to the support of these schools but to their very existence. At times, these opponents of Catholic education have used the word "boycott" to stigmatize the choice Catholic parents freely make between the public school and the Catholic school. Their initial assumption is that the state-established secular school has some claim on the primary allegiance of all citizens. In their book any citizen who, compelled by conscience, chooses to exercise his natural right to patronize his own school becomes guilty of disloyalty to a state enterprise.

Yet this attitude bespeaks a strange reversal of values honored in both the Judaeo-Christian and the American traditions. There is a primacy of spiritual values over the purely secular, and consequently there is a priority of choice in education, which is part of the religious freedom of parents. This is the oft-recurring theme of the pastoral letters of the American bishops.

One of the most complete statements of the entire philosophy of Catholic education is found in the encyclical letter of Pope Pius XI, "The Christian Education of Youth" (*Divini Illus Magistri*).[8] The starting point in the Catholic idea of education is the reality of the supernatural as revealed through, and in the person of, Jesus Christ the Saviour. The Catholic belief that man is a creature of God destined to share in the divine life answers the two questions upon which every philosophy of education is built: What is man? What is his purpose? This sharing in the divine life begins at the moment of baptism, when sanctifying grace and the virtues of faith, hope, and charity—man's supernatural faculties, as it were—are infused into his soul. That life, which begins on earth through faith, is perfected in a beatific union with God in glory hereafter. For a believer, this truth is not only the ultimate purpose and final objective of education; it is the theological integrating principle, the philosophical guide, and the basis of sanctions in the moral order.

Needless to add, there are millions of American Protestants who are as deeply convinced of these truths as any Catholic. Yet they can no longer look to the public school for help in passing on to their children even as primary a truth as the existence of a personal God or the reality of the supernatural order. Ironically, the Protestant churches have been put in a position where they must side with the State against institutional religion and promote secular rather than religious values in the schools.

As American society has taken on more and more a secular orientation, certain truths of the Christian philosophy of education have been pushed unobtrusively into the background. Because the State now plays the dominant role in education, there are public school apologists and philosophers of education who operate on the assumption that the school and the school-child exist primarily for the State. They must be continually reminded that this assumption can be valid only in a totalitarian state, whether one selects the Republic of Plato or the Cuba of Castro.[9]

By way of contrast, the Catholic Church still teaches that since education is coextensive with human life itself, different agencies in society share rights and responsibilities in this broad field. For man is born into three subsocieties of the larger society: the family, civil society (including the State), and the Church. Each has distinct rights, but all should be properly ordered to ensure balance and harmony within the total educational process.

When the religious dimension in education is absent, the natural harmony of the child's formation is upset. The Sunday school approach, upon which Protestants generally have relied, has not been a conspicuous success in recent decades, any more than parallel Catholic efforts to teach formal religion outside the public school.

X

Historically, since the Catholic youngster was not made to feel at home in the public school, he went to his own school, wherever possible. After the failure of the 1840 effort to have the New York parochial schools receive public support, Catholics began to expend their interest and energy almost exclusively on Catholic parochial and private schools, leaving the public schools as semi-Protestant domain.

In the decade after the Civil War, popular education began to take hold everywhere. In 1880, public school enrollment reached 1 million for the first time, but in 1900, it soared to 15 million, and in 1920, to 21 million. Under the impetus of the school legislation passed in 1884 by the Third Plenary Council of Baltimore, Catholic school enrollment likewise began to mount. At the turn of the century, there were 854,523 pupils in Catholic schools, and by 1920, this number had more than doubled to 1.8 million. The current enrollment in Catholic schools is 5.5 million, or 14 per cent of the nation's total elementary- and secondary-school population. But this achievement has not been without a price—in more than dollars. Thoughtful leaders within the Church are calling for a reappraisal of certain traditional practices and policies, for American Catholics also confront a period of decision.

NOTES

1. See p. 66 [*Catholic Education in America: A Documentary History*].

2. In fact, the word appears in the title of the most competent study yet made of this period: Ray A. Billington, *The Protestant Crusade, 1800–1860* (New York: The Macmillan Co., 1938).

3. As the Catholic-Protestant polemic fades farther and farther away, the chances increase that more historians and fewer apologetes will turn their attention to the dreadfully neglected field of American education.

4. See pp. 115–116 [*Catholic Education in America: A Documentary History*].

5. Ireland, Gibbons and Spalding were more perspicacious here than the Germanizing bishops of the Midwest. Their idea was to "Americanize" the Church, hence proving again its catholicity. This included a reasonable acceptance of the American school as something good and worth coming to terms with. For Ireland's views, see pp. 127–150; for Spalding's, see pp. 166–174.

6. See p. 167 [*Catholic Education in America: A Documentary History*].

7. See Neil G. McCluskey, *Catholic Viewpoint on Education* (Garden City, N.Y.: Doubleday-Image, 1962), p. 53. The chapter on "The Evolution of the Secular School" discusses this problem.

8. The encyclical has been published in convenient pamphlet form by the America Press, 920 Broadway, New York, N.Y. 10010.

9. Whenever the occasion has offered itself, the United States Supreme Court has reaffirmed the American principle that "the child is not the mere creature of the State" (*Pierce* v. *Society of Sisters,* 1925) and that "the custody, care and nurture of the child reside first in the parents" (*Prince* v. *Massachusetts, 1944*). Unambiguous support for the primacy of the family right is likewise to be found in the Universal Declaration of Human Rights, proclaimed by the General Assembly of the United Nations (December 10, 1948); "Parents have a prior right to choose the kind of education that shall be given to their children" (Article 26, par. 3).

VALUES EDUCATION: SOCIOLOGICAL PERSPECTIVE

Robert Arnove

What students learn in schools is not necessarily what is taught. What is learned may be more the outcome of what students experience. What students experience may be more the result of the properties of schools as formal organizations than the explicit content of instructional programs.

What is learned in school includes not only the cognitive domain of knowledge and problem-solving skills, but the affective and conative domains of attitudes, feelings, and self-concepts. According to the Dreeben and the Bowles and Gintis articles (as well as those of Friedenberg, Michaels, and Bowles) one of the most important functions of schooling is the inculcation of norms—situationally specific prescriptions for behavior—and the imparting of values, self-definitions, and modes of working that prepare individuals to occupy roles in the economy and society. (Note that one of the principal criticisms of the Coleman and Jencks studies is that they concentrated only on the cognitive outcomes of formal education.)

In discussing socialization, the eminent sociologist Talcott Parsons distinguishes *technical* and *motivational* components. In schools, the technical component is most frequently evaluated in relation to cognitive achievement, and the motivational in relation to moral development. Both the cognitive and moral domains are considered by school authorities to be crucial to the successful socialization of youth. The moral has been variously designated as "deportment" or "responsible citizenship" and includes such attributes as "respect for teacher, consideration and cooperativeness in relation to fellow pupils, and good 'work-habits' . . . leading on to capacity for 'leadership,' and 'initiative.' "[1] (For an idea of the importance of these traits examine the elementary school report cards or grading sheets used in a school district.)

According to Parsons, cognitive and moral areas are not clearly differentiated from each other when teachers judge the achievement of elementary grade pupils:

233

> Broadly speaking, then, we may say that the "high achievers" of the elementary school are both the "bright" pupils, who catch on easily to their more strictly intellectual tasks, and the more "responsible pupils," who "behave well" and on whom the teacher can "count" in her difficult problems of managing the class.[2]

Indeed, as Parson notes, the primary challenge of the first grades of elementary school appears to be to the moral rather than the intellectual capacities of pupils.

Dreeben, who like Parsons assumes a functionalist point of view, advances the argument that perhaps the most important contribution of schooling is the imparting of norms. The norms that Dreeben singles out for analysis are independence, achievement, universalism, and specificity. The argument is functionalist in that these norms are considered by Dreeben to be critical to the successful workings of an industrial economy and a political democracy. The four norms are unlikely to be learned in families, which are characterized by the antipodal norms of dependence, ascription, particularism, and diffuseness. Structurally, schools represent an important intermediary agent between the family and the public institutions of adult life. Schools are an institution where students acquire a repertoire of essential behaviors and prescriptions for behavior. As Jules Henry has noted: "In the broader cultural context the classroom is the children's first important experience with the administrative structure of the society. It is their first contact with what is fundamentally an impersonal mechanism for getting the culture's business done."[3]

The learning of these norms is integrally related to the school as a formal organization and to the classroom as a social system. As Dreeben notes, the types of tasks, constraints, and opportunities that occur in the setting of schools shape what is learned. The following characteristics of schools are relevant to norm acquisition: the age grouping of students as cohorts; the subjection of students to continuous public assessment on the basis of what is expected of students of a certain age group in the way of achievement; the judging of students on their individual performance of specific academic tasks according to standards of excellence; and the expectation that teachers will treat students categorically but also fairly according to explicit rules. These properties are conducive to learning how to form loose, transient relationships with a variety of people; compromise and accept failure; work within formal institutions characterized by professional and bureaucratic forms of authority; accept the evaluations of others as part of one's identity; and distinguish between a role and the person who occupies the role.

The functional point of view assumes that (1) students learn the same things in schools, and (2) what is learned is beneficial to most people. The paradigm also takes as given the existing economic and political institutions of a society; the role of the school is to prepare individuals to fit into and perhaps improve these institutions. Why institutions have taken the particular forms they presently exhibit, or how institutions and the norms they stress change over time, are not explored by the functionalist paradigm.

By contrast, the conflict point of view, represented by the radical political economists Bowles and Gintis, is that institutional change is rooted in the dynamics of the means of production and the struggle for domination between social classes that emerge in different historical periods (a Marxist position). The values that are taught in school correspond to the interests of dominant groups, notably the owners of capital. As noted in the sociological introduction to Problem II, the authors represent the point of view that the content and form of instruction is class related. Socialization is differential: students from working class and minority backgrounds learn how to play subordinate roles in the society, to be docile and accepting of authority; whereas students from dominant groups learn how to assume decision-making roles that depend on internalization of rules. The authors also discuss the linkages between what is learned at home, as the result of a family's position in the hierarchy of work, and what is taught at school. The thrust of the argument is that the values that subordinate groups learn run counter to their self-interest and perpetuate a repressive social system (also see the Freire reading in Problem IV).

The arguments of both schools of thought (functionalist-consensus and radical-conflict) enhance our understanding of the workings of schools, the nature of the hidden curriculum (that is, the social relations of learning, the expectations and rules that shape instruction), and the organizational properties of schools that influence learning. Moreover, the concepts discussed by the authors in this section have relevance for an understanding of the other resolutive themes of education for community, equality of educational opportunity, and education through freedom.

NOTES

1. Talcott Parsons, "The School Class as a Social System: Some of Its Functions in American Society," *Harvard Educational Review,* **29** (Fall 1959), 303–304.

2. Ibid., p. 304.

3. Jules Henry, "Spontaneity, Initiative, and Creativity in Suburban Classrooms," *American Journal of Orthopsychiatry,* **29** (April 1959), 278.

THE CONTRIBUTION OF SCHOOLING
TO THE LEARNING OF NORMS

Robert Dreeben

This paper is concerned with the familiar phenomenon known as schooling. It departs from the usual approaches to education in that the problems of instruction and its direct outcomes are of peripheral interest. The main argument is based on the observation that schools and the classrooms within them have a characteristic pattern of organizational properties different from those of other agencies in which socialization takes place and on the contention that what children learn derives as much from the nature of their experiences in the school setting as from what they are taught.

Traditional approaches to understanding the educational process usually deal with the explicit goals of schools as expressed in curriculum content: the cognitive skills involved in reading, arithmetic, and the like; subject matter content; national tradition; vocational skills; and a multitude of good things such as citizenship, self-confidence, tolerance, patriotism, cooperation, and benevolent attitudes of various kinds. They are also concerned with pedagogy: methods of instruction considered broadly enough to include motivation and quasi-therapeutic activities as well as didactics more narrowly conceived. One indication that curriculum and pedagogy occupy a central place in educational thinking is the existence of a massive literature reporting research devoted overwhelmingly to problems in these two areas and to evaluations of instructional effectiveness in bringing about curricular outcomes.[1]

There is no question but that schools are engaged in an instructional enterprise, but the preoccupation with instruction has been accompanied by the neglect of other equally important problems. It is my contention that the traditional conception of schooling as an instructional process, primarily cognitive in nature, is at best only partially tenable. That is, what pupils

Reprinted by permission of *Harvard Educational Review* from pp. 211–237, Vol. 37, No. 2, 1967. Copyright © 1967 by President and Fellows of Harvard College.

learn is in part some function of what is taught; but what *is* learned and from what experiences remain open questions. Doubtless, the dissemination of knowledge is high on the school's agenda; but does such dissemination represent its peculiar contribution?

Instruction and knowledge, even at a high level, are made available to children outside the school: through the family, the mass media, travel, museums, libraries, and personal contacts with a variety of people. Perhaps the inconclusiveness of research designed to measure the impact of teaching on learning is attributable in part to the fact that many social agencies other than schools contribute to the acquisition of similar knowledge generally thought to fall largely within the school's jurisdiction.

Even though other agencies may resemble schools in their instructional impact, schools do have structural characteristics that distinguish them sharply from other settings—most particularly the family—contributing to the socialization of children, characteristics whose obviousness and familiarity probably account for their neglect. For example:

1. Responsibility for the control of schools and for instruction in the classroom rests in the hands of adults who are not the kinsmen of pupils.
2. Children leave the household daily to attend school but return at the close of the day; that is, they continue their active membership and participation in the family.
3. Schools are distinguished structurally according to level; despite the similarities between elementary and secondary levels, there are conspicuous differences involving:
   a. variation in the heterogeneity of the student body related to school district size;
   b. degree of differentiation of the teaching staff based upon subject matter specialization;
   c. presence or absence of formal provision for tracking pupils based largely on past academic achievement;
   d. variation in the number of pupils that each teacher confronts daily.
4. Pupils progress through school grade-by-grade at yearly intervals, each time severing associations with one set of teachers and establishing associations with a new set (unlike the family where children's relationships with parents do not follow a sequential pattern of severance and re-establishment).
5. Pupils move through school as members of age-equal cohorts (unlike the family in which the age dispersion of children is characteristically larger than that of the classroom).
6. Classrooms, like families, consist of adult and non-adult positions, but the former have a much larger non-adult membership.

Whatever pupils learn from the didactic efforts of teachers, they also learn something from their participation in a social setting some of whose structural characteristics have been briefly identified. Implicit in this statement are the following assumptions: (a) the tasks, constraints, and opportunities available within social settings vary with the structural properties of those settings; (b) individuals who participate in them derive principles of conduct based on their experiences coping with those tasks, constraints, and opportunities; and (c) the content of the principles learned varies with the nature of the setting. To the question of what is learned in school, only a hypothetical answer can be offered at this point: pupils learn to accept social norms, or principles of conduct, and to act according to them.[2]

Social Norms

The concept of social norm has long been important in sociological thinking where it has been treated primarily as a determinant, a prior condition accounting in part for some pattern of behavior: a rule, expectation, sanction, or external constraint; an internal force, obligation, conviction, or internalized standard. Given some pattern of conduct or rate of behavior, sociologists characteristically ask, among other things, whether it represents conformity to or deviation from a norm or whether it is a phenomenon emerging from a situation in which several norms operate. Comparatively little attention has been paid to the question of how norms originate in social settings and how individuals learn them.

Norms are situationally specific standards for behavior: principles, premises, or expectations indicating how individuals in specifiable circumstances *ought* to act. For example, pupils are expected to arrive at school on time. To say that they accept this norm means that: (a) there is such a standard whose existence can be determined independently of pupils' conduct (in this case, the hour they arrive at school); and (b) pupils adhere to the standard in the sense they consider that their actions should be governed by it. Acceptance, then, refers to a self-imposed, acknowledgeable obligation of variable intensity. The content of the norm must be in somebody's mind and communicable by gesture, spoken word, written rule, or sanction.

There are both logical and empirical problems in using the concept "norm."[3] First, norm and behavior must be distinguished analytically, for there is a logical circularity in inferring norms from behavior and then using them to account for variations in behavior. Second, norm acceptance and related behavior are empirically distinct; that is, there is a range of behavioral alternatives relative to any norm. Conduct varies, for example, relative both to a given norm and to prevailing conditions, and some norms explicitly acknowledge permissible variation in conduct.[4]

The Functions of Schooling

Schooling contributes to pupils' learning what the norms are, accepting them, and acting according to them; norm content, acceptance, and behavior can, however, all vary independently. This ostensibly straightforward assertion, however, conceals complexities behind obvious facts. Children leaving the household each day to attend school is an event so familiar that one tends to forget how problematic it is. Herskovits reminds us that "the significance of the distinction between 'schooling' and 'education' is to be grasped when it is pointed out that while every people must train their young, the cultures in which any substantial part of this training is carried on outside the household are few indeed."[5] The separation of schooling from the household is most characteristic of industrial societies (though not restricted to them), where economic, political, and religious institutions also tend to be independent of the family—independent, that is, in the sense that dominant principles of conduct (social norms) governing relations among kin differ from those governing the conduct of persons in non-familial institutions.

Even though the norms of family life have an important and complex relationship to conduct in non-familial settings, I am concerned here not with that relationship but with aspects of the process by which individuals learn new norms; for when other social institutions in industrial societies have replaced the family as the predominant economic, political, and religious unit and differ from it structurally, principles of conduct appropriate among kin cannot be generalized to them. Since schooling follows a period of life when children are largely dependent on kin, and precedes the period of adulthood when individuals participate as economic producers and citizens, one naturally looks to the school to discover how the addition of new principles of behavior to the psychological repertoire takes place.

Four norms have particular relevance to economic and political participation in industrial societies; those of independence, achievement, universalism, and specificity. I have selected these, not because they form an exhaustive list, but because they are central to the dominant, non-familial activities of adults in American society.[6] In school, pupils participate in activities where they are expected to act as if they were conforming to these norms whether they actually accept them at a particular time or not. Through such participation, it is my belief, pupils will in time know their content,[7] accept them as binding upon themselves, and act in accordance with them in appropriate situations. How schooling contributes to the acquisition of these norms will be discussed in the following pages.

In speaking of independence, achievement, universalism, and specificity as norms, I mean that individuals accept the obligations, respectively: to act by themselves (unless collaborative effort is called for) and accept personal responsibility and accountability for their conduct and its consequences (independence); to perform tasks actively and master the environment according to standards of excellence (achievement); and to acknowledge the right of others to treat them as members of categories often based on a few discrete characteristics rather than on the full constellation of them representing the whole person (universalism and specificity).

In one sense, full adult status, at least for men, requires occupational employment; and one of the outcomes of schooling is employability. The ability to hold a job involves not only adequate physical capacities but the appropriate psychological skills to cope with the demands of work. The requirements of job-holding are multifarious; most occupations, for example, require among other things that individuals assume personal responsibility for the completion and quality of their work and individual accountability for its shortcomings and that they perform their tasks to the best of their ability. Public life, however, extends beyond occupational employment. Although people work in their occupational capacities and in association with others (as clients, patients, customers, parishioners, students, and so on in *their* occupational capacities), they also have non-occupational identities as voters, communicants, petitioners, depositors, applicants, and creditors, to name a few, in which people are classified similarly as members of the same category based on a small number of specific characteristics irrespective of how they differ in other respects.

"The prime social characteristic of modern industrial enterprise," Goode observes, "is that the individual is ideally given a job on the basis of his ability to fulfill its demands, and that this achievement is evaluated universalistically; the same standards apply to all who hold the same job."[8] Societies in which industrial enterprise is the primary form of economic organization tend to have occupational systems characteristically organized around normative principles different from those of kinship units. Some observers, recognizing that individuals must undergo psychological changes of considerable magnitude in order to make the transition from family to economic employment,[9] have noted yet understated the contribution of schooling. Eisenstadt, for example, in an otherwise penetrating analysis of age-grouping, restricts his treatment of the school's contribution to "adapting the psychological (and to some extent also physiological) learning potential of the child to the various skills and knowledges which must be acquired by him;"[10] his emphasis is too narrowly limited to the cognitive outcomes of schooling. Furthermore, while stressing the transition between family and occupation, most writers have largely ignored the contribution of schooling to the development of psychological capacities necessary for participating in other (non-economic) segments of society. It is my contention that the social experiences available to pupils in schools, by virtue of the nature and sequence of their structural arrangements, provide opportunities for children to learn norms characteristic of several facets of adult public life, occupation being but one.

In the early grades, a formal and prolonged process of separating children from the family begins. It does not involve severing or renouncing kinship ties nor relinquishing the normative principles of family life since most members of society, after all, remain part of some kinship unit throughout most of their lives. Schooling does, however, put demands on pupils to adopt principles of conduct different from those they have come to accept as family members—more precisely, to restrict the premises governing the family life to conduct among kinsmen, and to learn new premises that apply to settings outside the family. It is a process in which children learn both to generalize principles of conduct from one setting to another and at the same time to specify what principles are appropriate to which setting.

The Structural Basis of Sanctions

Learning to accept norms and act according to them, like other forms of learning, requires the use of sanctions. In both family and school, patterns of action appropriate to each setting are encouraged and discouraged by rewards and punishments taking the form of both specific, momentary acts and more elaborate patterns of action over time.

I assume that in encouraging and discouraging enduring patterns of behavior, a sustained relationship between the parties involved must exist, one that involves more than the reward and punishment of specific acts on a *quid pro quo* basis. In the family, the basis for encouraging and discouraging children's behavior lies in their dependence on parents from earliest childhood and in mutual affection—in effect, the maintenance of a continuous and diffuse relationship based on goodwill. Although rewards for specific acts can replenish the bank of goodwill, it is maintained by gratuitous expressions of concern, friendliness, support, sympathy, encouragement, and the like, not simply as responses to specific acts, but as indications of a more enduring solidarity. Punishment, even if severe, will then mean one thing if administered in the context of sustained affection and another where such feeling is absent.

Problems of reward and punishment confront teachers as well as parents, but the problems differ. First, since children in classrooms outnumber those in families, teachers, because of the limitations on their time and energy, can neither attend to nor sanction each child in the same ways that parents can; they must control a class without sacrificing the school's agenda to the imperatives of keeping order. Second, pupils' school work is customarily sanctioned by means of grades based on the quality of assignments completed. Grades, however, are not inherently rewarding or punishing, at least not at the outset. One critical problem of early elementary schooling is for teachers to establish grades *as* sanctions; and to the extent that pupils do not learn to accept them as such, grades cannot serve to reward good performance and punish poor. Secondary schools operate on the assumption—not always correct—that pupils have already come to accept the sanctioning quality of grades.

Teaching in the early grades presents a classic problem in the creation of goodwill—finding some appropriate equivalent in the classroom of affection in the family. That is, gratuitous pleasure not tied to specific acts in a relationship of exchange must be created in order to develop in pupils a diffuse and positive attachment both to the teacher and to the school. But the problem of sanctioning does not end with the creation of goodwill and the assignment of grades. The demands of schooling, particularly in the early years, can prove difficult, taxing, and often alien when contrasted with the more protective and indulgent environment of the home. The school day is long; there is much sitting in one place, following orders, completing assigned and not necessarily enjoyable tasks on time: teachers devote less time and interest to each child than parents do—this despite whatever intrinsic pleasures children may find in the school environment. Yet the school must convey to the pupil that certain forms of conduct acceptable at home will be held unacceptable at school, that certain rights he may legitimately claim from the household will not be honored in the classroom, that however alien they may seem, the tasks that school presents must be confronted and will hopefully come to represent new sources of gratification. To effect such changes, the school must have more resources than grades and goodwill in its kit of sanctions.

Resources available for sanctioning derive initially from two structured characteristics of classrooms: the visibility of pupils and their homogeneity of age. Classrooms are public places in that their membership is collective and visible. Many activities are carried on out loud and in front of everybody (reports, recitations, replies to questions, discussions, praise, chastisement, laughter); pupils perform publicly and are judged openly by the teacher and by other members of the class.[11]

The similarity of pupils in age is important for at least three reasons. First, age represents an index (even if inexact) of developmental maturity, and by implication, of capacity;[12] and even though children of the same age vary greatly in what they can do, age is still used as a common shorthand to gauge the assignment of tasks, responsibilities, privileges, and the like. Second, it provides classrooms with a built-in standard for comparison, a fixed point indicative of the level of those capacities directly relevant to the activities in which pupils are engaged. Each pupil, then, can be compared and compare himself with all others because the comparisons can be anchored to the standard. Third, it allows each pupil the experience of finding himself in the same boat with others in terms of the characteristics of their social surroundings and in the way they are treated by teachers.

Since many classroom activities are in effect judged in public, the pupil is bombarded with messages telling him how well he has done and—with a short inferential leap—how good he is. If he doesn't take the teacher's word for it, he need only look at the performance of others of the same age and in the same circumstances. The school, in effect, plays on his self-respect. Each pupil is exposed and vulnerable to the judgments of adults in authority and of his equals—those who resemble him in many respects.[13] If the child at home wonders whether he is loved, the pupil in school wonders whether he is a worthwhile person. In both settings, he can find some kind of answer by observing how others treat him and what they think of him.

Given the standards for and the patterns of behavior that children learn from their family experiences, the schools, in preparing them for adult public life, must effect changes of considerable magnitude, changes that require giving up certain patterns of conduct found gratifying in other settings and adopting new patterns whose gratification may at best take the form of promissory notes. If knowledge about other forms of socialization is applicable to schooling—and there is no reason in principle why it should not be—the sanctions required must affect people's emotions deeply as is true in some of the most demanding and stressful social situations involving psychological change: psychotherapy, religious conversion, brain-washing, deracination. It is my contention that the emotions aroused in schooling derive from events in which the pupil's sense of self-respect is either supported or threatened, and that school classrooms, permitting the public exposure and judgment of performance against a reasonably fixed reference point (age-adapted tasks), are organized so that the pupil's sense of personal adequacy, or self-respect, becomes the leverage for sanctioning.

Not all sanctions employed in school settings have the potentiality for arousing intense emotions, nor are they similarly diffuse in character. Some, like grades, compliments, admonitions, and chastisements, are contingent upon desirable and undesirable conduct; others, like friendly greetings, gentleness, sympathy, sarcasm, bitchiness, and so on through the whole gamut of words and gestures indicating approval, disapproval, and general attitude are non-contingent. All represent resources at the teacher's disposal—used consciously or unconsciously—and influence whether or not pupils will find their early experiences at school enjoyable enough to act according to its standards.

As suggested earlier, the school provides constraints and opportunities related to its structural properties, the behavior of its members, and its resources available for sanctioning. I have argued that pupils infer principles of conduct on the basis of their experiences in school, that they learn principles underlying the alternative ways of coping with a social situation having a particular set of properties. Over a period of years, they discover which patterns of conduct permit them to cope with the school's constraints and opportunities; and, to the extent that they find that certain patterns of action lead to the successful accomplishment of tasks and bring gratifications, they adopt those patterns as the right way to act—that is, they value them.[14]

The Learning of Social Norms

The social properties of schools are such that pupils, by coping with the sequence of classroom tasks and situations, are more likely to learn the principles—social norms—of independence, achievement, universalism, and specificity than if they had remained full-time members of the household.

Independence. Pupils learn to acknowledge that there are tasks to be done by them alone and to do them that way. Along with this self-imposed obligation goes the idea that others have a legitimate right to expect such independent behavior under certain circumstances.[15] Independence has a widely acknowledged though not unequivocal meaning. In using it here I refer to a cluster of meanings: doing things on one's own, being self-reliant, accepting personal responsibility for one's behavior, acting self-sufficiently;[16] and to a way of approaching tasks in whose accomplishment *under different circumstances* one can rightfully expect the help of others. The pupil, when in school, is separated from family members who have customarily provided help, support, and sustenance—persons on whom he has long been dependent.

A constellation of classroom characteristics and both teacher- and pupil-actions shape experiences in which the norm of independence is learned. In addition to the fact that school children are removed from persons with whom they have already formed strong relationships of dependency, the sheer size of a classroom assemblage limits each pupil's claim to personal contact with the teacher, and more so at the secondary levels than at the elementary.[17] This numerical property of classrooms reduces pupils' opportunities for establishing new relationships of dependency with adults and for receiving help from them.

Parents expect their children to act independently in many situations but teachers are more systematic in expecting pupils to adhere to standards of independence in performing academic tasks. There are at least two additional aspects of classroom operation, however, that bear directly on learning the norm of independence: rules about cheating and formal testing. First, as to cheating. The word itself is condemnatory in its reference to illegal and immoral acts. Most commonly, attention turns to how much cheating occurs, who cheats, and why. But these questions are of no concern here (though obviously they are elsewhere). My interest is in a different problem: to what types of conduct is the pejorative "cheating" assigned?

In school, cheating usually refers to acts in which two or more parties participate when the unaided action of only one is expected and pertains primarily to instructional activities. Illegal and immoral acts such as stealing and vandalism, whether carried out by individuals or groups, are not considered cheating because they have no direct connection with the central academic core of school activities. Nor is joint participation categorically proscribed; joint effort is called cooperation or collusion depending upon the teacher's prior definition of the task.

Cheating takes forms, most of which involve collective effort. A parent and a child may collaborate to produce homework; two pupils may pool their wisdom—or ignorance, as the case may be—in the interest of passing an examination. In both cases, the parties join deliberately; deliberateness, however, is not essential to the definition. One pupil can copy from another without the latter knowing; nor need the second party be a person, as in the case of plagiarism. The use of crib notes, perhaps a limiting case, involves no collusion; it consists, rather, in an illegitimate form of help. These are the main forms of school cheating of which there are many variations, routine to exotic. Thus, actions called cheating are those closely tied to the instructional goals of the school and usually involving assisted performance when unaided performance is expected.

The irony of cheating *in school* is that the same kinds of acts are morally acceptable and even commendable in other situations. One friend assisting another in distress, a parent helping a child—both praiseworthy; if one lacks the information to do a job, the resourceful thing is to look it up. In effect, many school activities called cheating are those in which customary forms of support and assistance in the family and among friends are expected.

In one obvious sense, school rules against cheating are designed to establish the content of moral standards. In another sense, the school attaches the stigma of immorality to certain types of behavior for social as distinct from ethical reasons; namely, to change the character of prevailing social relationships in which children are involved. In the case of homework, the school, in effect, attempts to redefine the relationship between parents and children by proscribing one form of parental support, unproblematic in other circumstances. The teacher has no direct control over parents, but tries to influence them at a distance by asking their adherence to a principle clothed in moral language whose violations are punishable. The line between legitimate parental support (encouraged when it takes the form of parents stressing the importance of school and urging their children to do well) and collusion is unclear; but by morally proscribing parental intervention beyond a certain point, the teacher attempts to limit the child's dependence upon family members in doing his school work. He expects the pupil, in other words, to work independently. The same argument applies to pupils and their friends: the teacher attempts to eliminate those parts of friendship that make it difficult or impossible for him to discover what a pupil can do on his own. In relationships with kin and friends, the customary sources of support in times of adversity, the school intervenes by restricting solidarity and, in the process, determines what the pupil can accomplish unaided. The pupil, for his part, discovers which of his actions he is held accountable for individually within the confines of tasks set by the school.

The comparison between schooling and occupational employment for which school is intended as preparation provides indirect support for this argument. The question here is the sense in which school experience is preparatory. Usually workers are not restricted in seeking help on problems confronting them; on the contrary, many occupations provide resources specifically intended to be helpful: arrangements for consultation, libraries, access to more experienced colleagues, and so on. Only in rare situations are people expected not to enlist the aid of family and friends in matters pertaining to work where the aid is appropriate. In other words, activities on the job analogous to school work do not carry comparable restrictions. Required, however, is that people in their occupational activities accept individual responsibility and accountability for the performance of assigned and self-initiated tasks. To the extent that the school contributes to the development of independence, the preparation lies more in the development of a frame of mind to act independently than in a vocationalism consisting of the capacity to perform a certain range of tasks without help.

Second, as to testing, and particularly the use of achievement tests. Most important for independence are the social conditions designed for the *administration* of tests, not their content or format. By and large, pupils are tested under more or less rigorously controlled conditions. At one end of the spectrum, formal, standardized tests are administered most stringently: pupils are physically separated, and the testing room is patrolled by proctors whose job is to discover contraband and to guarantee that no communication occurs—these arrangements being designed so that each examination paper represents independent work. At the other end, some testing situations are more informal, less elaborately staged, although there is almost always some provision that each pupil's work represents the product of only his own efforts.[18]

Testing represents an approach to establishing the norm of independence different from the proscription against cheating even though both are designed to reduce the likelihood of joint effort. Whereas the rules against cheating are directed more toward delineating the form of appropriate behavior, the restrictions built into the testing situation provide physical constraints intended to guarantee that teachers will receive samples of work that pupils do unassisted; the restrictions, that is, bear more on the product than on the motive. Actually, unless they stipulate otherwise, teachers expect pupils to do most of their everyday work by themselves;

daily assignments provide opportunities for and practice in independent work. Tests, because they occur at less frequent intervals than ordinary assignments, cannot provide comparably frequent opportunities; by the elaborate trappings of their administration, particularly with college entrance exams, and the anxiety they provoke, they symbolize the magnitude of the stakes.

It may be objected that in emphasizing independence I have ignored cooperation since an important item on the school agenda is instructing pupils in the skills of working with others. Teachers do assign work to groups and expect a collaborative product—and to this extent require the subordination of independent to collective efforts; judging the product according to collective standards, however, is another question.

To evaluate the contribution of each member of a working team, the teacher must either judge the quality of each one's work, in effect relying on the standard of independence, or rate each contribution according to the quality of the total product. The latter procedure rests on the assumption that each member has contributed equally, an untenable assumption if one has carried the rest or if a few have carried a weak sister. That occurrences of this kind are usually considered "unfair" suggests the normative priority of independence and the simple fact of life in industrial societies that institutions of higher learning and employers want to know how well each person can do and put constraints on the schools to find out. Thus, although the school provides opportunities for pupils to gain experience in cooperative situations, in the last analysis it is the individual assessment that counts.

Achievement.   Pupils come to accept the premise that they should perform their tasks the best they can, and act accordingly. The concept of achievement, like independence, has several referents. It usually denotes activity and mastery, making an impact on the environment rather than fatalistically accepting it, and competing against some standard of excellence. Analytically, the concept should be distinguished from independence since, among other differences, achievement criteria can apply to activities performed collectively.

Much of the recent literature treats achievement in the context of child-rearing within the family, as if achievement motivation were primarily a product of parental behavior.[19] Even though there is reason to believe that early childhood experiences in the family do contribute to its development, classroom experiences also contribute through teachers' use of resources beyond those ordinarily at the command of family members.

Classrooms are organized around a set of core activities in which a teacher assigns tasks to pupils and evaluates and compares the quality of their work. In the course of time, pupils differentiate themselves according to how well they perform a variety of tasks, most of which require the use of symbolic skills. Achievement standards are not limited in applicability to the classroom nor is their content restricted to cognitive areas. Schools afford opportunities for participation in a variety of extra-curricular activities, most conspicuously, athletics, but also music, dramatics, and a bewildering array of club and small group activities appealing to individual interests and talents.

The direct relevance of classroom work to learning achievement standards is almost self-evident; the experience is built into the assignment-performance-evaluation sequence of the work. Less evident, however, is that classroom activities force pupils to cope with various degrees of success and failure both of which can be psychologically problematic. Consistently successful performance requires that pupils deal with the consequences of their own excellence in a context of peer-equality in non-academic areas. For example, they confront the dilemma inherent in surpassing their age-mates in some respects but depending on their friendship and support in others, particularly in out-of-school social activities. The classroom thus provides not only the achievement experience itself but by-products of it, taking the form of the dilemma just described.

Similarly, pupils whose work is consistently poor not only must participate in activities leading to their academic failure but also experience living with that failure. They adopt various modes of coping with this, most of which center around maintaining personal self-respect in the face of continuing assaults upon it. Probably a minority succeed or fail consistently; a large proportion, most likely, do neither one consistently, but nonetheless worry about not doing well. Schooling, then, affords most pupils the experiences of both winning and losing; and to the extent that they gain some modicum of gratification from academic activities they learn to accept the general expectation of approaching their work with an achievement frame of mind. At the same time, they learn how to cope in a variety of ways, and more or less well, with success and failure.

Failure is perhaps the most difficult because it requires acknowledgement that the premise of achievement, to which failure itself can be attributed in part, is a legitimate principle for governing one's actions. Yet, endemic to industrial societies in which many facets of public life are based on achievement principles are situations that constrain people to live with personal failure; political defeat and occupational non-promotion being two cases in point.

As already suggested, the school provides a broader range of experiences than those restricted to the classroom and academic in nature; these experiences are based similarly on achievement criteria but differ in several important respects. The availability of alternatives to academic performance means that a pupil can experience success in achievement-oriented activities even if he lacks the requisite talents for doing well in the classroom.

How these alternative activities differ from those of the classroom is as important as the fact that they do, as evidenced by the case of athletics. Competitive sports resemble classroom activities in that both provide participants with the chance to demonstrate individual excellence; however, the former—and this is more true of team than individual sports—permit collective responsibility for defeat whereas the latter by and large allow only individual responsibility for failure. That is to say, the chances of receiving personal gratification for success are at least as great in sports as in the classroom, while the assault on personal self-respect for failure is potentially less intense. Athletics should not be written off as a manifestation of mere adolescent nonintellectualism as several recent writers have so treated it.[20]

A similar contention holds for music and dramatics; both provide the potentiality for individual accomplishment and recognition but without the persistent, systematic, and potentially corrosive evaluation typical of the classroom. Finally, in various club activities based on interest and talent, a pupil can do the things he is good at in the company of others who share an appreciation for them. In all these situations, either the rigors of competition and judgment characteristic of the classroom are mitigated; or the activity in question has its own built-in sources of support and personal protection, not to the same extent as in the family, but more than is available in the crucible of the classroom.

The school provides a wider variety of achievement experiences than does the family but at the same time has fewer sources for supporting and protecting pupils' self-respect in the face of failure. As pupils proceed through successive school levels, the rigors of achievement increase at least for those who continue along the main academic line. Moreover, at the secondary levels the number of activities governed according to the achievement principle increases as does the variety of these activities. As preparation for adult public life in which the application of this principle is widespread, schooling contributes to personal development in assuring that the majority of pupils not only will have performed tasks according to the achievement standard but will have had experience in an expanding number of situations in which activities are organized according to it.

Universalism and Specificity. Unlike independence and achievement, universalism and specificity are not commonly regarded as good things. Parents and teachers admonish children to act independently and to do their work well; few of them support the idea that people should willingly acknowledge their similarity to others in specifically categorical terms while ignoring obvious differences—denying, in a sense, their own individuality.

Ideologically, social critics have deplored the impersonal, ostensibly dehumanizing aspects of categorization, a principle widely believed to lie at the heart of the problem of human alienation—the attachment of man to machine, the detachment of man from man. Often ignored, however, is the connection between this principle and the idea of fairness, or equity. Seen from this vantage point, categorization is widely regarded as a good thing, especially when contrasted to nepotism, favoritism, and arbitrariness. People resent the principle when they think they have a legitimate reason to receive special consideration, or when their individuality appears to vanish by being "processed." Yet, when a newcomer breaks into a long queue instead of proceeding to the end of the line, they usually condemn him for acting unfairly (for not following the standard rule for all newcomers to a line) and do *not* express any sense of their own alienation (for abiding by the same categorical principle). The contrasts between individuality and dehumanization, fairness and special privilege, are similarly predicated on universalism and specificity; they differ in the ideological posture of the observer, and, more cynically, in his conception of self-interest.

The concepts of universalism and specificity have been formulated most comprehensively by Parsons, though only part of his formulation pertains directly to this discussion. As part of his concern with social systems, Parsons views universalism as one horn of a dilemma—the other being particularism—in role definition; under what circumstances does the occupant of one social position govern his actions by adopting one standard or the other in dealing with the occupant of another position? My concern, however, is not with a selection among alternative, conflicting standards but with the conditions under which individuals learn to accept the obligation to impose the standards of universalism and specificity upon themselves and to act accordingly.

Defining the central theme of universalism raises problems because the term has various meanings, not all of them clear.[21] The relevant distinction here is whether individuals are treated as members of categories or as special cases. In one respect or another, an individual can always be viewed as a member of one or more categories; he is viewed particularistically if, notwithstanding his similarity to others in the same category or circumstances, he still receives special treatment.[22]

The norm of specificity is easily confused with universalism despite its distinctiveness. It refers to the scope of one person's interest in another; to the obligation to confine one's interest to a narrow range of characteristics and concerns, or to extend them to include a broad range.[23] Implicit is the notion of relevance; the characteristics and concerns that should be included in the range, whether broad or narrow, are those considered relevant in terms of the activities in which the persons in question are involved. Doctors and storekeepers, for example, differ in the scope of their interest in persons seeking their services, but the content of their interests also varies according to the nature of the needs and desires of those persons.

It is my contention that the school's contribution to children's accepting these norms that penetrate so many areas of public life is critical because children's preschool experience in the family is weighted heavily on the side of special treatment and parental consideration of the whole child.

To say that children learn the norm of universalism means that they come to accept being treated by others as members of categories (in addition to being treated as special cases, as in the family). Schools provide a number of experiences that families cannot readily provide because of limitations in their social composition and structure, one of which is the systematic establishment and demarcation of membership categories. First, by assigning all pupils in a classroom the same or similar tasks to perform, teachers in effect make them confront the same set of demands; and even if there are variations in task content, class members still confront the same teacher and the obligations he imposes. Second, parity of age creates a condition of homogeneity according to developmental stage, a rough equalization of pupil capacities making it possible for teachers to assign similar tasks. Third, through the process of yearly promotion from grade to grade, pupils cross the boundaries separating one age category from another. With successive boundary crossings comes the knowledge that each age-grade category is associated with particular circumstances (e.g., teachers, difficulty of tasks, subject matter studied); moreover, pupils learn the relationship between categories and how their present positions relate to past and future positions by virtue of having experienced the transitions between them. In these three ways, the grade—more specifically, the classroom within the grade—with its age-homogeneous membership and clearly demarcated boundaries provides a basis for categorical grouping that the family cannot readily duplicate. Most important, as a by-product of repeated boundary-crossing, pupils acquire a relativity of perspective, a capacity to view their own circumstances from other vantage points, having themselves occupied them.[24]

Although each child holds membership in the category "children" at home, parents, in raising them, tend to take age differences into account and thereby accentuate the uniqueness of each child's circumstances and to belie in some measure the categorical aspects of "childhood." However, even if the category "children" breaks into its age-related components within the family, it remains intact when children compare themselves with friends and neighbors of the same age. In typical situations of this kind, children inform their parents that friends of the same age have greater privileges or fewer responsibilities than they. Parents, if they cannot actually equalize the circumstances, often explain or justify the disparity by pointing to the special situation of the neighbor family: they have more money, fewer children, a bigger house—whatever the reason; that is, parents point out the uniqueness of family circumstances and thereby emphasize the particularities of each child's situation. The school, in contrast, provides the requisite circumstances for making comparisons among pupils in categorical rather than particular terms.

The second school experience fostering the establishment of social categories is the re-equalization of pupils by means of the high-school track
system after they have differentiated themselves through academic
achievement in the lower grades, a mechanism that reduces the likelihood
that teachers will have to deal with special cases.[25] Teachers with a
variegated batch of pupils must adopt more individualized methods of instruction than those whose pupils are similar in their level of achievement,
and who in so doing would partially recreate a kinship-type of relationship
with pupils, treating segments of the class differently according to differences in capacity much as parents treat their children differently according to age-related capacities.

As far as level is concerned, the high school is a better place to learn the
principle of universalism than the lower school levels because pupils within
each track, and therefore of roughly similar capacity, move from classroom
to classroom, in each one receiving instruction in a different subject area
from a different teacher. They discover that over a range of activities they
are treated alike and that relatively uniform demands and criteria of evaluation are applied to them. That is to say, by providing instruction from different teachers in different subject matter areas and by at the same time
applying criteria for judging performance and task difficulty which remain
roughly constant within each track and across subjects, the school makes it
possible for pupils to learn which differences in experience are subordinated to the principle of categorization. The elementary classroom, oriented
more to instruction in different subjects by a single teacher, does not provide the necessary variations in persons and subjects for a clear-cut demonstration of the categorical principle.

Although the idea of categorization is central to the norm of universalism, there are additional and derivative aspects of it. One is the crucial distinction, widely relevant in industrial society, between the person and the
social position he occupies. A frequent demand made on individuals is to
treat others and be treated by them according to the identity that their
positions confer rather than according to who they are as people. Schooling
contributes to the capacity to make the distinction (and the obligation to do
so) by making it possible for pupils to discover that different individuals can
occupy a single social position but act in ways that can be discovered as attached to the position rather than to the different persons filling it. Even
though all members of a given classroom find themselves in the same circumstances, are about equal in age, and resemble each other, roughly, in
social characteristics related to residence, they still differ in many respects—sex, race, ethnicity, and physical characteristics being among the
most obvious. Their situation, therefore, provides the experience of finding
that common interests and shared circumstances are assigned a priority
that submerges obvious personal differences. The same contention holds
for adults. Male and female adults are found in both school and family set-

tings; in school, pupils can discover that an increasingly large number of different adults of both sexes can occupy the same position, that of "teacher." This discovery is not as easily made in the family because it is not possible to determine definitively whether "parent" represents two positions, one occupied by a male, the other by a female, or a single position with two occupants differing in sex.[26] The school, in other words, makes it possible for pupils to distinguish between persons and the social positions they occupy—a capacity crucially important in both occupational and political life—by placing them in situations where both the similarities between persons in a single position are made evident and the membership of each position is varied in its composition.

Regarding the norm of specificity, again the school provides structural arrangements more conducive to its acquisition than does the family. First, since the number of persons and the ratio of non-adults to adults is much larger in classrooms than in the household, the school provides large social aggregates in which pupils can form many casual associations (in addition to their close friendships), in which they invest but a small portion of themselves. As both the size and heterogeneity of the student body increase at each successive level, the opportunities for these somewhat fragmented social contacts increase and diversify. The relative shallowness and transiency of these relationships increase the likelihood that pupils will have experiences in which the fullness of their individuality is *not* involved as it tends to be in their relationships among kin and close friends.

Second, upon leaving the elementary school and proceeding through the departmentalized secondary levels, pupils form associations with teachers who have a progressively narrowing and specialized interest in them. (This comes about both because of subject matter specialization itself and because the number of pupils each teacher faces in the course of a day also grows larger.) Although it is true that children, as they grow older, tend to form more specific relationships with their parents—symptomatically, this trend manifests itself in adolescents' complaints of parental invasions of privacy—the resources of the school in providing the social basis for establishing relationships in which only narrow segments of personality are invested far exceed those of the family.

A second facet of universalism is the principle of equity, or fairness (I use the terms interchangeably). When children compare their lot—their gains and losses, rewards and punishments, privileges and responsibilities—with that of others and express dissatisfaction about their own, they have begun to think in terms of equity; their punishments are too severe, chores too onerous, allowance too small compared, for example, to those of siblings and friends. Children's comparisons with siblings, who are almost always different in age, usually prompt parents to resolve the sensed inequities by equalizing age hypothetically. "If you were as young as he, you wouldn't have to shovel the walk either." "He is only a child and doesn't know any better." The pained questions to which these statements are replies are familiar enough.

Among children in a family, age is critical in determining what is fair and unfair.[27] In a sense, it is the clock by which we keep developmental time, changing constantly though not periodically. The personal significance of age is heightened among children because any given age difference between them is "larger" the younger they are. Thus, the difference between a four-year-old and an eight-year-old is "greater" than that between a fourteen-year-old and an eighteen-year-old because, on the average, there are greater developmental changes occurring during the earlier four-year span than during the later one. When life's circumstances change rapidly, when one is still in the process of learning what is one's due and what is due others, and when younger children do not have to fight the battles that older ones have already won, determining whether one is being treated fairly on any given occasion can be difficult.

Among young children, then, age provides a variable standard for judging questions of equity, a more fixed standard among older ones.[28] In the context of the transition between childhood and adulthood, two children *within the same family* (except if they are twins), cannot easily settle a question of equity by referring to their ages—they may acknowledge that the older child is entitled to more, but not how much more—because they differ in age, because the meaning of age differences changes, and because there can be disagreement over the coefficient for converting age units into units of gain and loss.

In school classrooms, the age of children is nearly constant; the problem of settling equity questions attributable to age variations found in families does not arise. Teachers cannot treat all pupils identically, but they can use age similarity as a guide for assigning similar instructional tasks to all members of a class and to communicate, implicitly or explicitly, that they all share the same situation together.

Even though age differences found in the family (and their associated problems of equity) are not present, problems of fairness and unfairness do arise in classrooms; they originate when pupils who are supposed to be treated similarly are not so treated. Grades, for example, according to the usual procedure, must be assigned according to the quality of work completed; equivalent products should receive the same grade. Marking similar work differently, or unequal work the same, represents unfair grading; a similar principle holds for the punishment of offenses—the punishment should fit the crime, and similar forms of misbehavior should be treated alike—and for the assignment of tasks and responsibilities according to difficulty and onerousness. But there are secondary considerations that enter the process of evaluating performance: how hard pupils work and how much they have improved. These criteria cannot readily replace quality of performance unless teachers, pupils, and parents are willing to acknowledge the justice of various anomalies (so defined, at least, within the scope of American values): for example, pupils who do excellent work with little effort receiving lower grades than those who produce mediocre work through feverish activity.

The contrast between classroom and family is pronounced. Equity in the former is based by and large on how well pupils perform and how they are treated in a setting whose characteristics are alike for all. From the vantage point of an outside observer, objective conditions within the classroom are similar for each pupil as are the tasks assigned; pupils, in other words, find themselves in the same boat. Within the family, on the other hand, each child rides his own boat, and judgments about equity derive from that fact.

As argued earlier, equity involves a comparative assessment of one's circumstances: gains and losses, rewards and punishments, rights and duties, privileges and responsibilities. To determine whether his circumstances in a given situation are equitable, an individual must learn to make comparisons by which he can discover whose circumstances resemble his own and whose do not, who is treated like him and who is not; he must also discover the relationships between his circumstances and the way he is treated.

Schooling, then, through the structural properties of classrooms at each school level and through teachers' treatment of pupils, provides opportunities for making the comparisons relevant for defining questions of equity far more effectively than does the family. The process is similar to that (above described) of learning the norm of universalism in general. Both within the classroom and within each grade, age and, to a lesser extent, other personal and social characteristics provide a basis for discovering both similarities and differences in categorical terms. The existence of grade levels, distinguished primarily by the demandingness of work and demarcated by the device of yearly promotion, and the progression of pupils through them year by year make it possible for children to learn that *within the context of the school* certain qualities that determine their uniqueness as persons become subordinated to those specific characteristics in which they are alike. Thus, fourth and fifth graders, despite their individuality, are judged according to specific criteria of achievement; and the content and difficulty of their assigned tasks are regulated according to the developmental considerations symbolized by grade. The fourth grader having completed the third grade can grasp the idea that he belongs to a category of persons whose circumstances differ from those of persons belonging to another.

Family relationships are not organized on a cohort basis nor do they entail anything comparable to the systematic, step-by-step progression of grades in which the boundaries between one category and another are clearly demarcated. Although a child knows the difference between family members and non-members and can distinguish even the categorical distinctions within his own family, his experiences in a kinship setting do not allow him to find as clear an answer to the question of whether his circumstances are uniquely his own or whether they are shared. In other words, these relationships are not structured in such a way as to form a basis for making the categorical comparisons basic to the universalistic norm. Specifically, they provide little or no basis for the repeated experience of crossing boundaries from one category to another so important for learning to make the comparisons involved in judgments of equity. Moreover, since parents treat their children more in terms of the full range of personal characteristics—that is, according to the norm of diffuseness rather than that of specificity—the family setting is more conducive to the special rather than the categorical treatment of each child (since the boundaries of a category are more clearly delineated if one characteristic, not many, constitutes the basis of categorization).

A Conceptual Caveat

The argument of this paper rests on the assumption that schools, through their structural arrangements and the behavior patterns of teachers, provide pupils with certain experiences unavailable in other social settings and that these experiences, by virtue of their peculiar characteristics, represent conditions conducive to the acquisition of norms. I have indicated how pupils learn the norms of independence, achievement, universalism, and specificity as outcomes of the schooling process. A critical point, however, is how the relationship between experience and outcome is formulated.

There is no guarantee that pupils will come to accept the four norms simply because these experiences are available;[29] for example, they may lack the necessary social and psychological support from sources outside of school or sufficient inner resources to cope with the demands of schooling. These are reasons external to the school situation and may be sufficient to preclude both instructional and normative outcomes. Forces internal to the schooling process itself, however, may be equally preclusive since the same activities and sanctions from which some pupils derive the gratification and enhancement of self-respect necessary for both types of outcome may create experiences that threaten the self-respect of others. Potentialities for success *and* failure inhere in tasks performed according to achievement criteria. Independence manifests itself as competence and autonomy in some, as a heavy burden of responsibility in others. Universalistic treatment represents fairness to some, cold impersonality to others. Specificity may be seen as situational relevance or personal neglect.

Within industrial societies, where norms applicable to public life differ markedly from those governing conduct among kin, schools provide a sequence of experiences in which individuals, during the early stages of personality development, acquire new principles of conduct, principles instituting additions to those already accepted during early childhood. The family, as a social setting with characteristic social arrangements, lacks the resources and the "competence"[30] to effect the psychological transition for reasons earlier enumerated in detail. This is not to say that only the school can produce these changes. Of those institutions having some claim over the lives of children and adolescents in industrial societies—the family, child labor, job apprenticeship, mass media, tutoring, the church—only the schools at the present time provide adequate, though not always effective, task experiences, sanctions, and arrangements for the generalization and specification of normative principles throughout the many spheres of public life.

It is conceivable, of course, that families (and these other institutions as well as some yet to be invented) can provide the experiences necessary for the acquisition of these norms; family life provides opportunities for achievement, for assuming individual responsibility, and for categorical and specific treatment, yet it is more likely than schools to provide experiences that also undermine the acquisition of these norms. The crucial consideration is the relationship between structural arrangements and activities in determining whether one setting or another is more conducive to producing a given outcome, for if two activities interfere with each other or if the situation is inappropriate to the performance of an activity, the outcome is unlikely to appear.

An Ideological Caveat

Although I construe them as norms, independence and achievement have been regarded by many observers of the American scene as dominant cultural themes or values—general standards of what is desirable.[31] In view of this, it is important that the argument of this paper not be taken as a defense of national values, although it should not surprise anyone that the normative commitments of individuals who have passed through American schools are generally though not invariably consistent with national values. The main purpose of this analysis was to present a formulation, hypothetical in nature, of how schooling contributes to the emergence of certain psychological outcomes, not to provide an apology or justification for those outcomes on ideological grounds. I have avoided calling universalism and specificity cultural values, even though both are norms, since few if any observers include them among the broad moral principles desirable in American life. Their exclusion from the list of values should further confirm the analytic and non-apologetic intent of this discussion.[32]

Having the means to produce a desired result is not the same thing as an injunction to use them in producing it. Of the many considerations entering into the decision to employ available resources in creating even widely valued outcomes, the probable costs involved should give pause. For the norms in question here, whose desirability can be affirmed either on ideological grounds or in terms of their relevance to public life in an industrial society, conditions conducive to their development are also conducive to the creation of results widely regarded as undesirable. Thus, a sense of accomplishment and mastery, on the one hand, and a sense of incompetence and ineffectualness, on the other, both represent psychological consequences of continually coping with tasks on an achievement basis. Similarly with independence: self-confidence and helplessness can each derive from a person's self-imposed obligation to work unaided and to accept individual responsibility for his actions. Finally, willingness to acknowledge the rightness of categorical and specific treatment may mean the capacity to adapt to a variety of social situations in which only a part of one's self is invested, or it may mean a sense of personal alienation and isolation from human relationships.

From the viewpoint of ideological justification, the process of schooling is problematic in that outcomes morally desirable from one perspective are undesirable from another: and in the making of school policy the price to be paid must be a salient consideration in charting a course of action.

NOTES

I wish to thank Barrie D. Bortnick, Andrew Effrat, Michael B. Katz, Larry A. Weiss, and Charlene A. Worth for their invaluable help. The research and development reported herein was performed pursuant to a contract (OE 5-10-239) with the United States Department of Health, Education, and Welfare, Office of Education, under the provisions of the Cooperative Research Program, as a project of the Harvard University Center for Research and Development on Educational Differences. Copyright © 1967, Dreeben; reproduction in whole or in part permitted for any purposes by the United States Government.

This paper is adapted from Part IV of *On What is Learned in School,* to be published in 1968 by Addison-Wesley Publishing Company, Inc. The volume is in a series on The Foundations of Education, under the editorship of Byron Massialas. Used by permission of Robert Dreeben and the publisher. [This volume was published in 1968.]

1. In one near-encyclopedic volume on educational research, the instructional emphases are most clearly illustrated. Nine of twenty-three long chapters are devoted to "Research on Teaching Various Grade Levels and Subject Matters." Six deal with measurement: both problems of measurement *per se,* and of measuring particular types of educational outcomes (cognitive and non-cognitive). Two deal with the characteristics of teachers; two with methods and media; one with social interaction in classrooms. The major preoccupations of educators and educational researchers are summarized in the following statement from Benjamin S. Bloom, "Testing Cognitive Ability and Achievement," in N. L. Gage (ed.), *Handbook of Research on Teaching* (Chicago: Rand McNally, 1963), p. 379:

> While it may or may not be true that the most important changes in the learner are those which may be described as cognitive, i.e., knowledge, problem-solving, higher mental processes, etc., it is true that these are the types of changes in students which most teachers do seek to bring about. These are the changes in learners which most teachers attempt to gauge in their

own tests of progress and in their final examinations. These, also, are the changes in the learners which are emphasized in the materials of instruction, in the interaction between teachers and learners, and in the reward system which the teachers and the schools employ.

There is a brief treatment of the characteristics of learning environments but with primary emphasis on teaching techniques in George G. Stern, "Measuring Non-cognitive Variables in Research on Teaching." (*Ibid.*, pp. 425–433).

2. Several questions pertaining to the connection between the acquisition of norms and the structural properties of social settings are beyond the scope of this paper, and so in places the argument must remain elliptical. For a more detailed discussion, see the writer's forthcoming book: *On What is Learned in School* (Reading, Mass.: Addison-Wesley).

3. The empirical problems of identifying norms in a given situation are beyond the scope of this discussion. Suffice it to say that identifying them requires that one consider at least the following: verbal statements, behavior, situation, and emotional expressions— none of which when taken alone is sufficient—and the connections among them.

4. A variety of conditions can affect the relationship between norm acceptance and behavior. (a) There may be disagreements among persons about what norm applies in a particular situation: behavior where consensus is lacking may not represent conformity to any of the conflicting norms. (b) Behavioral conformity may depend on the explicitly or implicitly conditional nature of norms. For example, although lying is proscribed in principle, there are widely-acknowledged situations in which telling 'white lies' is acceptable. (c) People vary in their desire to conform; they calculate the likelihood and severity of punishment if they do not; they judge the opportunities to conform or deviate; and they determine where their interests lie.

5. Melville J. Herkovits, *Man and His Works* (New York: Alfred A. Knopf, 1919), p. 311.

6. For technical discussions of the relevance of these norms to industrialism, see Talcott Parsons, *The Social System* (Glencoe: Free Press, 1951) and S. N. Eisenstadt, *From Generation to Generation* (Glencoe: Free Press, 1956).

7. I do not imply that accepting a norm as binding upon oneself implies the ability to formulate its underlying general principle verbally.

8. William J. Goode, *World Revolution and Family Patterns* (New York: Free Press of Glencoe, 1963), p. 11.

9. See, for example, Ruth Benedict, "Continuities and Discontinuities in Cultural Conditioning," in Clyde Kluckhohn, Henry A. Murray, and David M. Schneider (eds.), *Personality* (New York: Alfred A. Knopf, 1953), pp. 522–31; Eisenstadt, *op. cit.*, pp. 115–85. An important exception to this neglect of the importance of schooling is Talcott Parsons' paper, "The School Class as a Social System," *Harvard Educational Review*, XXIX No. 4, 297–318.

10. Eisenstadt, *op. cit.*, p. 164.

11. Formal grades, both for assigned work and for general evaluation of performance over several months' time, are customarily given in some degree of privacy; once pupils receive them, whatever confidentiality the teacher maintains in assigning grades usually tends to be short-lived. Pupils themselves turn private into public knowledge, and parents have been known to do the same.

12. Perhaps the social expectations for and beliefs about the capacities of similar-aged children are narrower than their actual capacities (however these are measured). If so, age is an exaggeratedly "good" index of equal capacity even if the "goodness" represents a self-fulfilling prophesy. There is some controversy about the usefulness of the term "capacity" among psychometricians, but for present purposes, it is beside the point since people often think in terms of children's capacities and act accordingly.

13. "Remember that you are as good as any man—and also that you are no better. . . . [But] the man who is as good as his neighbors is in a tough spot when he confronts all of his neighbors combined." Louis Hartz, *The Liberal Tradition in America* (New York: Harcourt, Brace and Co., 1955), p. 56. The opinions of massed equals are not negligible.

14. For empirical confirmation of the fact that experience in the performance of particular tasks can produce changes in preferences, beliefs, and most importantly in values (norms) and their generalization from one situation to another without verbal instruction in the content of those outcomes, see Paul E. Breer and Edwin A. Locke, *Task Experience as a Source of Attitudes* (Homewood: Dorsey Press, 1965), especially chapter 6. A statement of the argument of how the actual performance of a task can effect changes in norms—how it *should* be performed—is beyond the scope of this paper.

15. My emphasis here differs from Parsons' in that he views independence primarily as a personal resource: ". . . It may be said that the most important single predispositional factor with which the child enters the school is his level of independence" (Parsons, *op. cit.,* p. 300). Although independence is very likely such a predisposition—whether it is the most important single one is moot—it is part of the school's agenda to further the development of independence to a point beyond the level at which family resources become inadequate to do so.

16. Winterbottom, for example, lumps independence and mastery together; the indices she uses to measure them involve ostensibly distinct phenomena in that the mastery items refer to tendencies toward activity rather than independence. Marian R. Winterbottom, "The Relation of Need for Achievement to Learning Experiences in Independence and Mastery," in John T. Akinson (ed.), *Motives in Fantasy, Action, and Society* (Princeton, N.J.: D. Van Nostrand Co., 1958), pp. 453–78. As a definitional guideline for this discussion, I have followed the usage of Bernard C. Rosen and Roy D'Andrade, "The Psychosocial Origins of Achievement Motivation," *Sociometry,* XXII No. 3, 1959, 186, in their discussion of achievement training; also, David C. McClelland, A. Rindlisbacher, and Richard DeCharms, "Religious and Other Sources of Parental Attitudes toward Independence Training," in David C. McClelland (ed.), *Studies in Motivation* (New York: Appleton-Century-Crofts, Inc., 1955), pp. 389–97.

17. Thus, the ratio of children per adult in households are 0.5, 1.0, 2.0, and 3.0 in one-, two-, four-, and six-child families, respectively, with two parents present; comparatively few families have more than six children. In classrooms, the ratios of different children per adult at the elementary and secondary levels are approximately 28.1 and 155.8, respectively; *The American Public School Teacher, 1960–61,* Research Monograph 1963-M2, Research Division, National Education Association, April, 1963, p. 51.

18. By describing the conditions surrounding the administration of tests, I do not thereby attempt to justify these procedures; other means might accomplish the same ends.

19. See, for example, Winterbottom, *op. cit.,* pp. 453–78; Rosen and D'Andrade, *op. cit.,* pp. 185–218; and Fred L. Strodtbeck, "Family Interaction, Values, and Achievement," in David C. McClelland et al., *Talent and Society* (Princeton: D. Van Nostrand Co., Inc., 1958), pp. 135–91.

20. For one attempt to treat athletics condescendingly as anti-intellectualism, see James S. Coleman, *The Adolescent Society* (New York: Free Press of Glencoe, 1961). I do not suggest that athletics has an yet undiscovered intellectual richness; rather, that its contributions should not be viewed simply in terms of intellectuality.

21. Although Parsons, in *The Social System,* p. 62, considers universalism and particularism to form a dichotomy, he distinguishes them on at least two dimensions: cognitive and cathectic:

> The primacy of cognitive values may be said to imply a *universalistic* standard, while that of appreciative values implies a *particularistic* standard. In the former case the standard is derived from the validity of a set of existential ideas, or the generality of a normative rule, in the latter from the particularity of the cathectic significance of an object or of the status of an object in a relational system.

22. The treatment of others does not become more particularistic as an increasing number of categories is taken into account. If age, sex, religion, ethnicity, and the like—

all examples of general categories—are considered, treatment is still categorical in nature because it is oriented to categorical similarities, even if they number more than one, and not to what is special or unique about the person or about a relationship in which he is involved.

23. In the case of specificity, "the burden of proof rests on him who would suggest that ego has obligations vis-à-vis the object in question which transcend this specificity of relevance" (Parsons, *The Social System,* p. 65). In the case of diffuseness, "the burden of proof is on the side of the exclusion of an interest or mode of orientation as outside the range of obligations defined by the role-expectation" (*Ibid.,* p. 66).

24. For a discussion of relativity of perspective, empathy, and parochialism in the context of the economic and political development of nations, see Daniel Lerner, *The Passing of Traditional Society* (New York: Free Press of Glencoe, 1958), pp. 43–75 and *passim.*

25. The secondary school track system by which pupils are segregated according to academic achievement has conventionally been interpreted as a distributive device for directing pupils toward one or another broad segment of the occupational hierarchy. Although the distinctive or allocative function of the track system has pre-empted most discussions, it should not be regarded as the only function; in fact, a very different view of it is taken here.

26. Children are not left completely without clues in this matter since they do not have other adult relatives who can be seen as distinct persons occupying the same position. Yet, families, even of the extended variety, do not provide the frequent and systematic comparisons characteristic of schooling.

27. There are, of course, events in family life where the explanation that renders inequities fair lies not in age but in circumstances—"Your brother could stay home from school and watch television because he was sick (and you weren't)"—and in other personal characteristics besides age, such as sex—"It isn't safe for girls to walk home alone at that hour (but it's O.K. for your brother)."

28. The contrast between age as a constant and as a variable in questions of equity is evident by comparison with Homan's treatment of age: "One of the ways in which two men may be 'like' one another is in their investments [age being one]. Accordingly the more nearly one man is like another in age, the more apt he is to expect their net rewards to be equal and to display anger when his own are less." In the context of this statement, age is the fixed criterion for assessing the fairness of rewards as one man compares his gain with that of another. George C. Homans, *Social Behavior: Its Elementary Forms* (New York: Harcourt, Brace & World, 1961), p. 75.

29. Nor should one conclude that these experiences contribute to the learning of only the four norms discussed here and no others.

30. For a discussion of competence as an organizational characteristic, see Philip Selznick, *Leadership in Administration* (Evanston, Ill.: Row, Peterson, and Co., 1957), pp. 18–56.

31. For a general discussion of the concept of "value" and of major American cultural themes see Robin M. Williams, Jr., *American Society* (New York: Alfred A. Knopf, 1960), pp. 397–470.

32. The hypothetical nature of this discussion should be kept in mind especially since there has been no empirical demonstration of the relationships between schooling and the acceptance of norms.

EDUCATION AND PERSONAL DEVELOPMENT: THE LONG SHADOW OF WORK

Samuel Bowles
Herbert Gintis

It is not obvious why the U.S. educational system should be the way it is. Since the interpersonal relationships it fosters are so antithetical to the norms of freedom and equality prevalent in American society, the school system can hardly be viewed as a logical extension of our cultural heritage. If neither technological necessity nor the bungling mindlessness of educators explain the quality of the educational encounter, what does?

Reference to the educational system's legitimation function does not take us far toward enlightenment. For the formal, objective, and cognitively oriented aspects of schooling capture only a fragment of the day-to-day social relationships of the educational encounter. To approach an answer, we must consider schools in the light of the social relationships of economic life. In this chapter, we suggest that major aspects of educational organization replicate the relationships of dominance and subordinancy in the economic sphere. The correspondence between the social relation of schooling and work accounts for the ability of the educational system to produce an amenable and fragmented labor force. The experience of schooling, and not merely the content of formal learning, is central to this process.

In our view, it is pointless to ask if the net effect of U.S. education is to promote equality or inequality, repression or liberation. These issues pale into significance before the major fact: The educational system is an integral element in the reproduction of the prevailing class structure of society. The educational system certainly has a life of its own, but the experience of work and the nature of the class structure are the bases upon which educational values are formed, social justice assessed, the realm of the possible delineated in people's consciousness, and the social relations of the educational encounter historically transformed.

Chapter 5 from *Schooling in Capitalist America: Educational Reform and The Contradictions of Economic Life,* by Samuel Bowles and Herbert Gintis, © 1976 by Basic Books, Inc., Publishers, New York.

In short, and to return to a persistent theme of this book, the educational system's task of integrating young people into adult work roles constrains the types of personal development which it can foster in ways that are antithetical to the fulfillment of its personal development function.

Reproducing Consciousness

> . . . children guessed (but only a few and down they forgot as up they grew autumn winter spring summer). . . .
>
> E. E. Cummings, 1940

Economic life exhibits a complex and relatively stable pattern of power and property relationships. The perpetuation of these social relationships, even over relatively short periods, is by no means automatic. As with a living organism, stability in the economic sphere is the result of explicit mechanisms constituted to maintain and extend the dominant patterns of power and privilege. We call the sum total of these mechanisms and their actions the reproduction process.

Amidst the sundry social relations experienced in daily life, a few stand out as central to our analysis of education. These are precisely the social relationships which are necessary to the security of capitalist profits and the stability of the capitalist division of labor. They include the patterns of dominance and subordinary in the production process, the distribution of ownership of productive resources, and the degrees of social distance and solidarity among various fragments of the working population—men and women, blacks and whites, and white- and blue-collar workers, to mention some of the most salient.

What are the mechanisms of reproduction of these aspects of the social relations of production in the United States? To an extent, stability is embodied in law and backed by the coercive power of the state. Our jails are filled with individuals who have operated outside the framework of the private-ownership market system. The modern urban police force as well as the National Guard originated, in large part, in response to the fear of social upheaval evoked by militant labor action. Legal sanction, within the framework of the laws of private property, also channels the actions of groups (e.g., unions) into conformity with dominant power relationships. Similarly, force is used to stabilize the division of labor and its rewards within an enterprise: Dissenting workers are subject to dismissal and directors failing to conform to "capitalist rationality" will be replaced.

But to attribute reproduction to force alone borders on the absurd. Under normal conditions, the effectiveness of coercion depends at the very least on the inability or unwillingness of those subjected to it to join together in opposing it. Laws generally considered illegitimate tend to lose their coercive power, and undisguised force too frequently applied tends to be self-defeating. The consolidation and extension of capitalism has engendered struggles of furious intensity. Yet instances of force deployed against a united and active opposition are sporadic and have usually given way to détente in one form or another through a combination of compromise, structural change, and ideological accommodation. Thus it is clear that the consciousness of workers—beliefs, values, self-concepts, types of solidarity and fragmentation, as well as modes of personal behavior and development—are integral to the perpetuation, validation, and smooth operation of economic institutions. The reproduction of the social relations of production depends on the reproduction of consciousness.

Under what conditions will individuals accept the pattern of social relationships that frame their lives? Believing that the long-term development of the existing system holds the prospect of fulfilling their needs, individuals and groups might actively embrace these social relationships. Failing this, and lacking a vision of an alternative that might significantly improve their situation, they might fatalistically accept their condition. Even with such a vision they might passively submit to the framework of economic life and seek individual solutions to social problems if they believe that the possibilities for realizing change are remote. The issue of the reproduction of consciousness enters each of these assessments.

The economic system will be embraced when, first, the perceived needs of individuals are congruent with the types of satisfaction the economic system can objectively provide. While perceived needs may be, in part, biologically determined, for the most part needs arise through the aggregate experiences of individuals in the society. Thus the social relations of production are reproduced in part through a harmony between the needs which the social system generates and the means at its disposal for satisfying these needs.

Second, the view that fundamental social change is not feasible, unoperational, and utopian is normally supported by a complex web of ideological perspectives deeply embedded in the cultural and scientific life of the community and reflected in the consciousness of its members. But fostering the "consciousness of inevitability" is not the office of the cultural system alone. There must also exist mechanisms that systematically thwart the spontaneous development of social experiences that would contradict these beliefs.

Belief in the futility of organizing for fundamental social change is further facilitated by social distinctions which fragment the conditions of life for subordinate classes. The strategy of "divide and conquer" has enabled dominant classes to maintain their power since the dawn of civilization. Once again, the splintered consciousness of a subordinate class is not the product of cultural phenomena alone, but must be reproduced through the experiences of daily life.

Consciousness develops through the individual's direct perception of and participation in social life.[1] Indeed, everyday experience itself often acts as an inertial stabilizing force. For instance, when the working population is effectively stratified, individual needs and self-concepts develop in a correspondingly stratified, individual needs and self-concepts develop in a correspondingly fragmented manner. Youth of different racial, sexual, ethnic, or economic characteristics directly perceive the economic positions and prerogatives of "their kind of people." By adjusting their aspiration accordingly, they not only reproduce stratification on the level of personal consciousness, but bring their needs into (at least partial) harmony with the fragmented conditions of economic life. Similarly, individuals tend to channel the development of their personal powers—cognitive, emotional, physical, aesthetic, and spiritual—in directions where they will have an opportunity to exercise them. Thus the alienated character of work, for example, leads people to guide their creative potentials to areas outside of economic activity: consumption, travel, sexuality, and family life. So needs and need-satisfaction again tend to fall into congruence and alienated labor is reproduced on the level of personal consciousness.[2]

But this congruence is continually disrupted. For the satisfaction of needs gives rise to new needs. These new needs derive from the logic of personal development as well as from the evolving structure of material life, and in turn undercut the reproduction of consciousness. For this reason the reproduction of consciousness cannot be the simple unintended by-product of social experience. Rather, social relationships must be consciously organized to facilitate the reproduction of consciousness.

Take, for instance, the organization of the capitalist enterprise. . . . Power relations and hiring criteria within the enterprise are organized so as to reproduce the workers' self-concepts, the legitimacy of their assignments within the hierarchy, a sense of the technological inevitability of the hierarchical division of labor itself, and the social distance among groups of workers in the organization. Indeed, while token gestures towards workers' self-management may be a successful motivational gimmick, any delegation of real power to workers becomes a threat to profits because it tends to undermine patterns of consciousness compatible with capitalist control. By generating new needs and possibilities, by demonstrating the feasibility of a more thoroughgoing economic democracy, by increasing worker solidarity, an integrated and politically conscious program of worker involvement in decision-making may undermine the power structure of the enterprise. Management will accede to such changes only under extreme duress of worker rebellion and rapidly disintegrating morale, if at all.

But the reproduction of consciousness cannot be insured by these direct mechanisms alone. The initiation of youth into the economic system is further facilitated by a series of institutions, including the family and the educational system, that are more immediately related to the formation of personality and consciousness. Education works primarily through the institutional relations to which students are subjected. Thus schooling fosters and rewards the development of certain capacities and the expression of certain needs, while thwarting and penalizing others. Through these insitutional relationships, the educational system tailors the self-concepts, aspirations, and social class identifications of individuals to the requirements of the social division of labor.

The extent to which the educational system actually accomplishes these objectives varies considerably from one period to the next. We shall see in later chapters that recurrently through U.S. history these reproduction mechanisms have failed, sometimes quite spectacularly. In most periods— and the present is certainly no exception—efforts to use the schools to reproduce and extend capitalist production relations have been countered both by the internal dynamic of the educational system and by popular opposition.

In earlier chapters we have identified the two main objectives of dominant classes in educational policy: the production of labor power and the reproduction of those institutions and social relationships which facilitate the translation of labor power intro profits. We may now be considerably more concrete about the way that educational institutions are structured to meet these objectives. First, schooling produces many of the technical and cognitive skills required for adequate job performance. Second, the educational system helps legitimate economic inequality. As we argued in the last chapter, the objective and meritocratic orientation of U.S. education, reduces discontent over both the hierarchical division of labor and the process through which individuals attain position in it. Third, the school produces, rewards, and labels personal characteristics relevant to the staffing of positions in the hierarchy. Fourth, the educational system, through the pattern of status distinctions it fosters, reinforces the stratified consciousness on which the fragmentation of subordinate economic classes is based.

What aspects of the educational system allow it to serve these various functions? We shall suggest in the next section that the educational system's ability to reproduce the consciousness of workers lies in a straightforward correspondence principle: For the past century at least, schooling has contributed to the reproduction of the social relations of production largely through the correspondence between school and class structure.

Upon the slightest reflection, this assertion is hardly surprising. All major institutions in a "stable" social system will direct personal development in a direction compatible with its reproduction. Of course, this is not, in itself, a critique of capitalism or of U.S. education. In any conceivable society, individuals are forced to develop their capacities in one direction or another. The idea of a social system which merely allows people to develop freely according to their "inner natures" is quite unthinkable, since human nature only acquires a concrete form through the interaction of the physical world and preestablished social relationships.

Our critique of education and other aspects of human development in the United States fully recognizes the necessity of some form of socialization. The critical question is: What for? In the United States the human development experience is dominated by an undemocratic, irrational, and exploitative economic structure. Young people have no recourse from the requirements of the system but a life of poverty, dependence, and economic insecurity. Our critique, not surprisingly, centers on the structure of jobs. In the U.S. economy work has become a fact of life to which individuals must by and large submit and over which they have no control. Like the weather, work "happens" to people. A liberated, participatory, democratic, and creative alternative can hardly be imagined, much less experienced. Work under capitalism is an alienated activity.

To reproduce the social relations of production, the educational system must try to teach people to be properly subordinate and render them sufficiently fragmented in consciousness to preclude their getting together to shape their own material existence. The forms of consciousness and behavior fostered by the educational system must themselves be alienated, in the sense that they conform neither to the dictates of technology in the struggle with nature, nor to the inherent developmental capacities of individuals, but rather to the needs of the capitalist class. It is the prerogatives of capital and the imperatives of profit, not human capacities and technical realities, which render U.S. schooling what it is. This is our charge.

The Correspondence Principle

In the social production which men carry on they enter into definite relations which are indispensible and independent of their will. . . . The sum total of these relations of production constitutes . . . the real foundation on which rise legal and political superstructures, and to which correspond definite forms of social consciousness.

Karl Marx,
CONTRIBUTION TO A CRITIQUE OF POLITICAL ECONOMY, 1857

The educational system helps integrate youth into the economic system, we believe, through a structural correspondence between its social relations and those of production. The structure of social relations in education not only inures the student to the discipline of the work place, but develops the types of personal demeanor, modes of self-presentation, self-image, and social-class identifications which are the crucial ingredients of job adequacy. Specifically, the social relationships of education—the relationships between administrators and teachers, teachers and students, students and students, and students and their work—replicate the hierarchical division of labor. Hierarchical relations are reflected in the vertical authority lines from administrators to teachers to students. Alienated labor is reflected in the student's lack of control over his or her education, the alienation of the student from the curriculum content, and the motivation of school work through a system of grades and other external rewards rather than the student's integration with either the process (learning) or the outcome (knowledge) of the educational "production process." Fragmentation in work is reflected in the institutionalized and often destructive competition among students through continual and ostensibly meritocratic ranking and evaluation. By attuning young people to a set of social relationships similar to those of the work place, schooling attempts to gear the development of personal needs to its requirements.

But the correspondence of schooling with the social relations of production goes beyond this aggregate level. Different levels of education feed workers into different levels within the occupational structure and, correspondingly, tend toward an internal organization comparable to levels in the hierarchical division of labor. As we have seen, the lowest levels in the hierarchy of the enterprise emphasize rule-following, middle levels, dependability, and the capacity to operate without direct and continuous supervision while the higher levels stress the internalization of the norms of the enterprise. Similarly, in education, lower levels (junior and senior high school) tend to severely limit and channel the activities of students. Somewhat higher up the educational ladder, teacher and community colleges allow for more independent activity and less overall supervision. At the top, the elite four-year colleges emphasize social relationships conformable with the higher levels in the production herarchy.[3] Thus schools continually maintain their hold on students. As they "master" one type of behavioral regulation, they are either allowed to progress to the next or are channeled into the corresponding level in the hierachy of production. Even within a single school, the social relationships of different tracks tend to conform to different behavioral norms. Thus in high school, vocational and general tracks emphasize rule-following and close supervision, while the college track tends toward a more open atmosphere emphasizing the internalization of norms.

These differences in the social relationships among and within schools, in part, reflect both the social backgrounds of the student body and their likely future economic positions. Thus blacks and other minorities are concentrated in schools whose repressive, arbitrary, generally chaotic internal order, coercive authority structures, and minimal possibilities for advancement mirror the characteristics of inferior job situations. Similarly, predominantly working-class schools tend to emphasize behavioral control and rule-following, while schools in well-to-do suburbs employ relatively open systems that favor greater student participation, less direct supervision, more student electives, and, in general, a value system stressing internalized standards of control.

The differential socialization patterns of schools attended by students of different social classes do not arise by accident. Rather, they reflect the fact that the educational objectives and expectations of administrators, teachers, and parents (as well as the responsiveness of students to various patterns of teaching and control) differ for students of different social classes. At crucial turning points in the history of U.S. education, changes in the social relations of schooling have been dictated in the interests of a more harmonious reproduction of the class structure. But in the day-to-day operation of the schools, the consciousness of different occupational strata, derived from their cultural milieu and work experience, is crucial to the maintenance of the correspondences we have described. That working-class parents seem to favor stricter educational methods is a reflection of their own work experiences, which have demonstrated that submission to authority is an essential ingredient in one's ability to get and hold a steady, well-paying job. That professional and self-employed parents prefer a more open atmosphere and a greater emphasis on motivational control is similarly a reflection of their position in the social division of labor. When given the opportunity, higher-status parents are far more likely than their lower-status neighbors to choose "open classrooms" for their children.[4]

Differences in the social relationships of schooling are further reinforced by inequalities in financial resources. The paucity of financial support for the education of children from minority groups and low-income families leaves more resources to be devoted to the children of those with more commanding roles in the economy; it also forces upon the teachers and school administrators in the working-class schools a type of social relationships that fairly closely mirrors that of the factory. Financial considerations in poorly supported schools militate against small intimate classes, multiple elective courses, and specialized teachers (except for disciplinary personnel). They preclude the amounts of free time for teachers and free space required for a more open, flexible educational environment. The well-financed schools attended by the children of the rich can offer much greater opportunities for the development of the capacity for sustained independent work and all the other characteristics required for adequate job performance in the upper levels of the occupational hierarchy.

Much of this description will most likely be familiar to the reader and has been documented many times.[5] But only recently has there been an attempt at statistical verification. We will review a number of excellent studies, covering both higher and secondary education. Jeanne Binstock investigated the different patterns of social relations of higher education by analyzing the college handbooks covering rules, regulations, and norms of fifty-two public junior colleges, state universities, teacher-training colleges, and private, secular, denominational, and Catholic colleges. Binstock rated each school along a host of dimensions,[6] including the looseness or strictness of academic structure, the extent of regulations governing personal and social conduct, and the degree of control of the students over their cultural affairs and extracurricular activities. Her general conclusion is quite simple:

> The major variations of college experiences are linked to basic psychological differences in work perception and aspiration among the major social class (occupational) groups who are its major consumers. Each social class is different in its beliefs as to which technical and interpersonal skills, character traits, and work values are most valuable for economic survival (stability) or to gain economic advantage (mobility). Each class (with subvariations based on religion and level of urban-ness) has its own economic consciousness, based on its own work experiences and its own ideas (correct or not) of the expectations appropriate to positions on the economic ladder above their own. . . . Colleges compete over the various social class markets by specializing their offerings. Each different type of undergraduate college survives by providing circumscribed sets of "soft" and "hard" skills training that generally corresponds both to the expectations of a particular social class group of customers and to specific needs for sets of "soft" and "hard" skills at particular layers of the industrial system.[7]

Binstock isolated several organizational traits consistently related to the various educational institutions she studied. First, she distinguished between behavioral control which involves rules over the student's behavior rather than intentions and stresses external compliance rather than internalized norms, and motivational control which emphasizes unspecified, variable, and highly flexible task-orientation, and seeks to promote value systems that stress ambiguity and innovation over certainty, tradition, and conformity. Second, Binstock isolated a leader-versus-follower orientation with some schools stressing the future subordinate positions of its charges and teaching docility, and others stressing the need to develop "leadership" self-concepts.

Binstock found that institutions that enroll working-class students and are geared to staff lower-level jobs in the production hierarchy emphasize followership and behavioral control, while the more elite schools that tend to staff the higher-level jobs emphasize leadership and motivational control. Her conclusion is:

> Although constantly in the process of reformation, the college industry remains a ranked hierarchy of goals and practices, responding to social class pressures, with graded access to the technical equipment, organizational skills, emotional perspectives and class (work) values needed for each stratified level of the industrial system.[8]

The evidence for the correspondence between the social relations of production and education, however, goes well beyond this structural level and also sheds light on the communality of motivational patterns fostered by these two spheres of social life. Juxtaposing the recent research of Gene

Smith, Richard Edwards, Peter Meyer, and ourselves, the same types of behavior can be shown to be rewarded in both education and work. In an attempt to quantify aspects of personality and motivation, Gene Smith has employed a relatively sensitive testing procedure, which he has shown in a series of well-executed studies[9] to be an excellent predictor of educational success (grade-point average). Noting that personality inventories traditionally suffer because of their abstraction from real-life environments and their use of a single evaluative instrument, Smith turned to student-peer ratings of forty-two common personality traits, based on each student's observation of the actual classroom behavior of his or her classmates. A statistical technique called factor analysis then allowed for the identification of five general traits—agreeableness, extroversion, work orientation, emotionality and helpfulness—that proved stable across different samples. Of these five traits, only the work-orientation factor, which Smith calls "strength of character"—including such traits as ". . . not a quitter, conscientious, responsible, insistently orderly, not prone to daydreaming, determined, persevering . . ."—was related to school success. Smith then proceeded to show that, in several samples, this work-orientation trait was three times more successful in predicting post-high-school academic performance than any combination of thirteen cognitive variables, including SAT verbal, SAT mathematical, and high school class rank.

Our colleague Richard C. Edwards has further refined Smith's procedure. As part of his Ph.D. dissertation on the nature of the hierarchical division of labor, he prepared a set of sixteen pairs of personality measures relevant to work performance.[10] Edwards argued that since supervisor ratings of employees are a basic determinant of hirings, firings, and promotions, they are the best measure of job adequacy and, indeed, are the implements of the organization's motivational system. Edwards, therefore, compared supervisor ratings of worker performance with the set of sixteen personality measures as rated by the workers' peers. In a sample of several hundred Boston area workers, he found a cluster of three personality traits—summarized as rules orientation, dependability, and internationalization of the norms of the firm—strongly predicting supervisor ratings of workers in the same work group. This result, moreover, holds up even when the correlation of these traits with such attributes as age, sex, social class background, education, and IQ is corrected for by linear regression analysis. In conformance with our analysis . . . , Edwards found that rules orientation was relatively more important at the lowest levels of the hierarchy of production, internalization of norms was predominant at the highest level, while dependability was salient at intermediate levels.[11]

Ewards' success with this test in predicting supervisor ratings of workers convinced us that applying the same forms to high school students would provide a fairly direct link between personality development in school and the requirements of job performance.

This task we carried out with our colleague Peter Meyer.[12] He chose as his sample the 237 members of the senior class of a single New York State high school.[13] Following Edwards, he created sixteen pairs of personality traits,[14] and obtained individual grade-point averages, IQ scores, and college-entrance-examination SAT-verbal and SAT-mathematical scores from the official school records.[15]

As we expected, the cognitive scores provided the best single predictor of grade-point average—indeed, that grading is based significantly on cognitive performance is perhaps the most valid element in the "meritocratic ideology." But the sixteen personality measures possessed nearly comparable predictive value, having a multiple correlation of 0.63 compared to 0.77 for the cognitive variables.[16] More important than the overall predictive value of the personality traits, however, was the pattern of their contribution to grades. To reveal this pattern, we first eliminated the effect of differences in cognitive performance in individual grades and then calculated the correlation between grades and the personality traits.[17] The results are presented in Figure 1.

The pattern of resulting associations clearly supports the correspondence principle and strongly replicates our initial empirical study of grading. . . .

FIGURE 1.
Personality Traits Rewarded and Penalized
(in a New York High School)

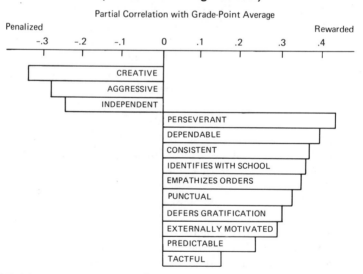

Partial Correlation with Grade-Point Average

NOTES: Each bar shows the partial correlation between grade-point average and the indicated personality trait, controlling for IQ, SAT-Verbal, and SAT-Mathematical. The penalized traits (left) indicate creativity and autonomy, while the rewarded traits (right) indicate subordinacy and discipline. The data are from Samuel Bowles, Herbert Gintis, and Peter Meyer. "The Long Shadow of Work: Education, the Family, and the Reproduction of the Social Division of Labor," *The Insurgent Sociologist,* Summer 1975, and is described in Appendix B (see Bibliography Appendix B). All partial correlations are statistically significant at the 1 percent level. . . .

The only significant penalized traits are precisely those which are incompatible with conformity to the hierarchical division of labor—creativity, independence, and aggressivity. On the other hand, all the personality traits which we would expect to be rewarded are, and significantly so. Finally, a glance at Figure 2 shows a truly remarkable correspondence between the personality traits rewarded or penalized by grades in Meyer's study and the pattern of traits which Edwards found indicative of high or low supervisor ratings in industry.

As a second stage in our analysis of Meyer's data, we used factor analysis to consolidate the sixteen personality measures into three "personality factors." Factor analysis allows us to group together those measured traits which are normally associated with one another among all individuals in the sample. The first factor, which we call "submission to authority," includes these traits: consistent, identifies with school, punctual, dependable, externally motivated, and persistent. In addition, it includes independent and creative weighted negatively. The second, which we call temperament, includes: not aggressive, not temperamental, not frank, predictable, tactful, and not creative. The third we call internalized control, and it includes: empathizes orders and defers gratification.[18]

FIGURE 2.
Personality Traits Approved by Supervisors

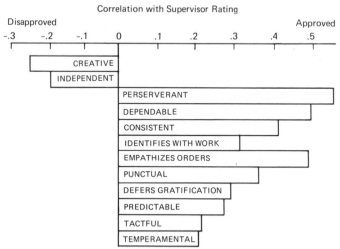

NOTES: The pattern of personality traits indicative of supervisor approval correspond to those rewarded in high school. Each bar shows the correlation between supervisor rating and the indicated personality trait. The results are similar to Figure 1, except that aggressive is insignificant and temperamental significant in the sample of workers. The data are from Richard C. Edwards, "Personal Traits and 'Success' in Schooling and Work." *Educational and Psychological Measurement,* in Press, 1976; "Individual Traits and Organizational Incentives: What Makes a "Good Worker?" *Journal of Human Resources,* Spring 1976, and are based on a sample of 240 workers in several government offices in the Boston area. All correlations are significant at the 1 percent level.

These three factors are not perfectly comparable to Edwards' three factors. Thus our submission to authority seems to combine Edwards' rules and dependability factors, while our internalized control is comparable to Edwards' internalization factor. In the case of the latter, both Edwards and Meyer's data depict an individual who sensitively interprets the desires of his or her superior and operates adequately without direct supervision over considerable periods of time.

Our theory would predict that at the high school level submission to authority would be the best predictor of grades among personality traits, while internalization would be less important. (The temperament factor is essentially irrelevant to our theory and might be expected to be unimportant.) This prediction was confirmed. Assessing the independent contributions of both cognitive measures and personality factors to the prediction of grades, we found that SAT math were the most important, followed by submission to authority and SAT-verbal scores (each equally important). Internalized control proved to be significantly less important as predictors. The temperament and IQ variables made no independent contribution.

Thus, at least for this sample, the personality traits rewarded in schools seem to be rather similar to those indicative of good job performance in the capitalist economy. Since moreover both Edwards and Meyer used essentially the same measures of personality traits, we can test this assertion in yet another way. We can take the three general traits extracted by Edwards in his study of workers—rules orientation, dependability, and internalization of norms—and find the relationship between those traits and grades in Meyer's school study. The results shown in Figure 3, exhibit a remarkable congruence.[19]

While the correspondence principle stands up well in the light of grading practices, we must stress that the empirical data on grading must not be regarded as fully revealing the inner workings of the educational system's reproduction of the social division of labor. In the first place, it is the overall structure of social relations of the educational encounter which reproduces consciousness, not just grading practices. Nor are personality traits the only relevant personal attributes captured in this data; others are modes of self-presentation, self-image, aspirations, and class identifications. The measuring of personality traits moreover is complex and difficult, and these studies probably capture only a small part of the relevant dimensions. Finally, both traits rewarded in schools and relevant to job performance differ by educational level, class composition of schools, and the student's particular educational track. These subtleties are not reflected in this data.

For all these reasons, we would not expect student grades to be a good predictor of economic success. In addition, grades are clearly dominated by the cognitive performance of students, which we have seen is not highly relevant to economic success. Still, we might expect that in an adequately controlled study in which work performances of individuals on the same job

FIGURE 3.
Predicting Job Performance and Grades in School
from the Same Personality Traits

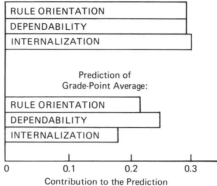

Prediction of
Supervisor Ratings:

RULE ORIENTATION
DEPENDABILITY
INTERNALIZATION

Prediction of
Grade-Point Average:

RULE ORIENTATION
DEPENDABILITY
INTERNALIZATION

0   0.1   0.2   0.3
Contribution to the Prediction

NOTES: The top three bars show the estimated normalized regression coefficients of the personality factors in an equation predicting supervisor ratings. The bottom three bars show the coefficients of the same three factors in an equation predicting high-school grade-point average. All factors are significant at the 1 percent level.

SOURCES: Bowles, Gintis, and Meyer (1975); Edwards (see full citations in Figures 1 and 2).

and with comparable educational experience are compared, grades will be good predictors. We have managed to find only one study even approaching these requirements—a study which clearly supports our position, and is sufficiently interesting to present in some detail.[20] Marshall S. Brenner studied one hundred employees who had joined the Lockheed-California Company after obtaining a high school diploma in the Los Angeles City school districts. From the employees' high school transcripts, he obtained their grade-point averages, school absence rates, a teachers' "work habits" evaluation, and a teachers' "cooperation" evaluation. In addition to this data, he gathered three evaluations of job performance by employees' supervisors: a supervisors' "ability rating," "conduct rating," and "productivity rating." Brenner found a significant correlation between grades and all measures of supervisor evaluation.

We have reanalyzed Brenner's data to uncover the source of this correlation. One possibility is that grades measure cognitive performance and cognitive performance determines job performance. However, when the high school teachers' work habits and cooperation evaluations as well as school absences were controlled for by linear regression, grades had no power to predict either worker conduct or worker productivity. Hence, we may draw two conclusions: First, grades predict job adequacy only through their noncognitive component; and second, teachers' evaluations of behavior in the classroom are strikingly similar to supervisors' ratings of behavior on the job. The cognitive component of grades predicts only the supervisors' ability rating—which is not surprising in view of the probability that both are related to employee IQ.[21]

Why then the association between more schooling and higher incomes? . . . we indicated the importance of four sets of noncognitive worker traits—work-related personality characteristics, modes of self-presentation, racial, sexual, and ethnic characteristics, and credentials. We believe that all of these traits are involved in the association between educational level and economic success. We have already shown how personality traits conducive to performance at different hierarchical levels are fostered and rewarded by the school system. A similar, but simpler, argument can be made with respect to modes of self-presentation. Individuals who have attained a certain educational level tend to identify with one another socially and to differentiate themselves from their "inferiors." They tend to adjust their aspirations and self-concepts accordingly, while acquiring manners of speech and demeanor more or less socially acceptable and appropriate to their level.[22] As such, they are correspondingly valuable to employers interested in preserving and reproducing the status differences on which the legitimacy and stability of the hierarchical division of labor is based. Moreover, insofar as educational credentials are an independent determinant of hiring and promotion, they will directly account for a portion of this association.[23]

Finally, family background also accounts for a significant portion of the association between schooling and economic attainment. Indeed, for white males, about a third of the correlation between education and income is due to the common association of both variables with socioeconomic background, even holding constant childhood IQ.[24] That is, people whose parents have higher-status economic positions tend to achieve more income themselves independent of their education, but they also tend to get more education. Hence the observed association is reinforced.

Indeed, there is a strong independent association between family background and economic success, illustrated in Figure 4. For the large national sample represented there, children of the poorest tenth of families have roughly a third the likelihood of winding up well-off as the children of the most well-to-do tenth, even if they have the same educational attainments and childhood IQ's. What is the origin of this effect? The inheritance of wealth, family connections, and other more or less direct advantages play an important role here. But there are more subtle if no less important influences at work here as well. We shall argue in the following section that the experiences of parents on the job tend to be reflected in the social relations of family life. Thus, through family socialization, children tend to acquire orientations toward work, aspirations, and self-concepts, preparing them for similar economic positions themselves.

FIGURE 4.
The Effect of Socioeconomic Background on Economic Success Is Strong even for Individuals with Equal Education and I.Q.

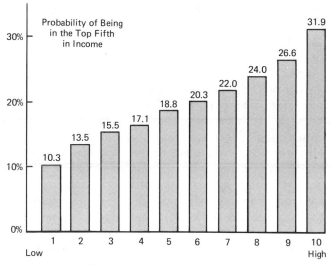

Family Socioeconomic Background (deciles)

NOTES: Each bar shows the estimated probability that a man is in the top fifth of the income distribution if he is from the given decile of socioeconomic background (as a weighted average of his father's education, occupational status, and his parents' income), and if he has an average childhood IQ and average number of years of schooling. That is, it measures the effect of socioeconomic background on income, independent of any effects caused by education or IQ differences.[24]

SAMPLE: Non-Negro males from nonfarm backgrounds, aged 35–44.

SOURCE: Samuel Bowles and Valerie Nelson, "The 'Inheritance of IQ' and the Intergenerational Reproduction of Economic Inequality," *The Review of Economics and Statistics,* Vol. 56, No. 1, February 1974.

Family Structure and Job Structure

> *According to the materialist conception, the determining factor in history is, in the last resort, the production and reproduction of immediate life. But this itself is of a two-fold character. On the one hand, the production of the means of subsistence, of food, clothing, and shelter and the tools requisite therefore; on the other, the production of human beings themselves, the propagation of the species. The social institutions under which people of a particular historical epoch and a particular country live are conditioned by both kinds of production; by the stage of development of labor, on the one hand, and of the family on the other.*
>
> Friedrich Engels,
> THE ORIGIN OF THE FAMILY, PRIVATE PROPERTY, AND THE STATE, 1884

Family experience has a significant impact on the well-being, behavior, and personal consciousness of individuals, both during maturation and in their daily adult lives. The social relationships of family life—relationships between husband and wife as well as between parents and children and among children—have undergone important changes in the course of U.S. economic development. The prospect for future changes is of crucial importance in the process of social transformation.[25]

Rather than attempt a broad analysis of family life, we shall limit our discussion to a few issues directly linked to our central concern: the reproduction of the social relations of production. Like the educational system, the family plays a major role in preparing the young for economic and social roles. Thus, the family's impact on the reproduction of the sexual division of labor, for example, is distinctly greater than that of the educational system.

This reproduction of consciousness is facilitated by a rough correspondence between the social relations of production and the social relations of family life, a correspondence that is greatly affected by the experiences of parents in the social division of labor. There is a tendency for families to reproduce in their offspring not only a consciousness tailored to the objective nature of the work world, but to prepare them for economic positions roughly comparable to their own. Although these tendencies can be countered by other social forces (schooling, media, shifts in aggregate occupational structure), they continue to account for a significant part of the observed intergenerational status-transmission processes.

This is particularly clear with respect to sexual division of labor. The social division of labor promotes the separation between wage and household labor, the latter being unpaid and performed almost exclusively by women. This separation is reflected within the family as a nearly complete division of labor between husband and wife. The occupational emphasis on full-time work, the dependence of promotion upon seniority, the career-oriented commitment of the worker, and the active discrimination against working women conspire to shackle the woman to the home while minimizing the likelihood of a joint sharing of domestic duties between husband and wife.

But how does the family help reproduce the sexual division of labor? First, wives and mothers themselves normally embrace their self-concepts as household workers. They then pass these onto their children through the differential sex role-typing of boys and girls within the family. Second, and perhaps more important, children tend to develop self-concepts based on the sexual divisions which they observe around them. Even families which attempt to treat boys and girls equally cannot avoid sex role-typing when the male parent is tangentially involved in household labor and child-rearing. In short, the family as a social as well as biological reproduction unit cannot but reflect its division of labor as a production unit. This sex typing, unless countered by other social forces, then facilitates the submission of the next generation of women to their inferior status in the wage-labor system and lends its alternative—child-rearing and domesticity—an aura of inevitability, if not desirability.

However, in essential respects, the family exhibits social patterns that are quite uncharacteristic of the social relations of production. The close personal and emotional relationships of family life are remote from the impersonal bureaucracy of the wage-labor system. Indeed, the family is often esteemed as a refuge from the alienation and psychic poverty of work life. Indeed, it is precisely because family structure and the capitalist relations of production differ in essential respects that our analysis sees schooling as performing such a necessary role in the integration of young people into the wage-labor system. We will return to this point in the next chapter.

Despite the tremendous structural disparity between family and economy—one which is never really overcome in capitalist society—there is a significant correspondence between the authority relationships in capitalist production and family child-rearing. In part, this is true of family life common at all social levels. The male-dominated family, with its characteristically age-graded patterns of power and privilege, replicates many aspects of the hierarchy of production in the firm. Yet here we shall be more concerned with the difference among families whose income-earners hold distinct positions in this hierarchy.

As we have seen, successful job performance at low hierarchical levels requires the worker's orientation toward rule-following and conformity to external authority, while successful performance at higher levels requires behavior according to internalized norms. It would be surprising, indeed, if these general orientations did not manifest themselves in parental priorities for the rearing of their children. Melvin Kohn's massive, ten-year study at the National Institute of Mental Health has documented important correspondences between authority in the social relationships of work and the social relationships of the family precisely of this type.

Kohn, in a series of papers and in his book, *Class and Conformity*, has advanced and tested the following hypothesis: Personality traits and values of individuals affect the economic positions they attain and, conversely, their job experiences strongly affect their personalities and values.[26] The most important values and behavior patterns in this interaction are those relating to self-direction and conformity,[27] with individuals of higher economic status more likely to value internal motivation and those of lower status more likely to value behavior that conforms with external authority. Thus, Kohn argues, individuals in higher-status jobs tend to value curiosity and self-reliance, to emphasize the intrinsic aspects of jobs such as freedom and choice, and to exhibit a high level of internalized motivation and a high degree of trust in interpersonal relationships. Conversely, people in lower-status jobs tend to value personal responsibility and the extrinsic aspects of jobs such as security, pay, and working conditions. Moreover, they exhibit more external motivations, a greater conformity to explicit social rules and they are less trustful of others.[28]

Kohn goes on to inquire which aspects of jobs produce these results and concludes that the statistically relevant job characteristic is the degree of occupational self-direction, including freedom from close supervision, the degree of initiative and independent judgment allowed, and the complexity and variety of the job.[29] Thus no matter what their economic status, whether white or blue collar, individuals with the same degree of occupational self-direction, tend to have similar values and traits. Self-direction versus close supervision and routinization on the job account for most of the status-related differences in personal preferences for self-direction, degree of internalized morality, trustfulness, self-confidence, self-esteem, and idea conformity.[30] He concludes:

> In industrial society, where occupation is central to men's lives, occupational experiences that facilitate or deter the exercise of self-direction come to permeate men's views, not only of work and their role in work, but of the world and of self. The conditions of occupational life at higher social class levels facilitate interest in the intrinsic qualities of the job, foster a view of self and society that is conducive to believing in the possibilities of rational action toward purposive goals, and promote the valuation of self-direction. The conditions of occupational life at lower social class levels limit men's view of the job primarily to the extrinsic benefits it provides, foster a narrowly circumscribed conception of self and society, and promote the positive valuation of conformity to authority.[31]

There remains, however, an important discrepancy between our interpretation and Kohn's. What Kohn calls "self-direction" we feel is usually better expressed as "internalized norms." That is, the vast majority of workers in higher levels of the hierarchy of production are by no means autonomous, self-actualizing, and creatively self-directed. Rather, they are probably supersocialized so as to internalize authority and act without direct and continuous supervision to implement goals and objectives relatively alienated from their own personal needs. This distinction must be kept clearly in mind to avoid the error of attributing "superior" values and behavior traits to higher strata in the capitalist division of labor.

Kohn then went on to investigate the impact of work-related values on child-rearing. He began, in 1956, with a sample of 339 white mothers of children in the fifth grade, whose husbands held middle-class and working-class jobs.[32] He inquired into the values parents would most like to see in their children's behavior. He found that parents of lower-status children value obedience, neatness, and honesty in their children, while higher-status parents emphasize curiosity, self-control, consideration, and happiness. The fathers of these children who were interviewed showed a similar pattern of values. Kohn says:

> Middle class parents are more likely to emphasize children's *self-direction*, and working class parents to emphasize their *conformity to external authority*. . . . The essential difference between the terms, as we use them, is that

self-direction focuses on *internal* standards of direction for behavior; conformity focuses on *externally* imposed rules.[33]

Kohn further emphasized that these values translate directly into corresponding authority relationships between parents and children, with higher-status parents punishing breakdowns of internalized norms, and lower-status parents punishing transgressions of rules:

> The principal difference between the classes is in the *specific conditions* under which parents—particularly mothers—punish children's misbehavior. Working class parents are more likely to punish or refrain from punishing on the basis of the direct and immediate consequences of children's actions, middle class parents on the basis of their interpretation of children's intent in acting as they do. . . . If self-direction is valued, transgressions must be judged in terms of the reasons why the children misbehave. If conformity is valued, transgressions must be judged in terms of whether or not the actions violate externally imposed proscriptions.[34]

In 1964, Kohn undertook to validate his findings with a national sample of 3,100 males, representative of the employed, male civilian labor force. His results clearly support his earlier interpretation: Higher-job-status fathers prefer consideration, curiosity, responsibility, and self-control in their children; low-status fathers prefer good manners, neatness, honesty, and obedience. Moreover, Kohn showed that about two-thirds of these social status-related differences are directly related to the extent of occupational self-direction. As a predictor of child-rearing values, the structure of work life clearly overshadows the other correlates of status such as occupational prestige or educational level.[35] He concludes:

> Whether consciously or not parents tend to impact to their children lessons derived from the conditions of life of their own social class—and this helps to prepare their children for a similar class position. . . .
> Class differences in parental values and child rearing practices influence the development of the capacities that children will someday need. . . . The family, then, functions as a mechanism for perpetuating inequality.[36]

Kohn's analysis provides a careful and compelling elucidation of one facet of what we consider to be a generalized social phenomenon: the reflection of economic life in all major spheres of social activity. The hierarchical division of labor, with the fragmentation of the work force which it engenders, is merely reflected in family life. The distinct quality of social relationships at different hierarchical levels in production are reflected in corresponding social relationships in the family. Families, in turn, reproduce the forms of consciousness required for the integration of a new generation into the economic system. Such differential patterns of child-rearing affect more than the worker's personality, as is exemplified in Kohn's study. They also pattern self-concepts, personal aspirations, styles of self-presentation, class loyalties, and modes of speech, dress, and interpersonal behavior. While such traits are by no means fixed into adulthood and must be reinforced at the workplace, their stability over the life cycle appears sufficient to account for a major portion of the observed degree of intergenerational status transmission.

Conclusion

You will still be here tomorrow, but your dreams may not.

Cat Stevens

The economic system is stable only if the consciousness of the strata and classes which compose it remains compatible with the social relations which characterize it as a mode of production. The prepetuation of the class structure requires that the hierarchical division of labor be reproduced in the consciousness of its participants. The educational system is one of the several reproduction mechanisms through which dominant elites seek to achieve this objective. By providing skills, legitimating inequalities in economic positions, and facilitating certain types of social intercourse among individuals, U.S. education patterns personal development around the requirements of alienated work. The educational system reproduces the capitalist social division of labor, in part, through a correspondence between its own internal social relationships and those of the workplace.

The tendency of the social relationships of economic life to be replicated in the educational system and in family life lies at the heart of the failure of the liberal educational creed. This fact must form the basis of a viable program for social change. Patterns of inequality, repression, and forms of class domination cannot be restricted to a single sphere of life, but reappear in substantially altered, yet structurally comparable, form in all spheres. Power and privilege in economic life surface not only in the core social institutions which pattern the formation of consciousness (e.g., school and family), but even in face-to-face personal encounters, leisure activities, cultural life, sexual relationships, and philosophies of the world. In particular, the liberal goal of employing the educational system as a corrective device for overcoming the "inadequacies" of the economic system is vain indeed. We will argue in our concluding chapter that the transformation of the educational system and the pattern of class relationships, power, and privilege in the economic sphere must go hand in hand as part of an integrated program for action.

To speak of social change is to speak of making history. Thus we are motivated to look into the historical roots of the present educational system in order to better understand the framework within which social change takes place. Our major question will be: What were the historical forces giving rise to the present correspondence between education and economic life and how have these been affected by changes in the class structure and by concrete people's struggles? How may we shape these forces so as to serve the goals of economic equality and liberated human development?

We shall show that the historical development of the educational system reflects a counterpoint of reproduction and contradiction. As we have already seen, capitalist economic development leads to continual shifts in the social relationships of production and the attendant class structure. These social relationships have involved class conflicts which, throughout U.S. history, have periodically changed in both form and content. In important respects the educational system has served to defuse and attenuate these conflicts. Thus the changing character of social conflict, rooted in shifts in the class structure and in other relations of power and privilege has resulted in periodic reorganizations of educational institutions. At the same time the educational system has evolved in ways which intensify and politicize the basic contradictions and conflicts of capitalist society.

NOTES

1. Herbert Gintis, "Welfare Criteria with Endogenous Preferences: The Economics of Education," *International Economic Review*, June 1974; Alfred Schutz and Thomas Luckmann, *The Structure of the Life-World* (Evanston, Illinois: Northwestern University Press, 1973); and Peter L. Berger and Thomas Luckmann, *The Social Construction of Reality: A Treatise in the Sociology of Knowledge* (Garden City, L.I., N.Y.: Doubleday and Co., 1966).

2. For an extended treatment of these issues, see Herbert Gintis, "Alienation and Power," in *The Review of Radical Political Economics*, Vol. 4, No. 5, Fall 1972.

3. Jeanne Binstock, "Survival in the American College Industry," unpublished Ph.D. dissertation, Brandeis University, 1970.

4. Burton Rosenthal, "Educational Investments in Human Capital: The Significance of Stratification in the Labor Market," unpublished honors thesis, Harvard University, 1972; and Edgar Z. Friedenberg, *Coming of Age in America* (New York: Random House, 1965).

5. Florence Howe and Paul Lauter, "The Schools Are Rigged for Failure," *New York Review of Books*, June 20, 1970; James Herndon, *The Way It Spozed to Be* (New York: Simon and Schuster, 1968); and Ray C. Rist, "Student Social Class and Taacher Expectations: The Self-Fulfilling Prophesy in Ghetto Education," *Harvard Educational Review*, August 1970.

6. Binstock (1970), *loc. cit.*, pp. 103–106.

7. *Ibid.*, pp. 3–4.

8. *Ibid.*, p. 6.

9. Gene M. Smith, "Usefulness of Peer Ratings of Personality in Educational Research," *Educational and Psychological Measurement*, 1967: "Personality Correlates of Academic Performance in Three Dissimilar Populations," Proceedings of the 77th Annual Convention, American Psychological Association, 1967; and "Nonintelligence Correlates of Academic Performance," mimeo. 1970.

10. Richard C. Edwards, "Alienation and Inequality: Capitalist Relations of Production in a Bureaucratic Enterprise," Ph.D. dissertation, Harvard University, July 1972.

11. Richard C. Edwards, "Personal Traits and 'Success' in Schooling and Work," *Educational and Psychological Measurement,* in press, 1975; and "Individual Traits and Organizational Incentives: What Makes a 'Good' Worker?" *Journal of Human Resources,* in press, 1976.

12. Peter J. Meyer, "Schooling and Reproduction of the Social Division of Labor," unpublished honors thesis, Harvard University, March 1972.

13. Personality data was collected for 97 per cent of the sample. Grade-point average and test scored data was available for 80 per cent of the sample, and family background data was available for 67 per cent. Inability to collect data was due usually to students' absences from school during test sessions.

14. These are described fully in Appendix B.

15. The school chosen was of predominantly higher income, so that most students had taken college entrance examinations.

16. The multiple correlation of IQ, SAT-verbal, and SAT-math with grade-point average (GPA) was $r = 0.769$, while their correlation with the personality variables was $r = 0.25$.

17. That is, we created partial correlation coefficients between GPA and each personality measure, controlling for IQ, SAT-V, and SAT-M. The numerical values are presented in Appendix B.

18. We emphasize that these groupings are determined by a computer program on the basis of the observed pattern of association among the sixteen variables. The fact that they are so clearly interpretable, rather than being hodgepodge, is a further indicator of the correctness of our analysis. We have not grouped the personality traits in terms of our preconceived theory, but observed rather how they are *naturally* grouped in our data. The results of the factor analysis are presented in Appendix B.

19. This is taken from Table 3 of Edwards (1975), *op. cit.;* and Samuel Bowles, Herbert Gintis, and Peter Meyer, "The Long Shadow of Work: Education, the Family and the Reproduction of the Social Division of Labor," in *The Insurgent Sociologist,* Summer 1975.

20. Marshall H. Brenner, "The Use of High School Data to Predict Work Performance," *Journal of Applied Psychology,* Vol. 52, No. 1, January 1968. This study was suggested to us by Edwards, and is analyzed in Edwards (1972), *loc. cit.*

21. The relevant regression equations are presented in Appendix B.

22. See Claus Offe, *Leistungsprinzip und Industrielle Arbeit* (Frankfurt: Europaische Verlanganstalt, 1970). Offe quotes Bensen and Rosenberg in Maurice Stein *et al.,* eds., *Identity and Anxiety* (New York: The Free Press, 1960), pp. 183–184:

> Old habits are discarded and new habits are nurtured. The would-be success learns when to simulate enthusiasm, compassion, interest, concern, modesty, confidence and mastery; when to smile and with whom to laugh and how intimate and friendly he can be with other people. He selects his home and his residential area with care; he buys his clothes and chooses styles with an eye to their probable reception in his office. He reads or pretends to have read the right books, the right magazines, and the right newspapers. All this will be reflected in the "right line of conversation" which he adapts as his own. . . . He joins the right party and espouses the political ideology of his fellows.

23. See Ivar Berg, *Education and Jobs: The Great Training Robbery* (Boston: Beacon Press, 1971); and Paul Taubman and Terence Wales, *Higher Education and Earnings* (New York: McGraw-Hill, 1974).

24. Calculated from an estimated normalized regression coefficient of 0.23 on socioeconomic background in an equation using background, early childhood IQ, and years of schooling to predict income for 35–44-year-old males. This is reported in Table 1 of Samuel Bowles and Valerie Nelson, "The 'Inheritance of IQ' and the Intergenerational Reproduction of Economic Inequality," *The Review of Economics and Statistics,* Vol. 56,

No. 1, February 1974, and in Appendix A. The corresponding coefficients for other age groups are 0.17 for ages 25–34; 0.29 for ages 45–54; and 0.11 for ages 55–64 years.

25. Margaret Benston, "The Political Economy of Women's Liberation," *Monthly Review,* September 1969; Marilyn P. Goldberg, "The Economic Exploitation of Women," in David M. Gordon, ed., *Problems in Political Economy* (Lexington, Mass.: D. C. Heath and Co., 1971); I. Gordon, *Families* (Cambridge, Mass.: A Bread and Rose Publication, 1970); Zaretzky, "Capitalism and Personal Life," *Socialist Revolution,* January–April 1973; and Juliet Mitchell, *Women's Estate* (New York: Vintage Books, 1973).

26. Melvin Kohn, *Class and Conformity: A Study in Values* (Homewood, Illinois: Dorsey Press, 1969).

27. Melvin Kohn and Carmi Schooler, "Occupational Experience and Cognitive Functioning: An Assessment of Reciprocal Effects," *American Sociological Review,* February 1973.

28. Kohn (1969), *loc. cit.;* chapters 5 and 10.

29. *Ibid.,* Chapter 10.

30. *Ibid.,* Table 10–7.

31. *Ibid.,* p. 192.

32. The occupational index used was that of Hollingshead, which correlates 0.90 with the Duncan index. Charles M. Bonjean, Richard J. Hill, and S. Dale McLemore, *Sociological Measurement: An Inventory of Scales and Indices* (San Francisco: Chandler, 1967).

33. Kohn (1969), *loc. cit.,* pp. 34–35.

34. *Ibid.,* pp. 104–105.

35. Two problems with the Kohn study may be noted. First, we would like to have more direct evidence of the ways in which and to what extent child-raising *values* are manifested in child-raising *practices.* And second, we would like to know more about the impact of differences in child-rearing practice upon child development.

36. Kohn (1969), *loc. cit.,* p. 200.

VALUES EDUCATION: PHILOSOPHICAL PERSPECTIVE

Elizabeth Steiner

The conflation of the desired and the desirable has led to conceiving values education as affective education. The development of feeling not of believing becomes the aim of values educators. Consequently, since values education is not encompassed in education directed toward the development of intelligence, education is broadened to include the development of preferences. This broadening is interpreted as preserving individual autonomy in the face of enculturating processes, i.e., nonintentional processes for transmitting culture. As seen in the sociological section, enculturating processes occur even in schools that are supposed to be educational institutions. Education is an intentional transmission of culture not a nonintentional one.

In my article on the teaching of values, I argue that desiring and valuing are distinct and so values education is cognitive not affective education. Development of intelligence suffices as the aim of values educators, and intelligence does not destroy personal freedom.

Another conflation, that of the desirable and the worthwhile, has led to conceiving values education as only theoretical education. The qualitative dimension of intelligence is neglected in education. In addition, I argue that desirability and worthwhileness are distinct, and hence values education must contain a qualitative cognitive dimension along with the theoretical. Intelligence must be developed to grasp unique, as well as general, essential or instrumental meaning.

According to content, ethical values can be sorted from other kinds of values, e.g., aesthetic. Ethical values are relevant to morals—right or good conduct. Richard S. Peters, a contemporary philosopher, explicates moral education as guiding one's cognitive development so that ethical principles of democracy—"impartiality, the consideration of interests, freedom, respect for persons, and probably truth-telling"—can be applied to living. But to so live, as Peters recognizes, conative development must also take place. "The moral life rests upon rational passions which permeate a whole range of ac-

286

tivities and which make them worthwhile for their own sake." As I state the matter in my article on teaching values, moral education goes beyond ethical education, a branch of values education, insofar as it guides the development of strong true character.

CONCRETE PRINCIPLES AND THE RATIONAL PASSIONS

Richard S. Peters

In education content is crucial. There is some point in raising aloft the romantic banners of "development," "growth ," and "discovery" when children are being bored or bullied. Romanticism is always valuable as a protest. But another sort of trouble starts when romantics themselves get into positions of authority and demand that children shall scamper around being "creative" and spontaneously "discovering" what it has taken civilized man centuries to understand. Some synthesis has to be worked out between established content and individual inventiveness. The basis for such a synthesis is to be found mainly in those public historically developed modes of experience whose immanent principles enable individuals to build up and revise an established content and to make something of themselves within it. In science, for instance, merely learning a lot of facts is a weariness of the spirit; but a Robinson Crusoe, untutored in a scientific tradition, could not ask a scientific question, let alone exhibit "creativity." Originality is possible only for those who have assimilated some content and mastered the mode of experience, with its immanent principles, by means of which this content has been established and repeatedly revised.

The same sort of Hegelian progression is detectable in morality. "Morality" to many still conjures up a "code" prohibiting things relating to sex, stealing, and selfishness. The very word "code" suggests a body of rules, perhaps of an arbitrary sort, that all hang together but that have no rational basis. To others, however, morality suggests much more individualistic and romantic notions, such as criterion-less choices, individual autonomy, and subjective preferences. Whether one experiences anguish in the attempt to be "authentic," produces one's commitment, like the white rabbit producing his watch from his waistcoat pocket, or proclaims, like Bertrand Russell, that one simply does not *like* the Nazis, the picture is roughly the

Reprinted by permission of the publisher from *Moral Education: Five Lectures* by James F. Gustafson, et al., Cambridge, Mass.: Harvard University Press. Copyright © 1970 by the President and Fellows of Harvard College.

same—that of the romantic protest. Synthesis must be sought by making explicit the mode of experience which has gradually enabled civilized people to distinguish what is a matter of morals from what is a matter of custom or law, and which has enabled them to revise and criticize the code in which they have been brought up, and gradually to stand on their own feet as autonomous moral beings. This they could never have done without a grasp of principles.

It is the details of this sort of synthesis that I propose to explore in this essay as a preliminary to discussing moral education; for it is no good talking about moral education until we have a more determinate conception of what is involved in being "moral." Because they are uncertain about this, many well-meaning parents and teachers are hamstrung in their attempts at moral education. If they incline toward the code conception, they tend to be authoritarian in their approach; if, on the other hand, they favor some variant of the romantic reaction, they may expect that children will go it alone and decide it all for themselves. A more adequate view of morality should reveal the proper place for both authority and self-directed learning in moral education. But I shall not have space to deal with details of such educational procedures in this essay—only to explore a middle road between these two extreme positions and to view the general contours of moral education from this vantagepoint.

The Function of Principles

There are some, like Alasdair MacIntyre,[1] who seem to hold that we have no middle way between allegiance to a surviving code and some kind of romantic protest. For, it is argued, moral terms such as "good" and "duty," once had determinate application within a close-knit society with clear-cut purposes and well-defined roles; but now, because of social change, they have broken adrift from these concrete moorings. A pale substitute is left in generalized notions such as "happiness" instead of concrete goals, and duty for duty's sake instead of duties connected with role performances that were manifestly related to the goals of the community. So we have a kind of moral schizophrenia in the form of irresolvable conflicts between "interest" and "duty" and no determinate criteria for applying these general notions, because their natural home has passed away. It is no wonder, on this view, that those who have not been brought up in one of the surviving tribalisms make such a fuss about commitment and criterionless choice; for there is nothing else except those ancient realities to get a grip on.

The Emergence of a Rational Morality Based on Principles

But even if this is how concepts such as "good" and "duty" originated, why this nostalgic fixation on those stuffy, self-contained little communities, such as Sparta, where they could be unambiguously applied? Could not one be equally impressed by the Stoic concept of a citizen of the world, by the law of nations forged by the Roman jurisprudents, and by the labors of lawyers such as Grotius to hammer out laws of the sea against piracy? The point is that both science and a more rational, universalistic type of morality gradually emerged precisely because social change, economic expansion, and conquest led to a clash of codes and to conflict between competing views of the world. Men were led to reflect about which story about the world was true, which code was correct. In discussing and reflecting on these matters they came to accept higher order principles of a procedural sort for determining such questions.

MacIntyre, it is true, applauds those like Spinoza who drew attention to values connected with freedom and reason. He admits the supreme importance of truth-telling;[2] he notes the massive consensus about basic rules for social living first emphasized by the natural law theorists, which H. L. Hart has recently revived as the cornerstone of a moral system.[3] Why then is he so unimpressed by this consensus that he gives such a onesided presentation of the predicament of modern man? Mainly, so it seems, because an appeal to such principles and basic rules cannot give specific guidance to any individual who is perplexed about what he ought to do.

Difficulties About Concrete Guidance

Two connected difficulties are incorporated in this type of objection to principles. The first, already mentioned, is that no concrete guidance can be provided by them for an individual who wants to know what he ought to do. This is usually illustrated by the case of the young man who came to Sartre wanting guidance about whether he should stay at home and look after his aged mother or go abroad and join the Free French. How could an appeal to principles help him? Well, surely he only had a problem because he already acknowledged duties connected with his status as a son and as a citizen. Would Sartre have said to him "You have to decide this for yourself" if the alternative to joining the Free French had been presented as staying at home and accepting bribes from the Germans for information? And surely if what is claimed to be missing is a principle for deciding between these duties, there are principles which would rule out some reasons which he might give for pursuing one of the alternatives. Supposing, for instance, he said that he was inclined toward going abroad because he wanted to determine precisely the height of St. Paul's Cathedral. Would Sartre have applauded his exercise of criterionless choice?

The existentialist emphasis on "choice" is salutary, of course, in certain contexts. It is important, for instance, to stress man's general responsibility for the moral system which he accepts. This needs to be said against those who smugly assume that it is just there to be read off. It needs to be said, too, in the context of atrocities such as Belsen. It also emphasizes the extent to which character is destiny and the role which choices play in shaping the individual's character. In this kind of development, conflict situations are particularly important, and if fundamental principles conflict there is not much more that one can say than that the individual must make up his own mind or use his "judgment." But we do not decide on our fundamental principles such as avoiding pain or being fair; still less do we "choose" them. Indeed, I would feel very uneasy in dealing with a man who did. And why should a moral theory be judged by its capacity to enable the individual to answer the question "What ought I to do now?" as distinct from the question "What, in general, are there reasons for doing?" Do we expect casuistry from a moral philosopher or criteria for making up our own minds?

The more important difficulty is the one MacIntyre has in mind, that fundamental principles such as "fairness" or "considering people's interests" give us such abstract criteria that they are useless because they always have to be interpreted in terms of a concrete tradition. I am very sympathetic to this objection, but I think that it also applies in varying degrees to all rational activities. To take a parallel: all scientists accept some higher order principle such as that one ought to test competing hypotheses by comparing the deduced consequences with observations. But this does not give them concrete guidance for proceeding. It has to be interpreted. To start with, what is to count as an observation? The amount of social tradition and previous theory built into most observation procedures, especially in the social sciences, is obvious enough. And how is the importance of one set of observations to be assessed in relation to others? This is not unlike saying in the moral case: Consider impartially the suffering of people affected by a social practice. But what is to count as suffering and how is one person's suffering to be weighed against another's? But do difficulties of this sort render the procedural principles of science useless? If not, why should fundamental moral principles be regarded as useless?

Fundamental principles of morality such as fairness and the consideration of interests only give us general criteria of relevance for determining moral issues. They prescribe what sort of considerations are to count as reasons. Within such a framework men have to work out arrangements for organizing their lives together. And just as in science there is a fair degree of consensus at a low level of laws, so in the moral case there are basic rules, e.g., considering contracts, property, and the care of the young, which any rational man can see to be necessary to any continuing form of social life, man being what he is and the conditions of life on earth being what they are. For, given that the consideration of interests is a fundamental principle of morality and given that there is room for a vast amount of disagreement about what, ultimately, a man's interests are, there are nevertheless certain general conditions which it is in any man's interest to preserve however idiosyncratic his view of his interests. These include not only the avoidance of pain and injury but also the minimal rules for living together of the type already mentioned. Above this basic level there is room for any amount of disagreement and development. People are too apt to conclude that just because some moral matters are controversial and variable, for instance sexual matters, the whole moral fabric is unstable. It is as if they reason: In Africa men have several wives, in Europe only one, in the U.S.A. only one at a time; therefore all morals are a matter of taste! As evils, murder and theft are just as culture-bound as spitting in the street!

The point surely is that stability and consensus at a basic level are quite compatible with change and experiment at other levels. Indeed to expect any final "solution," any secure resting place in social or personal life, is to be a victim of the basic illusion which is shared by most opponents of democracy, that of belief in some kind of certainty or perfection. But in determining what are basic rules and in seeking above this level ways of living which may be improvements on those we may have inherited, we make use of principles. Such principles have to be interpreted in terms of concrete traditions; they cannot prescribe precisely what we ought to do, but at least they rule out certain courses of action and sensitize us to features of a situation which are morally relevant. They function more as signposts than as guidebooks.

The Nature of Principles

A place for principles in the moral life must therefore be insisted on without making too far-flung claims for what they can prescribe without interpretation by means of a concrete tradition. Indeed I want to insist on the importance of such traditions for the learning of principles as well as for their interpretation. Before, however, this theme is developed in detail, more must be said about the nature of principles in order to remove widespread misunderstandings.

First of all, what are principles? A principle is that which makes a consideration relevant. Suppose that a man is wondering whether gambling is wrong and, in thinking about this, he takes account of the misery caused to the families of gamblers he has known. This shows that he accepts the principle of considering people's interests, for he is sensitized to the suffering caused by gambling rather than horror-struck at the amount of greenness in the world created by the demand for green tables. He does not, in other words, accept the principle of the minimization of greenness. He may or may not be able to formulate a principle explicitly. But this does not matter; for acceptance of a principle does not depend on the ability to formulate it and to defend it against criticism, as some, like Oakeshott,[4] who are allergic to principles, suggest. Rather it depends on whether a man is sensitized to some considerations and not to others.

Of course, formulation is necessary if one intends to embark on some moral philosophy in the attempt to justify principles. And it might well be said that the task of justifying them is a crucial one for anyone who is according them the importance I am according them. As, however, the central part of my *Ethics and Education* [5] was concerned with this very problem it would be otiose for me to present more than a thumbnail sketch of the arguments here. What I argued was that there are a limited number of principles which are fundamental but nonarbitrary in the sense that they are presuppositions of the form of discourse in which the question "What are there reasons for doing?" is asked seriously. The principles which have this sort of status are those of impartiality, the consideration of interests, freedom, respect for persons, and probably truth-telling. Such principles are of a procedural sort in that they do not tell us precisely what rules there should be in a society but lay down general guidance about the ways in which we should go about deciding such matters and indicate general criteria of relevance. It was argued that these principles are presuppositions of what is called the democratic way of life, which is based on the conviction that there is a better and a worse way of arranging our social life and that this should be determined by discussion rather than by arbitrary fiat.

Even if it is granted that arguments along these lines might be sustained for a few fundamental principles, further difficulties might still be raised. It might be said, for instance, that stress on the importance of principles in morality implies rigidity in the moral life. A picture is conjured up of Hardy-like characters dourly doing their duty whilst the heavens fall about them. Certainly some kind of firmness is suggested by a phrase "a man of principle." But here again, there are misunderstandings. A man of principle is one who is *consistent* in acting in the light of his sensitivity to aspects of a situation that are made morally relevant by a principle. But this does not preclude adaptability due to differences in situations, especially if there is more than one principle which makes different factors in a situation morally important.

Another time-honored objection is that principles are products of reason and hence inert. We may mouth them or assent to them, but this may be a substitute for acting in a morally appropriate way. Part of the answer to this objection is to be found in the answer to the criticism that links having principles with the ability to formulate them and to defend them. But there is a further point that needs to be made. Notions such as "fairness" and "the consideration of interests" are not affectively neutral. "That is unfair" is an appraisal which has more affinities with an appraisal such as "that is dangerous" than it has with a colorless judgment such as "that is oblong." Pointing out that someone is in pain is not at all like pointing out that he is 5 feet 6 inches tall.

The strength of the emotive theory of ethics derives from the fact that moral principles pick out features of situations which are not affectively neutral. This, however, does not make them inconsistent with living a life guided by reason; for this sort of life presupposes a whole constellation of such appraisals, e.g., that one should be consistent, impartial, and truthful, that one should have regard to relevance, accuracy, and clarity, and that one should respect evidence and other people as the source of arguments. It is only an irrationalist who welcomes contradictions in an argument, who laughs with delight when accused of inconsistency, or who is nonchalant when convicted of irrelevance. Science and any other rational activity presuppose such normative standards which are intimately connected with the passion for truth which gives point to rational activities. Unless people cared about relevance and had feelings about inconsistency science would not flourish as a form of human life. The usual contrast between reason and feeling is misconceived; for there are attitudes and appraisals which are the passionate side of the life of reason.

So much, then, for the usual objections to the conception of the moral life in which prominence is accorded to principles. I hope I have said enough to establish their place in it. I now want to show how they can be seen to function in relation to concrete traditions to which MacIntyre ascribes so much importance and how they can save us from the existentialist predicament which he views as the logical alternative to being encased in a surviving code.

The Complexity and Concreteness of the Moral Life

A man who accepts principles is too often represented as living in some kind of social vacuum and attempting to deduce from his principles a concrete way of living. This is an absurd suggestion. To start with, the disposition to appeal to principles is not something that men have by nature, any more than reason itself is some kind of inner gadget that men switch on when the occasion arises. If thinking is the soul's dialogue with itself, the dialogue within mirrors the dialogue without. To be critical is to have kept critical company, to have identified oneself with that segment of society which accepts certain principles in considering its practices. Rationality, of which science is a supreme example, is itself a tradition. Rational men are brought up in the tradition that traditions are not immune from criticism.

But criticism, thinking things out for oneself, and other such activities connected with a rational type of morality, cannot be exercised without some concrete content. For how can one be critical without being brought up in something to be critical of? How can one think things out for oneself unless one's routines break down or one's roles conflict? Adherence to principles must not be conceived of as self-contained; it must be conceived of as being bound up with and modifying some kind of content. Scientists cannot think scientifically without having any content to think about.

Complexity

In an open society this content is considerably more complex than in those small, self-contained communities where, according to MacIntyre, concepts such as "good" and "duty" had their naural home. The notion, for instance, that people are persons with rights and duties distinct from those connected with their roles is an alien notion in such close-knit communities. But once this is admitted, as was widely the case with the coming of Stoicism and Christianity, the content of the moral life becomes immediately much more complicated. For the norms connected with treating people as persons begin to interpenetrate those connected with roles and with the accepted goals of life. In trying to get a clear idea, therefore, about the contours of our moral life it is necessary to consider its complexity before we can grasp the concrete ways in which principles enter into it. At least five facets of our moral life must be distinguished.

First of all, under concepts such as "good," "desirable," and "worthwhile," fall those activities which are thought to be so important that time must be spent on initiating children into them. These include things such as science, poetry, and engineering and possibly a variety of games and pastimes. Most of these are intimately connected not only with occupations and professions but also with possible vocations and ideals of life. In our type of society they provide a variety of options within which an individual can make something of himself if he is encouraged to pursue his own bent as the principle of freedom demands.

Second, under the concepts of "obligation" and "duty," fall ways of behaving connected with social roles. Much of a person's moral life is taken up with his station and its duties, with what is required of him as a husband, father, citizen, and member of a profession or occupation.

Third, there are those duties, more prominent in an open society, which are not specifically connected with any social role but which relate to the following of general rules governing conduct between members of a society. Rules such as those of unselfishness, fairness, and honesty are examples. These affect the manner in which an individual conducts himself within a role as well as in his noninstitutionalized relationships with others. They are personalized as character traits.

Fourth, there are equally wide-ranging goals of life which are personalized in the form of "motives." These are purposes not confined to particular activities or roles, which derive from non-neutral appraisals of a man's situation. Examples are ambition, envy, benevolence, and greed. An ambitious man, for instance, is one who is moved by the thought of getting ahead of others in a whole variety of contexts. Both traits of character and motives can be thought of as virtues and vices. The traits of fairness and honesty are virtues; those of meanness and selfishness are vices. The motives of benevolence and gratitude are virtues; those of greed and lust are vices. Both character traits and motives, when looked at in a justificatory context, incorporate considerations that can be regarded as fundamental principles. Examples would be fairness and benevolence, which can be appealed to in order to criticize or justify not only other traits and motives, but also conduct covered by activities and role performances.

There are, finally, very general traits of character[6] which relate not so much to the rules a man follows or to the purposes he pursues as to the manner in which he follows or pursues them. Examples would be integrity, persistence, determination, conscientiousness, and consistency. These are all connected with what used to be called "the will."

The point in spelling out this complexity of our moral life is to rid us straightaway of any simpleminded view that moral education is just a matter of getting children to have "good personal relationships" or to observe interpersonal rules like those relating to sex, stealing, and selfishness. It emphatically is not. To get a boy committed to some worthwhile activity, such as chemistry or engineering, is no less part of his moral education than damping down his selfishness; so also is getting him really committed to the duties defining his role as a husband or teacher. These duties, of course, must be interpreted in a way which is sensitized by the principle of respect for persons; but no adequate morality could be constituted purely out of free-floating personal obligations.[7]

Concreteness

So much for the complexity of the content of the moral life which is to form the basis for any rational morality that appeals to principles. Let me now turn to the matter of concreteness in the interpretation of fundamental principles and moral ideals. The burden of the attack on principles by people like MacIntyre and Winch is to be found in Edmund Burke; it is that they are too abstract. "The lines of morality are not like the ideal lines of mathematics." My contention is that principles can be conceived of and must be conceived of as entering into the moral life in a perfectly concrete way without making them completely culture-bound.

Impartiality.[8] The most fundamental principle of all practical reasoning is that of impartiality. This is really the demand that excludes arbitrariness, which maintains that distinctions shall be made only where there are relevant differences. This is essential to reasoning, in that what is meant by a reason for doing A rather than B is some aspect under which it is viewed which makes it relevantly different. But though this principle gives negative guidance in that it rules out arbitrariness, making an exception of oneself, and so on, it is immediately obvious that it is quite impossible to apply without some other principle which determines criteria of relevance. The most obvious principle to supply such criteria is that of the consideration of interests, which is personalized in virtues such as benevolence and kindness.

The Consideration of Interests.   In practice the rays of this principle are largely refracted through the prism of our social roles and general duties as members of a society. If we are teachers, for instance, considering people's interests amounts, to a large extent, to considering the interests of children entrusted to our care. I once taught with a man who had such a wide-ranging concern for people's interests that he used to tell his class to get on with some work and to sit there with them, writing letters to old scholars, in order to get them to subscribe to an "Aid to India" fund. His present scholars were, of course, bored to death! He certainly had a somewhat abstract approach to considering people's interests!

Most Utilitarians, following Mill and Sidgwick, have stressed the importance of Mill's "secondary principles" in morality. The Utilitarian, Mill argued, has not got to be constantly weighing the effects of his actions on people's interests any more than a Christian has to read through the Bible every time before he acts. The experience of a society with regard to the tendencies of actions in relation to people's interests lies behind its roles and general rules. The principle that one should consider people's interests acts also as an ever-present corrective to, and possible ground of criticism of, rules and social practices which can also be appealed to when rules conflict. This point is well made by Stephen Toulmin in his book on ethics.[9] A man could stick too closely to his role and accept too uncritically what was expected of him generally as a member of society. He might be very much an organization man or a man of puritanical disposition, riddled with rules that might have lost their point, or without sensitivity to the suffering caused by unthinking insistence on the letter of the law. What would be lacking would be that sensitivity to suffering caused by actions and social practices which finds expression in virtues such as benevolence, kindness, and what Hume called "the sentiment of humanity."

Freedom.   Giving interpersonal support to the consideration of interests is the principle of freedom which lays it down that, other things being equal, people should be allowed to do what they want, or that, in other words, reasons should be given for constraining people in their pursuit of what they take to be good. This combines two notions, that of "wants" and that of "constraints," and immediately the concrete questions crowd in "What is it that people might want to do?" and "What sorts of constraints should be absent?" What, too, is to count as a constraint? Is it the want to walk about nude or to speak one's mind in public that is at issue? And are the constraints those of the bully or those of public opinion? The situation becomes even more complicated once we realize that, men being what they are, we are only in fact free from obnoxious constraints like those of the bully if we are willing to accept the milder and more leveling constraints of law. And so concreteness asserts itself. The principle only provides a general presumption, albeit one of far-reaching importance. At what point we decide that there are good reasons for constraining people because, for instance, they are damaging the interests of others, is a matter of judgment.

Closely related to the principle of freedom are ideals like "the self-development of the individual" and personal autonomy. But here again, concreteness is imperative, for what can "development" mean unless we build into the concept those modes of experience that it has taken the human race so long to evolve? And what sort of "self" is going to develop? Granted that this must come to a certain extent from the individual, who does this partly by his "choices," must not this "self" be fairly closely related to the normal stock of motives and character traits which are called virtues? And is it not desirable that higher order character traits, such as persistence and integrity, be exhibited in the development of this "self"? And how can the pressure for independence and the making of choices arise unless the individual genuinely feels conflicting obligations deriving from his occupancy of social roles and his acceptance of the general rules of a society? And what point is there in choice unless the individual thinks that what he decides can be better or worse, wise or foolish? And if he thinks that any particular act is not a pointless performance he must already accept that there are general principles which pick out relevant features of the alternatives open to him.

All of this adds up to the general conclusion that the ideals connected with the principle of freedom are unintelligible except against a background of desirable activities, roles, and rules between which the individual has to choose and that any proper choice (as distinct from random plumping) presupposes principles other than freedom in the light of which alternatives can be assessed.

Respect for Persons.   The same sort of point can be made about respect for persons, another fundamental principle which underlies and acts as a corrective to so many of our formalized dealings with other men. Indeed, much of the content of this principle has to be defined negatively in such concrete contexts. To show lack of respect for a person is, for instance, to treat him in a role situation as merely a functionary, to be impervious to the fact that he, like us, has aspirations that matter to him, is a center of evaluation and choice, takes pride in his achievements, and has his own unique point of view on the world. Or it is to treat him merely as a participant in an activity who is to be assessed purely in terms of his skill and competence in that activity. Worse at something becomes generalized to worse as a human being. In a similar way an excess of group loyalty or fellow-feeling can make a man seem not just different in some respects but generally inferior as a human being. Respect for persons, too, is at the bottom of our conviction that some motives are vices—lust, for instance, and envy and a certain kind of humility.

So much, then, by way of a brief sketch to illustrate the way in which I conceive of fundamental principles as entering into the moral life in a manner perfectly consistent with its complexity and concreteness. I now want to end by outlining my conception of moral education, which goes with this conception of the moral life.

Moral Education

One or two general remarks must first be made about the meaning of "education." There is a well-established generalized use of "education" which refers, roughly, to any processes of "rearing," "instruction," "training," etc., that go on at home and at school. But there is a more specific sense of education which emerged in the nineteenth century in which education is distinguished from training and which is used to pick out processes that lead to the development of an "educated man." In this more specific sense, education involves getting people to make something of themselves within activities that are thought to be worthwhile, in a way which involves an understanding that has some kind of depth and breadth to it. In this more specific sense of education, employed by most educators when they are thinking about their tasks, all education is, therefore, moral education, if we are to include the pursuit of good in morals and not just confine it to codes and more general dealings with other men. Again, we will have to leave on one side the vexatious question of justification in the sphere of "the good," of why, in other words, chemistry is more worthwhile than baseball or sun-bathing. We can pursue the implications of this view of education without getting immersed in that issue, which is a veritable "Serbonian bog where armies whole have sunk."[10]

The first implication is that educating people has very much to do with getting them "on the inside" of what is worthwhile, so that they come to pursue and appreciate it for what there is in it as distinct from what they may conceive of it as leading on to. It is in relation to this criterion of education that I want to make sense of notions such as commitment and being authentic, which starkly confront the instrumental attitude of "What is the use of it?" and "Where is this going to get one?" I have sympathy for the philosopher who was pressed at an interview for a chair to commit himself to the view that philosophy must have some practical use—whatever that means. He exclaimed in exasperation, "Look, we may have to say that sort of thing in order to get money from governments and businessmen for universities, but for heaven's sake do not let us become victims of our own propaganda."

The second implication is that educating people must involve knowledge and understanding. To be educated is not just to have mastered a know-how or knack, even if it is in the sphere of some very worthwhile activity such as cookery or ballet dancing. The Spartans were highly trained and skilled, but they are almost paradigms of a people who were not educated. Though depth of understanding is necessary to being educated, it is not sufficient, for a scientist can have a deep understanding of the "reasons why" of things and still be uneducated if all he understands is a specialized branch of science. "Education is of the whole man" is a conceptual truth in that being educated is inconsistent with being only partially developed in one's understanding—with seeing a car, for instance, as only a piece of machinery without aesthetic grace, without a history, and without potentialities for human good or ill. Let me now relate these two implications to the different facets of the moral life in order to show the indispensability of both content and principles and the proper place for the romantic ideal.

Commitment and Authenticity

One of the great enemies of education, in this specific sense, is second-handedness and instrumentality; hence Whitehead's polemic against inert ideas. What seems deplorable is not just that children should mug up some science because it is the done thing or in order to get good grades but that teachers should grind through their day with that dreadful fixed smile, or that people should be polite without sensing the point of it. Doing the done thing for conformity's sake seems a stifling corruption of the moral life, and, of course, it is an inherently unstable view; for a secondhand form of behavior is very susceptible to temptations and disintegrates when external pressures and incentives are withdrawn. This is tantamount to saying that moral education is centrally concerned with the development of certain types of motives, especially with what I have called the rational passions. When looked at in a justificatory context, some of these, e.g., benevolence, respect for persons, and the sense of justice, function as fundamental principles. But if such principles are to be operative in a person's conduct, they must become *his* principles. That means that they must come to function as motives, as considerations of a far-ranging sort that actually move him to act. Let us now consider the different facets of the moral life in the light of this commitment criterion of education.

Activities and Role-Performances. The trouble with the situation in which we are placed in education is not just that children do not always come to us glistening with a desire to learn what is worthwhile or with a predisposition toward mastering their duties; it is also that they are incapable of firsthand attitudes toward these activities and role performances until they are sufficiently on the inside of them to grasp them and be committed to what they involve. Although a child may have some degree of curiosity there is a great difference between this and the passion for truth which lies at the heart of an activity such as science, and until he feels strongly about this all-pervading principle that permeates science, it is difficult to see how his viewpoint can be anything but a bit external. He must, to a certain extent, be induced to go through the motions before he is in a position to grasp their point, and the point is given by the underlying principle, which personalizes one of the rational passions. To be rational is to care about truth; similarly, in the interpersonal sphere he must come to care about persons as centers of evaluation.

Of course there are all sorts of devices for bringing this about. In the old days, teachers, modeling the school on the army, used to employ a variety of coercive techniques. The progressives, in revolt, model the school more on the supermarket and try to gear their wares to children's wants and preferences. Then there are the less dramatic devices of stimulating by example and employing general guiding words such as "good" and "ought," which suggest that there are reasons but do not intimate clearly what the reasons are. The teacher's hope is that the proper reasons for doing things will become the pupil's actual reasons. This may come about by some process of identification. Admiration for a teacher may be turned outward toward involvement in the activities and forms of behavior to which he is committed, or an existing predisposition in the child, such as curiosity, may be gradually transformed by appropriate experience into the rational passion of respect for truth. This is likely to be greatly facilitated if the enthusiasm of the peer group is also enlisted, but this takes time and training. Let me illustrate this.

To be on the inside of an activity such as science or philosophy is not to have just a general curiosity or a merely abstract concern for truth. It is to be concretely concerned about whether particular points of view are true or false. These particularities are only intelligible within a continuing tradition of thought, which has been developed by people who adhere to a public stock of procedural principles. It is because of this concrete concern that they care desperately about things like the relevance of remarks, cogency in argument, and clarity of exposition; for how can one get to the bottom of anything without a concern about standards such as these which are indispensable to serious discussion? Sporadic curiosity is not enough; it has to be fanned into a steady flame and disciplined by adherence to the standards which regulate a common pursuit. The problem of education, as Whitehead saw only too well, is not just that of contriving the initial romance, it is that of bringing about acceptance of the precision and discipline required to wed a person to a pursuit. In this the support of the peer group is probably as important as the example and insistence of the teacher.

The judgment and skill which come with firsthand experience render activities more absorbing and worthwhile. The cultivation of personal relationships, for instance, and even sitting on committees, can become more and more absorbing as occupations for those who have a shrewd grasp of human behavior. Politics, as an activity, was quite different when practiced by Caesar rather than by Pompey, because of the skill and understanding Caesar brought to it. Although it is satisfying sometimes to relapse into routine activities requiring little effort (a point, I think, which Dewey appreciated too little), and although there is something to be said for occasional incursions into simple, and sometimes more brutish forms of enjoyment, it would be intolerable for a rational man to spend most of his life in such a circumscribed way. A minimum task of moral education is surely to equip people so that they will not be perpetually bored. Therefore, the case for skill and understanding, on grounds purely of individual satisfaction, is a strong one. There is also the point that, as soon as knowledge enters in as an important ingredient in an activity, an additional dimension of value, deriving from the concern for truth, is opened up.

In a pluralistic society like ours there must be a high degree of consensus at the level of those fundamental principles which underlie democratic procedures and, as I have already argued, it is obvious enough that there must be agreement about a level of basic rules which provide conditions necessary for anyone to pursue his interests. But above this level there is bound to be controversy. In this sphere of "the good" or of personal ideals, with which we are at the moment concerned, there are any number of options open to individuals. And the principle of freedom demands that there should be. It is in this sphere that talk of commitment and authenticity is particularly pertinent. One man may develop a lifelong passion for science. Another, more influenced by the Christian ideal, may find that his main sphere of commitment is in the sphere of personal relationships and the relief of suffering. Another may opt for an aesthetic type of activity.

On the other hand, another person may find almost complete fulfillment in devoting himself to the fulfillment of a role, that of a teacher for instance. There has been a lot of loose talk, deriving from Sartre's celebrated example of the waiter, about the incompatibility of authenticity with occupying a role. Playing a role, which involves either simulation or second-handedness, should not be confused with a genuine commitment to a role. And, of course, as has been emphasized repeatedly, there is no role which can *completely* contain one's concerns and duties as a human being.

Interpersonal Rules.   In the interpersonal sphere there may have to be firm insistence from the start on rules like those of keeping contracts, not stealing, punctuality, and honesty.[11] And why should children not *enjoy* mastering these rules as well as those of games? Unless, however, the reasons behind these rules eventually become the individual's reasons, the job is only half done. And this does not mean fostering a theoretical grasp of the conduciveness of such rules to the general good. That kind of notion never induced anyone to do anything except to preach theoretical revolution. Neither does it mean being swept by occasional gusts of sympathy when it dawns that somebody has suffered because he has been let down. It means, on the contrary, a steady but intense sensitivity to the consequences of actions, a constant and imaginative realization that in interpersonal relations one is dealing with persons who also have their unique point of view on the world and that this is something about them which matters supremely. In other words, it means the development of motives which personalize fundamental principles. It means also the development of judgment about particular moral matters that can only come to a person who has really got on the inside of this mode of experience. Making decisions and choices is too often represented as agonizing. For those who have attained some degree of wisdom it can be both a challenge and a delight.

It is not for a philosopher to pronounce on how children can be got on the inside of this more rational form of life, or on how the rational passions, which personalize fundamental principles, can best be awakened and developed. That is a matter for psychologists. The philosopher's role is only to indicate the sort of job that has to be done. But what he *can* say is that all talk of commitment and being authentic is vacuous unless this sort of job *is* done; for it is pointless to mouth these general injunctions unless concrete provision is made to implement them. What is to be lamented about young people today is not their lack of idealism but the difficulty of harnessing it to concrete tasks. Demonstrations, like mourning, are often symbolic expressions of feelings that have no obvious channel of discharge in appropriate action.

The Will. The importance of the rational passions can also be shown in the sphere of what used to be called "the will," where notions like those of integrity, determination, and resoluteness have their place. Of course this form of consistency is possible for people who adhere conscientiously to a simple code, perhaps because, like the colonel in *The Bridge over the River Kwai*, they accept unthinkingly some role-regulating principle such as "one ought always to obey orders" or "an officer must always care for his men." But such consistency is also possible for people with a more complicated morality if they genuinely care about the considerations which are incorporated in fundamental principles. Strength of character is so often represented in negative terms as saying no to temptation, as standing firm, as being impervious to social pressure. My guess is that rational people are able to do this only if they are passionately devoted to fairness, freedom, and the pursuit of truth and if they have a genuine respect for others and are intensely concerned if they suffer. As Spinoza put it: "Blessedness is not the reward of right living; it is the right living itself; nor should we rejoice in it because we restrain our desires, but, on the contrary, it is because we rejoice in it that we restrain them."[12] So much, then, for the first aspect of education, which concerns commitment to what is worthwhile. I now pass briefly to the second: that concerned with depth and breadth of understanding.

Depth and Breadth of Understanding

In any worthwhile activity or form of behavior there is a mode of acting or thinking, with its underlying principles, and some kind of established content which incorporates the experience of those who are skilled in this sphere. Depth is provided partly by the principles immanent in the mode of experience and partly by the degree to which it has been possible to discern the one in the many in the content.

The sin, of course, of the old formalism was to hand on content in a secondhand way without encouraging children to get on the inside of activities and to master the appropriate mode of experience for themselves. The converse sin of the progressive was to imagine that children could go it alone without any proper grasp of content or of the underlying mode of experience with its immanent principles. A more modern sin is to assume that a mode of experience, or a methodology, can be formalized and handed out and children saved the trouble of mastering any content. Don't bother, it is said, to teach children any historical facts, just teach them to think historically. This reminds me of the yearning, which one so often encounters, that one should hand out rules for Clear Thinking in twelve easy lessons or that one should set out philosophical method in advance of dealing with particular philosophical arguments. Enough, I hope, has been said about the intimate relationship between principles and concrete content to avoid that particular rationalistic delusion.

In the interpersonal sphere of morality there is, of course, a basic content, which every child must master, of rules to do with noninjury, property, contracts, and so on; but depth of understanding in this sphere is rather different. It is not like depth of understanding in the sciences, which consists in grasping more and more abstract theories; for in morality one comes very quickly to nonarbitrary stopping points in fundamental principles, such as the consideration of interests. Depth consists rather in the development of the imagination so that one can become more acutely aware of content to be given to these principles. What, for instance, is a man's interest? Above the level of physical and mental health what is to count? Surely not just what he thinks his interest to be? And so we start trying to understand various forms of worthwhile activity and personal ideals, not only in general but in relation to the capacity of particular individuals.

Respect for persons also opens up endless vistas for the imagination in making us vividly aware of the extent to which we drag our feet in failing to treat individuals and classes of people as persons in a full sense. It opens up, too, the whole realm of our understanding of persons. For understanding a person is more than being able to interpret his behavior in terms of wide-ranging psychological generalizations—even if there were any such generalizations that had been established—and it is not a mystic confrontation of "I" with "thou," about which there is little coherent that can be said. It is something about which a great deal can be said which is of cardinal importance for the moral life—about the way in which an individual's outlook is shaped by his roles, about his traits, and about his motives and aspirations. But most of this sort of knowledge we obtain by being with a person and sharing a common life with him, not by delving in psychological textbooks. This sort of knowledge is probably the most important sort for any moral agent to have; for our detailed appraisals of people are very closely intertwined with explanatory notions. Indeed, I made the point earlier that most motives and traits are also virtues or vices. And it may take a whole novel such as *Howards End* to explore concretely the range of an emotion like indignation.

Breadth of understanding, however, is of equal importance to depth in any concrete approach to the moral life. It has been argued that this life itself is a complex affair involving roles, activities, motives, and interpersonal rules. It also involves the disposition to be critical of this wideranging content in which any generation must necessarily be nurtured. The individual, too, may be confronted with conflicts arising from this heritage. How is he to be critical in an intelligent way about a social practice or about a particular feature of government policy unless he has some understanding of history and of the sorts of facts and unintended consequences of actions with which the social sciences are concerned? How is he to choose realistically between alternatives open to him unless he knows some facts?

It is absurd to encourage children to be critical and autonomous and not to insist on them learning facts which may inform their criticism and choices. In England, at the moment, we have all sorts of variants on the topic-centered curriculum, which is meant to induce moral commitment and to sensitize children to social issues. Discussion, of course, is the thing; it is regarded as almost sinful nowadays to instruct children in anything! But too often all that such discussions achieve is to confirm people's existing prejudices. They are not used as launching pads to dispatch children to the realm of some hard facts in the light of which they might make up their minds in an informed manner.

The same sort of point can be made about the necessity of breadth if children are to choose for themselves the sphere of activity within the wide range of what is desirable, to which they are to become personally committed and which may form the nucleus of a personal ideal. Not only must they have some breadth of content in order to be provided with concrete samples of the sorts of things between which they must choose; they must also make a concrete study of some of the forms of experience which have a special position in informing their choice. By this I mean studies such as literature, history, religion, and the social sciences, which, if imaginatively entered into, enlarge one's perspective of the predicament of man and so put one's own choice in a less abstract setting. The romantic ideal must at least have a classical background, if it is to function as more than a mere protest.

Conclusion

It might be said that my conception of moral education is indistinguishable from the ideal of a liberal education. I do not mind putting it this way provided that "liberal" implies no wishy-washiness and is used with awareness of the distinct emphases that it intimates.

A liberal education, to start with, is one that stresses the pursuit of what is worthwhile for what is intrinsic to it. It is hostile to a purely instrumental view of activities, to the bonds that link whatever is done to some palpable extrinsic end. The moral life, I have argued, rests upon rational passions which permeate a whole range of activities and which make them worthwhile for their own sake.

A liberal education is secondly one that is not narrowly confined to particular perspectives. I have argued both for a broad interpretation of the moral life and for the necessity of breadth of understanding to give concrete backing to the ideal of freedom, which is the most obvious ideal of liberalism.

Thirdly, a liberal education is one that is incompatible with authoritarianism and dogmatism. This is because a liberal education is based ultimately on respect for truth which depends on reasons and not on the word or will of any man, body, or book. This means, of course, not that there is not an important place for authority in social life, but that it has to be rationally justified—as indeed it can be in the bringing up of children. The use of authority must not be confused with authoritarianism. Respect for truth is intimately connected with fairness, and respect for persons, which, together with freedom, are fundamental principles which underlie our moral life and which are personalized in the form of the rational passions. The central purpose, however, of my essay, has been to show that adherence to such principles is a passionate business and that they can and should enter in a very concrete way into a man's activities, roles, and more personal dealings with other men.

NOTES

1. A. MacIntyre, *A Short History of Ethics* (London, Routledge & Kegan Paul, 1967).

2. See ibid., pp. 95–96.

3. H. L. Hart, *The Concept of Law* (London, Oxford University Press, 1961), chaps. viii, ix.

4. See M. Oakeshott, "The Tower of Babel," in *Rationalism in Politics* (London, Methuen, 1962).

5. London, Allen and Unwin, 1966.

6. For fuller treatment of the concept of "character" see R. S. Peters, "Moral Education and the Psychology of Character," *Philosophy* (January 1962); reprinted in *Philosophy and Education,* 2nd ed., ed. I. Scheffler (Boston, Allyn and Bacon, 1966).

7. It might well be asked whether any kind of priority is to be given to one or other of these distinct elements in the moral life. Are a man's motives in performing a role morally more crucial than the efficiency with which he performs it? Are his ideals, deriving from his concept of the good, more or less important than his adherence to interpersonal rules? Can "duty" be reconciled with "interest"? Are higher order traits, such as determination and integrity, to be admired irrespective of the purposes a man pursues or the rule he follows? The devil, according to all accounts, is damnably persistent. Is it possible to discern any rational unity in a moral life which emphasizes the importance of man as a person and not just as an occupant of a role? Or is MacIntyre right in thinking that such a moral life must necessarily be schizophrenic? These are difficult questions whose answer can be sought only by going into details of moral philosophy.

8. For extensive treatment of fundamental principles see Peters, *Ethics and Education,* chaps. iv, vi, vii, viii.

9. See S. C. Toulmin, *The Place of Reason in Ethics* (Cambridge, Cambridge University Press, 1950), chap. 11.

10. See Peters, "Education and the Educated Man," in *Proceedings of the Philosophy of Education Society of Great Britain,* January 1970.

11. For further treatment of this interpersonal realm of morality in relation to stages of child development see R. S. Peters, "Reason and Habit: The Paradox of Moral Education," in *Moral Education in a Changing Society,* ed. W. R. Niblett (London, Faber, 1963); reprinted in *Philosophy and Education,* 2nd ed., ed. I. Scheffler (Boston, Allyn and Bacon, 1966).

12. Spinoza, *Ethics,* part V., prop. XLII.

THE TEACHING OF VALUES AND MORAL EDUCATION

Elizabeth Steiner

Today, there is concern that our schools are teaching WASP values and, thus, excluding the values of other groups in the society. For example, the values of groups such as Chicanos and Blacks are thought to be excluded through the teaching in our schools. This concern appears to be based on one or more of the following beliefs:

B1. The values of the dominant group in society are not necessarily the most worthwhile.
B2. All values of a given society are worthy of perpetuation.
B3. The values of one person or group cannot be judged by another person or group.
B4. To teach values is to destroy personal freedom.

I shall agree that the concern is justified in terms of B1, but not in terms of B2, B3, and B4. I shall do so by showing how B1 is warranted and how B2, B3, and B4 are not. In the course of so showing, I shall offer some thoughts on the teaching of values and moral education.

Valuing is not appetitive but intellectual. It is not desiring but the prizing of that which is desired. Desiring is a positive feeling toward or a wanting of an object. Valuing is believing in the desirability of the object. Obviously, not all organisms that desire are capable of valuing; worms and such. Also, history makes obvious that human beings are value-makers *par excellance*. The record reveals assent and dissent toward objects of desire. Through the years, values were attributed to some objects and withheld from others.

The process of value conferral or the apprizing process can be in respect to either essential or instrumental meaning of the object. Essential mean-

This paper was presented in 1977 at a Symposium on Philosophy of Education held under the auspices of the Philosophical Society at State University of New York at Fredonia.

ing is the sense of an object which attaches to its very nature; it is its requisite and inherent sense. The requisite and inherent sense of lying is deception; of painting, aesthetic production in line and color. Instrumental meaning is the sense of an object which attaches to it through its use as a means. Both lying and painting, of course, could be means to fortune. Gould's and Picasso's lives so attest.

To apprize is to fixate belief in an object through qualitative cognition. That is to say, one bases assent as to desirability of an object solely on its unique essential or instrumental meaning. Unique essential and instrumental meaning is to be contrasted with general essential and instrumental meaning. To have general sense is to have significance in terms of a class, i.e., as an instance of a kind.

Perhaps qualitative cognition which is the heart of apprizing can be exemplified best in acts of aesthetic appreciation. In aesthetic appreciation, value is placed upon an object that has certain kind of qualities, because the meaning embodied in these qualities is comprehended. Thus, Gericault's *Epsom Derby* is valued for the way the horses really run on the canvas; and Rouault's *Flight into Egypt* for making it seem that we are actually there in an unbounded landscape, with sky extending over us in a chill dawn.

Given that one must appreciate what one desires in order to place value upon it and that this entails comprehending its embodied meaning, there remains a question as to the adequacy of the values. Surely, human beings have prized the wrong objects. They have been mistaken as to what is valuable in terms of goodness, beauty, or practicality.

Values, hence, must be subjected to evaluatings. They must be appraised. This appraising is a matter of quantitative cognitive. The objects must be considered insofar as they are instances of e-values. E-values are true values as to goodness, beauty, and practicality and are set forth in ethics, aesthetic, and praxiology respectively.

Schema 1 is an attempt to summarize the analysis of desiring, valuing, and evaluating.

SCHEMA 1.
Desiring, Valuing, and Evaluating

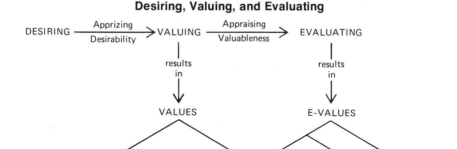

In the light of this analysis, it becomes clear that the values to be taught are not necessarily the values of the dominant group in the society. The values of the dominant group are not necessarily the most worthwhile. B1 is warranted, since the values to be taught are the e-values or the true values. Might does not make right as to goodness, beauty, or practicality. Those in power are not necessarily the philosopher-kings. That is to say, those in power are not necessarily those who are wise, i.e., those who know what is good, beautiful, and practical. In fact, it probably would be safe to say that those in power have never been and are not now the wise. But whether those in power ever have been, are now, or in the future will be wise is not the essential point in warranting the belief that the values of the dominant group in society are not necessarily the most worthwhile. The essential point is that wisdom is required over and above dominance in order that values be also valuable or be e-values and that wisdom is not a necessary consequent of dominance.

In regard to B2, all values of a given society are worthy of perpetuation, the analysis makes patent its falsity. Only values that are adequate or are e-values are worthy of continuing. Not all culture should be transmitted. This is true irrespective of the group or person involved. For instance, the Chicano value of machismo is not valuable. It expresses itself in action such as male chauvinism. Machismo is destructive of personhood, and so is unethical and should not be taught.

However, some believe that judgments like the one just noted ought not be made except by Chicanos or by individuals. What Chicanos or an individual should value should be judged by the Chicanos or by the individual involved. This belief, a specification of B3 that the values of one person or group cannot be judged by another person or group, is a rejection of the objectivity of value judgments. This rejection can arise either from the supposed relativism of judgmental criteria or of judges.

Consider first the supposed relativism of judgmental criteria. It is thought that what is good or beautiful or practical is relative to the person or to the group. Goodness, beauty, and practicality are supposed not the same for all human beings. What is valuable for one is supposed not valuable for another. This position denies evaluation, since there would be no basis for judging the person's or group's values even by the person or group itself. The person or group would be able to engage in valuation, i.e., apprize their desires as desirable in the light of the object's unique essential or instrumental meaning, but they would not be able to judge the essentiality or instrumentality in terms of goodness, beauty, or practicality. No intersubjectivity would be possible. To state the matter differently, no truth or falsity of values would be possible, i.e., no e-values or knowledge of good (ethics), knowledge of the beautiful (aesthetics), or knowledge of the practical (praxiology) would be possible. One consequence of this position is to rule out moral action, since there would be no ethical basis for human action. Morality too would give way to individual or cultural relativism.

At this point, relativists will expect me to counter their position. Although I am tempted to insert my Neo-Kantian theory of justification, I shall not here. Rather this paper is addressed to those who take seriously the question, "What ought I do?"

Turning to the supposed relativism of judges. It is thought that only the person or group that holds the values can fully know them and not be biased in judging them. A non-Chicano woman, for example, is taken as incapable of knowing Chicano values and as biased against them. The situation would be taken as better with a Chicano woman, for at least she is Chicano even though she supposedly cannot know male values and is biased against them. It would follow from this position that only Chicanos can teach Chicano values and only men, male values. To generalize the position, we can only judge and teach the values that we hold.

Critiquing this position depends upon senses of 'to know.'[1] One can know in a quantitative, a qualitative, and a performative sense. To know in a quantitative sense is to know a state of affairs as a class or as an instance of a class; it is knowing-that. To know in a qualitative sense is to know a state of affairs as unique; it is knowing-that-one. To know in a performative sense is to know a state of affairs as an actor; it is a knowing-how-to-do. Given these three senses of 'knowing,' knowing is extended beyond thinking to feeling and acting.

In the light of this extension, is the generalization that we only can judge and teach the values which we hold warranted? I shall argue that it is not. Even if it could be argued that to know values qualitatively and performatively requires that one espouse them or be a member of a group that does, nevertheless knowing values in the sense of being able to feel them and act upon them is not necessary for judging them. What is necessary is a quantitative stance in which one determines membership in the class of goodness or beauty or practicality. Hence, espousing the values to be judged rather than not espousing them could be a biasing factor. To subject one's person and society to judgment is not always easy and demands a special discipline.

In considering the part of the generalization which is about teaching values, attention must be paid to the different senses of 'teaching values.' One can teach about values or teach values from a standpoint of either process or product. To teach about values is to teach about the values people have and do hold, i.e., what the values are, why people have and do hold them, and so on. The psychology of values, the sociology of values, and the politics of value would be subjects about values. The Values Clarification movement in the teaching of values[2] also teaches about values insofar as students are guided, as the name implies, in making clear their values whatever they are. There is no consideration of valuableness, and so values are not criticized. Destructive self-seeking values stand proudly alongside constructive alturistic values.

Students can be taught values in the sense of how to value. What is involved is teaching appreciation. Again one can and probably should turn to the arts for insight into such teaching. Such teaching always involves the substantive as well as the methodological. Values are taught as well as the process of valuing. Also the values taught are those that are valuable; the art teacher picks masterworks for the class in art appreciation. Usually the teacher discusses why the values in these masterworks are e-values which are aesthetic. Art criticism also enters into the teaching.

Unless the basis of appraising values and hence sorting out the e-values is made clear and is justified as in art appreciation classes, teaching of values relative to goodness, beauty, or practicality will be much like the Values Analysis[3] approach set forth by the National Council for the Social Studies as an alternative to Values Clarification. In this approach, the principle governing appraisal must be merely acceptable to the evaluator. Consequently, evaluation is made arbitrary and so of no sense. Rather students must be taught a sound basis for appraisal of values.

Often the teaching of ethics is confused with the teaching of morals, and the teaching of morals is taken to be a kind of value teaching. But morals involves action as well as ethics. Ethics, of course, only encompasses e-values relative to goodness. Moral education, therefore, is a teaching-studenting process directed toward conative and cognitive development relative to goodness. A student's capacity for intending must be guided so that motive power for goodness is developed. The student's character must become strong. A student's beliefs in the good must be guided in their development so that a basis for good action emerges. A student's character must become true. Finally, a student's cognitive structures for performance must be guided in their development so that the student acquires action capabilities. A strong true character implies one that can and does act good.

Given this explication of the teaching of values and morals, the generalization that we only can teach the values which we hold is not true of the teaching of quantitative knowledge of values. All quantitative knowledge, including that of values, requires a universal stance. To be value theoretical, one must take a stance beyond one's own values or beyond the values of a particular group. At first glance, the generalization does appear true of qualitative and performative knowledge of values. In qualitative and performative knowledge of values, what is wanted is the kind of experience one would have if one held the values. But there is no reason why one cannot be directed to experience what a given group experiences or even what another individual has experienced. This is precisely what one does in teaching qualitative and performative knowledge. The generalization that only those who hold the values can teach their application does not hold.

The final belief to discuss is B4, to teach values is to destroy human freedom. To teach values does not destroy freedom in either of its senses. In one sense, 'freedom' means to be without restraint. To teach someone does not involve forcing them to live by that teaching. One can know morals and not be moral. Teaching *qua* teaching is not restrictive. In its other sense, 'freedom' means the capacity to exercise choice. Teaching does not take away this capacity, but makes it possible to exercise it. Knowledge indeed makes one free. Unless one has a knowledge of e-values, a good, beautiful, and practical life cannot be chosen.

NOTES

1. George S. Maccia, "Pedagogical Epistemology," *Proceedings of the Ohio Valley Philosophy of Education Society*, ed. by W. E. Brownson and J. E. Carter (Terre Haute: Indiana State University Press, 1973), pp. 57–76.

2. L. Raths, M. Harmin, and S. Simon, *Values and Teaching* (Columbus, Ohio: Merrill, 1966).

3. *Values Education: Rationale, Strategies, and Procedures*, 41st Yearbook of the National Council for the Social Studies, ed. by L. E. Metcalf (Washington, D.C., 1971).

PROBLEM IV

Educate How?

RESOLUTIVE THEME

Education Through Freedom

EDUCATION THROUGH FREEDOM: HISTORICAL PERSPECTIVE

B. Edward McClellan

Few problems have been as persistent or worrisome to American educators as the problem of freedom and control. In its most obvious form, the problem has manifested itself as a question of classroom discipline. Many teachers, burdened with custodial as well as educational duties and confronted with frequently hostile students, have come to regard the establishment of minimum control in the classroom as the first test of professional competence. Legendary accounts of failure on this score have at once documented the difficulty of the task and heightened the anxiety of the teachers who have had to face it.

Although the question of classroom discipline has always had a special immediacy about it, it is only one part of a more general problem of freedom in education. Educators have also had to make judgments about the freedom of teachers to articulate unpopular views; the freedom of school libraries to include controversial literature; the freedom of students to choose their courses, set the pace of their learning, express their political opinions, or even determine their mode of dress.

The readings included in this section offer historical perspectives on the problem of freedom in two general areas. David Swift's "The Problem of Control" sketches the history of classroom discipline from the eighteenth century when children attended schools irregularly until the twentieth century when attendance was both regular and prolonged. He finds that both the nature of the problem and the response of educators to it have changed dramatically over the centuries. By explaining these changes in terms of the changing role of the school in society, Swift shows clearly how the problem of discipline has always been affected by both fundamental educational aims and by the composition of the school's student population.

Paul Violas examines a second facet of the problem of freedom and control in education. His topic is academic freedom, and he explores the subject through a careful study of the restraints placed on public school teachers in the middle decades of the twentieth century. In his article, "Fear and Constraints on Academic Freedom of Public School Teachers, 1930–1960," Violas advances two notions that are particularly worthy of consideration. First, he suggests that the very sensitivity of modern public education to national needs—whether those needs be rooted in economic depression or international conflict—has served to restrict academic freedom. Second, he argues that even champions of academic freedom have often favored the idea less for its value in the search for truth than for its utility in the achievement of social reform.

As both Swift and Violas suggest, Americans have always carefully circumscribed the freedom of public school teachers and students. Readers may find it useful to ponder just how often this restraint has been the product of the internal, organizational needs of schools for order and how often it has been the result of controls imposed from the outside. It may also be interesting to ask why a society that has traditionally given its colleges and universities so much freedom has allowed its elementary and secondary schools so little. Finally, readers may wish to explore whether the conditions that have in the past restricted freedom show any signs of disappearing from contemporary American society and education.

THE PROBLEM OF CONTROL

David Swift

When considering the problems which pupils pose for public schools, we are likely to think first of educational problems, such as remedial instruction for slow learners, more effective methods for average children, and stimulation of gifted students to the full utilization of their potentialities. In addition, however, pupils also present problems of a custodial nature. On one hand, the school must try to keep all children in school, preferably until they graduate from the twelfth grade. At the same time, it is imperative that they be kept under control. Taken separately, these custodial tasks are not easy, and together they become formidable.

The public school has been delegated the responsibility of educating all children. Regardless of their background, ability or inclination, the school must keep them almost until they reach adulthood. If they drop out before that time, it is considered to be a failure not merely of the individual pupil but also of the school. Therefore, the motivation of pupils is a major concern of the school. It must do everything in its power to encourage them to remain, at least until they receive a high school diploma and, preferably, even longer. This task is complicated by the tremendous diversity among pupils. Universal compulsory education brings into the schools a student body characterized by an extremely broad range of social origins, motivations and abilities. Many of these pupils lack the willingness to learn the traditional skills and, in fact, resent having to come to school at all. If given a choice, they would stay home, work, or engage in other activities more pleasurable than those involved in formal education. But, they have little choice in the matter. Whether they want to or not, they must attend school, and it is the school's responsibility to see that they do.

Keeping all youngsters in school, however, is only one part of the job. Pupils also pose problems in control. This is a crucial problem, and its con-

Reprinted by permission of the publisher from pp. 31–62 of *Ideology and Change in the Public Schools* (Columbus, Ohio: Merrill Publishing Co.), 1971.

sequences extend far beyond educational issues. When, for one reason or another, a pupil fails to learn, it is regretable, but it is primarily an individual misfortune, in the sense that it does not have an immediate disruptive effect upon other students, the teacher, or the school. Overt misbehavior is a different matter. One mischievous boy or girl can upset an entire class, interrupting the education of other pupils and interfering with the instructor's attempts to teach.

If pupils get too far out of hand there is the danger of physical injury or property damage. In addition, teachers are expected to keep their classes under control; their inability to do so may cast doubts upon their competence and can lead to dismissal. Perhaps the most general reason for wanting to avoid disorder is simply that the work of teachers and administrators is easier when the school is running smoothly. At any rate, while the education of all pupils is certainly desirable, a modicum of law and order is considered to be essential.

The essence of the problem of control lies in the fundamental conflict between the aims of the pupils and those of the teacher. This conflict was aptly described by Waller:

> Teacher and pupil confront each other in the school with an original conflict of desires, and however much that conflict may be reduced in amount, or however much it may be hidden, it still remains. The teacher represents the adult group, ever the enemy of the spontaneous life of groups of children. The teacher represents the formal curriculum, and his interest is in imposing that curriculum upon the children in the form of tasks; pupils are much more interested in life in their own world than in the desiccated bits of adult life which teachers have to offer. The teacher represents the established social order in the school, and his interest is in maintaining that order, whereas pupils have only a negative interest in that feudal superstructure. Teacher and pupil confront each other with attitudes from which the underlying hostility can never be altogether removed.[1]

.   .   .

The Traditional Era

Misbehavior was a prevalent problem in the traditional American school, and it often attained serious proportions. In 1837, for example, over three hundred schools in Massachusetts alone were broken up by rebellious pupils.[2] Disruption of ten percent of the schools in the state[3] during a single year is especially notable in view of the fact that Massachusetts had been a leader in education since earliest colonial times, and was still, in many respects, ahead of the rest of the nation. Therefore, these figures may present an unduly optimistic picture of the country as a whole. We can assume that conditions in other states were not much better and frequently were considerably worse.[4]

In addition to minor mischief, which undoubtedly went on much of the time, two more serious forms of misbehavior directly challenged the teacher's authority: locking the teacher out of the school, and physically assaulting him. At the least, either of these would disrupt the school for several hours, if not the rest of the day. Frequently, however, these episodes led to the dismissal of the teacher and the closing of the school until a replacement could be found.

The first of these two types of rebellion was known as "putting out" or "turning out" the teacher. He was removed from the classroom either by subterfuge or by force, and then was prevented from getting back in. This process was discussed by Horace Greeley:

> At the close of the morning session of the first of January, and perhaps on some other day that the big boys chose to consider or make a holiday, the moment the master left the house in quest of his dinner, the little ones were started homeward, the doors and windows suddenly and securely barricaded, and the older pupils, thus fortified against intrusion, proceeded to spend the afternoon in play and hilarity. I have known a master to make a desperate struggle for admission, but the odds were too great. If he appealed to the neighboring fathers, they were apt to advise him to desist, and let matters take their course. I recollect one instance, however, where a youth was shut out who, procuring a piece of board, mounted from a fence to the roof of the schoolhouse and covered the top of the chimney nicely with his board. Ten minutes thereafter, the house was filled with smoke, and its inmates, opening the doors and windows, were glad to make terms with the outsider.[5]

The other serious type of rebellion involved physical interference with, or attacks upon, the teacher. Sometimes these confrontations evolved out of a situation which the rebels felt to be grossly unfair, as in unreasonable punishment administered to a classmate. Mild and just chastisement was not likely to stimulate other pupils to attack the teacher.

> If, however, the whipping was continued beyond what was considered by the older boys as reasonable, and the boy happened to be a favorite with his fellows, some protest on the part of the big boys might be made; and if that did not effect the object, forcible, if not indeed armed, intervention might be the result.[6]

Castigation of a big boy was particularly crucial because it ". . . required greater effort, the punishment was usually more severe, and the chances of interference were materially enhanced."[7]

On other occasions, trouble might even grow out of a seemingly innocuous, good-humored contest between teacher and pupils. For example, one account of a nineteenth-century school related:

> In the school were several bad boys who were good wrestlers, and prided themselves on athletic sports and feats. [The teacher] was a pretty good wres-

tler himself, or thought he was. Indulging in the sport with some of them he was downed successively by two or three and soon, as a result, lost control of the school, as they found they could handle him, and so concluded to have their own way.[8]

The seriousness of such incidents resided in the possibility that they might lead to a permanent loss of control. A teacher who had been defeated in these encounters was likely to have difficulty restoring and maintaining order. If the situation got too far out of hand, as it sometimes did, his usefulness at that school was at an end, and the loss of his job was apt to follow. For instance, the teacher who engaged in the wrestling matches and subsequently lost control over his class consulted the trustees of the school:

. . . it was thought best that he should resign as the signs were unmistakable that an insurrection was brewing; and if he had insisted on staying, in all probability he would have been thrown out with little ceremony. . . .[9]

Johnson noted that when pupils had "put out" two or three teachers in succession, the school got the reputation of being "hard," with the result that the school authorities might have to offer liberal wages and seek out a teacher who could subdue the young rebels.[10]

For such reasons, the basic task of the traditional teacher was considered to be *schoolkeeping* rather than *school teaching*. "The teacher's job was to maintain order—to keep the class intact. In the upper grades, as often as not, this meant that the teacher had to be able physically to subdue the larger members of the class."[11] Severity in a teacher was considered to be a virtue. Unless he made frequent and forceful use of the rod, many parents felt uneasy and doubted that the children could be learning much.[12] The average schoolmaster used extremely primitive methods for controlling his pupils. He relied mainly on a three-foot ruler, known as a *ferule*, and the *heavy gad*, a flexible sapling about five feet in length. These implements were applied "with force and frequency" to boys and girls, to young and old alike.[13] Cubberly aptly summed up the situation when he commented, "There was little 'soft pedagogy' in the management of either town or rural schools in the days before the Civil War."[14]

American schools were not alone in their use of severe discipline. In centuries past, schools everywhere had relied upon harsh methods of control. However, this general tendency may have been further accentuated by material conditions prevalent in the American colonies and on the frontier. As historian Bernard Bailyn has pointed out, these difficult conditions undermined the authority of parents. Their traditional ideas and customs were of little help in facing unfamiliar problems posed by the wilderness. Instead, such conditions put a premium upon youthful strength and originality. Moreover, abundant land coupled with a scarcity of labor offered young adults opportunities to become economically independent. The elders, attempting desperately to prevent what they interpreted to be the disintegration of their families and the decay of the entire culture, threatened to impose severe sanctions against disobedience. In Massachusetts and Connecticut, for example, the death penalty was authorized as a suitable punishment for disobeying one's parents.[15] Although it is unlikely that many rebellious children were subjected to this extreme penalty, its existence does suggest that control was considered to be a serious problem and that severe measures were thought to be appropriate.

Subsequent generations witnessed some amelioration of punishment, but harsh discipline persisted throughout the traditional period. A schoolhouse constructed in Sunderland, Massachusetts, in 1793, contained a whipping post set firmly in the floor of the schoolroom.[16] Descriptions of nineteenth-century schools indicate, ". . . the walls of the schoolroom were marred by the dents made by ferules hurled at misbehaving pupils' heads with an aim that sometimes proved untrue."[17]

By the middle of the nineteenth century, some attempts were being made to curb brutal disciplinary procedures, but these efforts did not necessarily meet with immediate success. In 1844, for example, the Boston Board of Education passed a rule requiring a full report of every case in which flogging was used. This ruling, however, apparently had little effect. During inspection tours the following year, the board members found that whippings in a "representative" school of four hundred pupils averaged sixty-five per day. In their subsequent report, the committee mentioned "severe injuries" following corporal punishment of pupils, and stated that in most cases the offense was "very trifling."[18]

Because of the importance of classroom control, it will be helpful to get a clear picture of the methods used in traditional schools. Johnson's description of typical disciplinary practices in the middle of the nineteenth century will enable us to appreciate the contrast with the much milder progressive methods to be discussed later and, insofar as harsh punishment may actually aggravate discipline, may give us some idea of the genesis of many traditional behavior problems:

> "Spare the rod and spoil the child" was a Bible text which received the most literal acceptance both in theory and practice. Even the naturally mild-tempered man was an "old-fashioned" disciplinarian when it came to teaching, and the naturally rough and coarse-grained man was as frightful as any ogre in a fairy tale.
>
> In summer, unless the teacher was an uncommonly poor one, or some of the scholars uncommonly wild and mischievous, the days moved along very harmoniously and pleasantly. In winter, when the big boys came in, some of them grown men, who cared vastly more about having a good time than getting learning, an important requisite of the master was "government." He ruled his little empire, not with a rod of iron, but with a stout three-foot

ruler, known as a "ferule," which was quite as effective. The really severe teacher had no hesitation in throwing this ruler at any child he saw misbehaving, and it is to be noted that he threw first and spoke afterward. Very likely he would order the culprit to bring him the ferule he had cast at him, and when the boy came out on the floor would further punish him. Punishment by spatting the palm of the hand with the ruler was known as "feruling." The smarting of blows was severe while the punishment lasted, but this was as nothing to a "thrashing." The boy to be thrashed was himself sent for the apple-tree twigs with which he was to be whipped. Poor fellow! Whimpering, and blinded by the welling tears, he slowly whittles off one after the other of the tough twigs. This task done, he drags his unwilling feet back to the schoolroom.

"Take off your coat, sir!" says the master.

The school is hushed into terrified silence. The fire crackles in the wide fireplace, the wind whistles at the eaves, the boy's tears flow faster, and he stammers a plea for mercy. Then the whip hisses through the air, and blows fall thick and fast. The boy dances about the floor, and his shrill screams fill the schoolroom. His mates are frightened and trembling, and the girls are crying. . . .

The list of milder punishments was a varied one. If the master saw two boys whispering, he would, if circumstances favored, steal upon them from behind and visit unexpected retribution upon them by catching them by the collars and cracking their heads together. Frequently an offender was ordered out on the floor to stand for a time by the master's desk, or he was sent to a corner with his face to the wall, or was asked to stand on one leg for a time. In certain cases he was made to hold one arm out at right angles to his body—a very easy and simple thing to do for a short time, but fraught with painful discomfort if long continued. Sometimes the punishment was made doubly hard by forcing the scholar to support a book or other weight at the same time. When the arm began to sag, the teacher would inquire with feigned solicitude what the trouble was, and perhaps would give him a rap on his "crazy bone" with the ruler to encourage him to persevere. This process soon brought a child to tears, and then the teacher was apt to relent and send him to his seat.

Making a girl sit with the boys, or a boy with the girls, was another punishment. The severity of this depended on the nature of the one punished. For the timid and bashful it was a terrible disgrace. . . .

Some of the punishments produced very striking spectacular effects to which the present-day mind would feel quite averse. Fancy the sight of a boy and girl guilty of some misdemeanor standing in the teacher's heavy armchair, the girl wearing the boy's hat and the boy adorned with the girl's sunbonnet. Both are redfaced and tearful with mortified pride. They preserve a precarious balance on their narrow footing with difficulty, and every movement of one causes the other to grasp and clutch to prevent inglorious downfall.

To sit on the end of a ruler, which the teacher presently knocked from under the boy, was considered by some pedagogues an effective punishment. One teacher used to have the offending boy bend over with his head under the table. Then the teacher whacked the culprit from behind with his heavy ruler, and sent him shooting under the table and sprawling across the floor. Among the most ingenious and uncomfortable in the varied list of punishments was the fitting a cut from a green twig, partially split, to the offender's nose. In cases of lying, this rude pair of pinchers was attached to the scholar's tongue.[19]

In short, life in the traditional school was often harsh and hectic, for master and pupils alike. It remained this way, with few fundamental changes, for more than two hundred years, from the early colonial period to the middle of the nineteenth century. Only in the final few years before the Civil War was there any hint of the forces which, during the following decades, would transform the nature of American public education.

A number of factors contributed to the stability of this traditional pattern: prevailing attitudes regarding public education, the isolation of one-room rural schools, the characteristics of the teacher's job, the homogeneity of the student body, the low economic investment in the schools, and the marginal place of the school in the activities of the community.

During the traditional era the public school was not expected to educate everyone. Compulsory education as we know it today did not exist. Before the Civil War only one state had enacted compulsory attendance laws— Massachusetts made schooling mandatory in 1852.[20] In most parts of the country, free public schools were just being established on a broad scale during the 1840s and 1850s. Many districts had only the most rudimentary educational facilities, and other communities, especially in the South, had none at all.

Consequently, education was mostly a matter of individual choice, with the decision left to the pupil and his family. If he came to school, it was mainly because his parents wanted him to, and he was more or less willing to do so. As far as the school was concerned, it didn't really matter whether or not he attended but, if he did come, he had to abide by the teacher's demands or accept the frequently severe consequences. If school became intolerable, he was free to leave. In the case of a backward or unruly pupil this was all to the good, from the teacher's point of view, because the class would be easier to manage without him. Pupils who returned after an interlude of truancy might be punished by the schoolmaster, but basically the responsibility for attendance rested with the pupil and his parents.

Thus, the traditional public school, when it existed at all, was a selective institution, accommodating only those hardy souls who were able to adapt to its inflexible demands. Those who could not, or would not, dropped out. It should be noted that this applied to teachers as well as to pupils. Usually it was the pupils who left, one by one, as punishment or study reached the point of being unbearable, but occasionally, as we have seen, when several students joined forces, it was the schoolmaster who was compelled to leave. However, the sporadic disruptions and closings of the school by rebellious pupils did not generate enough pressure to alter the traditional patterns of the school or to encourage critical reappraisals of its methods.

Although school closings may not have been welcomed—except by the pupils, who received an unscheduled holiday—the closing of a school apparently worked no great hardship on anyone except the teacher, and he was not in a position to do much about it. His duties were simple and it was easy to replace him. Because his instructional effectiveness was defined, in large part, by his capacity to maintain order, his inability to do so was interpreted as evidence that he was incompetent and therefore should not be teaching. He had no colleagues to whom he might turn for support. Most schools before the late-nineteenth century were in the country and the majority had only one teacher. School administrators did not appear until the 1840s and '50s.[21] This isolation gave little chance even for communication with other teachers, from whom the embattled schoolmaster might have learned of similar problems and of possible solutions. There were few teacher-training institutions, educational journals, and no occupational associations through which to take concerted action. Thus, for the great majority of teachers, the struggle to maintain control was a solitary one, and there would be few to mourn those who failed.

Moreover, the economic consequences of student revolts were far less serious than they are today. In fact, school districts actually saved money when the school was closed. The lone teacher was the only paid employee. There were no other personnel—no superintendents, secretaries, principals, custodians, counselors, or coordinators—who would also have to be paid, or laid off, if the teacher left. Shutting down the school did not mean a waste of money. Quite the contrary: there was actually a saving because not even the meager salary of the teacher had to be expended.

In addition, the financial investment in the school plant was small. Most schoolhouses were crude, one-room structures, furnished with a few rough benches and a stove. They were devoid of equipment; there were no free textbooks or supplies, and blackboards did not become common until well into the nineteenth century. Thus, even the more rambunctious students could do little material damage and there was nothing worth stealing when the school was closed.

Pupils who left school early were not seriously handicapped by their lack of formal education in their endeavors to earn a living. As for the more general benefits of universal education, the public was far from unanimous in its support, and even members of the school board were sometimes ambivalent about it, especially when they considered the expenses it involved. When students dropped out, or when the school closed down for a while, it was not generally viewed as a calamity because education itself was not considered to be of paramount importance.

Acceptance of the idea of education for all had been delayed by factional fears that one group might gain control of the schools and impose its beliefs and customs upon others. In addition, universal education had to await the development of stable methods of financial support. While many people agreed in theory to the principle of education for everyone, they were less prepared to pay the taxes needed to support such education, especially for the benefit of other people's children. Even after some public support was available, students often had to pay partial tuition fees. These assessments, known as *rate bills* because parents were charged according to the number of children they had in school and the length of time they attended, were not entirely abolished until after the Civil War.[22] Charges for textbooks and supplies often provided a further barrier.

Even where adequate and completely free schools existed, other factors prevented many children from attending. America was still a rural nation. As late as 1870, seventy-two percent of the people were living outside of cities and towns.[23] Transportation was a common problem. The miles of poor roads and open country which separated some farms from the district school made attendance difficult for many children, even under the best of circumstances, and poor weather presented an almost insurmountable obstacle. In addition, many youths were kept at home to work around the house or in the fields.

Consequently, in 1850, less than half of the nation's youth between the ages of five and nineteen were enrolled in public schools. Moreover, education at that time was limited to whites; less than two percent of the non-Caucasians in the five-to-nineteen age group were attending school.[24] Furthermore, even the white population was predominantly of northwest European stock; the waves of immigrants from central and southern Europe had not yet arrived. Thus the student body of the traditional school was relatively homogeneous, and most pupils were thought to have some chance of success in the same simple, undiversified curriculum that had sufficed in their grandparents' day.

To sum up, awareness of individual differences in pupil ability did not emerge until late in the nineteenth century. In earlier times, it was not considered to be a reflection on the school when a pupil dropped out but was, instead, attributed to laziness or a similar deficiency in the character of the child. Education was still seen as somewhat of a luxury, though not necessarily an enjoyable one, to be experienced only under a fortuitous configuration of circumstances. The education of everyone was not considered to be the responsibility of the traditional school. Under such conditions the traditional school could be a selective enterprise, offering a simple curriculum to a relatively homogeneous student body. Harsh discipline may have frightened many children into submission, but it also forced others to leave school entirely.

The Transitional Era

After the Civil War, traditional patterns of attendance and discipline were shattered by a number of profound changes in American society. These

changes, associated to a considerable degree with urbanization, industrialization and immigration, transformed the character of the student
body, increased the school's responsibility toward pupils, made control
more urgent, and rendered unusable the orthodox, time-honored methods
of discipline.

One of the most obvious changes was the spectacular population increase. In 1850 there were twenty-three million people in the United
States. By the end of the century the population had more than tripled, to
seventy-six million, and by 1950 it had doubled again.[25] Growth in itself,
however, would not have so changed the character of everyday life if the
increase had merely consisted of the establishment of more communities
like those which already existed. But this was not the case; urbanization
brought profound alterations. In 1830, three-fourths of the population was
still rural but, by 1920, half of the people were living in cities.[26]

Industrialization and urbanization were accompanied by changes in family structure. The extended family, common in agrarian societies, was broken up as some of its members moved to the cities, leaving behind friends,
relatives and neighbors. The family in the city often found itself in an unfamiliar milieu where few others knew them or cared about them.

As a result of these changes, a new role emerged for the child. In a rural
setting he had been a useful member of the family, contributing to its
maintenance by working directly in the production of food and marketable
goods, or by assisting with household chores. This changed drastically,
however, under the impact of urbanization and industrialization. City children were no longer assets; they had become liabilities. There was a brief
transitional period during which children could still work in factories or
in home industries but, as sentiments against child labor were followed
by legislation outlawing the practice, even this opportunity for contributing
to family support was eliminated. Consequently the urban youth, in comparison to his rural counterpart, had less productive work to occupy his
time, and had fewer adults or older siblings around to supervise his increased leisure. In addition, crowded metropolitan conditions, especially in
tenement areas, provided few opportunities for wholesome recreation, or
for harmless dissipation of youthful energy. Moreover, there were many
others in the same situation living within a block or two. The stage was set
for juvenile delinquency. As early as 1870, the annual report of the Philadelphia schools estimated that ". . . upwards of 20,000 children not attending any school, public, private or parochial, are running the streets in
idleness or vagabondism. . . ."[27]

The desire to forestall youthful mischief, concern of working men over
competition from cheap child labor, and genuinely altruistic regard for
child welfare probably all contributed to the rising demand for universal
compulsory education. Following Massachusetts' pioneer legislation of
1852, Vermont made education mandatory in 1867. By 1919, all of the

states had enacted compulsory education laws.[28] Although this legislation did not mean that every young person was actually attending school, it does at least give some indication of the situation.

More important, however, the enactment of these laws signified that a new burden had been placed upon the school, vastly complicating its work and requiring a radical change in its treatment of pupils.[29] Now that a large share of the responsibility was in the school's hands, motivation for attending school shifted from being solely the concern of the pupil and his family to also being a concern of the school. This meant that the school's previous operating principles had become inapplicable. Teachers and administrators could no longer employ a "take it or leave it" attitude toward their students. Under the traditional pattern it had been up to the pupil to adjust to the school. If he was unable or unwilling to do so, the school could expel him, if he did not leave voluntarily. Now, however, the shoe was on the other foot; the school had to adapt itself to the pupils. If pupils were unwilling to cooperate with traditional expectations, a new system had to be devised which they would be willing to tolerate.

The school's responsibility for encouraging all pupils to continue their schooling as long as possible was increasingly accepted by educators as well as laymen. For school personnel themselves, it became a fact of life which they seldom questioned. Even when individual teachers complained about the policy of keeping every pupil in school, they nevertheless accepted it as inevitable. Of course, many pupils still dropped out before they graduated, but the school now had the responsibility of doing all it could to keep them in.

The rapid growth of cities and the obligation to educate all children confronted metropolitan schools with the difficult problem of providing for the deluge of pupils.[30] Urban districts were seldom able to keep up with their soaring enrollments. Costs of construction increased, and less land was available for building additional rooms or for enlarging playgrounds. The result was that city schools became increasingly crowded,[31] and this in turn increased tensions among pupils, and aggravated problems of control. The more congested the classroom became, the more difficult it was for pupils to study or even to remain relatively quiet. In addition, behavior in the classroom was also affected by the inadequacy of playground facilities. A spacious yard would give pupils the opportunity to work off tensions built up in class. They could release their energy through physical activity or, if they preferred, they could find a quiet corner in which to relax. In this respect, rural schools, with their almost unlimited space, held a big advantage. Life inside the little country schoolhouse may have been grim but at least, during recess or at noon, the whole out-of-doors was a playground. The urban pupil was less fortunate in this respect. His yard was smaller and he had to share it with hundreds of others. Because of such crowding his activities were further limited by rules and adult supervision. The urban pupil had less opportunity to release tension and, therefore, was probably more inclined to be a restless, potential behavior problem.

Furthermore, if disturbances did occur, they could have more serious consequences in the larger, urban schools than in small, isolated rural schools. There were more pupils who might participate in the disorder. There were other personnel, other teachers and administrators whose work might be made more difficult by the outbreak. Also, the disruptions would be immediately noticed, and perhaps feared, by residents and shopkeepers whose homes and businesses adjoined the school. Finally, there was a greater financial investment in the buildings, equipment, supplies, and grounds of the urban school. In these respects, crowding of city schools gave a new urgency to the maintenance of law and order. Control over pupils in the urban school was far from being the solitary concern of one lone teacher. There were other people who also had an interest in the maintenance of discipline and the smooth operation of the school.

To complicate things further, the student body became considerably more varied, and consequently more difficult to handle. Not only were there more pupils, but also they were more heterogeneous than in traditional times, varying more widely in age, ability, religion, social and economic status, place of birth, race, and language. The previous differences among the earlier settlers from northwestern Europe were dwarfed by the entry of heretofore unfamiliar groups from southern and eastern Europe, not to mention Orientals, Negroes and Latin-Americans. The age-range broadened, with more younger pupils and also more older pupils in their late teens. In 1871, ninety-one percent of the nation's seven million public school pupils were in elementary schools.[32] By 1920, ten percent of all public school pupils were enrolled in high school or postgraduate courses.[33]

The percentage of non-white pupils, infinitesimal during the traditional era, began to rise very rapidly during the Civil War decade. In 1860, less than two percent of the non-white children, aged five to nineteen, were in public schools. By 1870 the proportion had increased to ten percent, and by 1920, fifty-four percent of the non-white school-age population was actually enrolled.[34]

As the age of compulsory attendance rose, there were more likely to be full grown men and women in school. These older students were less inclined than were the younger ones to submit to traditional methods of discipline. If nothing else, their size alone would be a deterrent to the frequent whippings given to smaller students. And, increasingly, there were pupils whose poor scholastic performance was clearly not the simple consequence of laziness. Some of these students came from unsettled or impoverished families, others were handicapped physically or mentally, and still others did not speak English. By 1909, fifty-eight percent of the pupils in thirty-seven of the nation's largest cities had foreign-born parents.

In New York, the percentage was seventy-two, in Chicago, sixty-seven, and in Boston, sixty-four. In Chelsea, Massachusetts, and Duluth, Minnesota, the percentage reached seventy-four.[35] Of course, there had been pupils with similar handicaps in traditional times, but, as their numbers increased toward the end of the nineteenth century, the shortcomings of orthodox methods of instruction and control became more and more obvious. The inadequacy of such time-honored methods as meting out a sharp rap with a ruler for a poorly prepared recitation was more apparent than ever before.[36]

On one hand, then, the advent of universal compulsory education brought a far more heterogeneous group of pupils into the schools and forced a fundamental change in the school's responsibilities. This, in turn, necessitated modification of the school's attitudes toward its pupils. On the other hand, traditional methods of control were rendered unusable by at least two changes. First, a gradual softening of attitudes regarding acceptable methods of child treatment meant that neither the public-at-large nor school personnel were as willing to use the harsh punishments of the past. Prohibition of corporal punishment was written into the codes of most school districts, and the possibility of lawsuits by parents provided a further restraint.

Second, changes in the composition of the teaching staff meant that corporal punishment was less practical than before, even in districts where it was still permitted. During the eighteenth and early-nineteenth centuries most teachers were men, but in later times the majority of American public school teachers have been women. It is possible that the advent of industrialization offered educated men other opportunities which were more appealing than public school teaching. Perhaps, too, there was increasing desire by school boards to hire women rather than men. Women could be paid less than men, a point which became more important as the number of teachers in a school district increased. There also emerged the belief that women were better attuned to children, better able to understand them and to establish satisfactory relations with them.[37]

The change began around 1830[38] and by 1870 the majority of teachers were women. The ratio of male teachers continued to drop steadily. In 1920, only fourteen percent of the teaching staff were men. The proportion still has not climbed much above this level.[39]

This radical change in the teaching staff undoubtedly had some effect upon methods of control. Women, for various reasons, are less likely than men to rely on brute force. In the first place, women seldom have the size and the physical strength needed to control obstreperous pupils by sheer force. Many sixth-grade boys, for example, are as tall as their teachers, and even younger pupils may match an adult's strength. Of course, there are exceptions to these generalizations. We need not look far to find mild-mannered men of slight build or robust women who would be capable of thrashing almost every pupil in the school. All things considered, however, women's assets in the problem of maintaining control consist less of physical strength than of gentle inducements to cooperation.

Female capacities and limitations became increasingly important as women assumed a larger and larger share of teaching positions in public schools. This, along with a general softening of cultural attitudes regarding the treatment of children, rendered traditional reliance on corporal punishment unacceptable and pointed the way to new methods of control, which will be discussed in the next pages.

In sum, four major changes made the school's task more difficult after 1870. First, a large part of the responsibility for pupil attendance shifted from the pupil to the school. Second, pupils were more varied than before. Third, traditional methods of control were no longer practical or acceptable. Finally, the consequences of disorder became more serious.

The Progressive Era

As a result of these changes, public schools in the twentieth century, and especially city schools, have been confronted with custodial problems quite different from those of the traditional era. The age-old task of maintaining order is still present, but former methods of coping with it can no longer be used. To make matters even more difficult, a new burden has been placed upon the schools in the form of the obligation to educate all of the nation's youth.

By 1920, 77.8 percent of the population between the ages of five and seventeen were receiving some sort of formal education, and by 1940, the proportion had risen to 85.3 percent. The vast majority of these pupils were attending public schools.[40] Although the flow of immigrants from abroad was stemmed by restrictive legislation in the 1920s, internal migration continued to supply the schools with challenging problems. The depression and drought of the 1930s and the booming war industries and manpower shortages of the 1940s brought to the cities many people from the Midwest and South whose differences from the mainstream of middle-class American culture were only slightly less pronounced than those of earlier immigrants from foreign countries.

Consequently public schools were attempting to accommodate a student body characterized by a very wide range of social origins, motivations and abilities. In earlier times, pupils who were not scholastically inclined dropped out after a few years, while children from poor families were not likely to attend at all. The relatively select group of students who remained had some chance to succeed in the traditional academic program. In the last few decades, however, there have been many pupils who are unable or unwilling to learn under those conditions.

In addition to these problems, resulting from the greater variety of students, there was also a very significant shift in the responsibility for the students. The school was expected to educate them or, at least, to keep them in school until they graduated from the twelfth grade. As a result, dropouts could no longer be shrugged off merely as "misfits;" the school was sharing the blame for their failure. The school could not continue as a selective institution, forcing its students either to accept its rigid demands or to leave. It now had to adapt its ways to fit the students, in an effort to encourage them to remain. Keeping all pupils in school was not an easy task. In spite of many attempts to persuade them to remain, many youngsters were still dropping out.

The handling of these pupils is complicated by the American tradition of equality. Not only must every child be educated but, in addition, it is believed that he should receive the same kind of education as everyone else. Although this tradition is in part responsible for many pupils being in school in the first place, it discourages the establishment of separate schools and makes it difficult to set up clearly distinct curricula for different types of pupils. Differentiation does appear in junior and senior high school, but it is somewhat covert and is not carried to the degree that characterizes some European systems. Consequently, all pupils, representing virtually the entire spectrum of human ability, must ideally be accommodated within the same schools.

There is a vital relationship between the school's responsibility for pupil attendance and methods of control. When pupils attend voluntarily they are more apt to comply with the school's expectations regarding behavior. They have some desire to remain in school, even if it is only a half-hearted desire, prompted largely by their parents. Therefore they are more willing to tolerate its rules. On the other hand, when pupils are forced to attend, regardless of their own inclinations or their parents' wishes, they may be less likely to cooperate with the teacher and are more apt to create disciplinary problems.

Thus, along with this newer problem of retention, the school still faced the age-old problem of control. The one-room country school was rapidly fading into the past but the possibility of losing control still confronted public school teachers. As a study of Chicago's schools observed, "One of the teacher's basic work problems is that of maintaining constant control over the actions of her pupils."[41] Moreover, "it is important to remember that the problem of discipline is one that is always present for the teacher. Even where a solution seems to have been reached, the teacher fears the possibility of an outbreak of disorder."[42] Even well-behaved classes are aware of the possibility of breaking the teacher's control. The teacher of one such class said: "There's the whole roomful of them sitting on the edge of their seats with their eyes gleaming, waiting to see how much this one is going to get away with."[43]

Most breaches of school rules would seem mild and inconsequential to laymen and even to some administrators. Talking or whispering, for example, or chewing gum, making faces, leaving one's seat without permission, and many similar actions may not seem serious when indulged in by only a few pupils. However, the danger lies in the possibility of escalation. Many teachers fear that if these minor infractions are allowed to continue unchecked, they may lead to more serious disturbances. There seems to be practically no limit to the kinds of problems which may arise in public schools. For example, another Chicago study provided some illustrations of the things which actually had occurred in elementary schools:

> The reports which these teachers gave of what *can* be done by a group of children are nothing short of amazing. A young white teacher walked into her new classroom and was greeted with the comment, "Another damn white one." Another teacher was "rushed" at her desk by the entire class when she tried to be extremely strict with them. Teachers report having been bitten, tripped and pushed on the stairs. Another gave an account of a second-grader throwing a milk bottle at the teacher and of a first-grader having such a temper tantrum that it took the principal and two policemen to get him out of the room.
>
> In another school following a fight on the playground, the principal took 32 razor blades from children in a first grade room. Some teachers indicated fear that they might be attacked by irate persons in the neighborhoods in which they teach. Other teachers report that their pupils carry long pieces of glass and have been known to threaten other pupils with them, while others jab each other with hypodermic needles. One boy got angry at his teacher and knocked in the fenders of her car.[44]

While incidents like these are less frequent in schools outside of urban slums, they nevertheless occur often enough to keep alive in the minds of school personnel the spectre of insurrection. Most teachers, even if they have escaped the experience themselves, know of colleagues who have lost control of their classes, at least momentarily, or who, because of their inability to maintain order, were transferred to undesirable positions or were fired.[45] Threats to the teacher's control may be more obvious in the lower class school, but they are also present in middle class and well-to-do schools. The difference is that more privileged pupils are usually more subtle in their defiance of school rules. The relative rarity of spectacular incidents in middle and upper class schools is offset, to a considerable degree, by more serious repercussions which these incidents may have on the occasions when they do occur. Parents of higher social status are more likely to take an interest in occurrences in the school. They are more apt to be disturbed by events which would pass unnoticed in a lower class school. They are more inclined to protest to school officials, and their protests generally carry more weight.

For example, when a slum child falls to the floor as a result of being tripped by a classmate, the incident is likely to end there, at least as far as the teacher is concerned. However, when this happens to a pupil from a middle class or upper-middle class family, there is a higher probability that the parents will complain to the principal or even to the superintendent about it, and in turn, the teacher may have to explain why such things were allowed to happen in her class. Or, the parents may threaten the school and the teacher with a lawsuit because of alleged negligence and incompetence. Teachers and other school personnel are quite vulnerable to such pressures and threats, and their desire to forestall such unpleasant possibilities provides added incentive to maintain control of the classroom. Again, it is not that loss of control happens often, but rather the grim possibility that it *can* happen, anywhere, which causes teachers to be concerned with the problem.

The general effect of this continuing struggle was described by a high school teacher:

> . . . there's that tension all the time. Between you and the students. It's hard on your nerves. Teaching is fun if you enjoy your subject, but it's the discipline that keeps your nerves on edge, you know what I mean? There's always that tension. Sometimes people say, "Oh you teach school. That's an easy job, just sitting around all day long." They don't know what it's really like. It's hard on your nerves.[46]

The Functions of Progressive Education

Thus, faced with problems of retention and control, and unable to use traditional methods of maintaining order, new procedures were necessary. Instead of using force and coercion, public schools now sought the pupils' willing participation. This was done by minimizing pressures, especially those of an academic nature, and, in general, by making school as pleasant as possible. Whatever the pedagogical merits or shortcomings of this approach might have been, it did enable the school to win the cooperation of many pupils who would have resisted a more traditional program.

It may be helpful, therefore, to consider several aspects of the progressive school from the standpoint of pupil retention and control. First, punishment is much milder. Second, attention is given to the psychological needs of pupils. Third, many subjects are offered in place of a single academically oriented course of study. Fourth, counseling and testing guide marginal pupils to classes in which chances of failure or frustration are minimized. Fifth, teaching methods take into account the interests of pupils. Sixth, standards of grading and promotion are more flexible. Finally, extracurricular activities appeal to some pupils who would find little else of interest in the school. In short, every effort is made to make the modern school as pleasant as possible, and these efforts are facilitated by various aspects of what is commonly called progressive education.

Milder Discipline. The relaxing of discipline has removed much of the sting from education. Harsh punishments of a bygone era have all but disappeared. Where not explicitly forbidden by law, corporal punishment is discouraged by public sentiment, educational theory, school district policies, and the feelings of school personnel. Some teachers and principals still, on occasion, wield a paddle, give a quick spat with a ruler, twist an ear or in some other manner inflict momentary pain, but this happens with far less frequency and ferocity than before.

Even traditional sanctions not involving physical punishment are used with restraint: ridicule, sarcasm, detention, extra assignments, or suspension for a few days are generally avoided whenever possible. Permanent expulsion is relatively rare.[47] Although compulsory education laws may provide loopholes for use in extreme cases, the schools are reluctant to resort to them. These procedures for expulsion are troublesome. Furthermore, it may be perceived as an indication of failure on the part of the school. In addition, many teachers and administrators are restrained by humanitarian considerations; they are reluctant to cast the erring youth into society, especially when they know that his next step will be into juvenile hall or that, at best, he will have difficulty getting a job without a high school diploma.

Thus, the conscious motivation for the repudiation of harsh punishment was largely a concern for the well-being of the pupil. In general, people today have more compassion for children's feelings than their forefathers did. This sympathy has been strengthened by the emergence of pedagogical and psychological theories advocating the elimination of harsh punishment, on the grounds that it adversely affects the child's natural development. Again, the emphasis has been upon the welfare and happiness of the pupil. As Dewey put it, "The child has a right to enjoy his childhood." [48]

At the same time, the abolition of severe disciplinary measures also has had custodial consequences. It lessens the possibility of kindling pupil resentment, a resentment which might even lead to overt retaliation against the teacher and the school. The pupil who has been severely chastised is likely to feel angry about it, no matter how much it might seem that he deserved it. A description of a typical incident in a mid-nineteenth-century school observed that the boy who had just been whipped ". . . in his heart vows vengeance, and longs for the day when he shall have the age and stature to thrash the teacher in return." [49]

The culprit himself was not the only one disturbed by severe castigation. It affected his classmates, too, and these effects were not always those which the teacher would have wanted. Harsh punishment, whatever its chastening effects might have been, also promoted an increased consciousness of the existence of two separate groups, teachers and pupils, and it made very clear the subordination of the latter to the former. The more obvious the differences between the two, the more likely were conflicts between them. When people think of themselves as relatively similar, pursuing the same general goals together, they are less likely to clash than if they perceive themselves as members of sharply differentiated groups, struggling for mutually exclusive ends. Speaking of the incident referred to in the previous paragraph, the chronicler of the nineteenth-century punishment observed, "When the sobbing boy is sent to his place, whatever his misdemeanor may have been, the severity of the punishment has won him the sympathy of the whole school, and toward the master there are only feelings of fear and hate."[50]

Sensitivity to Pupils' Needs. Second, the progressive school facilitates control by recognizing the psychological needs of the pupil, especially in showing greater concern for him as an individual. According to progressive ideology, each child should be approached as a unique human being whose personal characteristics must be thoroughly understood. Nothing, not even subject matter, should obscure this aim.

This concern is not intended merely to locate the pupil's strengths and weaknesses so that he may be helped toward mastery of his school work. Instead, it is a concern for the pupil himself, for his happiness and his physical, social and psychological well-being. By treating each pupil as an individual, the child-centered school tries to build his self-respect and to give him a sense that he is valued in his own right. The teacher, therefore, deemphasizes the status gap between herself and her students and plays the role of a friendly parent or sibling, providing the warmth and security of a primary relationship. Most pupils would respond to such treatment anyway, but it is especially important for those whose home life is not very satisfying.

Here, too, the basic motivation behind the recognition of individual needs was concern for the welfare of the child. Its usefulness as a mechanism of social control has rarely been considered. Nevertheless, it does have important custodial consequences for the school. The more content the child is, the less likely will he be to cause disciplinary problems for the teacher. Even though the origins may lie outside the school—within his family, for example—his frustrations may erupt at school, upsetting routine in the classroom, in the hallways, on the playground, or on the way to and from school. Giving the pupil the feeling that he is respected and liked by the teacher lessens the possibility that his unhappiness will upset the operation of the school. An elementary school principal observed:

> At home, their parents ignore them or curse and whip them. But here at school we treat them as individuals, build them up, give them self-respect. They have to be really worked up before they'll turn their backs on this.[51]

Sensitivity to individual needs also helps to prevent the formation of a united front against the teacher. One rebellious pupil can be disruptive enough, but control becomes even more difficult when several students join forces. If pupils feel little connection with the school, if they do not believe that their teacher really knows them or cares about them, they are more likely to get into mischief or to support other pupils who create trouble. On the other hand, the more they like their teacher, the more satisfaction they receive from her in friendship, praise, and encouragement, the less apt they are to be uncooperative, or to support rebellion against her. Thus, it behooves the teacher to establish positive relations with her pupils. One of the best ways to do this is to give each one the feeling that she believes he is important and that no one else could take his place.

Of course, this goal is difficult to achieve even under the best of circumstances, and teaching conditions are rarely ideal. However, even if the teacher does not succeed in reaching every pupil, her partial success is nevertheless worthwhile because class control is not an all-or-nothing matter. If the teacher can reduce the number of active trouble-makers to two or three, it is still an improvement over opposition by the entire class. There are usually a couple of pupils in each room who would be hard to handle in any situation, but the others, the "uncommitted majority," may hold the balance of power in the struggle for class control. At the least, the teacher may dissuade them from joining in mischief against her. And, if she can win the majority to her side, their disapproval of the rebellious behavior may be a more effective restraint upon the culprits than any sanction the teacher herself could impose. The teacher's ability to reach out into the masses of pupils and to give each one a feeling that he means something to her not only gives the pupil a sense of satisfaction but is also essential for the teacher.[52] Her sensitivity to individual pupils, her college training in psychology, and her experience in human relations can be powerful tools for maintaining control over her class.[53]

Diversified Curriculum.   A third way in which progressive education has eased problems of control is by offering a variety of courses in place of a single, academically oriented program. This reduces intellectual pressures to the point where they are tolerable to many marginal students. Because academic subjects require mental effort and the restriction of bodily activity, they are less apt to be enjoyed than are courses like shop, art, homemaking, or physical education. When an academic, "solid" course is required of all public school students, regardless of their ability or motivation, serious disciplinary problems may occur. On the other hand, pupils are more likely to enjoy courses which do not require concentration or the prolonged cessation of movement. A study of Chicago schools, for instance, observed, "Teachers of physical education report fewer problems of discipline and lack of motivation. They say that children like their classes and are cooperative in them because they like to play."[54] Waller aptly summed up the situation when he stated that, "It is only because teachers wish to force students to learn that any unpleasantness ever arises to mar their relationship."[55]

The variety of courses ameliorates a problem which is particularly acute in the United States. Egalitarian values in this country discourage the establishment of completely separate schools or courses of study, but differences of ability and motivation between one pupil and the next are nevertheless so pronounced that they cannot be ignored. Broadening the curriculum and reducing the number of academic courses required of all students offers a workable compromise. This compromise presents the appearance of offering the same educational opportunities to everyone, yet it allows a considerable degree of flexibility in the assignment of pupils. It is especially useful in handling troublemakers and potential dropouts, many of whom would encounter difficulties in compulsory academic courses.[56]

Counseling and Testing.   A fourth point, related to the previous one, involves counseling and testing programs. Because it is no longer necessary for everyone to follow the same path to graduation, the selection of courses for each pupil has become an important aspect of American secondary education. In fact, it is so important, for the school as well as for the student, that it cannot be left to chance. Aptitude testing, counseling, and detailed records of health, behavior, scholastic progress, and home conditions facilitate the placement of students in classes where they are least likely to encounter frustration. Youths who might not get along in academic work are guided away from it and assigned to courses where mental effort is presumably not imperative. For example, an art teacher in a California high school complained:

> All I get in here are the rejects from other classes. Most of them are really sad; they're practically human vegetables. I have six classes and it's the same thing all day long. I probably don't have more than three or four kids with an I.Q. above 90.
> Art classes are a dumping ground for clods who can't do anything else. They think that if a kid can't work with his head, he can do work with his hands. If a kid screws up in an English class, they throw him in here.[57]

Guiding potential discipline problems into non-academic courses is only part of the problem. Because these classes often require extra equipment and special supplies, they are more expensive than regular classes. Therefore, only a minimal number are usually provided and space in them is limited. In order to insure enough room for potential troublemakers or dropouts, the average and good students are likely to be steered away from these non-academic courses. The same art teacher, quoted above, commented wistfully:

The other day after school a couple of girls came into my room to work on decorations for the senior prom. You could see they were alert youngsters, the kind you'd really like to work with. They saw the projects my classes were working on and one of them said that she wished she could take art. She said she had asked her counselor about it several times but he always told her they were full, there wasn't any room.

That's not true. I have empty seats in here, but they're being saved for the clods who can't make it anywhere else.[58]

Thus, one result of counseling is the reduction of pressures on pupils who might otherwise cause problems of control.[59] Of course, this is not the justification usually given for counseling programs, but these services do minimize haphazard or "mistaken" assignments which might make retention and control more difficult. The development of these services was encouraged by progressive education.[60] It is possible that counselors, aptitude tests, and detailed records covering many phases of the pupils' school and family life might have evolved anyway, out of the sheer necessity for organizational survival, but they have received further support from progressive beliefs that individual differences are important and should be the focus of scientific study.

New Teaching Methods.   Fifth, tensions which might lead to custodial problems have been relieved by progressive teaching methods. These methods reduce intellectual demands and, instead, emphasize learning through meaningful activity. Many children and adolescents would find it difficult to sit quietly for several hours a day, puzzling over a problem in long division, analyzing sentences, or memorizing long lists of facts. As Dewey stated, "Nature has not adapted the young animal to the narrow desk, the crowded curriculum, the silent absorption of complicated facts. His very life and growth depend upon motion, yet the school forces him into a cramped position for hours at a time."[61] The progressive approach permits and even encourages students to leave their desks and to engage in a variety of interesting projects, even to the point of working with other pupils.

Interest in school work may also be maintained by the use of a variety of teaching methods and equipment. Such devices as plays, murals, dioramas, models, projects, games, tape recorders, movies, committees, television, and field trips are more palatable to most pupils than the limited instructional techniques used in previous times, and are less likely to arouse frustration and resentment. An indication of the effectiveness of such methods appeared in a newspaper near the end of summer vacation. When a reporter asked, "Are you eager for school to start?" a ten-year-old boy replied:

I sure am! There's nothing to do in the summer but hang around the parks. At school I like the movies in the auditorium and the field trips. School is more of a vacation than vacation is.[62]

Flexible Standards.   Sixth, lenient policies of grading and promotion have removed the threat of failure, which otherwise would have been a source of anxiety for many pupils and their parents. As an English observer of comparative education has noted:

> . . . the common school principle behind American education, which makes it automatic for every boy and girl to pass from the primary school to some form of secondary education in the high school, frees both parents and children from the anxiety neuroses which abound in Europe [where there is an examination hurdle which determines their educational future].[63]

With an extremely heterogenous student body it is difficult to maintain standards which will guide the intellectually capable pupils to better performance, but which will not discourage pupils with less ability. By reducing emphasis upon grades and by virtually eliminating the danger of failure, the school maintains the cooperation and interest of most pupils, especially those whose motivation and ability are low. American students learn relatively early in their school careers that the path to promotion and graduation presents few intolerable demands. They know that, with minimum effort, they will receive passing grades and will be promoted at the end of the year and, as long as they don't create too many disturbances, they will eventually receive a high school diploma. Pupils are occasionally expelled for extremely bad behavior, but no matter how little studying one does, it is almost impossible to "flunk out" of elementary or high school.[64]

Again the dual aspects of progressive education are evident. Besides preventing damage to the pupil's self-image, social promotion averts a potentially serious custodial problem for the school by avoiding disturbances which are likely to occur when a larger, older pupil is put back into a classroom with younger children. Occasionally pupils who cause a lot of trouble, instead of being demoted or held back, are skipped ahead a grade or two, "kicked upstairs" in order to rid the school of them a year or so earlier. For example, in one such instance known to the writer, an aggressive boy who had been held back a year in elementary school was moved forward an extra grade as soon as he entered junior high. At the end of the year he was skipped again, missing the last year of junior high and going on to senior high school. In this way, the junior high had to put up with him for only one year instead of the usual three.[65]

Thus, progressive education's emphasis upon the needs of the whole child rather than merely his intellectual development provides a useful rationale for the promotion of inept pupils who might otherwise cause serious problems of control and retention.

Extracurricular Activities.   Finally, extracurricular activities offer incentives to remain in school and to obey its rules. These activities appeal to many pupils who would not be interested in intellectual endeavors. Baseball games, dances, carnivals, football, rallies, hobby clubs, assemblies, basketball, talent shows, and track meets can be powerful inducements for cooperation, offering to otherwise apathetic adolescents pleasures which would not be available outside the school. Though some of these activities may have existed on a smaller scale before the advent of progressive education, they now occupy a much more important place in the school program.[66] Mallison writes:

> One marked feature of the American high school is the emphasis placed on extra-curricular and out-of-school activities. . . . There are schools at which something is going on every night, and on Saturdays as well, organized by the pupils on an often extremely elaborate scale. The fact that most of the drive behind these activities comes from the pupils themselves is evidence that they are genuinely interested.[67]

Such activities have contributed to a reversal of the former pattern of sanctions: instead of behaving in order to avoid corporal punishment, pupils today are more likely to behave and to stay in school because they don't want to miss the fun which school offers. For example, the principal of a large high school in a California ghetto remarked:

> The worst thing that could happen to many of these kids is suspension. I can paddle the daylights out of them and they'll just laugh at me. But kick 'em out for a few days and that usually brings them around. It gets pretty dull and lonely at home. Suspension puts them away from their friends and school activities. That really hurts.[68]

The custodial potentialities of athletics are especially noteworthy. Competitive sports provide an outlet for some of the very pupils whose size, energy, and aggressiveness would almost inevitably have embroiled them in mischief in the traditional school. Now, however, instead of bullying weaker students, attacking the teacher, or otherwise causing trouble, their energies are diverted away from the school and are dissipated against each other, or ultimately, against rivals from another school. The highly structured nature of these contests provides further control over the release of potentially destructive energies; practice sessions and the actual games are held at certain times in specified places, and are conducted according to detailed rules under the watchful eyes of peers, adults and official referees. Even if violations of these rules occur, in the form of "unnecessary roughness" or "unsportsmanlike conduct," for example, they are far less disruptive there, on the athletic field, then they would be in the classroom.

The custodial benefits of competitive sports are not limited to redirecting youthful energy into relatively harmless areas. In addition, the athlete actually becomes dependent upon the school, because it is the means by which he achieves his pleasure and his status. Thus, he is put in the position of staying in school and conforming to most of its expectations so that he can enjoy its rewards. He may not like everything about it but he must tolerate it in order to receive the benefits it offers. Without the school there would be no team, no games, no rallies, no sweaters, no throngs of admirers, no cheering sections chanting his name, no mention of him on the sports page of the local newspaper.

Perhaps the alchemy of athletics is best exemplified by the new meanings associated with the school's name. Of course, not all athletically capable pupils would have been unsuccessful in a traditional setting. Nevertheless, for many of them, the name of the school would have signified frustration, unhappiness and failure. For the present-day athlete, however, the school's name has taken on more pleasant connotations, as a symbol of his success and prowess in sports. The school's initial, displayed on his sweater or jacket, is one of the most coveted awards the high school student can receive.

Thus, athletics, whatever its other functions might be, is also an instrument of social control.[69] It does not solve all custodial problems faced by contemporary public schools but it does forestall many of them, especially with regard to some of the pupils who are potentially most troublesome. Perhaps the main drawback of sports, from a custodial point of view, is that not all of the problem pupils are big enough or agile enough to qualify for the team. As one observer points out, however, the progressive school provides other possibilities for success:

> Inadequacy in the most glamorous sports is not by any means total failure in the bid for popularity, because all kinds of opportunities are provided for each child to be at least in something the king of the hour.[70]

A variety of other positions are available, ranging from team managers and yell-leaders to monitors responsible for student behavior. Thus, in one form or another, extracurricular activities do much to simplify the school's problems of retention and control.

Conclusion

The advent of mass compulsory education created custodial as well as educational problems. The necessity for accommodating a large and varied student body which could not be controlled by traditional methods of corporal punishment, segregation, failure, or expulsion forced American public schools to seek new solutions. Controversial phenomena like "pupil-centered" curriculum and the relaxing of academic standards, whatever their educational value might have been, alleviated urgent problems confronting the schools.

It may be illuminating to compare the school with another institution whose custodial function is more obvious: the prison. The comparison between the two is not as far fetched as it might at first seem, especially if we consider progressive, minimal security prisons. Both the prison and the school have a non-voluntary clientele, and both face custodial problems of retention and control. Of course, there are differences. Pupils are younger than prisoners, they go home every night, they attend coeducational institutions, and so forth. Basically, however, both the school and the prison must retain within their walls large numbers of "clients" who are forced, regardless of their own wishes, to spend time there. Thus, both institutions are confronted with problems of control.

It is worth noting that a prison's custodial problems, like those of the school, are also affected by its orientations. A recent study, for example, found that the prisons' general outlook had a noticeable effect upon the attitudes of its inmates.[71] Two contrasting orientations were observed, which were analogous to the traditional and progressive approaches in education. The "traditional" prison's main concern was containment, with little effort directed toward rehabilitation. There were many regulations, discipline was strict, and prison personnel remained aloof from the inmates. In contrast, the "progressive" prison was oriented toward treatment. There were maximal provisions for guidance and counseling, considerable interaction between staff and inmates, and a sincere effort toward constructively changing the prisoner.

The study revealed that inmates' attitudes toward prisons, staff, and treatment programs were most hostile in the institutions whose primary goal was containment, without much effort toward rehabilitation. Convicts' attitudes were more favorable in other prisons where there was considerable interaction between staff and inmates, where there was maximal opportunity for counseling and guidance, and where guards and administrators made a sincere effort to help the inmates.[72] The harsh conditions in the custodial prison led inmates to view the prison itself as the source of many of their problems, so they were more likely to unite against it. In contrast, the humane atmosphere of the progressive institution reduced deprivations to the point where inmates were unlikely to join forces against the prison and its staff.

The similarity between this and the contemporary public school is striking. In neither institution was the progressive orientation introduced officially as a means of control. Instead, the welfare of the inmate or the pupil was the reason given for adopting the new system. Nevertheless, in both the prison and the school, the progressive approach has softened the sting of compulsory attendance, alleviating critical problems of retention and control.

There is an old saying that "even the tyrant must sleep;" a progressive ideology makes it easier for him to do so.

NOTES

1. Waller, *The Sociology of Teaching,* pp. 195–96.

2. Johnson, *Old Time Schools,* p. 121.

3. *Ibid.,* p. 129.

4. Where not otherwise indicated, the sources for historical details in this and sub-sequent chapters are Cubberly's *Public Education in the United States,* rev. ed., and Butts and Cremin's *A History of Education in American Culture.*

5. Horace Greeley, in Clifton Johnson's *Old Time Schools,* 123–26.

6. Ruth S. Freeman, *Yesterday's Schools,* p. 77.

7. *Ibid.*

8. *Ibid.,* pp. 78–79.

9. *Ibid.*

10. Johnson, *Old Time Schools,* p. 121.

11. Butts and Cremin, *History of Education,* p. 286.

12. Johnson, *Old Time Schools,* p. 121.

13. *Ibid.,* pp. 121–22.

14. Cubberly, *Public Education,* rev. ed., p. 328.

15. Bailyn, *Education in the Forming of American Society.*

16. Cubberly, *Public Education,* rev. ed., p. 57.

17. Johnson, *Old Time Schools,* p. 123.

18. Caldwell and Curtis, *Then and Now in Education: 1845:1923,* pp. 20–21.

19. Johnson, *The Country School in New England,* pp. 47–52.

20. Butts and Cremin, *History of Education,* p. 357. A compulsory education law had been enacted two centuries earlier. Although it eventually fell into disuse, it is worth noting. The Massachusetts law of 1642 heralded the first occasion, at least in the English-speaking world, that a legislative body representing the state had ordered that all children should be taught to read. Town officials were directed to see that all parents and masters of apprentices were training their children "in learning and labor and other employments profitable to the commonwealth" and that they were learning "to read and understand the principles of religion and the capital laws of the country." Fines were to be imposed on those who neglected to give adequate instruction. However, the results were unsatisfactory, so five years later the "Old Deluder Satan" Act ordered the establishment of elementary and secondary schools, under penalty of fines for failing to do so. Thus, by the middle of the seventeenth century, the idea of compulsory attendance in publicly supported schools had appeared in legislation and was, for a while, being enforced in the courts (Cubberly, *Public Education,* rev. ed., pp. 17–18).

21. Cubberly, *Public Education,* rev. ed., p. 320.

22. Wisconson was one of the first states to abolish the *rate bill,* in 1848. Other midwestern states followed suit during the 1850s (Indiana, 1852; Ohio, 1853; Illinois, 1855; and Iowa, 1858). However, rate bills were not eliminated in New York until 1867, in Connecticut until 1868, and in Michigan until 1869 (Butts and Cremin, *History of Education,* pp. 247, 249, 252).

23. U.S. Bureau of the Census, *Historical Statistics . . . ,* p. 14.

24. *Ibid.,* p. 213. "In some of the districts near to the reservations, Indian children were sometimes sent to school, but not very regularly" (Freeman, *Yesterday's Schools,* p. 64).

25. U.S. Bureau of the Census, *Historical Statistics . . . ,* p. 7.

26. *Ibid.,* p. 14.

27. *Report of the Commissioner of Education . . . for the Year 1870,* p. 273.

28. After the 1954 Supreme Court decision, several states repealed their compulsory education laws or adopted other means for avoiding racially integrated schools.

29. See Cremin's statement, *Transformation of the School,* pp. 127–28.

30. There had been a few large schools before, with sixty or more pupils jammed into a single-room rural school, and some of the Lancastrian monitorial schools held several hundred students. These, however, had been the exception rather than the rule.

31. The reduction of the class size to sixty pupils per teacher was often considered an unattainable ideal (Cremin, *Transformation of the School,* p. 21).

32. U.S. Bureau of the Census, *Historical Statistics . . . ,* p. 207.

33. *Ibid.* In terms of actual numbers, the increase was more spectacular. There were only eighty thousand public school pupils in 1870, compared to 2,200,000 in 1920.

34. *Ibid.*

35. Cremin, *Transformation of the School,* p. 72.

36. *Ibid.* As Cremin observed: "The mere fact that children in a single schoolroom spoke a half-dozen languages, none of them English, inevitably altered the life of that schoolroom. And the problem went far beyond language, for each language implied a unique heritage and unique attitudes toward teacher, parents, and schoolmates— indeed, toward the school itself."

37. Eby and Arrowood, *Development of Modern Education,* p. 719. By the middle of the nineteenth century, for example, Horace Mann was proclaiming women to be more sympathetic than men, and better adapted to elementary teaching. Therefore, he advocated the employment of more women teachers in common schools.

38. Butts and Cremin, *History of Education,* p. 283.

39. Research Division, NEA, in Lieberman, *Education as a Profession,* p. 242.

40. U.S. Bureau of the Census, *Historical Statistics . . . ,* p. 207.

41. Becker, *Role and Career Problems of the Chicago Public School Teacher,* p. 60.

42. *Ibid.,* pp. 62–63.

43. *Ibid.,* p. 63. Another teacher explained ". . . the biggest problem you face in the public school is discipline. You have to get them in order and keep them that way before you can teach" (*Ibid.,* p. 61).

44. Wagenschein, *Reality Shock,* pp. 58–59. For reports of similar problems in California, see James Herndon, *The Way it Spozed To Be.* Two Harlem teachers, Mary Frances Greene and Orletta Ryan, describe their situation in *The Schoolchildren.*

45. Riesman observes that the teacher ". . . has been taught that bad behavior on the children's part implies poor management on her part" (Riesman *et al., The Lonely Crowd,* p. 84). Similarly, Brookover comments. ". . . in most communities, the adults, including the older teachers, expect the teacher to maintain authority over the children" (Brookover, *A Sociology of Education,* p. 233).

46. Becker, *Role and Career Problems,* p. 63.

47. For example, only four students were expelled from San Francisco's high schools during the 1968–69 school year, although principals had asked for the expulsion of sixty. The board of education permitted the other fifty-six to return to their schools (*San Francisco Examiner,* October 26, 1969).

48. John and Evelyn Dewey, *Schools of Tomorrow,* p. 14.

49. Johnson, *Country School,* p. 49.

50. *Ibid.*

51. A California elementary principal in a conversation with the author.

52. In offering "Hints for New Teachers" on classroom control, the Richmond (California) Federation of Teachers suggested: "Work upon the ego of each student. Every individual is worth something—has some special talent or trait. The sooner you recognize and publicly acknowledge this worth, the sooner you will be on your way to winning the class" (R.F.T. *Newsletter,* October 8, 1969).

53. The use of psychology in pupil control is mentioned by David Riesman. He speaks of teachers as ". . . young college graduates who have been taught to be more concerned with the child's social and psychological adjustment than with his academic progress. . . . This greater knowledge . . . prevents the children from uniting in a wall of distrust or conspiracy against the school. . . ." (Riesman *et al.*, *The Lonely Crowd*, p. 80).

54. Wagenschein, *Reality Shock*, p. 56.

55. Waller, *Sociology of Teaching*, p. 355. Describing an early progressive school which emphasized manual training, a 1904 newspaper announced, "They need no truant officer at Menomonie." Cremin added, "Boys who might have become disciplinary problems elsewhere actually remained in school after hours to work in the machine and carpentry shops" (Cremin, *Transformation of the School*, p. 144).

56. Although curricular diversity is not limited to progressive systems of education, and would probably emerge in any nation which is trying to educate all children, its appearance in American public schools was facilitated by progressive beliefs that individual differences among children should be recognized, and that pupils' interests and needs should shape the curriculum.

57. From a conversation with the author.

58. *Ibid.*

59. This need of the school to minimize pupil frustrations may be a factor behind the complaints that counselors "discriminate" by their alleged readiness to assign minority-group pupils to vocational instead of college preparatory classes.

60. Burton Clark has observed a similar process at the junior college level, whereby the pupil who appears to have little chance of success in academic endeavors is guided into an alternative curriculum more in keeping with his limited scholastic achievement (Clark, "The 'Cooling-Out' Function in Higher Education," pp. 569–76).

61. John and Evelyn Dewey, *Schools of Tomorrow*, p. 15.

62. *San Francisco Chronicle*, August 23, 1959.

63. Mallinson, *An Introduction to the Study of Comparative Education*. p. 159.

64. Expulsion because of low grades was so rare in California that even the threat of it, in a small high school a hundred miles away, was enough to make the front page of the *San Francisco Chronicle* in 1958. The article reported, "So far as local educators know, there have never been expulsions on such grounds in California. 'We don't feel this problem in San Francisco,' school superintendent Harold Spears said, 'I can't see anybody booted out just because he didn't have his grades up' " (*San Francisco Chronicle*, February 17, 1958).

To keep up appearances, administrators sometimes order a change in a pupil's grade, raising the mark given by the teacher (*e.g., San Francisco Chronicle*, March 5, 1958). In elementary schools, the principals often review report cards before they are sent home to the parents. High grades are rarely challenged; even when a child receives ten or twelve As, there is usually no question. A low grade, however, is more likely to be protested by the principal, and frequently it is not the pupil but the teacher who must defend the low mark she has given.

65. During the 1959–60 school year, ninety-seven percent of all pupils in Los Angeles elementary schools received regular promotions both semesters, while only two percent were retained. One percent of the elementary pupils were accelerated, and half of these accelerations were due to over-age rather than to high ability or achievement. It is also interesting to note that the retention rate had dropped considerably during a period of approximately thirty years, from nine percent in 1927, to two percent in 1957–60 (Bowman, "Promotion, Retention, and Acceleration in the Los Angeles City Elementary Schools," in *Educational Research Projects Reported by California County and District School Offices 1960–61*, C.T.A. Research Bulletin 153).

66. One indication of their increasing importance is the change of terminology associated with them. Originally called *extra-curricular*, they are currently referred to as *co-curricular* activities.

67. Mallinson, *Comparative Education*, pp. 182–83.

68. From a conversation with the author.

69. For example, following racial disturbances which closed a San Francisco high school, ". . . the only wholly 'normal' event on the Balboa campus was a lengthy football practice . . ." (*San Francisco Chronicle,* September 24, 1969).

70. King, *Other Schools and Ours,* p. 117.

71. Berk, "Organizational Goals and Inmate Organizations," *A.J.S.,* March, 1966, pp. 522–34.

72. These differences did not appear to be due to selective input of the inmates into various prisons, but rather to the differences between the prisons (*Ibid.,* p. 528).

FEAR AND THE CONSTRAINTS ON ACADEMIC FREEDOM OF PUBLIC SCHOOL TEACHERS, 1930–1960

Paul Violas

Freedom and fear are rather strange bedfellows. A study of the history of the idea of academic freedom for public school teachers from 1930 to 1960, however, reveals an intimate relationship between the two. During this period over twelve hundred articles dealing with various aspects of the concept of public school teachers' academic freedom appeared in educational, legal, and popular journals. An analysis of these articles discloses the academic freedom dialogue reflected the fears emerging from successive crises in American society.

The thirty year period was trisected by three of the most traumatic events in American social history: the Great Depression, World War II, and the Cold War. During each era, the trauma which dominated it gave rise to a peculiar set of social fears. These fears had an important impact on the academic freedom dialogue because: first, the objectives of the school were ascribed in response to society's fears; and, second, the justification of academic freedom rested upon the teachers' function in implementing those objectives.

Reprinted by permission of the author and *Educational Theory,* from pp. 70–80, Volume 21, Number 1, Winter, 1971.

This relationship, however, was complex. The crescendo of fear did not necessarily mean a closure on teachers' freedom. On the contrary, it often provided the impetus for development of the rationale which enhanced certain aspects of academic freedom. All too often, this rationale supporting teachers' freedom was based on a sacrifice of the freedom of students. Because of the limitations of space, all of the dialogue cannot be examined here. This paper will analyze the dialogue surrounding one academic freedom issue during each of the three eras and illustrate the impact of the relationship of fear and freedom.

The portrait of the academic freedom dialogue during the 1930's was strongly colored by the fears arising from social issues stemming from the economic dislocations caused by the Great Depression. The feelings of fear and frustrations which one can sense in the literature of the era, however, was not directed toward the entire economic or social system. While the overwhelming majority of Americans had not lost faith in the system, it was obvious, nevertheless, that all was not right. Some evil had penetrated the Edenic American Garden. It was necessary, then, to dislodge the evil without destroying the Garden. When the evil had been expelled, America would again become the New Israel. The national mood was for reform rather than revolution, and the support accorded to Franklin Roosevelt and his New Deal evidenced that most Americans favored a patchwork approach to reform—reform which amounted to little more than a minor reshuffling of the deck. Within this context there were two satanic enemies; the selfish businessmen who had stacked the deck and those who would overthrow the system—the revolutionaries who wanted a new game rather than a new deal to continue the old game.

The school, as often in the past, was viewed as a vehicle to alleviate social problems.[1] An important objective now assigned to the schools was the creation of safeguards against the dual threat to the Garden. This objective required that the schools produce a special kind of citizen—a citizen who possessed what was termed "critical intelligence." This kind of intelligence would lead the citizen to understand that both the selfish businessmen and the revolutionaries would contaminate Edenic America. Many writers were able to translate this objective into a persuasive rationale for increased teacher freedom. An analysis of the dialogue concerning the question of loyalty oaths provides a typical example of this process.

During the thirties, considerable effort was directed toward the passage of laws requiring loyalty oaths for teachers. By 1935, over twenty states had passed such laws.[2] The major thrust of these laws was to eliminate radical teachers. Most of the support for loyalty oaths stemmed from the belief that there existed a real danger to the Republic in the person of teachers who were imposing un-American and subversive doctrines on the nation's school children. The 1934 American Legion National Convention passed a resolution demanding that schools hire only teachers who were "citizens of unquestioned patriotism and advocates of American ideals."[3] William Kelty of the Y.M.C.A. contended, "There are forces at work in the schools, as elsewhere, that are insidiously undermining the confidence of children in their government. Teachers have been guilty of subversive indoctrination of their classes . . . the truly American forces are taking steps to eradicate the un-American ones. One of the most important moves in this campaign has been the loyalty pledge."[4] The president of the New York City Board of Education wrote to the Board of Examiners instructing them to go beyond the mere requirement of the loyalty oath and "make personality and character your first consideration, and that under the head of character you consider loyalty and love of country."[5] These writers typified those who feared the radical as the greatest threat to the American system and believed the best weapon to expurgate the Garden was the loyalty oath.

This position, however, conflicted with the liberal reformers who were certain that selfish business interests posed the greater threat. They argued that loyalty oaths hindered the development of "critical intelligence" necessary to return America to its promise. One approach suggested that the oaths were neither needed nor effective. In 1936, the N.E.A. passed a resolution condemning loyalty oaths for teachers. This resolution attacked the basic premise of the oath supporters as it stated, "We hold that the loyalty of the teachers of America is beyond question."[6] In a somewhat different mood, H. L. Mencken had expressed the same disdain for the supposed threat of radical teachers as he commented on the proposed Maryland oath law: "The Halloway-American Legion Bill is foolish enough to be worthy of its sponsors. Its ostensible aim is to smoke out schoolmarms who poison their pupils with Marxian heresies . . . it is almost as rare for one of them to hatch sedition as it is for one of them to go up in a balloon."[7]

If the opponents of loyalty oaths believed there were too few un-American teachers to make oaths necessary, they even more strongly denied that such oaths would inhibit any few disloyal teachers that might exist. Abraham Lefkowitz pointed out that, "since these so-called dangerous 'reds' do not believe in bourgeois morality, they will be the first to take such silly oaths and then laugh at bourgeois stupidity and morality."[8] But, if these oaths could not solve American society's problems, their opponents believed they were detrimental to the development of that solution.

The opponents of loyalty oaths contended the depression had shown that a major responsibility of the schools was to develop students with "critical intelligence." They argued it could only be accomplished by professional teachers who were free from fear. Loyalty oaths would cause fear and inhibit this development. William H. Kilpatrick stated that the Constitution was held as a symbol of those supporting the status quo. The oaths, he believed, would be used to retard responsible social change and reduce reasonable social criticism.[9] Florence Curtis Hanson argued that the loyalty oath laws would produce fear among teachers. "Such legislation creates an

atmosphere of fear in which it is impossible to develop critical intelligence.
. . . Effective teaching can be carried on only under conditions of freedom
from fear of official discipline for thinking thoughts that may be different
from those approved by the guardians of status quo."[10] These writers believed the "guardians of the status quo" represented the same selfish business interests which had caused the depression. In a sense, this demand for
the expulsion of the influence of the guardians of the status quo was not significantly different from the nature of the demand to eliminate the radical
influence in the school. The presence of either would prevent the teacher
from doing the right things to the student, i.e., equip him with "critical intelligence" that he might understand reality in a way to insure the continuation of the American system.

Perhaps the most interesting, and most visible, of such oaths was the
"little red rider" which appeared as an amendment to a June, 1935 appropriations bill providing funds for the Washington, D.C. public schools. The
amendment stated: "Hereafter no part of any appropriation for the public
schools shall be available for the payment of the salary of any person teaching or advocating Communism."[11] The United States Controller-General
interpreted this to mean that school employees could not discuss Communism either in or out of school.[12] Before each payday, every teacher was
required to sign a statement swearing that he had not violated this edict.
The effect of this was the omission of any discussion or reading material
dealing with Communism, or the history, geography and current events of
the U.S.S.R., in Washington Public Schools.[13] Representative Thomas
Blanton, author of the rider, went so far as to send a questionnaire to the
teachers on June 11, 1936, asking if they believed in God, approved of the
writings of George S. Counts or Charles H. Beard or were members of the
N.E.A. and, if so, who had suggested such membership.[14] Reactions
against such measures were swift and forceful. They came from both individuals and educational organizations. A concentrated effort against the law
resulted in its repeal in May, 1937. The most effective arguments against
the law focused on its debilitating effect on the development of effective,
i.e., "critically intelligent," citizens.

It is interesting to note that the arguments both for and against loyalty
oaths were not based on the need for individual freedom. The conservative
who believed the radical posed the greatest threat to American Society
wanted the school to produce students whose outlook corresponded to this
world view. The liberals opposing the oaths based their rationale on the
necessity of developing students whose world view saw the selfish business
interest as the greatest threat. The rationale for increased teacher freedom
was dominated by the desire to utilize this freedom to alleviate a social
problem. A concern for the freedom of the individual teacher, apart from
its social utility, did not constitute even a minor eddy in the main stream of
the rhetoric.

The World War II Era saw a new threat and the development of a different complex of fears which then directed the academic freedom dialogue. This threat, represented by the Fascist dictators of Germany, Italy, and Japan, was both visible and foreign based. The Garden had been cleansed and now the crusade was sanctioned to protect democracy against totalitarianism. This crusade required a unified national effort. Groups and individuals who contributed toward that effort consequently were awarded increased esteem. Such groups included the American industrialists, women workers and veterans' organizations. Any tendency which seemed to weaken the drive for national unity, the war effort, or "democracy" was immediately suspect.

Within this context, the schools were assigned two somewhat conflicting roles: to extend and protect democracy and, to aid in the drive for national unity. Because these roles were somewhat contradictory, their impact on the function of the teacher was felt in contradictory ways. The need to protect democracy lent credence to the arguments for increased academic freedom, while the necessity for unity suggested restrictions.

The most interesting example of the effect of these fears on the academic dialogue concerned the development of the rationale for the exclusion of teachers from the profession because of their association with undesirable groups. In an important sense this rationale was similar to the dialogue of the depression era. The production of student attitudes conducive to effecting national unity became a primary objective of the schools. Educators now campaigned to purge teachers who might detract from that objective because of their associations with groups which displayed any tendency away from the norms of "Americanism." It is also interesting to note that this rationale developed during the war years by educators was not entirely dissimilar from the later rationale expounded by the professional patriots of the McCarthy Era.

The chairman of the N.E.A. Academic Freedom Committee, responding to the pressures of nationalism and fears of European war, declared, "the time has come when we should rethink and rewrite the statement of principles which was adopted in 1937."[15] The direction the rethinking and rewriting was going to take was accurately forecast when he continued:

> There is, we realize, always a danger that certain persons may hide under the cloak of academic freedom and disseminate propaganda in our public schools in behalf of doctrines that will not bear public scrutiny. Occasionally one finds an individual who takes advantage of academic freedom in a subtle way in an effort to undermine the fundamentals of democratic government. The Committee must not and will not be a shield for Fifth Columnists in the United States of America![16]

The statement of principles drafted by William S. Taylor affected a significant closure on the concept of teacher's freedom in extra-school citizenship.[17] It cautioned teachers that intellectual integrity was indispensable to education and to qualify as teachers they must be certain that their associations would not prostitute their integrity. The Committee bluntly asserted: "Any suspicion, therefore, that the teacher is externally controlled or otherwise unduly influenced in reaching his opinions or in expressing them honestly must call into question his intellectual integrity and so work against the desired integrity in all whom he influences."[18] It is important that there was no discussion about how to determine whether a teacher was, in fact, "externally controlled." The statement simply said, "any suspicion." Not even a well-founded suspicion was required to "call into question his intellectual integrity." Significantly, the N.E.A. Committee on Academic Freedom did not find it necessary to even discuss the question of what kind of external control would in fact compromise one's "intellectual integrity."[19] Should, for example, a Baptist, or a Catholic, or a Republican, or a Communist have been disqualified as a teacher because each of them might in some way have been externally controlled? Or did this prohibition apply only to bad external control? If so, who would define "bad"? The reflex expressed in 1941 by the N.E.A. Academic Freedom Committee was one which teachers would hear again at a later time. The 1941 N.E.A. National Convention adopted a resolution with reference to this question which was more precise than its Academic Freedom Committee. The resolution read: "The N.E.A. is opposed to the employment in any school, college or university, of any person who advocates or who is a member of any organization that advocates changing the form of government of the United States in any means not provided for under the federal constitution."[20] This resolution, while more precise than the Academic Freedom Committee's statement, nevertheless, made association, rather than acts, cause for summary condemnation and punishment.

The American Federation of Teachers under the direction of its President George S. Counts, took similar action in its 1941 Convention. After revoking the charters of three of its local unions, No. 5, No. 192, and No. 537, for Communist domination, the convention amended its constitution to exclude from membership an "applicant whose political actions are subject to totalitarian control such as Fascist, Nazi, or Communist."[21] The rationale offered by the A.F.T. paralleled that of the N.E.A. point for point and could be subjected to the same criticism as the rationale of the N.E.A. It is interesting during this time that such criticism was not voiced in the academic freedom dialogue.

What did appear was an attack on the Rapp-Coudert Committee. This committee was set up by the New York State Legislature in 1939 to examine state aid to education and investigate subversive activities in the schools. Oddly enough, the same 1941 American Federation of Teachers' Convention passed a resolution condemning the aims and methods of this committee. It charged that teachers should not be dismissed "until legitimate and specific charges for dismissal have been presented and substantiated in a fair public trial."[22]

Although a member of the 1941 N.E.A. Academic Freedom Committee, William H. Kilpatrick also challenged the activities of the Rapp-Coudert Committee.[23] He believed if it was indeed true that Communist teachers had rejected democratic standards of truth and honesty, then this rejection should be scored against their right to remain teachers. He argued, however, it was important to show that the individual teacher had actually subscribed to the alleged Communist tenets regarding truth and then show that this subscription had adversely affected his teaching. He said, "It is not hated ideas but wrong conduct which calls for penalty."[24] His arguments against guilt by association and his demands for proof of wrong actions represented, unfortunately, only a small minority view-point. Even Kilpatrick's lonely voice was raised only against legislative committees. Its impact was considerably diminished by the appendage of his name to the 1941 N.E.A. Academic Freedom Committee report.

Moreover, less than four months after his attack on the Rapp-Coudert Committee, Kilpatrick wrote an article defending the American Federation of Teachers' expulsion of the allegedly Communist dominated locals.[25] He argued that liberal democratic methods demanded free and open discussion as a means to apply intelligence to problematic situations in order to arrive at optimal solutions. The Communists, according to Kilpatrick, rejected open discussion and relied upon "obstructive and browbeating tactics so as seriously to hamper the legitimate deliberations."[26] When this happened, he believed "the bounds of toleration have been passed."[27] In effect Kilpatrick argued that the Communist locals should be denied entrance to the arena of open discussion because they had not abided by the ground rules and had sought to destroy the process to gain their own ends. This may have been a valid account of the activities of those locals. The difficulty, however, occurred as this analysis was generalized from this specific instance and Kilpatrick's argument used against all Communist teachers.

Such an argument was presented in 1942 by V. T. Thayer.[28] He believed it was time for liberals to rethink their traditional commitment to complete freedom of speech and of teaching. This commitment was based on the belief that in a completely free exchange of ideas man would use his reason to determine truth. Education was the agency, according to Thayer, charged with instructing future generations with this method, therefore, it must not attempt to inculcate dogmas or beliefs. Its commodity was method, not conclusions.

The teacher who was a Communist or a Fascist could not meet the qualifications Thayer set for membership in this agency. His first reason acknowledged its close allegiance with those who saw the teacher as an exemplar. He argued, "No conscientious teacher can ignore the fact that there is a relationship between his life outside school and his influence within the classroom."[29] Because his out-of-school behavior was to be an example for his students, it was obvious to Thayer that "conduct becoming a teacher cannot rightfully include membership in any group or party dedicated to a policy of undermining the essential structure of our government or our way of life."[30] Thayer apparently did not think it necessary to show the individual's compliance or involvement with the organization plans. Nor did he explain what he meant by "undermining our way of life."

Thayer's second reason for expelling Communists and Fascists from the teaching profession borrowed heavily from Kilpatrick's argument against the three Communist dominated A.F.T. locals. He contended that the Communist teachers violated the belief that the teacher should be free from dogma and restraint which would prohibit his arrival at undictated conclusions. The key assumption in Thayer's argument was the statement that "The Communist Party, and doubtless Fascist groups as well, secretly controls the activities of its members for purposes that can properly be termed subversive."[31] Armed with this assumption, which he considered a fact, Thayer believed that it was no longer necessary to demand proof of wrong action before the expulsion of a teacher from the profession. Proof of association with an undesirable group, i.e., membership in a Communist or Fascist Party, was accepted as sufficient cause for punishment.

Long before the red-baiting, Cold War Era, leading educators had developed the guilt by association arguments which they would again hear from men like Senator Joseph McCarthy and Congressman Richard Nixon. The rationale supporting this closure on academic freedom was based on what the teacher was supposed to do to the student—i.e., develop attitudes facilitating the intensification for national unity. It was necessary to expel those teachers whose associations indicated that they might be ineffective examples for the molding of effective citizens.

Several conditions obtaining in the Cold War Era produced a new fear. The increasing hostilities between the United States and the Soviet Union dashed the earlier hopes for world peace which had attended the end of World War II. A series of sensational espionage trials in the U.S., Canada, and Great Britain not only informed Americans that their international enemies had acquired the means to destroy American urban areas, but also that they had acquired this capacity through the conspiratorial efforts of faceless and silent traitors, some of whom were undoubtedly still lurking undetected. Thus, the awesome and constant fear of total annihilation was reinforced with the fear of internal conspiracy.

These fears were reflected in the definition of the role of the school. As in World War II, the school was to protect democracy against a totalitarian threat. The Communist threat, however, appeared more insidious in that it seemed to involve a significant internal conspiracy. The school had to do more than simply facilitate national unity. Its role now included the preparation of the sentinels of democracy. The teacher's function was to insulate the student from the evil effects of Communism and to outfit him for efficient service in the nation's struggle. One significant aspect of the academic freedom dialogue concerned the degree to which the teacher should be confined by this role.

An example of this was the demand that the teacher become an instrument of national policy and indoctrinate his students for patriotism and against Communism. The writers who supported this idea wanted education to be used as an instrument of social control and teachers to become agents for obtaining that control. The N.E.A. lent credence to this position when its Educational Policies Commission stated in a 1949 bulletin: "If the schools develop programs that contribute to the nation's needs in this time of crisis, and if they can convince the public that these contributions are useful, then education can command the support it will deserve as an instrument of national policy." [32] This statement suggests not only that education should attempt to become an instrument of national policy, but, that it will be less susceptible to attack and perhaps better financed if it does so.

When Massachusetts established the position of director of civic education in 1951, Henry W. Holmes, former Dean of Harvard's Graduate School of Education supported the creation by endorsing the statement subscribed to by the Massachusetts Association of School Superintendents. This statement called for the use of the school as an instrument of national policy. It listed several reasons for supporting the post. They included the following:

> *First*, the fight against Communism calls for all the weapons in the arsenal. If we neglect education, we are missing an opportunity so important that it may be impossible to make up, later, for what we fail to do now. . . .
> *Third*, the Department of Education is the key place for a leader . . . as we see it; *education for citizenship is a grass roots investment in national security; the schools are asking for help in meeting this great need; and the Massachusetts plan is to put an experienced leader in a key spot.* [33]

Similarly, William F. Russell, Dean of Teachers College, Columbia University asserted that the schools might be more secure if they could convince the public that they were aiding in the national defense. He said, "The basic reason for the attacks on the schools is that many people believe that the schools are not doing as much as they should for the national defense; or that what they are doing is hurting the national defense; or that doing something else might strengthen the national defense." [34] In a later article, Russell asserted that patriotic history could be one way of aiding national defense. He argued that an analysis of the post-war crisis "points to the supreme importance, in the better prosecution of the cold war, of bringing every American into close relationship with the glorious history of his country. When he knows it he will thrill to it. He will sense that he is a part of it. He will make the sacrifices."[35] This statement left little doubt about the kind of history and the kind of education the Dean of Teachers College supported.

Erling H. Hunt agreed that the social studies provided an effective avenue for developing right answers regarding the dangers of Communism.[36] Although he argued for a "full study of facts" and contended that "Americans are strong enough and smart enough to compare the theory and the realities of American democracy and Communism, and come out with the right answers," he still favored inoculation.[37] Hunt said, "So far as Communism is concerned, the schools are, I believe, basically responsible for inoculating young citizens against it. But the serum must be strong enough to be effective. I grant that there are risks in inoculation, but the risks of no inoculation are far greater."[38] Apparently Professor Hunt would support full and open study by American public school teachers and students only when there were guarantees that such study would lead to acceptable answers. This analysis is supported by his statement: "Perhaps we can safely admit that our democracy has not yet achieved perfection . . . and yet have plenty of margin of attractiveness for our youth."[39] In a "full study of facts," it would seem that the admissability of a fact would be determined by its validity not by its effect on the conclusion the teacher wanted his students to reach.[40]

Although the belief that education should be an instrument of national security did not go unchallenged during the Cold War Era, its proponents were the most vociferous and occupied the most prestigious positions in the educational establishment.

Throughout this thirty year period the academic freedom dialogue was closely related to societal fears. Arguments for increased or decreased academic freedom rested on the function of the teacher. This function was determined by the purposes which society assigned to the schools. When one examines the history of American education and particularly its recent history, it becomes clear that most often those purposes have been in response to the fears and anxieties felt in American society. The idea of academic freedom for the public school teacher, then, has been shaped by what American society, in response to its fears, has decided that the teacher should do to the student to render him a more effective citizen.

NOTES

1. For a history of the idea that the school could solve America's social problems see: Henry J. Perkinsen, *The Imperfect Panacea* (New York: Random House, 1968).

2. "Loyalty Oaths for Teachers," *School and Society*, vol. 42, No. 1078, August 24, 1935, pp. 267–269. "Loyalty Oaths," *Social Frontier*, vol. 2, No. 1, October, 1935, p. 23.

3. Quoted in "Educational Resolutions by the American Legion," *School and Society*, vol. 40, No. 1943, December 22, 1943, p. 839.

4. "Is It 'Misguided Patriotism'?" *School and Society,* vol. 41, No. 1066, June 1, 1935, p. 735. See also Glenn W. Moon, "Club Activity as Training for Democracy," *Social Education,* vol. 3, No. 1, January, 1939, pp. 103–107.

5. Quoted in "Qualifications for Teachers in the New York City Schools," *School and Society,* vol. 40, No. 1033, October 13, 1934, p. 484.

6. "Platform and Resolutions," *NEA Addresses and Proceedings,* vol. 74, 1936, p. 216.

7. "Chasing the Reds," *Teachers College Record,* vol. 36, No. 8, May, 1935, p. 721.

8. "Academic Freedom and Progress," *The American Teacher,* vol. 19, No. 4, March–April, 1935, p. 11. See also "Teachers' Loyalty Oath," *The American Teacher,* vol. 19, No. 5, May–June, 1935, p. 24.

9. "Loyalty Oath—A Threat to Intelligent Teaching," *Social Frontier,* vol. 1, No. 9, June, 1935, pp. 10–15.

10. "Loyalists' Oaths," *Social Frontier,* vol. 2, No. 2, November, 1935, pp. 47–49. See also Charles L. Bane, "Oaths for Teachers," *School and Society,* vol. 42, No. 1080, September 7, 1935, pp. 330–331. Franklin W. Johnsen, "The Teacher's Oath," *School and Society,* vol. 43, No. 1121, June 20, 1936, pp. 832–835; and "Teachers' Loyalty Oath," p. 25.

11. Quoted in "The Little Red Rider," *School and Society,* vol. 43, No. 1111, April 11, 1936, p. 513.

12. *Ibid.,* pp. 513–514.

13. Caroline Williams, "Congress Legislates Character," *Social Frontier,* vol. 3, No. 22, January, 1937, pp. 107–110.

14. Ellen Thomas, "Sequelae of the 'Red Rider,'" *Progressive Education,* vol. 13, No. 8, December, 1936, pp. 606–608.

15. William S. Taylor, "Academic Freedom," *NEA Addresses and Proceedings,* vol. 78, 1940, p. 879.

16. *Ibid.,* p. 879.

17. "Principles of Academic Freedom," *NEA Journal,* vol. 30, No. 5, May, 1941, pp. 142–143.

18. *Ibid.,* p. 142.

19. It seems from the context in which the phrase "externally controlled" is used that it is meant to indicate control from outside one's own rational decision-making process as by some body of dogma or set of preconceptions which short-circuit the process of inquiry. The context does not seem to indicate control from outside the country as by some foreign power. This lack of preciseness, however, which forces speculation from context, is part of the difficulty with the statement.

20. Resolutions Committee, *NEA Addresses and Proceedings,* vol. 79, 1941, p. 906.

21. "The Twenty-Fifth Annual Convention," *The American Teacher,* vol. 26, No. 1, October, 1941, p. 8.

22. *Ibid.,* p. 23.

23. "The Coudert Investigation," *Frontiers of Democracy,* vol. 7, No. 58, January 15, 1941, pp. 102–103.

24. *Ibid.,* p. 103.

25. "Liberalism, Communist Tactics and Democratic Efficiency," *Frontiers of Democracy,* vol. 7, No. 60, March 15, 1941, pp. 167–168.

26. *Ibid.,* p. 168.

27. *Ibid.,* p. 168.

28. "Should Communists and Fascists Teach in the Schools?" *Harvard Educational Review,* vol. 12, No. 1, January, 1942, pp. 7–19.

29. *Ibid.,* p. 14.

30. *Ibid.,* p. 16.

31. *Ibid.,* p. 17.

32. *American Education and International Tensions,* Washington, D.C., 1949, p. 35.

33. "Civil Education: Massachusetts Steps Ahead," *School and Society,* vol. 75, No. 1948, April 19, 1952, p. 242. Author's emphasis.

34. "The Caravan Goes On," *Teachers College Record,* vol. 54, No. 1, October, 1952, p. 4.

35. "Education and the Cold War," *Teachers College Record,* vol. 55, No. 3, December, 1953, p. 118.

36. "Teaching the Contrasts Between American Democracy and Soviet Communism," *Teachers College Record,* vol. 55, No. 3, December, 1953, pp. 122–127.

37. *Ibid.,* p. 123.

38. *Ibid.,* p. 123.

39. *Ibid.,* p. 125.

40. Other writers who also argued that teachers should insure the acceptance by their students of those attitudes and beliefs most beneficial to the national security included: Louis William Norris, "The Teacher as Prophet," *School and Society,* vol. 71, No. 1831, January 21, 1950, pp. 36–39; and Philip H. Phenix, "Teachers Education and the Unity of Culture," *Teachers College Record,* vol. 60, No. 6, March, 1959, pp. 337–343.

EDUCATION THROUGH FREEDOM: SOCIOLOGICAL PERSPECTIVE

Robert Arnove

The sociological study of this topic concerns itself with those organizational characteristics of schools that circumscribe the choice and autonomy of students and teachers. Those characteristics are the compulsory nature of schooling and the tendency of schools to approximate total institutions. Schools contain coercive elements; and as large-scale bureaucratic organizations, batch-processing masses of students, they emphasize control often to the detriment of learning. Another sociological consideration is the relationship between the objective structural situation of individuals and their perceptions and definitions of that situation.

A salient feature of schooling is that it is compulsory, usually until age sixteen. Schools represent a type of institution where the clients (students) have little or no choice concerning their participation in the organization; and the institution itself has little say concerning who is admitted.[1] Other institutions that share these features sadly enough, are prisons, mental institutions, and reformatories.[2] Indeed, the penalty for truancy may very well be institutionalization in a state reformatory.

Etzioni has developed a typology of organizations based on the kinds of power exercised (coercive, remunerative, and normative) and the basis for members' involvement (alienative, calculative, and moral).[3] Schools, at least at the elementary and secondary levels, tend to represent institutions in which coercion is the major means of control over highly alienated members.[4] At the higher education level, schools represent institutions that attract students because of the goals or missions they stand for, and their instrumental value to the attainment of ends such as improved social status, attractive employment, and greater income. This analysis does not exclude consideration of the fact that large numbers of students, notwithstanding compulsory attendance laws, enjoy being in school, consider it intrinsically rewarding or integrally related to some desired future outcomes.

In a sense, all organized systems of education—not just schools—

360

represent an imposition of adult values on children. As Jules Henry has observed in *Culture Against Man,* the purpose of education systems is to make children's attitudes look organized to adults. Far from liberating individuals, the purpose of education is to prevent the creative genius from getting out of hand.[5] All societies must depend on its members to engage in mundane, routine activities by which the business of a society is accomplished. The task of teachers is to focus student attention and direct behavior toward the attainment of societal goals.

The tension between control and learning has been a continuing theme in the sociology of education.[6] To focus attention on learning a certain amount of teacher control and order is necessary in the classroom. But control is imperative in schools in which large numbers of students have to be processed efficiently; this is particularly the case with urban high schools, which are built to accommodate as many as several thousand students. Teachers and administrators are sometimes judged more in relation to their ability to create the semblance of control and order, than with regard to their effectiveness in fostering learning. Edgar Friedenberg, in "The Modern High School: A Profile," details the excessive preoccupation of school officials with petty regulations: "Indeed Milgrim High's most memorable arrangements are its corridor passes and its johns; they dominate social interaction."

Schools are evolving into total institutions. According to Goffman, total institutions are distinguished by their quality of being all encompassing.[7] Schools not only minutely regulate students but they increasingly scrutinize and evaluate every aspect of the individual. Schools, which are called upon to select and allocate students to socioeconomic positions in the society, assess individuals not only according to cognitive achievement but personality attributes and social and emotional adjustment.[8] The question raised by Friedenberg in his various essays on American adolesence is where can the individual hide—find a place where his/her identity is respected and allowed to develop?

In response to the control schools attempt to exercise over them, students may withdraw or rebel. They strike back at the system by flaunting of the rules; and increasingly they turn to more serious vandalism as well as physical assault on school personnel. But rarely, as the Michaels and Friedenberg articles point out, do they object to it in principle: "The [school] administration, like forces of law and order generally in the United States, is accepted as part of the way things are and work" (Friedenberg). To repeat Mills, in *The Sociological Imagination,* "Individuals cannot cope with their personal troubles in such ways as to control the structural transformations that usually lie behind them." To objectify and name the injustices individuals collectively experience, to view their problems as manifestations of social arrangements that can be changed through human efforts, is the basis of Paulo Freire's *Pedagogy of the Oppressed.* In this process of awakening and liberation, sociology can play a constructive role in enriching our understanding of how social structures affect the individual, and the nature of the transformations required.

NOTES

1. There are of course exceptions. Before mainstreaming, students who were variously labeled as retarded, disabled, visually and aurally impaired, were referred to special education institutions. Recently, a number of alternatives have been created for disruptive students, as means of siphoning-off malcontents and other students classroom teachers are unable to instruct or control.

2. For a more detailed discussion, see Richard D. Carlson, "Environmental and Organizational Consequences: The Public School and Its Clients," in Daniel E. Griffiths (ed.), *Behavioral Science and Educational Administration Yearbook* (Washington, D.C.: National Society for the Study of Education, 1964), part II, chap. 12.

3. Amitai Etzioni, *A Comparative Analysis of Complex Organizations* (New York: The Free Press, 1961), chap. 1–3.

4. Ronald G. Corwin, *Education in Crisis: A Sociological Analysis of Schools and Universities in Transition* (New York: Wiley, 1974), p. 15.

5. Jules Henry, *Culture Against Man* (New York: Random House, 1963), pp. 285–286; and Yehudi Cohen, "Schools and Civilizational States," in Joseph and Fischer (ed.), *The Social Sciences and the Comparative Study of Educational Systems* (Scranton, Pa.: International Textbook Co., 1970), pp. 116–119.

6. See Willard Waller, *The Sociology of Teaching* (New York: Wiley, 1965); Charles Bidwell, "The School as a Formal Organization," in James March (ed.), *Handbook of Organizations* (Chicago, Ill.: Rand McNally, 1965), pp. 972–1022; C. Wayne Gordon, *The Social System of the High School* (New York: The Free Press, 1957); and William G. Spady, "The Authority System of the School and Student Unrest: A Theoretical Exploration," in C. Wayne Gordon (ed.), National Society for the Study of Education's 1974 Yearbook on Education, *Uses of the Sociology of Education* (Chicago, Ill.: University of Chicago Press, 1974), pp. 36–77.

7. Irving Goffman, "The Characteristics of Total Institutions," in Amitai Etzioni (ed.), *Complex Organizations: A Sociological Reader* (New York; Holt, 1961), pp. 312–340.

8. See, for example, Aaron Cicourel and John Kitsuse, *The Educational Decision-Makers* (Indianapolis: Bobbs, 1963).

THE MODERN HIGH SCHOOL: A PROFILE

Edgar Z. Friedenberg

Not far from Los Angeles, though rather nearer to Boston, may be located the town of Milgrim, in which Milgrim High School is clearly the most costly and impressive structure. Milgrim is not a suburb. Although it is only fifty miles from a large and dishonorable city and a part of its conurbation, comparatively few Milgrimites commute to the city for work. Milgrim is an agricultural village which has outgrown its nervous system; its accustomed modes of social integration have not yet even begun to relate its present, recently acquired inhabitants to one another. So, though it is not a suburb, Milgrim is not a community either.

Milgrim's recent, fulminating growth is largely attributable to the rapid development of light industry in the outer suburbs, with a resulting demand for skilled labor. But within the past few years, further economic development has created a steady demand for labor that is not so skilled. In an area that is by no means known for its racial tolerance or political liberalism, Milgrim has acquired, through no wish of its own, a sizable Negro and Puerto Rican minority. On the shabby outskirts of town, a number of groceries label themselves Spanish-American. The advanced class in Spanish at Milgrim High School makes a joyful noise—about the only one to be heard.

Estimates of the proportion of the student body at Milgrim who are, in the ethnocentric language of demography, non-white, vary enormously. Some students who are clearly middle-class and of pinkish-gray color sometimes speak as if they themselves were a besieged minority. More responsible staff members produce estimates of from 12 to 30 per cent. Observations in the corridors and lunchrooms favor the lower figure. They also establish clearly that the non-whites are orderly and well behaved, though somewhat more forceful in their movements and manner of speech than their light-skinned colleagues.

What is Milgrim High like? It is a big, expensive building, on spacious but barren grounds. Every door is at the end of a corridor; there is no reception area, no public space in which one can adjust to the transition from the outside world. Between class periods the corridors are tumultuously crowded; during them they are empty. But at both times they are guarded by teachers and students on patrol duty. Patrol duty does not consist primarily in the policing of congested throngs of moving students, or the guarding of property from damage. Its principal function is the checking of corridor passes. Between classes, no student may walk down the corridor without a form, signed by a teacher, telling where he is coming from, where he is going, and the time, to the minute, during which the pass is valid. A student caught in the corridor without such a pass is sent or taken to the office; there a detention slip is made out against him, and he is required to remain after school for two or three hours. He may do his homework during this time, but he may not leave his seat or talk.

There is no physical freedom whatever at Milgrim. Except during class breaks, the lavatories are kept locked, so that a student must not only obtain a pass but find the custodian and induce him to open the facility. Indeed Milgrim High's most memorable arrangements are its corridor passes and its johns; they dominate social interaction. "Good morning, Mr. Smith," an attractive girl will say pleasantly to one of her teachers in the corridor. "Linda, do you have a pass to be in your locker after the bell rings?" is his greeting in reply. There are more classifications of washrooms than there must have been in the Confederate Navy. The common sort, marked just "Boys" and "Girls," are generally locked. Then there are some marked, "Teachers, Men" and "Teachers, Women," unlocked. Near the auditorium are two others marked simply, "Men" and "Women," which are intended primarily for the public when the auditorium is being used for some function. During the school day cardboard signs saying "Adults Only" are placed on these doors. Girding up my maturity, I used this men's room during my stay at Milgrim. Usually it was empty; but once, as soon as the door clicked behind me, a teacher who had been concealed in the cubicle began jumping up and down to peer over his partition and verify my adulthood.

He was not a voyeur; he was checking on smoking. At most public high schools, students are forbidden to smoke, and this is probably the most common source of friction with authorities. It focuses, naturally, on the washrooms which are the only place students can go where teachers are not supposed to be. Milgrim, for a time, was more liberal than most; last year its administration designated an area behind the school where seniors might smoke during their lunch period. But, as a number of students explained to me during interviews, some of these seniors had "abused the privilege" by lighting up before they got into the area, and the privilege had been withdrawn. No student, however, questioned that smoking was a privilege rather than a right.

The concept of privilege is important at Milgrim. Teachers go to the head of the chow line at lunch; whenever I would attempt quietly to stand in line the teacher on hall duty would remonstrate with me. He was right, probably; I was fouling up an entire informal social system by my ostentation. Students on hall patrol also were allowed to come to the head of the line; so were seniors. Much of the behavior that Milgrim depends on to keep it going is motivated by the reward of getting a government-surplus peanut butter or tuna fish sandwich without standing in line.

The lunchroom itself is a major learning experience, which must make quite an impression over four years time. There are two large cafeterias which are used as study halls during the periods before and after the middle of the day. The food, by and large, is good, and more tempting than the menu. The atmosphere is not quite that of a prison, because the students are permitted to talk quietly under the frowning scrutiny of teachers standing around on duty, during their meal—they are not supposed to talk while standing in line, though this rule is only sporadically enforced. Standing in line takes about a third of their lunch period, and leaves plenty of time for them to eat what is provided them. They may not, in any case, leave the room when they have finished, any more than they could leave a class. Toward the end of the period a steel gate is swung down across the corridor, dividing the wing holding the cafeterias, guidance offices, administrative offices, and auditorium from the rest of the building. Then the first buzzer sounds, and the students sweep out of the cafeteria and press silently forward to the gate. A few minutes later a second buzzer sounds, the gate is opened, and the students file out to their classrooms.

During the meal itself the atmosphere varies in response to chance events and the personality of the teachers assigned supervisory duty; this is especially true in the corridor where the next sitting is waiting in line. The norm is a not unpleasant chatter; but about one teacher in four is an embittered martinet, snarling, whining, continually ordering the students to stand closer to the wall and threatening them with detention or suspension for real or fancied insolence. On other occasions, verbal altercations break out between students in the cafeteria or in line and the *student* hall patrolmen. In one of these that I witnessed, the accused student, a handsome, aggressive-looking young man, defended himself in the informal but explicit language of working-class hostility. This roused the teacher on duty from his former passivity. He walked over toward the boy, and silently but with a glare of contempt, beckoned him from the room with a crooked finger and led him along the corridor to the administrative office: the tall boy rigid in silent protest, the teacher, balding and stoop-shouldered in a wrinkled suit, shambling ahead of him. The youth, I later learned, was suspended for a day. At some lunch periods all this is drowned out by Mantovani-type pop records played over the public address system.

What adults generally, I think, fail to grasp even though they may actually know it, is that there is no refuge or respite from this: no coffee-break, no taking ten for a smoke, no room like the teachers' room, however poor, where the youngsters can get away from adults. High schools don't have club rooms; they have organized gym and recreation. A student cannot go to the library when he wants a book; on certain days his schedule provides a forty-five-minute library period. "Don't let anybody leave early," a guidance counselor urged during a group-testing session at Hartsburgh, an apparently more permissive school that I also visited. "There really isn't any place for them to go." Most of us are as nervous by the age of five as we will ever be, and adolescence adds to the strain; but one thing a high-school student learns is that he can expect no provision for his need to give in to his feelings, or swing out in his own style, or creep off and pull himself together.

The little things shock most. High-school students—and not just, or even particularly, at Milgrim—have a prisoner's sense of time. They don't know what time it is outside. The research which occasioned my presence at Milgrim, Hartsburgh, and the other schools in my study required me to interview each of twenty-five to thirty students at each school three times. My first appointment with each student was set up by his guidance counselor; I would make the next appointment directly with the student and issue him the passes he needed to keep it. The student has no *open* time at his own disposal; he has to select the period he can miss with least loss to himself. Students well-adapted to the school usually pick study halls; poorer or more troublesome students pick the times of their most disagreeable classes; both avoid cutting classes in which the teacher is likely to respond vindictively to their absence. Most students, when asked when they would like to come for their next interview replied, "I can come any time." When I pointed out to them that there must, after all, be some times that would be more convenient for them than others, they would say, "Well tomorrow, fourth period" or whatever. But hardly any of them knew when this would be in clock time. High-school classes emphasize the importance of punctuality by beginning at regular but uneven times like 10:43 and 11:27, which are, indeed, hard to remember; and the students did not know when this was.

How typical is all this? The elements of the composition—the passes, the tight scheduling, the reliance on threats of detention or suspension as modes of social control are nearly universal. The usurpation of any possible *area* of the student initiative, physical or mental, is about as universal. Milgrim forbids boys to wear trousers that end more than six inches above the floor, and has personnel fully capable of measuring them. But most high schools have some kind of dress regulation; I know of none that accepts and relies on the tastes of students.

There are differences to be sure, in tone; and these matter. They greatly affect the impact of the place on students. Take, for comparison and contrast, Hartsburgh High. Not fifteen miles from Milgrim, Hartsburgh is an utterly different community. It is larger, more compact, and more suburban; more of a place. Hartsburgh High is much more dominantly middle class and there are few Negroes in the high school there.

First impressions of Hartsburgh High are almost bound to be favorable. The building, like Milgrim, is new; unlike Milgrim's, it is handsome. External walls are mostly glass, which gives a feeling of light, air, and space. At Hartsburgh there is none of the snarling, overt hostility that taints the atmosphere at Milgrim. There are no raucous buzzers; no bells of any kind. Instead, there are little blinker lights arranged like the Mexican flag. The green light blinks and the period is over; the white light signals a warning; when the red light blinks it is time to be in your classroom. Dress regulations exist but are less rigorous than at Milgrim. Every Wednesday, however, is dress-up day; boys are expected to wear ties and jackets or jacket-sweaters, the girls wear dresses rather than skirts and sweaters. The reason is that on Wednesday the school day ends with an extra hour of required assembly and, as the students explain, there are often outside visitors for whom they are expected to look their best.

Students at Hartsburgh seem much more relaxed than at Milgrim. In the grounds outside the main entrance, during lunch period, there is occasional horseplay. For ten minutes during one noon hour I watched three boys enacting a mutual fantasy. One was the audience who only sat and laughed, one the aggressor, and the third—a pleasant, inarticulate varsity basketball player named Paul—was the self-appointed victim. The two protagonists were portraying in pantomime old, silent-movie type fights in slow motion. The boy I did not know would slowly swing at Paul, who would sink twisting to the ground with grimaces of anguish; then the whole sequence would be repeated with variations, though the two boys never switched roles. In my interviews with Paul I had never solved the problems arising from the fact that he was eloquent only with his arms and torso movements, which were lost on the tape recorder, and it was a real pleasure to watch him in his own medium. This was a pleasure Milgrim would never have afforded me. Similarly, in the corridors at Hartsburgh I would occasionally come upon couples holding hands or occasionally rather more, though it distressed me that they always broke guiltily apart as soon as they saw me or any adult. One of my subjects, who was waiting for his interview, was dancing a little jig by himself in the corridor when I got to him. This was all rather reassuring.

It was also contrary to policy. There is a regulation against couples holding hands and they are punished if caught by the kind of teacher who hates sexuality in the young. The air and space also, subtly, turn out to be illusions if you try to use them. Hartsburgh High is built around a large, landscaped courtyard with little walks and benches. I made the mistake of trying to conduct an interview on one of these benches. When it was over we could not get back into the building except by disturbing a class, for the doors onto this inviting oasis can only be opened from inside, and nobody ever goes there. Since the courtyard is completely enclosed by the high-school building, this arrangement affords no additional protection from intruders; it merely shuts off a possible place for relaxation. The beautiful glass windows do not open enough to permit a body to squirm through and, consequently, do not open enough to ventilate the rooms, in which there are no individual controls for the fiercely effective radiators. Room temperature at Hartsburgh is a matter of high policy.

Teachers do not hide in the washrooms at Hartsburgh; but the principal recently issued a letter warning that any student caught in the vicinity of the school with "tobacco products" would be subject to suspension; students were directed to have their parents sign the letter as written acknowledgment that they were aware of the regulation and return it to school. Staff, of course, are permitted to smoke. At Hartsburgh a former teacher, promoted to assistant principal, serves as a full-time disciplinarian, but students are not dragged to his office by infuriated teachers, as sometimes happens at Milgrim. Instead, during the first period, two students from the school Citizenship Corps go quietly from classroom to classroom with a list, handing out summonses.

Along with having a less rancorous and choleric atmosphere than Milgrim, Hartsburgh seems to have more teachers who like teaching and like kids. But the fundamental pattern is still one of control, distrust, and punishment. The observable differences—and they are striking—are the result almost entirely, I believe, of *structural* and demographic factors and occur despite very similar administrative purposes. Neither principal respects adolescents at all or his staff very much. Both are preoccupied with good public relations as they understand them. Both are inflexible, highly authoritarian men. But their situations are different.

At Milgrim there is a strong district superintendent; imaginative if not particularly humane, he is oriented toward the national educational scene. He likes to have projects, particularly in research and guidance. Guidance officers report through their chairman directly to him, not to the building principal; the guidance staff is competent, tough, and completely professional. When wrangles occur over the welfare of a student they are likely to be open, with the principal and the guidance director as antagonists; both avoid such encounters if possible, and neither can count on the support of the district office; but when an outside force—like an outraged parent— precipitates a conflict, it is fought out. At Hartsburgh, the district superintendent is primarily interested in running a tight ship with no problems. To this end, he backs the authority of the principal whenever this might be challenged. The guidance office is vestigial and concerned primarily with college placement and public relations in the sense of inducing students to behave in socially acceptable ways with a minimum of fuss.

In these quite different contexts, demographic differences in the student bodies have crucial consequences. At Milgrim, the working-class students are not dominant—they have not got quite enough self-confidence or nearly enough social savvy to be—but they are close enough to it to be a real threat to the nice, college-bound youngsters who set the tone in their elementary and junior high school and who expect to go on dominating the high school. These view the rapid influx of lower-status students as a rising wave that can engulf them, while the newcomers, many of whom are recent migrants or high-school transfers from the city, can remember schools in which they felt more at home.

The result is both to split and to polarize student feeling about the school, its administration, and other students. Nobody likes Milgrim High. But the middle-class students feel that what has ruined it is the lower-class students, and that the punitive constraint with which the school is run is necessary to keep them in line. In some cases these students approach paranoia: one girl—commenting on a mythical high school described in one of our semi-projective research instruments—said, "Well, it says here that the majority of the students are Negro—about a third" (the actual statement is "about a fifth").

The working-class students are hard-pressed; but being hard-pressed they are often fairly realistic about their position. If the Citizenship Corps that functions so smoothly and smugly at Hartsburgh were to be installed at Milgrim, those who actually turned people in and got them in trouble would pretty certainly receive some after-school instruction in the way social classes differ in values and in the propensity for non-verbal self-expression. At Milgrim, the working-class kids know where they stand and stand there. They are exceptionally easy to interview because the interviewer need not be compulsively non-directive. Once they sense that they are respected, they respond enthusiastically and with great courtesy. But they do not alter their position to give the interviewer what they think he wants, or become notably anxious at disagreeing with him. They are very concrete in handling experience and are not given to generalization. Most of them seem to have liked their elementary school, and they share the general American respect for education down to the last cliché—but then one will add, as an afterthought, not bothering even to be contemptuous, "Of course, you can't respect *this* school." They deal with their situation there in correspondingly concrete terms. Both schools had student courts last year, for example, and Hartsburgh still does, though few students not in the Citizenship Corps pay much attention to it. Student traffic corpsmen give out tickets for corridor offenses, and these culprits are brought before an elected student judge with an administrative official of the school present as adviser. But Milgrim had a student court last year that quickly became notorious. The "hoody element" got control of it, and since most of the defendants were their buddies, they were either acquitted or discharged on pleas of insanity. The court was disbanded.

The struggle at Milgrim is therefore pretty open, though none of the protagonists see it as a struggle for freedom or could define its issues in terms of principles. The upper-status students merely assent to the way the school is run, much as middle-class white Southerners assent to what the sheriff's office does, while the lower-status students move, or get pushed, from one embroilment to the next without ever quite realizing that what is happening to them is part of a general social pattern. At Hartsburgh the few lower-status students can easily be ignored rather than feared by their middle-class compeers who set the tone. They are not sufficiently numerous or aggressive to threaten the middle-class youngsters or their folkways; but, for the same reason, they do not force the middle-class youngsters to make common cause with the administration. The administration, like forces of law and order generally in the United States, is accepted without deference as a part of the way things are and work. Americans rarely expect authority to be either intelligent or forthright; it looks out for its own interests as best it can. Reformers and troublemakers only make it nervous and therefore worse; the best thing is to take advantage of it when it can help you and at other times to go on living your own life and let it try to stop you.

This is what the Hartsburgh students usually do, and, on the whole, the results are pleasant. The youngsters, being to some degree ivy, do not constantly remind the teachers, as the Milgrim students do, that their jobs have no connection with academic scholarship. Many of the teachers, for their part, act and sound like college instructors, do as competent a job, and enjoy some of the same satisfactions. The whole operation moves smoothly. Both Milgrim and Hartsburgh are valid examples—though of very different aspects—of American democracy in action. And in neither could a student learn as much about civil liberty as a Missouri mule knows at birth.

What is learned in high school, or for that matter anywhere at all, depends far less on what is taught than on what one actually experiences in the place. The quality of instruction in high school varies from sheer rot to imaginative and highly skilled teaching. But classroom content is often handled at a creditable level and is not in itself the source of the major difficulty. Both at Milgrim and Hartsburgh, for example, the students felt that they were receiving competent instruction and that this was an undertaking the school tried seriously to handle. I doubt, however, that this makes up for much of the damage to which high-school students are systematically subjected. What is formally taught is just not that important, compared to the constraint and petty humiliation to which the youngsters with a few exceptions must submit in order to survive.

The fact that some of the instruction is excellent and a lot of it pretty good *is* important for another reason; it makes the whole process of compulsory schooling less insulting than it otherwise would be by lending it a superficial validity. Society tells the adolescent that he is sent to school in order to learn what he is taught in the classroom. No anthropologist and very few high school students would accept this as more than a rationalization; but rationalizations, to be at all effective, must be fairly plausible. Just as the draft would be intolerable if the cold war were wholly a piece of power politics or merely an effort to sustain the economy, so compulsory school attendance would be intolerable if what went on in the classrooms were totally inadequate to students' needs and irrelevant to their real intellectual concerns. Much of it is, but enough is not, to provide middle-class students, at least, with an answer when their heart cries out "For Christ's sake, what am I doing here?"

But far more of what is deeply and thoroughly learned in the school is designed to keep the heart from raising awkward, heartfelt issues—if design governs in a thing so subtle. It is learned so thoroughly by attendance at schools like Milgrim or even Hartsburgh that most Americans by the time they are adult cannot really imagine that life could be organized in any other way.

First of all, they learn to assume that the state has the right to compel adolescents to spend six or seven hours a day, five days a week, thirty-six or so weeks a year, in a specific place, in charge of a particular group of persons in whose selection they have no voice, performing tasks about which they have no choice, without remuneration and subject to specialized regulations and sanctions that are applicable to no one else in the community nor to them except in this place. Whether this law is a service or a burden to the young—and, indeed, it is both, in varying degrees—is another issue altogether. As I have noted elsewhere,[1] compulsory school attendance functions as a bill of attainder against a particular age group. The student's position is that of a conscript, who is protected by certain regulations but in no case permitted to use their breach as a cause for terminating his obligation. So the first thing the young learn in school is that there are certain sanctions and restrictions that apply only to them; that they do not participate fully in the freedoms guaranteed by the state, and that *therefore, these freedoms do not really partake of the character of inalienable rights.*

Of course not. The school, as schools continually stress, acts *in loco parentis;* and children may not leave home because their parents are unsatisfactory. What I have pointed out is no more than a special consequence of the fact that students are minors, and minors do not, indeed, share all the rights and privileges—and responsibilities—of citizenship. Very well. However one puts it, we are still discussing the same issue. The high school, then, is where you really learn what it means to be a minor.

For a high school is not a parent. Parents may love their children, hate them, or like most parents, do both in a complex mixture. But they must nevertheless permit a certain intimacy and respond to their children as persons. Homes are not run by regulations, though the parents may think they are, but by a process of continuous and almost entirely unconscious emotional homeostasis, in which each member affects and accommodates to the needs, feelings, fantasy life, and character structure of the others. This may be, and often is, a terribly destructive process; I intend no defense of the family as a social institution. But children grow up in homes or the remnants of homes; are in physical fact dependent on parents, and too intimately related to them to permit their area of freedom to be precisely defined. This is not because they have no rights or are entitled to less respect than adults, but because intimacy conditions freedom and growth in ways too subtle and continuous to be defined as overt acts.

Free societies depend on their members to learn early and thoroughly that public authority is not like that of the family; that it cannot be expected—or trusted—to respond with sensitivity and intimate perception to the needs of individuals but must rely basically, though as humanely as possible, on the impartial application of general formulae. This means that it must be kept functional, specialized, and limited to matters of public policy; the meshes of the law are too coarse to be worn close to the skin. Especially in an open society, where people of very different backgrounds and value systems must function together, it would seem obvious that each must understand that he may not push others further than their common undertaking demands, or impose upon them a manner of life that they feel to be alien.

After the family, the school is the first social institution an individual must deal with—the first place in which he learns to handle himself with strangers. The school establishes the pattern of his subsequent assumptions as to what relations between the individual and society are appropriate and which constitute invasions of privacy and constraints on his spirit—what the British, with exquisite precision, call "taking a liberty." But the American public school evolved as a melting pot, under the assumption that it had not merely the right but the duty to impose a common standard of genteel decency on a polyglot body of immigrants' children and thus insure their assimilation into the better life of the American dream. It accepted, also, the tacit assumption that genteel decency was as far as it could go. If America has generally been governed by the practical man's impatience with other individuals' rights, it has also accepted the practical man's determination to preserve his property by discouraging public extravagance. With its neglect of personal privacy and individual autonomy the school incorporates a considerable measure of Galbraith's "public squalor." The plant may be expensive—for this is capital goods; but little is provided graciously, liberally, simply as an amenity, either to teachers or students, though administrative offices have begun to assume an executive look.

The first thing the student learns, then, is that as a minor, he is subject to peculiar restraints; the second is that these restraints are general, not limited either by custom or by the schools' presumed commitment to the curriculum. High-school administrators are not professional educators in the sense that a physician, an attorney, or a tax accountant are professionals. They do not, that is, think of themselves as practitioners of a specialized instructional craft, who derive their authority from its requirements. They are specialists in keeping an essentially political enterprise from being strangled by conflicting community attitudes and pressures. They are problem-oriented, and the feelings and needs for growth of their captive and unenfranchised clientele are the least of their problems; for the status of the "teen-ager" in the community is so low that even if he rebels, the school is not blamed for the conditions against which he is rebelling. He is simply a truant or a juvenile delinquent; at worst the school has "failed to reach him." What high-school personnel become specialists in, ultimately, is the *control* of large groups of students even at catastrophic expense to their opportunity to learn. These controls are not exercised primarily to facilitate instruction, and particularly, they are in no way limited to matters bearing on instruction. At several schools in our sample boys had been ordered—sometimes on the complaint of teachers—to shave off beards. One of these boys had played football for the school; he was told that, although the school had no legal authority to require him to shave, he would be barred from the banquet honoring the team unless he complied. Dress regulations are another case in point.

Of course these are petty restrictions, enforced by petty penalties. American high schools are not concentration camps. But I am not complaining about their severity; what disturbs me is what they teach their students concerning the proper relationship of the individual to society, and in this respect the fact that the restrictions and penalties are unimportant in themselves makes matters worse. Gross invasions are more easily recognized for what they are; petty restrictions are only resisted by "troublemakers." What matters in the end is that the school does not take its own business of education seriously enough to mind it.

The effects on the students are manifold. The concepts of dignity and privacy, notably deficient in American adult folkways, are not permitted to develop here. The school's assumption of custodial control of students implies that power and authority are indistinguishable. If the school's authority is not limited to matters pertaining to education, it cannot be derived from its educational responsibilities. It is a naked, empirical fact, to be accepted or contraverted according to the possibilities of the moment. In such a world, power counts more than legitimacy; if you don't have power, it is naïve to think you have rights that must be respected . . . wise up. High school students experience regulation only as control, not as protection; they know, for example, that the principal will generally uphold the teacher in any conflict with a student, regardless of the merits of the case. Translated into the high-school idiom, *suaviter in modo, fortiter in re* becomes "If you get caught, it's just your ass."

Students do not often resent this; that is the tragedy. All weakness tends to corrupt, and impotence corrupts absolutely. Identifying, as the weak must, with the more powerful and frustrating of the forces that impinge upon them, they accept the school as the way life is and close their minds against the anxiety of perceiving alternatives. Many students like high school; others loathe and fear it. But even the latter do not object to it on principle; the school effectively obstructs their learning of the principles on which objection might be based; though these are among the principles that, we boast, distinguish us from totalitarian societies.

Yet, finally, the consequence of continuing through adolescence to submit to diffuse authority that is not derived from the task at hand—as a doctor's orders or the training regulations of an athletic coach, for example, usually are—is more serious than political incompetence or weakness of character. There is a general arrest of development. An essential part of growing up is learning that, though differences of power among men lead to brutal consequences, all men are peers; none is omnipotent, none derives his potency from magic, but only from his specific competence and function. The policeman represents the majesty of the state, but this does not mean that he can put you in jail; it means, precisely, that he cannot—at least not for long. Any person or agency responsible for handling throngs of young people—especially if he does not like them or is afraid of them—is tempted to claim diffuse authority and snare the youngster in the trailing remnants of childhood emotion which always remain to trip him. Schools succumb to this temptation, and control pupils by reinvoking the sensations of childhood punishment, which remain effective because they were originally selected, with great unconscious guile, to dramatize the child's weakness in the face of authority. "If you act like a bunch of spoiled brats, we'll treat you like a bunch of spoiled brats," is a favorite dictum of sergeants, and school personnel, when their charges begin to show an awkward capacity for independence.

Thus the high school is permitted to infantilize adolescence; in fact, it is encouraged to by the widespread hostility to "teen-agers" and the anxiety about their conduct found throughout our society. It does not allow much maturation to occur during the years when most maturation would naturally occur. Maturity, to be sure, is not conspicuously characteristic of American adult life, and would almost certainly be a threat to the economy. So perhaps in this, as in much else, the high school is simply the faithful servant of the community.

There are two important ways in which it can render such service. The first of these is through its impact on individuals: on their values, their conception of their personal worth, their patterns of anxiety, and on their mastery and ease in the world—which determine so much of what they think of as their fate. The second function of the school is Darwinian; its biases, though their impact is always on individual youngsters, operate systematically to mold entire social groups. These biases endorse and support the values and patterns of behavior of certain segments of the population, providing their members with the credentials and shibboleths needed for the next stages of their journey, while they instill in others a sense of inferiority and warn the rest of society against them as troublesome and untrustworthy. In this way the school contributes simultaneously to social mobility and to social stratification. It helps see to it that the kind of people who get ahead are the kind who will support the social system it represents, while those who might, through intent or merely by their being, subvert it, are left behind as a salutary moral lesson.

NOTES

1. See "An Ideology of School Withdrawal," June 1963.

TEACHING AND REBELLION AT UNION SPRINGS

Patricia Michaels

In 1967 I got a job teaching high school in a small industrial community in upstate New York. I didn't think the job would have political significance for me. I had been involved in civil rights demonstrations and anti-Vietnam marches and in general I identified with the movement. I had also taught in an urban ghetto school. No liberal or left activity existed in Union Springs, so I saw my job there as a retreat from politics and as an opportunity to teach without the pressures of the ghetto. But, in fact, teaching in Union Springs turned out to be a profoundly political experience. I learned there that decent human relations and meaningful work and education are impossible in this country even in those little red schoolhouses that seemed impervious to the crisis affecting the rest of society.

One of my first discoveries was that most of my students, who looked like Wonder Bread children, were non-college bound and hostile to school. I asked them why they hadn't quit when they were 16. Most replied, like a chorus, "Because to get a good job you have to go to school." They understood that the boredom and discipline were preparation for the future. One boy parroted an administrator on the subject of keeping his shirttails in: "When you work in a factory you're going to have to follow rules you don't like, so you'd better get used to them now."

After a few weeks of teaching, I began to discover that the school was designed to teach the majority of students to adjust to the lives already laid out for them after high school. It reinforced what they had learned at home and in grade school: to blunt feelings, distrust feelings you do have, accept boredom and meaningless discipline as the very nature of things. The faculty and the administration saw themselves as socializers in this process. This point was brought home to me at one faculty meeting following an as-

Reprinted from pp. 37–46 of *Myth and Reality*, edited Glenn Smith and Charles R. Kniker (Boston, Allyn and Bacon, Inc., 1972).

sembly. In an effort to bring culture to Union Springs, the school sponsored a cello concert, one of several longhair events. The students, tired of having their "horizons broadened," hooted and howled throughout the concert. The cellist was almost as indignant as the teachers and administration. The teachers expressed the sentiment that somehow they had failed to do their job; to train kids to accept things they did not like. Teacher after teacher admitted that while the assembly may have been boring, so were many things in life. *They* had made it; so could the kids. "Culture isn't supposed to be fun," said the principal, "but if you get something out of it, that's all that counts. For most of our kids this is the only time they'll ever get to hear a cellist and their lives will be richer for it."

The school was also designed to promote a definition of work that excluded emotional satisfaction. To the degree that the kids accepted this definition, they distrusted the very classes they enjoyed. Students would often tell me, "This isn't English, it's too much fun," or "School is where you learn—not have a good time." Enjoyment was drinking, speeding cars, minor lawbreaking activities that involved little creativity or effort. Having defined school (i.e., work) as joyless, joy, they thought, must be effortless.

They didn't connect their feelings of depression and anger with the socialization they were undergoing. While putting themselves down as failures, they would tell me everything that was wrong with the school. The petty vandalism, the screaming in the halls, the "cutting up" in class were their means of psychological survival. They didn't see this behavior as an attack on the school system. They were certain, too, that it they didn't shape up, they would pay a terrible price.

Their response to the first novel we read in class, Warren Miller's *The Cool World*, reflected their sense of futility. They admired Duke, the gang-leader hero, and thought he was "cool" because he said what he felt and did what he wanted. At the same time, he was "stupid" because his actions could only lead to poverty, violence, and death. They were infuriated at the ending of the novel when Duke "gets rehabilitated." In the endings that they wrote as an exercise, they had Duke killed or imprisoned. As one boy wrote, "This was the only honest ending because the price you pay for doing what you want is defeat in one form or another."

Resigned to the "realities" of life, they had difficulty accepting praise. They had been taught that they were unworthy and to distrust anyone who thought they were not. Praise challenged their self-image. John B., for example, was a senior who planned to pump gas after he got out of the army. He also wrote poetry. He alternated between being proud of his work and telling me that it was "bull-shit." He was threatened by his creativity. The school had "tracked" him into a "low achiever" class since grade one, and after 18 years he wasn't about to challenge that authoritative definition. The only other job he considered was as a state policeman. "At least you'd have some power," he told me.

The student body was split between the working-class "greasers" and the middle-class "scholars" or honors students. The students from working-class homes saw the honors kids as sellouts, phonies, and undeservedly privileged. The honors kids, for example, had a lounge. The rest of the student body congregated in the bathrooms.

The honors students were more ambivalent in their attitudes toward the greasers. Their own school experience was a grind, and they both resented and envied the relative casualness of the other students.

A few college-bound kids protested against my lenience in grades and the lack of discipline in my classes. They demanded that I lower the grades of the "less gifted" and enforce school rules. Some honors students admitted that behind their demands was a conception of learning as drudgery. Success, in turn, meant the failure of others. But this, they added, was the way things are. Society, they were convinced, owed them nothing. Reality was the status quo, and people should be judged by how well they coped with that reality.

The "scholars'" game in school consisted of conning the teachers. Establish your reputation and slide through. At times, they acknowledged the hypocrisy of the game, but rarely acted on it. While the "scholars" had nothing but contempt for the administration and most of the faculty, they couldn't get close to the other kids because of their unwillingness to give up the privileges that came with being honors students.

The student body was also divided along sexual lines. Men at Union Springs were more individually rebellious; they expressed their hatred of the school in ways that were considered "manly": haphazard disobedience, drinking before coming to school, vandalism. The women, however, were passive about school on a daily basis, since their major concern was the prestige that came from having a boyfriend and their status among the men.

One day I assigned my senior class an article about a girl who had been thrown out of college for living with her boyfriend. The boys in the class acknowledged that while they wouldn't marry a girl who did "that," they didn't think it was the school's right to punish her. The girls said nothing. In their compositions they expressed anger at the injustice of punishing the girl and not the boy. One girl wrote: "It's always the girl who suffers in this situation; nothing ever happens to the boy."

The following day I spoke with the girls (the boys were out of the room) and asked why they hadn't said in class what they had written on their papers. They said that they were afraid. One girl told me that the only time she would talk freely in a class was if no boys whom she liked romantically were present.

On another occasion a boy criticized my assigning a novel that contained obscene language, because, he said, it embarrassed him to read those words in front of girls. At the end of the class, a few girls told me that while people should be free to read and write what they wanted, they were glad at least one boy respected them enough to watch his language.

In spite of these divisions among the students, the oppressiveness of the school sometimes brought them together in action. Smoking in the bathrooms was the most controversial issue in the school. Breaking the smoking rules enraged the teachers. Several of them spent their free time catching the smokers, bringing them into the office, and getting them suspended for three days. The administration, in an act of desperation (20 cigarette butts had been found on the floor in one day), removed the entrance doors to the bathrooms. After unsuccessfully petitioning the principal, 25 students lined up in front of the men's room and refused to proceed to their first-period class. The principal threatened to call the police if they wouldn't obey his order to move.

Inside the faculty room, some teachers said they wanted to bust heads and hoped that the administration would allow it. Others joked about how our students were trying to imitate the college kids.

In an assembly later that afternoon, the principal announced that he was replacing the bathroom doors, but only because of the responsible behavior of the majority of students. "All over the country," he said, "bearded rebels are tearing up the schools and causing trouble, and now we have their younger versions at Union Springs. We know," he added, "that while the troublemakers demonstrate, the cream of the crop is dying in Vietnam. These are the true heroes. The boys who stood in front of the men's room this morning are the riffraff."

The students had not thought of the demonstrators as riffraff. They were among the most popular kids in school. But neither had they seen them as part of a national movement. By making that association, the principal had helped to break down some of the students' antagonisms toward the left. Later, when SDS people tried to link up with students at Union Springs, some of the groundwork had already been laid by the principal.

By my second year at Union Springs, I was intensely sensitive to the repressiveness of the school system and my own role in it. My way of dealing with that was to make my classes more relevant to students' lives. I told them to write about what they felt in the language with which they were most comfortable. The first papers I received were filled with obscenity, and I criticized them on stylistic rather than moral grounds. In the second papers, the students' efforts to shock me changed into honest attempts at good writing. I told one class of seniors who were working on short stories that I would mimeograph and distribute some of their work. The most popular story was a satire concerning soldiers in Vietnam; it was sprinkled with obscenity. I said that I would reprint the story as promised, but I wanted the class to be aware of the risk. They all agreed that the author had written what he felt and that there was nothing objectionable about the piece.

A few weeks later the principal told me that I would have to "cease and desist" from accepting students' work that made use of "poor" language. The principal also criticized me for playing rock music in my classes. "You're allowing too much freedom in your classes." He told me that while these methods were all right for "Negro kids," since "that's the kind of life they're used to," or for responsible college-bound students, they were not all right for youngsters whose future success in the army or on their jobs depended on their following rules.

As a result of my classes, he said, students were becoming defiant and teachers and parents were complaining. He said that I was doing a disservice to students in allowing them a freedom that they were not going to have later on.

Up to that point I had not thought of my work as political. In fact, I had berated myself because I hadn't spent more time talking about the war, blacks, tracking, and so on. Movement friends I had spoken with warned me that far from "radicalizing" my students, I was providing them with a "groovy classroom," making school more palatable and adjustment to a corrupt system easier for them. After speaking with the principal, however, I concluded that my classroom methods were political. In order for the students to fit into the society, they had to believe certain things about themselves, about their teachers, and about their work. By permitting my students to use their own language in the classroom and to wander the halls without passes, by helping them to discover that schoolwork could be creative, I was challenging the values of the school and, therefore, those of society. That was the beginning for the students of understanding the relation between their lives and the movement.

I told the principal that I could not comply with his order but would discuss the issue with my class. He warned me that I was close to losing my job and he couldn't figure out why I wanted to be a martyr for the students.

The next day I told my class what had happened. They agreed that we should continue to do what we were doing, although a few students argued that I was teaching revolution and disrespect for authority. One boy told me that his father said that if I were teaching in Russia I would have been jailed long ago. Other students defended our classroom activities, saying that this was the first time they'd been able to express themselves in school. "Everybody in town is calling Mrs. Michaels a Communist," one girl said. "Everything they don't like around here they call Communist. We've done nothing wrong and neither has she. Those who don't like it here should transfer to another class, and not ruin it for the rest of us."

Although the students expressed concern about my losing my job, they knew that the issue was them, as well as myself. It wasn't *my* class that was on the line, but *our* class. Crucial to their understanding of the issue as it deepened was my continuing to inform them of developments. By breaking down the traditional teacher-student relationship, I could speak with them not only about their own oppression but mine as well. In that process, the students had begun to listen to me when I raised questions about the war, the draft, and the tracking system, although they weren't ready yet to ask those questions for themselves.

In January of my second year, a local SDS chapter sponsored a festival and several workshops for high school students. I announced the events to my students and urged them to go. In spite of warnings from administrators, teachers, and parents, a number of students attended. Several teachers showed up to "learn about SDS," but the students knew that they were spies.

The SDS organizer asked the students if they wanted the teachers to stay. "They are part of the reason we're here," one boy said. "We can never talk honestly in their presence and we can't now. They have to leave." When the teachers refused to go, the students walked out of the room and set up another workshop—a liberating experience, defiance without punishment, a taste of collective power.

The festival changed the students' attitude toward the left. Their disdain for the "peace freaks" was based on a stereotype of the cowardly college student. Their brothers were fighting in Vietnam and if the leftists took their beliefs seriously, they "would be fighting too." One boy told me that the only time he took college demonstrators seriously was when he saw them on TV at the Chicago convention. The students at Union Springs disliked the college protestors because they saw them as a privileged group and they couldn't figure out why they were rebelling.

Students at Union Springs felt ambivalent about leftist culture. Although they talked about "filthy hippies," they listened to the Doors and the Rolling Stones. Rock music was vital to their lives. To hate hippies was difficult for them because Mick Jagger was one, too. The longhaired radicals who spoke to them at the SDS festival acted tough, brave, and "tuned" into the kids' experiences. That the principal and teachers defined these people as outlaws only made them more attractive.

The festival and the presence of high school students at an SDS function frightened the community. The newspapers were filled with letters for the next few weeks condemning the SDS and the students who attended. Kids brought the newspapers to school and we discussed reasons for the community's and administration's terror at SDS presence. Gradually the kids began to connect the local issue with the anti-Communist, pro-war rhetoric they had heard all their lives. They had begun to identify their own rebellion with the rebellion of the people they had earlier called "rioters," "peace creeps," and "commies."

Earlier that year I had talked with some students about Cuba. They had insisted that Castro was a dictator who filled the prisons with anyone who disagreed with him, and that the United States ought to invade the island.

When I questioned the reliability of media reporting, they didn't respond. Only after they read the distortions about themselves in the local newspaper stories did my argument have some meaning for them. When they were not involved in their own struggle, they accepted what the TV and the newspapers told them. They had even resented my raising questions about Cuba, Vietnam, or blacks. As one student told me after I talked with him about the war, "Our government couldn't be doing all of those terrible things." What made those "terrible things" believable to him was his new-found consciousness of what the school had been doing to him every day and how the principal and teachers responded when he began to act.

In the months that followed the SDS conference, I talked with students in class, during free period, and in my home, where many of them became frequent visitors, about everything from Vietnam to dating problems. In April of that year, some of them joined an SDS demonstration against Westmoreland.

As the opportunity to rebel began to develop at Union Springs High, many of the women held back. They didn't see the relevance of the rebellion to their own lives, and some even discouraged the boys from participating since it disrupted the normal social life of the school. The girls who did participate, however, were the most militant and committed of the rebels. Some were girls whose dating unpopularity had made high school hell for them and who identified with me because in my classroom they could assert themselves in ways that won them respect. Others were girls who were more assured of their popularity and, because they were not hung up in the individualism of the boys, could act together more easily.

The male students, on the other hand, were beginning to challenge the traditional values of individualism and competitiveness that had made it difficult for them to rebel together. Previously much of their prestige had depended upon *individual* defiance. As one boy told me earlier that year: "I talk back to teachers, but when everybody starts doing it, it doesn't mean anything anymore."

About two weeks after the Westmoreland demonstration, seven students decided that they were going to boycott an honors assembly and asked if they could use my room. The assembly was an annual ritual to humiliate the majority of students and to honor the handful who had "achieved." The students felt that their refusal to participate was justified, but were uncomfortable about the action. One boy said, "Listen, I don't like this: 'Cutting up' in class is fun, but this is different, It's too serious. I'm not scared or anything, but everybody's acting like it's such a big deal." The boy may have expected punishment for his action, but felt threatened because he had involved himself with six others in a collective decision to defy the school system. If they escaped without punishment, he would be only one among seven heroes. If they got into trouble, his act couldn't be dismissed as a prank. Another boy replied, "This is different from setting a cherry bomb off in the halls and running away. We're identifying ourselves and we're trying to figure out why we're doing it. If you don't see that, you'd better leave."

In early May, I was fired. Many students prepared to sit in. They made signs, held meetings, and argued with their parents, who urged them not to get involved. The administration responded with threats of police, suspensions, and warnings to seniors who "might not graduate" if they participated. Administrators phoned the parents of the student leaders and urged them to keep their kids at home. Police watched the entrance of my house. On the morning of the sit-in, teachers in the halls urged the students to hurry to class. Many students did stay home. Others were confused and stood around the halls. About 50 sat in. Six students were suspended for five days, and one boy was beaten by the vice-principal when he refused to move on to class.

The next morning the principal met with the students and tried to calm them. There wasn't anything they or he could do to get me back in school, he said. But he would listen to their grievances about the school. After a few days of restlessness and more meetings with students, Union Springs High had ostensibly returned to normal.

But many students had changed during my two years there. When I first met them, they had been resigned to the limited world that the school had defined for them. They didn't believe that they were capable of creating anything larger. Experiences in my classes and their struggle opened the possibility of new definitions of work, of teachers, and of themselves. When they had to defend those discoveries to parents, contemporaries, and school personnel, the students learned how to work together.

I did not come to Union Springs to be a political organizer. I came to teach. But I refused to be the teacher that both the administration and the students expected me to be. I had rejected the role of cop and socializer not out of any revolutionary commitment, but out of my need to relate to my students. This same need made me reject the labels "lower track," "non-college bound," and "slow learner" that were placed on my students. My refusal to play the traditional teacher role was linked to my refusal to accept them as inferior because they had been treated as such. By breaking down their stereotypes of themselves and of me, I also helped them break down their self-confining images of the world around them.

One letter I received from a female student indicated the achievement as well as the limitations of my work at Union Springs: "Up until you came to us, I'm sure no student knew where he or she stood in the school. They didn't know the powers they had. Now we know them and are trying to use them as best we can. It's going to take time to get organized, but the way things are going now, I'm sure the time will come. I remember the time I was accused of smoking. The principal told me that I had no alternative but to admit I was smoking. I told him that I wasn't and that he could get the

Supreme Court on it if he wanted to, but he couldn't prove it. That was the first time I really used the power I had and I won. It didn't seem like much power when it was all over, but I can still remember looking at his face and noticing that his smirk was gone and that he really looked afraid of me. I don't know if you realize it or not, but that small power has affected almost every kid in school and I think that's why you were fired."

Energy had been released at Union Springs, but where will students go with this energy, what will they do with it in that same school this year, in the army, in the factories, and in their marriages? The students were ready to join a movement. Right now there is no movement for them to join. Those who are still in school write me that Union Springs is quiet again. Those who are out say pretty much the same thing. The movement that speaks to the needs they experienced and acted on at Union Springs is yet to be created.

EDUCATION THROUGH FREEDOM: PHILOSOPHICAL PERSPECTIVE

Elizabeth Steiner

One sense of freedom is negative; it is freedom-from or the absence of constraint or restraint preventing choice. According to Paulo Freire, education when it is based on a banking conception is not through freedom-from. Education based on a banking conception "mirror[s] the oppressive society as a whole." The students are prevented from choosing; "the teacher chooses and enforces his choice, and the students comply." The students are manipulated by "indoctrinating them to adapt to the world of oppression." If education is to be through freedom-from, Freire avers that it must be based upon a problem-posing conception of education. "The students—no longer docile listeners—are now critical co-investigators in dialogue with the teacher."

In the notion of critical investigator is a positive sense of freedom, freedom-for or the presence of choosing for oneself. To choose one must know, and so freedom-for depends upon discipline which, in Whitehead's words, is "the ordered acquirement of knowledge."

Alfred North Whitehead (1862–1947) held that freedom and discipline were the two essential elements of education. The educational process, as a part of reality, consists of actual occasions. Any actual occasion begins as a burst of creative novelty, continues by making itself of the past from which it arises, and finally completes itself. The unfolding of reality is thus cyclical. Each cycle consists of three phases: ingathering, ordering, and realizing. This rhythm reveals itself in education as stages. The first phase of the educative development of the individual is the *romantic* one, a stage of interest. There is no constraining or restraining of the student to get things straight, but rather "plenty of independent browsing and first-hand experiences, involving adventures of thought and action." Hence, education begins in freedom-from. With the preschool child it is the romantic encounter with objects; later it is with literature, art, and history; and still later, in early adolescence, it is with science. The second stage is that of *precision*. Discipline enters, as the acquisition of knowledge is emphasized; one gets "to know the fundamental details and the main exact generalizations, and of acquiring an easy mastery of technique." "There is no getting away from the fact that things have been found out, and that to be effective in the modern world you must have a store of definite acquirement of the best practice." "The untutored art of genius is . . . a vain thing, fondly invented." The third stage is that of *generalization*. "He relapses into the discursive adventures of the romantic stage, with the advantage, that his mind is now a disciplined regiment instead of a rabble." Wise choices for living now can be made. To summarize, education begins in freedom-from and through discipline ends in freedom-for.

THE PROBLEM-POSING CONCEPT OF EDUCATION AS AN INSTRUMENT FOR LIBERATION

Paulo Freire

A careful analysis of the teacher-student relationship at any level, inside or outside the school, reveals its fundamentally *narrative* character. This relationship involves a narrating Subject (the teacher) and patient, listening objects (the students). The contents, whether values or empirical dimensions of reality, tend in the process of being narrated to become lifeless and petrified. Education is suffering from narration sickness.

The teacher talks about reality as if it were motionless, static, compartmentalized, and predictable. Or else he expounds on a topic completely alien to the existential experience of the students. His task is to "fill" the students with the contents of his narration-contents which are detached from reality, disconnected from the totality that engendered them and could give them significance. Words are emptied of their concreteness and become a hollow, alienated, and alienating verbosity.

The outstanding characteristic of this narrative education, then, is the sonority of words, not their transforming power. "Four times four is sixteen; the capital of Pará is Belém." The student records, memorizes, and repeats these phrases without perceiving what four times four really means, or realizing the true significance of "capital" in the affirmation "the capital of Pará is Belém," that is, what Belém means for Pará and what Pará means for Brazil.

Narration (with the teacher as narrator) leads the students to memorize mechanically the narrated content. Worse yet, it turns them into "containers," into "receptacles" to be "filled" by the teacher. The more completely he fills the receptacles, the better a teacher he is. The more meekly the receptacles permit themselves to be filled, the better students they are.

Education thus becomes an act of deposition, in which the students are the depositories and the teacher is the depositor. Instead of communicating, the teacher issues communiqués and makes deposits which the students patiently receive, memorize, and repeat. This is the "banking" concept of education, in which the scope of action allowed to the students extends only as far as receiving, filing, and storing the deposits. They do, it is true, have the opportunity to become collectors or cataloguers of the things they store. But in the last analysis, it is men themselves who are filed away through the lack of creativity, transformation, and knowledge in this (at best) misguided system. For apart from inquiry, apart from the praxis, men cannot be truly human. Knowledge emerges only through invention and re-invention, through the restless, impatient, continuing, hopeful inquiry men pursue in the world, with the world, and with each other.

In the banking concept of education, knowledge is a gift bestowed by those who consider themselves knowledgeable upon those whom they consider to know nothing. Projecting an absolute ignorance onto others, a characteristic of the ideology of oppression, negates education and knowledge as processes of inquiry. The teacher presents himself to his students as their necessary opposite; by considering their ignorance absolute, he justifies his own existence. The students, alienated like the slave in the Hegelian dialectic, accept their ignorance as justifying the teacher's existence—but, unlike the slave, they never discover that they educate the teacher.

The *raison d'être* of libertarian education, on the other hand, lies in its drive towards reconciliation. Education must begin with the solution of the teacher-student contradiction, by reconciling the poles of the contradiction so that both are simultaneously teachers *and* students.

This solution is not (nor can it be) found in the banking concept. On the contrary, banking education maintains and even stimulates the contradiction through the following attitudes and practices, which mirror oppressive society as a whole:

a. the teacher teaches and the students are taught;
b. the teacher knows everything and the students know nothing;
c. the teacher thinks and the students are thought about;
d. the teacher talks and the students listen—meekly;
e. the teacher disciplines and the students are disciplined;
f. the teacher chooses and enforces his choice, and the students comply;
g. the teacher acts and the students have the illusion of acting through the action of the teacher;
h. the teacher chooses the program content, and the students (who were not consulted) adapt to it;
i. the teacher confuses the authority of knowledge with his own professional authority, which he sets in opposition to the freedom of the students;

j. the teacher is the Subject of the learning process, while the pupils are mere objects.

It is not surprising that the banking concept of education regards men as adaptable, manageable beings. The more students work at storing the deposits entrusted to them, the less they develop the critical consciousness which would result from their intervention in the world as transformers of that world. The more completely they accept the passive role imposed on them, the more they tend simply to adapt to the world as it is and to the fragmented view of reality deposited in them.

The capability of banking education to minimize or annul the students' creative power and to stimulate their credulity serves the interests of the oppressors, who care neither to have the world revealed nor to see it transformed. The oppressors use their "humanitarianism" to preserve a profitable situation. Thus they react almost instinctively against any experiment in education which stimulates the critical faculties and is not content with a partial view of reality but always seeks out the ties which link one point to another and one problem to another.

Indeed, the interests of the oppressors lie in "changing the consciousness of the oppressed, not the situation which oppresses them";[1] for the more the oppressed can be led to adapt to that situation, the more easily they can be dominated. To achieve this end, the oppressors use the banking concept of education in conjunction with a paternalistic social action apparatus, within which the oppressed receive the euphemistic title of "welfare recipients." They are treated as individual cases, as marginal men who deviate from the general configuration of a "good, organized, and just" society. The oppressed are regarded as the pathology of the healthy society, which must therefore adjust these "incompetent and lazy" folk to its own patterns by changing their mentality. These marginals need to be "integrated," "incorporated" into the healthy society that they have "forsaken."

The truth is, however, that the oppressed are not "marginals," are not men living "outside" society. They have always been "inside"—inside the structure which made them "beings for others." The solution is not to "integrate" them into the structure of oppression, but to transform that structure so that they can become "beings for themselves." Such transformation, of course, would undermine the oppressors' purposes; hence their utilization of the banking concept of education to avoid the threat of student *conscientização*.

The banking approach to adult education, for example, will never propose to students that they critically consider reality. It will deal instead with such vital questions as whether Roger gave green grass to the goat, and insist upon the importance of learning that, on the contrary, *R*oger gave green grass to the *r*abbit. The "humanism" of the banking approach masks the effort to turn men into automatons—the very negation of their ontological vocation to be more fully human.

Those who use the banking approach, knowingly or unknowingly (for there are innumerable well-intentioned bank-clerk teachers who do not realize that they are serving only to dehumanize), fail to perceive that the deposits themselves contain contradictions about reality. But, sooner or later, these contradictions may lead formerly passive students to turn against their domestication and the attempt to domesticate reality. They may discover through existential experience that their present way of life is irreconcilable with their vocation to become fully human. They may perceive through their relations with reality that reality is really a *process*, undergoing constant transformation. If men are searchers and their ontological vocation is humanization, sooner or later they may perceive the contradiction in which banking education seeks to maintain them, and then engage themselves in the struggle for their liberation.

But the humanist, revolutionary educator cannot wait for this possibility to materialize. From the outset, his efforts must coincide with those of the students to engage in critical thinking and the quest for mutual humanization. His efforts must be imbued with a profound trust in men and their creative power. To achieve this, he must be a partner of the students in his relations with them.

The banking concept does not admit to such partnership—and necessarily so. To resolve the teacher-student contradiction, to exchange the role of depositor, prescriber, domesticator, for the role of student among students would be to undermine the power of oppression and serve the cause of liberation.

Implicit in the banking concept is the assumption of a dichotomy between man and the world: man is merely *in* the world, not *with* the world or with others; man is spectator, not re-creator. In this view, man is not a conscious being (*corpo consciente*); he is rather the possessor of *a* consciousness: an empty "mind" passively open to the reception of deposits of reality from the world outside. For example, my desk, my books, my coffee cup, all the objects before me—as bits of the world which surrounds me— would be "inside" me, exactly as I am inside my study right now. This view makes no distinction between being accessible to consciousness and entering consciousness. The distinction, however, is essential: the objects which surround me are simply accessible to my consciousness, not located within it. I am aware of them, but they are not inside me.

It follows logically from the banking notion of consciousness that the educator's role is to regulate the way the world "enters into" the students. His task is to organize a process which already occurs spontaneously, to "fill" the students by making deposits of information which he considers to constitute true knowledge.[2] And since men "receive" the world as passive entities, education should make them more passive still, and adapt them to the world. The educated man is the adapted man, because he is better "fit" for the world. Translated into practice, this concept is well suited to the purposes of the oppressors, whose tranquility rests on how well men fit the world the oppressors have created, and how little they question it.

The more completely the majority adapt to the purposes which the dominant minority prescribe for them (thereby depriving them of the right to their own purposes), the more easily the minority can continue to prescribe. The theory and practice of banking education serve this end quite efficiently. Verbalistic lessons, reading requirements,[3] the methods for evaluating "knowledge," the distance between the teacher and the taught, the criteria for promotion: everything in this ready-to-wear approach serves to obviate thinking.

The bank-clerk educator does not realize that there is no true security in his hypertrophied role, that one must seek to live *with* others in solidarity. One cannot impose oneself, nor even merely co-exist with one's students. Solidarity requires true communication, and the concept by which such an educator is guided fears and proscribes communication.

Yet only through communication can human life hold meaning. The teacher's thinking is authenticated only by the authenticity of the students' thinking. The teacher cannot think for his students, nor can he impose his thought on them. Authentic thinking, thinking that is concerned about *reality*, does not take place in ivory tower isolation, but only in communication. If it is true that thought has meaning only when generated by action upon the world, the subordination of students to teachers becomes impossible.

Because banking education begins with a false understanding of men as objects, it cannot promote the development of what Fromm calls "biophily," but instead produces its opposite: "necrophily."

> While life is characterized by growth in a structured, functional manner, the necrophilous person loves all that does not grow, all that is mechanical. The necrophilous person is driven by the desire to transform the organic into the inorganic, to approach life mechanically, as if all living persons were things.
> . . . Memory, rather than experience; having, rather than being, is what counts. The necrophilous person can relate to an object—a flower or a person—only if he possesses it; hence a threat to his possession is a threat to himself; if he loses possession he loses contact with the world. . . . He loves control, and in the act of controlling he kills life.[4]

Oppression—overwhelming control—is necrophilic; it is nourished by love of death, not life. The banking concept of education, which serves the interests of oppression, is also necrophilic. Based on a mechanistic, static, naturalistic, spatialized view of consciousness, it transforms students into receiving objects. It attempts to control thinking and action, leads men to adjust to the world, and inhibits their creative power.

When their efforts to act responsibly are frustrated, when they find themselves unable to use their faculties, men suffer. "This suffering due to impotence is rooted in the very fact that the human equilibrium has been disturbed."[5] But the inability to act which causes men's anguish also causes them to reject their impotence, by attempting

> . . . to restore [their] capacity to act. But can [they], and how? One way is to submit to and identify with a person or group having power. By this symbolic participation in another person's life, [men have] the illusion of acting, when in reality [they] only submit to and become a part of those who act.[6]

Populist manifestations perhaps best exemplify this type of behavior by the oppressed, who, by identifying with charismatic leaders, come to feel that they themselves are active and effective. The rebellion they express as they emerge in the historical process is motivated by that desire to act effectively. The dominant elites consider the remedy to be more domination and repression, carried out in the name of freedom, order, and social peace (that is, the peace of the elites). Thus they can condemn—logically, from their point of view—"the violence of a strike by workers and [can] call upon the state in the same breath to use violence in putting down the strike."[7]

Education as the exercise of domination stimulates the credulity of students, with the ideological intent (often not perceived by educators) of indoctrinating them to adapt to the world of oppression. This accusation is not made in the naïve hope that the dominant elites will thereby simply abandon the practice. Its objective is to call the attention of true humanists to the fact that they cannot use banking educational methods in the pursuit of liberation, for they would only negate that very pursuit. Nor may a revolutionary society inherit these methods from an oppressor society. The revolutionary society which practices banking education is either misguided or mistrusting of men. In either event, it is threatened by the specter of reaction.

Unfortunately, those who espouse the cause of liberation are themselves surrounded and influenced by the climate which generates the banking concept, and often do not perceive its true significance or its dehumanizing power. Paradoxically, then, they utilize this same instrument of alienation in what they consider an effort to liberate. Indeed, some "revolutionaries" brand as "innocents," "dreamers," or even "reactionaries" those who would challenge this educational practice. But one does not liberate men by alienating them. Authentic liberation—the process of humanization—is not another deposit to be made in men. Liberation is a praxis: the action and reflection of men upon their world in order to transform it. Those truly committed to the cause of liberation can accept neither the mechanistic concept of consciousness as an empty vessel to be filled, nor the use of banking methods of domination (propaganda, slogans—deposits) in the name of liberation.

Those truly committed to liberation must reject the banking concept in its entirety, adopting instead a concept of men as conscious beings, and consciousness as consciousness intent upon the world. They must abandon the educational goal of deposit-making and replace it with the posing of the problems of men in their relations with the world. "Problem-posing" education, responding to the essence of consciousness—*intentionality*—rejects communiqués and embodies communication. It epitomizes the special characteristic of consciousness: being *conscious of*, not only as intent on objects but as turned in upon itself in a Jasperian "split"—consciousness as consciousness *of* consciousness.

Liberating education consists in acts of cognition, not transferrals of information. It is a learning situation in which the cognizable object (far from being the end of the cognitive act) intermediates the cognitive actors—teacher on the one hand and students on the other. Accordingly, the practice of problem-posing education entails at the outset that the teacher-student contradiction be resolved. Dialogical relations—indispensable to the capacity of cognitive actors to cooperate in perceiving the same cognizable object—are otherwise impossible.

Indeed, problem-posing education, which breaks with the vertical patterns characteristic of banking education, can fulfill its function as the practice of freedom only if it can overcome the above contradiction. Through dialogue, the teacher-of-the-students and the students-of-the-teacher cease to exist and a new term emerges: teacher-student with students-teachers. The teacher is no longer merely the-one-who-teaches, but one who is himself taught in dialogue with the students, who in turn while being taught also teach. They become jointly responsible for a process in which all grow. In this process, arguments based on "authority" are no longer valid; in order to function, authority must be *on the side of* freedom, not *against* it. Here, no one teaches another, nor is anyone self-taught. Men teach each other, mediated by the world, by the cognizable objects which in banking education are "owned" by the teacher.

The banking concept (with its tendency to dichotomize everything) distinguishes two stages in the action of the educator. During the first, he cognizes a cognizable object while he prepares his lessons in his study or his laboratory; during the second, he expounds to his students about that object. The students are not called upon to know, but to memorize the contents narrated by the teacher. Nor do the students practice any act of cognition, since the object towards which that act should be directed is the property of the teacher rather than a medium evoking the critical reflection of both teacher and students. Hence in the name of the "preservation of culture and knowledge" we have a system which achieves neither true knowledge nor true culture.

The problem-posing method does not dichotomize the activity of the teacher-student: he is not "cognitive" at one point and "narrative" at another. He is always "cognitive," whether preparing a project or engaging in dialogue with the students. He does not regard cognizable objects as his private property, but as the object of reflection by himself and the students. In this way, the problem-posing educator constantly re-forms his reflections in the reflection of the students. The students—no longer docile listeners—are now critical co-investigators in dialogue with the teacher. The teacher presents the material to the students for their consideration, and re-considers his earlier considerations as the students express their own. The role of the problem-posing educator is to create, together with the students, the conditions under which knowledge at the level of the *doxa* is superseded by true knowledge, at the level of the *logos*.

Whereas banking education anesthetizes and inhibits creative power, problem-posing education involves a constant unveiling of reality. The former attempts to maintain the *submersion* of consciousness; the latter strives for the *emergence* of consciousness and *critical intervention* in reality.

Students, as they are increasingly posed with problems relating to themselves in the world and with the world, will feel increasingly challenged and obliged to respond to that challenge. Because they apprehend the challenge as interrelated to other problems within a total context, not as a theoretical question, the resulting comprehension tends to be increasingly critical and thus constantly less alienated. Their response to the challenge evokes new challenges, followed by new understandings; and gradually the students come to regard themselves as committed.

Education as the practice of freedom—as opposed to education as the practice of domination—denies that man is abstract, isolated, independent, and unattached to the world; it also denies that the world exists as a reality apart from men. Authentic reflection considers neither abstract man nor the world without men, but men in their relations with the world. In these relations consciousness and world are simultaneous: consciousness neither precedes the world nor follows it.

> La conscience et le monde sont dormes d'un même coup: exterieur par essence à la conscience, le monde est, par essence relatif à elle.[8]

In one of our culture circles in Chile, the group was discussing (based on a codification[9]) the anthropological concept of culture. In the midst of the discussion, a peasant who by banking standards was completely ignorant said: "Now I see that without man there is no world." When the educator responded: "Let's say, for the sake of argument, that all the men on earth were to die, but that the earth itself remained, together with trees, birds, animals, rivers, seas, the stars . . . wouldn't all this be a world?" "Oh no," the peasant replied emphatically. "There would be no one to say: 'This is a world.' "

The peasant wished to express the idea that there would be lacking the consciousness of the world which necessarily implies the world of consciousness. *I* cannot exist without a *not-I*. In turn, the *not-I* depends on that existence. The world which brings consciousness into existence becomes the world *of* that consciousness. Hence, the previously cited affirmation of Sartre: *"La conscience et le monde sont dormés d'un même coup."*

As men, simultaneously reflecting on themselves and on the world, increase the scope of their perception, they begin to direct their observations towards previously inconspicuous phenomena:

> In perception properly so-called, as an explicit awareness [*Gewahren*], I am turned towards the object, to the paper, for instance. I apprehend it as being this here and now. The apprehension is a singling out, every object having a background in experience. Around and about the paper lie books, pencils, ink-well, and so forth, and these in a certain sense are also "perceived", perceptually there, in the "field of intuition"; but whilst I was turned towards the paper there was no turning in their direction, nor any apprehending of them, not even in a secondary sense. They appeared and yet were not singled out, were not posited on their own account. Every perception of a thing has such a zone of background intuitions or background awareness, if "intuiting" already includes the state of being turned towards, and this also is a "conscious experience," or more briefly a "consciousness of" all indeed that in point of fact lies in the co-perceived objective background.[10]

That which had existed objectively but had not been perceived in its deeper implications (if indeed it was perceived at all) begins to "stand out," assuming the character of a problem and therefore of challenge. Thus, men begin to single out elements from their "background awarenesses" and to reflect upon them. These elements are now objects of men's consideration, and, as such, objects of their action and cognition.

In problem-posing education, men develop their power to perceive critically *the way they exist* in the world *with which* and *in which* they find themselves; they come to see the world not as a static reality, but as a reality in process, in transformation. Although the dialectical relations of men with the world exist independently of how these relations are perceived (or whether or not they are perceived at all), it is also true that the form of action men adopt is to a large extent a function of how they perceive themselves in the world. Hence, the teacher-student and the students-teachers reflect simultaneously on themselves and the world without dichotomizing this reflection from action, and thus establish an authentic form of thought and action.

Once again, the two educational concepts and practices under analysis come into conflict. Banking education (for obvious reasons) attempts, by mythicizing reality, to conceal certain facts which explain the way men exist in the world; problem-posing education sets itself the task of demythologizing. Banking education resists dialogue; problem-posing education regards dialogue as indispensable to the act of cognition which unveils reality. Banking education treats students as objects of assistance; problem-posing education makes them critical thinkers. Banking education inhibits creativity and domesticates (although it cannot completely destroy) the *intentionality* of consciousness by isolating consciousness from the world, thereby denying men their ontological and historical vocation of becoming more fully human. Problem-posing education bases itself on creativity and stimulates true reflection and action upon reality, thereby responding to the vocation of men as beings who are authentic only when engaged in inquiry and creative transformation. In sum: banking theory and practice, as immobilizing and fixating forces, fail to acknowledge men as historical beings; problem-posing theory and practice take man's historicity as their starting point.

Problem-posing education affirms men as beings in the process of *becoming*—as unfinished, uncompleted beings in and with a likewise unfinished reality. Indeed, in contrast to other animals who are unfinished, but not historical, men know themselves to be unfinished; they are aware of their incompletion. In this incompletion and this awareness lie the very roots of education as an exclusively human manifestation. The unfinished character of men and the transformational character of reality necessitate that education be an ongoing activity.

Education is thus constantly remade in the praxis. In order to *be*, it must *become*. Its "duration" (in the Bergsonian meaning of the word) is found in the interplay of the opposites *permanence* and *change*. The banking method emphasizes permanence and becomes reactionary; problem-posing education—which accepts neither a "well-behaved" present nor a predetermined future—roots itself in the dynamic present and becomes revolutionary.

Problem-posing education is revolutionary futurity. Hence it is prophetic (and, as such, hopeful). Hence, it corresponds to the historical nature of man. Hence, it affirms men as beings who transcend themselves, who move forward and look ahead, for whom immobility represents a fatal threat, for whom looking at the past must only be a means of understanding more clearly what and who they are so that they can more wisely build the future. Hence, it identifies with the movement which engages men as beings aware of their incompletion—an historical movement which has its point of departure, its Subjects and its objective.

The point of departure of the movement lies in men themselves. But since men do not exist apart from the world, apart from reality, the movement must begin with the men-world relationship. Accordingly, the point of departure must always be with men in the "here and now," which constitutes the situation within which they are submerged, from which they emerge, and in which they intervene. Only by starting from this situation—which determines their perception of it—can they begin to move. To do this authentically they must perceive their state not as fated and unalterable, but merely as limiting—and therefore challenging.

Whereas the banking method directly or indirectly reinforces men's fatalistic perception of their situation, the problem-posing method presents this very situation to them as a problem. As the situation becomes the object of their cognition, the naïve or magical perception which produced their fatalism gives way to perception which is able to perceive itself even as it perceives reality, and can thus be critically objective about that reality.

A deepened consciousness of their situation leads men to apprehend that situation as an historical reality susceptible of transformation. Resignation gives way to the drive for transformation and inquiry, over which men feel themselves to be in control. If men, as historical beings necessarily engaged with other men in a movement of inquiry, did not control that movement, it would be (and is) a violation of men's humanity. Any situation in which some men prevent others from engaging in the process of inquiry is one of violence. The means used are not important; to alienate men from their own decision-making is to change them into objects.

This movement of inquiry must be directed towards humanization—man's historical vocation. The pursuit of full humanity, however, cannot be carried out in isolation or individualism, but only in fellowship and solidarity; therefore it cannot unfold in the antagnoistic relaitons between oppressors and oppressed. No one can be authentically human while he prevents others from being so. Attempting *to be more* human, individualistically, leads to *having more*, egotistically: a form of dehumanization. Not that it is not fundamental *to have* in order *to be* human. Precisely because it *is* necessary, some men's *having* must not be allowed to constitute an obstacle to others' *having*, must not consolidate the power of the former to crush the latter.

Problem-posing education, as a humanist and liberating praxis, posits as as fundamental that men subjected to domination must fight for their emancipation. To that end, it enables teachers and students to become Subjects of the educational process by overcoming authoritarianism and an alienating intellectualism; it also enables men to overcome their false perception of reality. The world—no longer something to be described with deceptive words—becomes the object of that transforming action by men which results in their humanization.

Problem-posing education does not and cannot serve the interests of the oppressor. No oppressive order could permit the oppressed to begin to question: Why? While only a revolutionary society can carry out this education in systematic terms, the revolutionary leaders need not take full power before they can employ the method. In the revolutionary process, the leaders cannot utilize the banking method as an interim measure, justified on the grounds of expediency, with the intention of *later* behaving in a genuinely revolutionary fashion. They must be revolutionary—that is to say, dialogical—from the outset.

NOTES

1. Simone de Beauvoir, *La Pensée de Droite, Aujourd'hui* (Paris); ST, *El Pensamiento politico de la Derecha* (Buenos Aires, 1963), p. 34.

2. This concept corresponds to what Sartre calls the "digestive" or "nutritive" concept of education, in which knowledge is "fed" by the teacher to the students to "fill them out." See Jean-Paul Sartre, "Une idée fundamentale de la phénoménologie de Husserl: L'intentionalité," *Situations I* (Paris, 1947).

3. For example, some professors specify in their reading lists that a book should be read from pages 10 to 15—and do this to "help" their students!

4. Fromm, *op. cit.*, p. 41.

5. *Ibid.*, p. 31.

6. *Ibid.*

7. Reinhold Niebuhr, *Moral Man and Immoral Society* (New York, 1960), p. 130.

8. Sartre, *op. cit.*, p. 32.

9. See Chapter 3. —Translator's note [*Pedagogy of the Oppressed*].

10. Edmund Husserl, *Ideas—General Introduction to Pure Phenomenology* (London, 1969), pp. 105–106.

THE RHYTHMIC CLAIMS OF FREEDOM AND DISCIPLINE

Alfred North Whitehead

The fading of ideals is sad evidence of the defeat of human endeavour. In the schools of antiquity philosophers aspired to impart wisdom, in modern colleges our humbler aim is to teach subjects. The drop from the divine wisdom, which was the goal of the ancients, to text-book knowledge of subjects, which is achieved by the moderns, marks an educational failure, sustained through the ages. I am not maintaining that in the practice of education the ancient were more successful than ourselves. You have only to read Lucian, and to note his satiric dramatizations of the pretentious claims of philosophers, to see that in this respect the ancients can boast over us no superiority. My point is that, at the dawn of our European civilisation, men started with the full ideals which should inspire education, and that gradually our ideals have sunk to square with our practice.

But when ideals have sunk to the level of practice, the result is stagnation. In particular, so long as we conceive intellectual education as merely consisting in the acquirement of mechanical mental aptitudes, and of formulated statements of useful truths, there can be no progress; though there will be much activity, amid aimless re-arrangement of syllabuses, in the fruitless endeavour to dodge the inevitable lack of time. We must take it as an unavoidable fact, that God has so made the world that there are more topics desirable for knowledge than any one person can possibly acquire. It is hopeless to approach the problem by the way of the enumeration of subjects which every one ought to have mastered. There are too many of them, all with excellent title-deeds. Perhaps, after all, this plethora of material is fortunate; for the world is made interesting by a delightful ignorance of important truths. What I am anxious to impress on you is that though knowledge is one chief aim of intellectual education, there is another ingredient, vaguer but greater, and more dominating in its importance. The ancients called it "wisdom." You cannot be wise without some basis of knowledge; but you may easily acquire knowledge and remain bare of wisdom.

Now wisdom is the way in which knowledge is held. It concerns the handling of knowledge, its selection for the determination of relevant issues, its employment to add value to our immediate experience. This mastery of knowledge, which is wisdom, is the most intimate freedom obtainable. The ancients saw clearly—more clearly than we do—the necessity for dominating knowledge by wisdom. But, in the pursuit of wisdom in the region of practical education, they erred sadly. To put the matter simply, their popular practice assumed that wisdom could be imparted to the young by procuring philosophers to spout at them. Hence the crop of shady philosophers in the schools of the ancient world. The only avenue towards wisdom is by freedom in the presence of knowledge. But the only avenue towards knowledge is by discipline in the acquirement of ordered fact. Freedom and discipline are the two essentials of education, and hence the title of my discourse to-day, "The Rhythmic Claims of Freedom and Discipline."

The antithesis in education between freedom and discipline is not so sharp as a logical analysis of the meanings of the terms might lead us to imagine. The pupil's mind is a growing organism. On the one hand, it is not a box to be ruthlessly packed with alien ideas: and, on the other hand, the ordered acquirement of knowledge is the natural food for a developing intelligence. Accordingly, it should be the aim of an ideally constructed education that the discipline should be the voluntary issue of free choice, and that the freedom should gain an enrichment of possibility as the issue of discipline. The two principles, freedom and discipline, are not antagonists, but should be so adjusted in the child's life that they correspond to a natural sway, to and fro, of the developing personality. It is this adaptation of freedom and discipline to the natural sway of development that I have elsewhere called The Rhythm of Education. I am convinced that much disappointing failure in the past has been due to neglect of attention to the importance of this rhythm. My main position is that the dominant note of education at its beginning and at its end is freedom, but that there is an intermediate stage of discipline with freedom in subordination: Furthermore, that there is not one unique threefold cycle of freedom, discipline, and freedom; but that all mental development is composed of such cycles, and of cycles of such cycles. Such a cycle is a unit cell, or brick; and the complete stage of growth is an organic structure of such cells. In analysing any one such cell, I call the first period of freedom the "stage of Romance," the intermediate period of discipline I call the "stage of Precision," and the final period of freedom is the "stage of Generalisation."

Let me now explain myself in more detail. There can be no mental development without interest. Interest is the *sine qua non* for attention and apprehension. You may endeavour to excite interest by means of birch rods, or you may coax it by the incitement of pleasurable activity. But without interest there will be no progress. Now the natural mode by which living organisms are excited towards suitable self-development is enjoyment. The infant is lured to adapt itself to its environment by its love of its mother and its nurse; we eat because we like a good dinner: we subdue the forces of nature because we have been lured to discovery by an insatiable curiosity: we enjoy exercise: and we enjoy the unchristian passion of hating our dangerous enemies. Undoubtedly pain is one subordinate means of arousing an organism to action. But it only supervenes on the failure of pleasure. Joy is the normal healthy spur for the élan vital. I am not maintaining that we can safely abandon ourselves to the allurement of the greater immediate joys. What I do mean is that we should seek to arrange the development of character along a path of natural activity, in itself pleasurable. The subordinate stiffening of discipline must be directed to secure some long-time good; although an adequate object must not be too far below the horizon, if the necessary interest is to be retained.

The second preliminary point which I wish to make, is the unimportance—indeed the evil—of barren knowledge. The importance of knowledge lies in its use, in our active mastery of it—that is to say, it lies in wisdom. It is a convention to speak of mere knowledge, apart from wisdom, as of itself imparting a peculiar dignity to its possessor. I do not share in this reverence for knowledge as such. It all depends on who has the knowledge and what he does with it. That knowledge which adds greatness to character is knowledge so handled as to transform every phase of immediate experience. It is in respect to the activity of knowledge that an over-vigorous discipline in education is so harmful. The habit of active thought, with freshness, can only be generated by adequate freedom. Undiscriminating discipline defeats its own object by dulling the mind. If you have much to do with the young as they emerge from school and from the university, you soon note the dulled minds of those whose education has consisted in the acquirement of inert knowledge. Also the deplorable tone of English society in respect to learning is a tribute to our educational failure. Furthermore, this overhaste to impart mere knowledge defeats itself. The human mind rejects knowledge imparted in this way. The craving for expansion, for activity, inherent in youth is disgusted by a dry imposition of disciplined knowledge. The discipline, when it comes, should satisfy a natural craving for the wisdom which adds value to bare experience.

But let us now examine more closely the rhythm of these natural cravings of the human intelligence. The first procedure of the mind in a new environment is a somewhat discursive activity amid a welter of ideas and experience. It is a process of discovery, a process of becoming used to curious thoughts, of shaping questions, of seeking for answers, of devising new experiences, of noticing what happens as the result of new ventures. This general process is both natural and of absorbing interest. We must often have noticed children between the ages of eight and thirteen absorbed in its ferment. It is dominated by wonder, and cursed be the dullard who destroys wonder. Now undoubtedly this stage of development requires help, and even discipline. The environment within which the mind is working must be carefully selected. It must, of course, be chosen to suit the child's stage of growth, and must be adapted to individual needs. In a sense it is an imposition from without; but in a deeper sense it answers to the call of life within the child. In the teacher's consciousness the child has been sent to his telescope to look at the stars, in the child's consciousness he has been given free access to the glory of the heavens. Unless, working somewhere, however obscurely, even in the dullest child, there is this transfiguration of imposed routine, the child's nature will refuse to assimilate the alien material. It must never be forgotten that education is not a process of packing articles in a trunk. Such a simile is entirely inapplicable. It is, of course, a process completely of its own peculiar genus. Its nearest analogue is the assimilation of food by a living organism: and we all know how necessary to health is palatable food under suitable conditions. When you have put your boots in a trunk, they will stay there till you take them out again; but this is not at all the case if you feed a child with the wrong food.

This initial stage of romance requires guidance in another way. After all the child is the heir to long ages of civilisation, and it is absurd to let him wander in the intellectual maze of men in the Glacial Epoch. Accordingly, a certain pointing out of important facts, and of simplifying ideas, and of usual names, really strengthens the natural impetus of the pupil. In no part of education can you do without discipline or can you do without freedom; but in the stage of romance the emphasis must always be on freedom, to allow the child to see for itself and to act for itself. My point is that a block in the assimilation of ideas inevitably arises when a discipline of precision is imposed before a stage of romance has run its course in the growing mind. There is no comprehension apart from romance. It is my strong belief that the cause of so much failure in the past has been due to the lack of careful study of the due place of romance. Without the adventure of romance, at the best you get inert knowledge without initiative, and at the worst you get contempt of ideas—without knowledge.

But when this stage of romance has been properly guided another craving grows. The freshness of inexperience has worn off; there is general knowledge of the groundwork of fact and theory: and, above all, there has been plenty of independent browsing amid first-hand experiences, involving adventures of thought and of action. The enlightenment which comes from precise knowledge can now be understood. It corresponds to the obvious requirements of common sense, and deals with familiar material. Now is the time for pushing on, for knowing the subject exactly, and for retaining in the memory its salient features. This is the stage of precision. This stage is the sole stage of learning in the traditional scheme of education, either at school or university. You had to learn your subject, and there was nothing more to be said on the topic of education. The result of such an undue extension of a most necessary period of development was the production of a plentiful array of dunces, and of a few scholars whose natural interest had survived the car of Juggernaut. There is, indeed, always the temptation to teach pupils a little more of fact and of precise theory than at that stage they are fitted to assimilate. If only they could, it would be so useful. We—I am talking of schoolmasters and of university dons—are apt to forget that we are only subordinate elements in the education of a grown man; and that, in their own good time, in later life our pupils will learn for themselves. The phenomena of growth cannot be hurried beyond certain very narrow limits. But an unskilful practitioner can easily damage a sensitive organism. Yet, when all has been said in the way of caution, there is such a thing as pushing on, of getting to know the fundamental details and the main exact generalisations, and of acquiring an easy mastery of technique. There is no getting away from the fact that things have been found out, and that to be effective in the modern world you must have a store of definite acquirement of the best practice. To write poetry you must study metre; and to build bridges you must be learned in the strength of material. Even the Hebrew prophets had learned to write, probably in those days requiring no mean effort. The untutored art of genius is—in the words of the Prayer Book—a vain thing, fondly invented.

During the stage of precision, romance is the background. The stage is dominated by the inescapable fact that there are right ways and wrong ways, and definite truths to be known. But romance is not dead, and it is the art of teaching to foster it amidst definite application to appointed task. It must be fostered for one reason, because romance is after all a necessary ingredient of that balanced wisdom which is the goal to be attained. But there is another reason: The organism will not absorb the fruits of the task unless its powers of apprehension are kept fresh by romance. The real point is to discover in practice that exact balance between freedom and discipline which will give the greatest rate of progress over the things to be known. I do not believe that there is any abstract formula which will give information applicable to all subjects, to all types of pupils, or to each individual pupil; except indeed the formula of rhythmic sway which I have been insisting on, namely, that in the earlier stage the progress requires that the emphasis be laid on freedom, and that in the later middle stage the emphasis be laid on the definite acquirement of allotted tasks. I freely admit that if the stage of romance has been properly managed, the discipline of the second stage is much less apparent, that the children know how to go about their work, want to make a good job of it, and can be safely trusted with the details. Furthermore, I hold that the only discipline, important for its own sake, is self-discipline, and that this can only be acquired by a wide use of freedom. But yet—so many are the delicate points to be considered in education—it is necessary in life to have acquired the habit of cheerfully undertaking imposed tasks. The conditions can be satisfied if the tasks correspond to the natural cravings of the pupil at his stage of progress, if they keep his powers at full stretch, and if they attain an obviously sensible result, and if reasonable freedom is allowed in the mode of execution.

The difficulty of speaking about the way a skilful teacher will keep romance alive in his pupils arises from the fact that what takes a long time to describe, takes a short time to do. The beauty of a passage of Virgil may be rendered by insisting on beauty of verbal enunciation, taking no longer than prosy utterance. The emphasis on the beauty of a mathematical argument, in its marshalling of general considerations to unravel complex fact, is the speediest mode of procedure. The responsibility of the teacher at this stage is immense. To speak the truth, except in the rare case of genius in the teacher, I do not think that it is possible to take a whole class very far along the road of precision without some dulling of the interest. It is the unfortunate dilemma that initiative and training are both necessary, and that training is apt to kill initiative.

But this admission is not to condone a brutal ignorance of methods of mitigating this untoward fact. It is not a theoretical necessity, but arises because perfect tact is unattainable in the treatment of each individual case. In the past the methods employed assassinated interest; we are discussing how to reduce the evil to its smallest dimensions. I merely utter the warning that education is a difficult problem, to be solved by no one simple formula.

In this connection there is, however, one practical consideration which is largely neglected. The territory of romantic interest is large, ill-defined, and not to be controlled by any explicit boundary. It depends on the chance flashes of insight. But the area of precise knowledge, as exacted in any general educational system, can be, and should be, definitely determined. If you make it too wide you will kill interest and defeat your own object: if you make it too narrow your pupils will lack effective grip. Surely, in every subject in each type of curriculum, the precise knowledge required should be determined after the most anxious inquiry. This does not now seem to be the case in any effective way. For example, in the classical studies of boys destined for a scientific career—a class of pupils in whom I am greatly interested—What is the Latin vocabulary which they ought definitely to know? Also what are the grammatical rules and constructions which they ought to have mastered? Why not determine these once and for all, and then bend every exercise to impress just these on the memory, and to understand their derivatives, both in Latin and also in French and English. Then, as to other constructions and words which occur in the reading of texts, supply full information in the easiest manner. A certain ruthless definiteness is essential in education. I am sure that one secret of a successful teacher is that he has formulated quite clearly in his mind what the pupil has got to know in precise fashion. He will then cease from half-hearted attempts to worry his pupils with memorising a lot of irrelevant stuff of inferior importance. The secret of success is pace, and the secret of pace is concentration. But, in respect to precise knowledge, the watchword is pace, pace, pace. Get your knowledge quickly, and then use it. If you can use it, you will retain it.

We have now come to the third stage of the rhythmic cycle, the stage of generalisation. There is here a reaction towards romance. Something definite is now known; aptitudes have been acquired; and general rules and laws are clearly apprehended both in their formulation and their detailed exemplification. The pupil now wants to use his new weapons. He is an effective individual, and it is effects that he wants to produce. He relapses into the discursive adventures of the romantic stage, with the advantage that his mind is now a disciplined regiment instead of a rabble. In this sense, education should begin in research and end in research. After all, the whole affair is merely a preparation for battling with the immediate experiences of life, a preparation by which to qualify each immediate moment with relevant ideas and appropriate actions. An education which does not begin by evoking initiative and end by encouraging it must be wrong. For its whole aim is the production of active wisdom.

In my own work at universities I have been much struck by the paralysis of thought induced in pupils by the aimless accumulation of precise knowl-

edge, inert and unutilised. It should be the chief aim of a university professor to exhibit himself in his own true character—that is, as an ignorant man
thinking, actively utilising his small share of knowledge. In a sense, knowledge shrinks as wisdom grows: for details are swallowed up in principles.
The details of knowledge which are important will be picked up *ad hoc* in
each avocation of life, but the habit of the active utilisation of well-under-
stood principles is the final possession of wisdom. The stage of precision is
the stage of growing into the apprehension of principles by the acquisition
of a precise knowledge of details. The stage of generalisations is the stage of
shedding details in favour of the active application of principles, the details
retreating into subconscious habits. We don't go about explicitly retaining
in our own minds that two and two make four, though once we had to learn
it by heart. We trust to habit for our elementary arithmetic. But the essence of this stage is the emergence from the comparative passivity of
being trained into the active freedom of application. Of course, during this
stage, precise knowledge will grow, and more actively than ever before,
because the mind has experienced the power of definiteness, and responds
to the acquisition of general truth, and of richness of illustration. But the
growth of knowledge becomes progressively unconscious, as being an incident derived from some active adventure of thought.

So much for the three stages of the rhythmic unit of development. In a
general way the whole period of education is dominated by this threefold
rhythm. Till the age of thirteen or fourteen there is the romantic stage,
from fourteen to eighteen the stage of precision, and from eighteen to two
and twenty the stage of generalisation. But these are only average characters, tinging the mode of development as a whole. I do not think that any
pupil completes his stages simultaneously in all subjects. For an example, I
should plead that while language is initiating its stage of precision in the
way of acquisition of vocabulary and of grammar, science should be in its
full romantic stage. The romantic stage of language begins in infancy with
the acquisition of speech, so that it passes early towards a stage of precision; while science is a late comer. Accordingly a precise inculcation of
science at an early age wipes out initiative and interest, and destroys any
chance of the topic having any richness of content in the child's apprehension. Thus, the romantic stage of science should persist for years after the
precise study of language has commenced.

There are minor eddies, each in itself a threefold cycle, running its
course in each day, in each week, and in each term. There is the general
apprehension of some topic in its vague possibilities, the mastery of the relevant details, and finally the putting of the whole subject together in the
light of the relevant knowledge. Unless the pupils are continually sustained
by the evocation of interest, the acquirement of technique, and the excite-
ment of success, they can never make progress, and will certainly lose
heart. Speaking generally, during the last thirty years the schools of En-

gland have been sending up to the universities a disheartened crowd of young folk, inoculated against any outbreak of intellectual zeal. The universities have seconded the efforts of the schools and emphasised the failure. Accordingly, the cheerful gaiety of the young turns to other topics, and thus educated England is not hospitable to ideas. When we can point to some great achievement of our nation—let us hope that it may be something other than a war—which has been won in the class-room of our schools, and not in their playing-fields, then we may feel content with our modes of education.

So far I have been discussing intellectual education, and my argument has been cramped on too narrow a basis. After all, our pupils are alive, and cannot be chopped into separate bits, like the pieces of a jig-saw puzzle. In the production of a mechanism the constructive energy lies outside it, and adds discrete parts to discrete parts. The case is far different for a living organism which grows by its own impulse towards self-development. This impulse can be stimulated and guided from outside the organism, and it can also be killed. But for all your stimulation and guidance the creative impulse towards growth comes from within, and is intensely characteristic of the individual. Education is the guidance of the individual towards a comprehension of the art of life; and by the art of life I mean the most complete achievement of varied activity expressing the potentialities of that living creature in the face of its actual environment. This completeness of achievement involves an artistic sense, subordinating the lower to the higher possibilities of the indivisible personality. Science, art, religion, morality, take their rise from this sense of values within the structure of being. Each individual embodies an adventure of existence. The art of life is the guidance of this adventure. The great religions of civilisation include among their original elements revolts against the inculcation of morals as a set of isolated prohibitions. Morality, in the petty negative sense of the term, is the deadly enemy of religion. Paul denounces the Law, and the Gospels are vehement against the Pharisees. Every outbreak of religion exhibits the same intensity of antagonism—an antagonism diminishing as religion fades. No part of education has more to gain from attention to the rhythmic law of growth than has moral and religious education. Whatever be the right way to formulated religious truths, it is death to religion to insist on a premature stage of precision. The vitality of religion is shown by the way in which the religious spirit has survived the ordeal of religious education.

The problem of religion in education is too large to be discussed at this stage of my address. I have referred to it to guard against the suspicion that the principles here advocated are to be conceived in a narrow sense. We are analysing the general law of rhythmic progress in the higher stages of life, embodying the initial awakening, the discipline, and the fruition on the higher plane. What I am now insisting is that the principle of progress is from within: the discovery is made by ourselves, the discipline is self-discipline, and the fruition is the outcome of our own initiative. The teacher has a double function. It is for him to elicit the enthusiasn by resonance from his own personality, and to create the environment of a larger knowledge and a firmer purpose. He is there to avoid the waste, which in the lower stages of existence is nature's way of evolution. The ultimate motive power, alike in science, in morality, and in religion, is the sense of value, the sense of importance. It takes the various forms of wonder, of curiosity, of reverence, or worship, or tumultuous desire for merging personality in something beyond itself. This sense of value imposes on life incredible labours, and apart from it life sinks back into the passivity of its lower types. The most penetrating exhibition of this force is the sense of beauty, the aesthetic sense of realised perfection. This thought leads me to ask, whether in our modern education we emphasize sufficiently the functions of art.

The typical education of our public schools was devised for boys from well-to-do cultivated homes. They travelled in Italy, in Greece, and in France, and often their own homes were set amid beauty. None of these circumstances hold for modern national education in primary or secondary schools, or even for the majority of boys and girls in our enlarged system of public schools. You cannot, without loss, ignore in the life of the spirit so great a factor as art. Our aesthetic emotions provide us with vivid apprehensions of value. If you maim these, you weaken the force of the whole system of spiritual apprehensions. The claim for freedom in education carries with it the corollary that the development of the whole personality must be attended to. You must not arbitrarily refuse its urgent demands. In these days of economy, we hear much of the futility of our educational efforts and of the possibility of curtailing them. The endeavour to develop a bare intellectuality is bound to issue in a large crop of failure. This is just what we have done in our national schools. We do just enough to excite and not enough to satisfy. History shows us that an efflorescence of art is the first activity of nations on the road to civilisation. Yet, in the face of this plain fact, we practically shut out art from the masses of the population. Can we wonder that such an education, evoking and defeating cravings, leads to failure and discontent? The stupidity of the whole procedure is, that art in simple popular forms is just what we can give to the nation without undue strain on our resources. You may, perhaps, by some great reforms, obviate the worse kind of sweated labour and the insecurity of employment. But you can never greatly increase average incomes. On that side all hope of Utopia is closed to you. It would, however, require not very great effort to use our schools to produce a population with some love of music, some enjoyment of drama, and some joy in beauty of form and colour. We could also provide means for the satisfaction of these emotions in the general life of the population. If you think of the simplest ways, you will see that the strain on material resources would be negligible; and when you have done that, and when your population widely appreciates what art can give—its joys and its terrors—do you not think that your prophets and your clergy and your statesmen will be in a stronger position when they speak to the population of the love of God, of the inexorableness of duty, and of the call of patriotism?

Shakespeare wrote his plays for English people reared in the beauty of the country, amid the pageant of life as the Middle Age merged into the Renaissance, and with a new world across the ocean to make vivid the call of romance. To-day we deal with herded town populations, reared in a scientific age. I have no doubt that unless we can meet the new age with new methods, to sustain for our populations the life of the spirit, sooner or later, amid some savage outbreak of defeated longings, the fate of Russia will be the fate of England. Historians will write as her epitaph that her fall issued from the spiritual blindness of her governing classes, from their dull materialism, and from their Pharisaic attachment to petty formulae of statesmanship.